EISENSTEIN

EISENSTEIN
A Life in Conflict

Ronald Bergan

LITTLE, BROWN AND COMPANY

A *Little, Brown* Book

First published in Great Britain by
Little, Brown and Company 1997

Copyright © Ronald Bergan 1997

A CIP catalogue record for this book
is available from the British Library.

ISBN 0 316 87708 5

Typeset in Sabon by M Rules
Printed and bound in Great Britain by
Clays Ltd, St Ives plc

Little, Brown and Company (UK)
Brettenham House
Lancaster Place
London WC2E 7EN

For Naum Kleiman

I love to watch children dying.
Do you note, behind protruding nostalgia,
the shadowy billow of laughter's surf?
But I –
in the reading room of the streets –
have leafed so often through the volume of the coffin.
Midnight
with sodden hands has fingered
me
and the battered paling,
and the crazy cathedral galloped
in drops of downpour upon the cupola's bald pate.
I have seen Christ escape from an icon,
and the slush tearfully kiss
the wind-swept fringe of his tunic.
At bricks I bawl,
thrusting the dagger of desperate words
into the swollen pulp of sky:
'Sun!
Father mine!
If at least *thou* wouldst have mercy and stop tormenting me!
For my blood thou spilled gushes down this nether road.
That is my soul yonder
in tatters of torn cloud
against a burnt-out sky
upon the rusted cross of the belfry!
Time!
You lame icon-painter,
will you at least daub my countenance
and frame it as a freak of this age!
I am as lonely as the only eye
of a man on his way to the blind!'

A Few Words About Myself,
Vladimir Mayakovsky (1894–1930)

Contents

PART III   BACK IN THE USSR

Author's Note

Each time a book in English is published on a Russian subject, the same theme, albeit with variations, appears in the author's note: how does one transcribe from the Cyrillic to the Latin alphabet? So, for the purposes of this book, I have followed the (admittedly imprecise) rule that renders well-known Russian names in the form in which they are customarily used in English e.g. Chekhov and Tchaikovsky. I have largely opted for the final 'y' – Mayakovsky rather than Mayakovski, though this rule, too, is subject to common usage variations, so that the reader will find Lavrenti Beria and Dmitri Shostakovich. I have also chosen the middle 'y', which gives Shumyatsky rather than Shumiatski and Katayev as opposed to Kataev, while leaving Dostoevsky without his 'y' as is customary.

Several names which occur frequently in my narrative are accorded different spellings in different sources, and I was left to choose, for example, between Nikolai Cherkasov or Cherkassov, between Pera Atasheva and Attasheva, Dimitri or Dmitri and Fedor or Fyodor. Working on a combination of instinct and common usage, I decided to use the latter versions of these, and other similarly variable names. In short, I have aimed for consistency, though logic might sometimes have suffered.

I faced a dilemma regarding *Strike* and *Battleship Potemkin*. These titles have tended to a literal translation since the Russian language takes no article, either definite or indefinite. However, languages which do take articles, such as French, have rendered these great films correctly for their own language (*La Grève*, *La Cuirassé Potemkin*) so I have chosen to use correct English as in *The Strike* and *The Battleship Potemkin*.

There was a slight problem, too, with the title of *The General Line*, Eisenstein's film on collectivisation. When it was completed, Comrade Stalin decided that the policy presented in the film was no longer the Party's 'general line', and made Eisenstein change the title to *The Old and the New* (sometimes *Old and New*). Since both titles are used in various texts on the film and by Eisenstein himself, it has sometimes been assumed that these were two different films. I have preferred to use *The General Line* throughout, except when *The Old and the New* is used in direct quotation.

For all quotes from the Russian, I have used English and French translations. Thankfully, the translations of Richard Taylor, Michael Glenny and William Powell in the inestimably useful BFI publications of Eisenstein's writings are generally excellent. Those from other sources are sometimes less so, therefore, in the interests of clarity, I have taken the occasional liberty of altering a word or a phrase. On the whole, however, I have left unchanged those letters written by Eisenstein in English, retaining his spelling mistakes and stylistic idiosyncrasies.

Eisenstein was as much a theorist of the cinema as a director, and I make no apology for quoting liberally from his copious writings, since these bring us closer to an understanding of the man and of the workings of his extraordinary mind. They not only pave a way into his films, but are an essential component of his entire oeuvre. Perhaps he would have written less if he had been more busily engaged in making films, or even directing in the theatre, but his avid impulse to communicate by all means at his disposal resulted in the substantial quantity of drawings, speeches and essays.

I have in Eisenstein, however, a great guide. He wrote, 'Quotations! Quotations! Quotations! Someone once said, "It is only those who have no hope of themselves being cited who cite nobody." Quotations! Quotations! Quotations! . . . I see quotations as outrunners on either side of a galloping shafthorse. Sometimes they go too far, but they help one's imagination to bowl along two distinct paths, supported by the parallel race. But don't let go of the reins!'

I have tried to take Eisenstein's advice, though he proved most difficult to rein in.

Ronald Bergan
London 1997

Acknowledgements

I would like to record my heartfelt thanks to the following people for their invaluable assistance to me in the writing of this biography. Between them they gave me guidance, patiently answered endless questions, and generously lent me books, tapes and film footage.

In Riga my path was eased by Ieva Pitruka, Augusts Sukuts and Janet Vognere of Arsenâls; in Moscow by film director Andrei Konchalovsky and, of course, Naum Kleiman of the Eisenstein Museum. I had help in New York from Elena Pinto-Simon of the Tisch School of Arts, in Berlin from the Ukrainian film writer Oksana Bulgakowa. At home, I owe a debt of gratitude to film director Vito Rocco, to Rik Boulton of King Key Movies, to Professors Ian Christie and Richard Taylor of, respectively, the Universities of Kent and Swansea, Irina Hamilton at the Latvian Embassy, Eric Liknaitzky of Contemporary Films, and film and theatre critic Clive Hirschhorn. A special thank you to Richard Taylor again, and to William Powell and Michael Glenny for allowing me to quote liberally from their translations, which were essential to my purpose. I much appreciated also the generous assistance given by John Atkinson of BFI Publications.

My gratitude is due to Catherine Grégoire for putting up with a *ménage à trois* – herself, me and Eisenstein – for so long; to Andrew Wille, my patient and understanding editor at Little, Brown; and lastly and most, Robyn Karney, who transforms the job of copy-editing into the art of co-writing.

Prologue

Yo!

First of all I must warn you. These notes are completely amoral. And I must at this point disillusion anyone who is expecting a series of amoral episodes, seductive details, or indecent descriptions. There is nothing of the sort: this is not Casanova's diary, or the history of a Russian director's amorous adventures.

– Sergei Eisenstein from the Foreword to his
Memoirs written in May 1946.

P.S. To begin with a postscript . . . Sergei Mikhailovich Eisenstein died on February 11, 1948, less than three weeks after celebrating his fiftieth birthday. Almost two years previously, following a severe heart attack, Eisenstein wrote, 'On February 2 this year [1946], a heart muscle ruptured. There was a haemorrhage. (An infarction.) By some incomprehensible, absurd and pointless miracle, I survived. All the facts of science dictated that I should die. For some reason I survived. I therefore consider that everything from now on is a postscript to my own life . . . P.S. . . .'[1]

While recovering in the Kremlin Hospital during this unexpected 'after-life', Eisenstein began writing his memoirs in the 'stream of consciousness' manner he had learnt, principally, from his reading of James Joyce. He decided to call the book *Yo!*, the Spanish for 'I'. Naum Kleiman, the world's foremost keeper of the Eisenstein flame, suggests that this was to give the memoirs 'an ironic distance, diluting its "concentrated egoism" . . . There were echoes of his longing for Mexico, where Eisenstein had really been happy,

1

"himself", and where he had learned to speak Spanish . . . He must have thought of Mayakovsky's poem "I" and his autobiographical sketch "I Myself" . . .'[2]

The title of this chapter also refers to the 'I' of the biographer, though I affirm that the first person singular outside quotation marks will not reappear until the very last chapter.

Eisenstein's fragmentary memoirs, which remained incomplete (like so many of Eisenstein's projects, though this time it was death that intervened), were published in German as *Yo! Ich Selbst*, and in English as *Beyond the Stars*, because, according to the translators, 'we, like Eisenstein himself, believe it [the title] aptly distinguishes his approach to cinema from that of Hollywood.'[3] It was Eisenstein who had expressed the wish for a 16th-century engraving of a monk gazing 'beyond the stars' to illustrate the dustjacket for a book of his theoretical essays on the cinema, subtly signifying that 'the book dealt with problems of cinema – everything, apart from the stars and the spontaneous human participants in film.'[4]

However, this does not mean, as some commentators blindly continue to insist, that Eisenstein was a cold, intellectual artist uninterested in the 'human participants' in his films, but only in the theories behind them. The quote above was merely a reference to a particular collection of essays. Among the many Hollywood 'stars' that Eisenstein adored were Charlie Chaplin, Douglas Fairbanks, Harold Lloyd, George Arliss, Greta Garbo, Henry Fonda and Judy Garland, nor was he unresponsive to Hollywood films, which he watched avidly. One has only to read his perceptive essays on Chaplin, Walt Disney, D. W. Griffith and John Ford's *Young Mr Lincoln* to recognise this.

He was also enraptured by the *commedia dell'arte*, the great actors of the past such as the two 19th-century Frenchmen, the mime Jean-Gaspard Deburau and the Romantic actor Frederic Lemaître, and those of the classical Russian tradition, to whose style he paid homage in *Ivan the Terrible*. In addition, there was his admiration for the performers he discovered at Stanislavsky's Moscow Arts Theatre, and for the hypnotic and gaunt Vsevolod Meyerhold, on whom Eisenstein drew for his portrait of Tsar Ivan, as well as a fascination with Mei Lan-fan, the most celebrated of all Chinese actors from the Peking Opera.

Were the eyes of the same commentators who have preached the dogma of Eisenstein's coldness too blinded by Eisenstein's dazzling style in *The Strike* to feel the real pain in the suicide of the wrongly-accused worker, or of the starving child crying beside his empty plate; or to sense the suffering of each individual victim on the Odessa steps in *The Battleship Potemkin*? Surely *The General Line* and *Ivan the Terrible* encompass two of the most extraordinary performances in cinema history, on the one hand by Marfa Lapkina, a simple peasant woman who had never acted before or since, and, on the other, by Nikolai Cherkassov, a renowned actor of stage and screen. And, most frustratingly, is it not impossible to be other than deeply moved by the glimpses of what remains of the boy Vitka Kartachov's portrayal in the edited version of the rescued stills from the vanished *Bezhin Meadow*? The notion that the films of Eisenstein lack flesh-and-blood characters is one of the many misconceptions that have clung to his name since 1924 when his first feature, *The Strike*, appeared.

But the perception of Eisenstein as the calculating, didactic theorist, whose films 'lack humanity' still persists. I cannot consider his films without quoting his own words as he gazed on Leonardo da Vinci's *Virgin of the Rocks* in the Louvre. 'Look at it. I *know* that the sense of balance, harmony and perfection that this work conveys to me comes partly from the geometric arrangement of line and form, from the positioning of the figures and setting . . . Yet this knowledge in no way diminishes the intense emotion, the feeling of ecstasy that overwhelms me. The logic behind it makes everything clearer, but only *after* the emotional response.'[5]

Apart from the stereotyped view of Eisenstein as a cold-blooded montage maniac, his name still provokes knee-jerk reactions such as 'a Stalinist hack'. But as Professor Richard Taylor explained, 'The English, unlike their neighbours in continental Europe, have never experienced the trauma of occupation (internal or external) and find it difficult to envisage the day-to-day compromises that may have been made to ensure survival. To reduce Eisenstein to an intelligible cipher carries with it the enormous danger of oversimplification, precisely because the daily choices that people had to make are unintelligible to those of us fortunate not have experienced them for ourselves.'[6] In fact, there is a strong case to suggest, as did the English writer Herbert Marshall, a student of Eisenstein's at the G. I. K. (State Cinema Institute), that 'Eisenstein deliberately and consciously risked his life and freedom to show the degeneration of Stalin in Ivan [the Terrible] and his *oprichniki* [his entourage] . . . No other Soviet film director got away with such a challenge. All other artists were reduced to impotence and silence.'[7]

Though Eisenstein wrote profoundly about art, science, philosophy, metaphysics and religion, there is little in his writings on either political theory or practice, apart from his mandatory public utterances when he merely mouthed the prevalent orthodoxy. These differed markedly from his private utterances and passions. There is no doubt that, like the majority of his generation, he embraced the Revolution, wanting it to continue in the innovatory manner in which it had begun, and he was forever suspicious of capitalism, but a man of Eisenstein's wide culture and universal interests could never had condoned Stalin's regime or the restrictive rules it imposed on art. He remained faithful to the Communist principles that were at the root of the Revolution.

It is what I profoundly consider to be the many distortions of Eisenstein's life and work that first prompted me to embark on this biography. I also sought to throw some new light on the mysteries and contradictions of his complex character, to put the recently published writings in English into some chronological sequence, and to include newly-discovered material. With *glasnost* now allowing more access to the archives, I also hope to have thrown more light on his homosexuality, and other elements in his life that no-one else has been able to reveal previously. And there are, of course, the unpublished diaries. Why did Pera Attasheva, Eisenstein's widow, withhold them from publication? What dark secrets do they contain? Why do they still remain hidden from the public eye?

The diary is the generic term used for a number of scattered and diverse writings, some in notebooks or pads, others on the backs of envelopes, theatre programmes or scraps of paper, begun in 1919 during his earliest days in the theatre at the front in the Civil War. Mostly 'automatic writing', they were ideas he jotted down as they came to him, and only sometimes revised. In an even less disciplined manner than the memoirs, his thoughts would scurry off in all directions as they made certain connections, comparable to some of the method behind the dynamic montage in *October*. (A priest = the bourgeois = Alexander Kerensky = mechanical peacock = vanity = corruption = power = Napoleon . . . and so on.) For example, he wrote, 'Yesterday I was at the Ministry of Foreign Affairs where Maxim Litvinov [People's Commissar for Foreign Affairs] introduced me to a young Englishman with whom I discussed Chesterton. There is a description of Chesterton on the threshold of the church where he was converted, that has a charming symbol and internal sense. When he was asked if he had a twopenny catechism, Chesterton searched his pockets feverishly to see whether his customary absentmindedness had got the better of him again. And the first thing he took out and hastily shoved back into the depths of his pocket was also worth two pennies, but it was a detective story not a catechism . . .' Eisenstein would then go into the mechanics of the detective story in general, its similarities to the tenets of the Catholic Church, double nature and meanings, moving into Greek mythology etc etc.

At the risk of immediately losing prurient readers, I can confidently state, from what I have seen and learned, that there is virtually nothing in the diaries about his love affairs or emotional life. Unlike his multitude of drawings, many of them bordering on the pornographic, Eisenstein did not use the diaries as a safety valve for his pent-up sexuality, but as a way of elaborating on his ideas of art and life. Many of these scribblings were notes about the theatre, set out in the numbered paragraph style of Spinoza or Kant, and were preparations for his books on directing, which he had started writing in Moscow in the early 1920s.

Yet Pera Attasheva decided to keep the diaries closed. One of her main reasons was the adverse comment Eisenstein made about some of the films of his colleagues. Though they were rarely personal attacks, Pera did not wish to hurt his victims when many of them were still alive. For example, he called Grigori Roshal's popular family saga *Gospoda Skotininy*, 'a piece of shit' and Yuri

Raizman's *Stepan Razin*, 'Stinker Raizman'. (Actually, Eisenstein was very fond of Raizman as a man.) In his diaries, Eisenstein accused some managers at Sovkino of lining their own pockets from the budget of *October* while complaining that the film was too expensive, and he reviled the hypocrisy of the director Alexander Ivanovsky, who had been a general in the White Army during the Civil War, for saying that *October* was not Bolshevik enough. Among the writings were also comments that could be dangerously interpreted as 'anti-Soviet' (the Russian equivalent of the McCarthyite 'un-American'), particularly Eisenstein's contemplation of religion during his stay in Mexico, and one unequivocally negative early reference to Stalin.

There is another problem about publishing the diary in that, like Ezra Pound's *Cantos*, it is written in many languages, sometimes three in one sentence. He would start in Russian, then move into German, until he discovered that an English word might be more exact than a German one . . . and so on.

Before Pera's death in 1965, she gave the 'diary' to a circle of friends, who decided to begin typing it out. By the early 1980s, a manuscript was prepared for a twelve-volume edition. But, as Naum Kleiman explained, 'Then *perestroika* came and there was no money for publication. That is the dark side of *perestroika*.'[8] However, nobody needs reminding of the bright side of *perestroika*, one advantage being that fear no longer hides the truth. There is a warmer climate (metaphorically, most of the time) in which to write a biography of a Soviet artist such as Eisenstein.

For me, Eisenstein, though his films are thoroughly Russian in content and context, belongs directly in the current of 20th-century Western art with other 'cosmopolitan' Russians like Igor Stravinsky, Sergei Rachmaninov, Vassili Kandinsky, Marc Chagall, Vladimir Nabokov, George Balanchine and Sergei Diaghilev. But, like Pushkin's Eugene Onegin, they were able to say, 'I will leave this terrible state of Russia to have nostalgia in Italy' (or Switzerland, France, the USA). Though the polymath, polyglot Eisenstein himself suffered nostalgia for the West while remaining in 'the terrible state of Russia', he continued, in comparative isolation, to widen his knowledge of the arts and sciences, using everything, including his friendships, personal feelings and desires, which all interconnect his memoirs, diaries, drawings, theoretical essays and films, to form an integrated oeuvre, in which an understanding of one element enriches and illuminates the others. As the Soviet director Sergei Yutkevich remarked, 'the director, as Eisenstein imagines him, is simultaneously an architect, a poet, a painter, a composer – but above all, a film artist in the most honourable and highest sense of the term. An artist, thinking synthetically, an artist-innovator, tracing out new paths, the untiring discoverer and creator of new forms able to shake the mind and heart, and win the sympathy of the spectator.'[9]

I began my search for Eisenstein in England, to which he paid a short visit in 1929, where I studiously combed through the Ivor Montagu collection (Montagu was the English Marxist friend of Eisenstein's who invited him to lecture in London and was with him in Hollywood); the personal ephemera of Marie Seton (a previous Eisenstein biographer), and the Eisenstein Exhibition collection of letters, drawings and other Eisensteinia brought together by David Elliott and Ian Christie in 1988. Then there was a chat to Ian Christie, Russian cinema expert, and a trip to the University of Wales in Swansea to see Richard Taylor, professor of politics, who edited Eisenstein's collected writings from 1988 to 1996, a picture of Lenin, and a constructivist Soviet propaganda poster behind him in his office. Yet, although I had come closer to Eisenstein intellectually, I still didn't feel physically very close to him.

I felt just as far away from Eisenstein as I sat in the library of New York University, off Washington Square, where I perused the many folders of the Jay Leyda collection. Leyda, who studied with Eisenstein in Moscow, and was an assistant on *Bezhin Meadow*, did more than anyone else to defend and maintain Eisenstein's reputation in the USA. If only I had met Leyda, but he died in 1988, three weeks after the ninetieth anniversary of Eisenstein's birth, and four days after the fortieth anniversary of his death. I was also denied a meeting with Pera Attasheva's sister, Zina Voynov, a documentary director and film editor who lived in New York but who, alas, was ill with Alzheimer's disease.

But in a wintry Gothenburg in Sweden, during a film festival, I met the Russian director Andrei Konchalovsky for the first time.

His mother had been a friend of Eisenstein's. During World War II, they had been evacuated to Alma Ata in Kazakhstan, where Eisenstein was filming *Ivan the Terrible*. 'Eisenstein spoke English to my mother all the time,' Konchalovsky told me. 'I was only seven years old and I didn't understand what they were saying. But she had spent some time in the USA, and both of them were very nostalgic about America. Eisenstein showed me around the dark and cold sets of *Ivan the Terrible*. I remember his big, white hand holding my small one.' So now, I had, at least, shaken the same hand that had held Eisenstein's.

In Gothenburg, I was hoping to meet, for the first time, Naum Kleiman, Pera Attasheva's heir and the man who had spent most of his life preserving Eisenstein's memory in the Eisenstein Museum (or the 'scientific-memorial cabinet' as it is sometimes referred to), a small apartment in Moscow filled with the director's books and memorabilia, a place I definitely planned to visit. But I missed Kleiman by a day.

In Riga, Eisenstein's birthplace, I was asked to join a panel of Eisenstein 'experts', including Kleiman, after the showing of a Russian documentary entitled *Sergei Eisenstein Autobiography*. The director Oleg Kovalov claimed that 'the most important aspect of my film is not Eisenstein's life, but the mystery he took to his grave.' For me, the only mystery was how such a film could have been made. As I watched it, I got angrier and angrier, realising that his hodgepodge of images taken from Eisenstein's films and those of his contemporaries, as well as from newsreels, cut together with no respect for the dynamic or construction of the original shot or sequence, was merely doing the memory of Eisenstein a disservice. It was almost a parody of Eisenstein's 'montage of attractions'.

When the lights came up, I was told that none of the other members of the panel had turned up, and I was to address the audience alone. So there I was, someone from England, speaking in English, through an interpreter, to an audience of Latvians and Russians about a Latvian-born Russian film director. I started by making negative comments about the documentary we had just witnessed. The reaction was antagonistic. I was told I didn't understand that it was meant to be an impressionistic view of Eisenstein's life and work. I then explained what I felt was my mission as regards Eisenstein in the West: to clear up the misconceptions, to show how accessible he was, how I felt he could have made a wonderful Hollywood musical, and that people have been put off by the myriad theories and theorists surrounding his films. 'I want to rescue Eisenstein from the academics and give him back to the people!' I proclaimed. There was a long silence, before a bearded gentleman rose. 'I am an academic,' he said, and left the cinema.

Flashback to the 1996 Edinburgh Festival, where there was a showing of *Ivan the Terrible Part II*, for some reason in the 'Films of 1947' section. (It was completed in 1946, and not shown until 1958 after 'the thaw'.) I was asked to introduce it. The audience, many of them prepared to be bored, filed in solemnly to see what they had been told was a great Russian film classic, about a period of Russian history of which they knew little. The reaction was heartening. During the enthusiastic question-and-answer session that followed the screening, the names of Shakespeare, Grand Opera, Russian icons, Franz Kafka, Charlie Chaplin, Walt Disney, the Hollywood Musical, the Kabuki Theatre, the Peking Opera, the circus, and the homoerotic underground films of Kenneth Anger (an Eisenstein disciple) were all mentioned. It was clear that the bizarre beauty and power of the once-derided film had been appreciated and understood. The modernist Eisenstein was communicating directly to a modern audience, almost half a century after his death. They had not only caught up with Eisenstein, but had caught *on* to him.

Back in Riga, I visited the Museum of Literature in order to track down some drawings by Eisenstein which I was told were held there. At the top of a winding staircase a little, old woman sat in the dark at the door of the museum. When I arrived, she switched on the lights of the first room. I said, 'Eisenstein?'. She looked at me blankly and gestured to the first room, the walls of which were covered with paintings and photographs of pompous-looking bearded men. I went into the next room, at the entrance of which was another little, old woman sitting in the dark. She put on the lights of this room. The walls were covered with more paintings and photographs of pompous-looking bearded men. I said, 'Eisenstein?' She, too, looked blank and gestured to the next room. I moved through to an identical third room, which was guarded by an identical old woman. Finally, I reached an office, where two teenage girls sat behind a desk doing nothing. They spoke a smattering of English. They had never heard of Eisenstein. I wrote the name down. They looked through their index cards in the files. Eventually, one of them triumphantly produced a card marked 'M. O. Eizensteins – Architect.' I nodded vigorously, realising that it referred to Eisenstein's father. I asked for the material they had on him. They conferred, and I was gestured to wait there, while one of them disappeared. I waited. I waited, smiling from time to time at the remaining girl. An older woman returned. I had to sign a form. She gestured me to wait. I waited and waited. About thirty minutes passed before she re-emerged with a pile of folders. I had to sign a form for each of them before I could open them. Inside were hundreds of sketches by S.M. Eisenstein, the son of the famous Riga architect. These wondrously inventive and witty drawings date from Sergei's sketchbook of 1915 to sketches he did for the prospective *Ivan the Terrible Part III* in 1946. Their stylistic range reflected the influence of artists as disparate as Honoré Daumier, George Grosz, Pablo Picasso and Walt Disney. There is a strange couple, an old man with a beard walking with a taller, much younger woman, who seems to be wearing a cat stole. There is a clown, a grotesquely fat Nero, a hunchback, a dandy leaning on his walking stick.

The drawings of the figures of Christ seen on the walls in *Ivan the Terrible* were taken from Paul Gauguin's *Yellow Christ*. Many of the sketches for the film were also derived, as Eisenstein admitted, from the 'ecstatic angularity' of the paintings of satanic monks by Alessandro Magnasco (1667–1749). 'It was his monks, rather than El Greco's, who stylistically determined how my Ivan the Terrible – Cherkassov – should look and move.'[10]

Emerging from the Museum, I walked around the city where Eisenstein was a child and adolescent, that most 'impressionable' period. People passing me on the pavement in Valdemara Street wondered why I was paying so much attention to No. 6, a rather unremarkable and neglected building. I alone was looking up at the small plaque which reads: 'Sergets Eisenstein, film artist, was born and lived here between 1898–1916.' On the other hand, Albert Street is a tourist attraction, especially for the bizarre houses designed by Mikhail Osipovich Eisenstein in the *art nouveau* style of the *fin de siécle*, which his son claimed to despise but whose influence, despite himself, is conspicuous in his work.

Mikhail Osipovich, who cast a long, dark shadow over most of his son's life, died in exile in Berlin in July 1920, when Eisenstein was twenty-two. I sought out this heavy father's grave in the small Russian cemetery on the outskirts of Berlin. Not knowing where to find the grave, I asked a small, bearded man in a woolly cap, watering some plants, whom I took to be the gardener, if he knew where Mikhail Eisenstein was buried. He told me he was the priest and directed me to the grave. He then indicated the grave of Vladimir Nabokov's father not far from Eisenstein's.

The priest then showed me inside the little Russian Orthodox church with the sky-blue onion dome. As he doffed his cap, I took off my fur hat. He crossed himself before entering and then again while kneeling before an icon of the Virgin Mary. He was silent. I wasn't sure if one was allowed to speak. He broke the silence by pointing out some of the features of the church and the art work, all of which had been smuggled out of Russia after the Revolution. The place reminded me of the church that is vandalised in *Bezhin Meadow*, though the priest had nothing of the demonic qualities of Eisenstein's priests.

Also in Berlin, I finally caught up, all too briefly, with the elusive Naum Kleiman. He was very busy in meetings with a German composer who was writing an original score to accompany a new print of *The General Line* – a film which had never had music specially written for it. Kleiman was following the tradition set by Eisenstein when he got the Austrian-born Edmund Meisel to write the pulsating scores for *The Battleship Potemkin* and *October*. In fact, Eisenstein had hoped that Meisel would write the music for *The General Line*, and had outlined his ideas in detail. 'See you in Moscow,' Kleiman said to me, rushing across Friedrichstrasse near the cinema where *Potemkin* was first shown in Berlin.

*

Like Chekhov's three sisters, I had been trying to get to Moscow for some time, but was prevented from doing so by a variety of obstacles. Eventually, I arrived in the capital where, but for three years spent abroad, Eisenstein had lived for almost three decades from 1920 until his death in 1948. Now I could get even closer to my subject by meeting the few people still alive who knew him, by chatting to Naum Kleiman while sitting among the books Eisenstein so loved – 'large and small, fat and slender, rare editions and cheap paperbacks, they cry out through their dustcovers or are perhaps sunk in contemplation in a solid, leather skin as if wearing soft slippers'[11] – and by steeping myself in the atmosphere of this somewhat overpowering city, where whatever I saw carried resonances of Eisenstein.

At the top of Arbat Street, where they were selling T-shirts marked MacLenin – Lenin's profile against the famous hamburger joint's logo – there remained the cinema that first showed *The Battleship Potemkin*, when the facade was decorated like a battleship, and the usherettes were dressed in sailor suits. Now, needing a new paint job, it was showing a porn movie. Opposite was the old building that once housed the Proletkult Theatre where Eisenstein began his professional career.

A visit to the Pushkin Museum of Fine Arts allowed me to see the many paintings that had impinged themselves on Eisenstein's mind. Hogarth and Goya, two of his favourite artists, are well represented, and there are Japanese and Chinese prints, Géricault's *Revolt*, and Sano di Pietro's *The Beheading of John the Baptist*, a subject Eisenstein returned to again and again in the drawings he made in Mexico.

At the Bolshoi, where Eisenstein directed a production of Wagner's *Die Walküre*, I saw a performance of Rimsky-Korsakov's *The Tsar's Bride*, the intrigues of which echo those in *Ivan the Terrible*. In the resplendent Armory Palace, I saw Ivan the Terrible's opulent regalia; in the Assumption Cathedral, where Ivan was crowned Tsar, his carved throne, and in the Cathedral of the Archangel, his tomb, all within the walls of the Kremlin, all of which were redolent of the atmosphere of Eisenstein's final film. Looking at these extraordinary relics, one could see that Eisenstein's invention made them even more extraordinary on the screen. In the magnificent Tretyakov Museum of Russian Art, I sat in front of Ilya Repin's *Ivan the Terrible Murdering His Child*. Ivan, staring wildly, holds in his arms his dead son, the child's head soaked in blood. In his film, Eisenstein recreated a similar posture, but substituted the dying Tsarina for the child.

Today, in the garden of the New Tretyakov Art Gallery lie the remains of monuments of Lenin and Michael Kalinin (a Stalin henchman), reminding me of the opening scene of *October* when the statue of Tsar Alexander III is toppled by the people. Like the reverse shot in *October*, history was repeated in reverse when, after *perestroika*, statues of discredited leaders, including Stalin himself, were treated in the same way. Felix Dzerzhinsky, the founder of the infamous CHEKA (Extraordinary Commission for Struggle with Counterrevolution and Sabotage) once stood proudly outside his former office on Lubyanka Square, opposite KGB headquarters. Now he lies on his side. Only one poem, Shelley's 'Ozymandias', could come to mind at such a sight: 'Two vast and trunkless legs of stone, stand in the desert. Near them, on the sand, half-sunk, a shattered visage lies, whose frown, and wrinkled lip, and sneer of cold command, Tell that its sculptor well those passions read . . .'

At the Revolution Museum, among the vibrant posters proclaiming the Bolshevik cause, stands Repin's portrait of Alexander Kerensky, the villain in *October*. On the posters, healthy, happy, good-looking farm workers beckon the observer to join them. It is clear that the tenebrous *Bezhin Meadow*, and even the sunnier *The General Line*, both films concerning agricultural collectivisation, would not have sat well with those who produced these posters. Dominating one room is a picture of 'Uncle' Joe Stalin surrounded by adoring children, and one which has a couple of them clinging to him, reminiscent of the kids being carried on horseback by the victorious hero in *Alexander Nevsky*.

I joined a line of people filing dutifully past Lenin's tomb, and then along the Kremlin wall where are buried the dead Soviet leaders (all except Nikita Kruschev, who can be found in the cemetery where Eisenstein's grave lies). Stalin's sepulchre was the only one honoured with fresh floral tributes, the others having to make do with plastic flowers.

There was only one place left to visit, a place where I would literally get as close to Eisenstein as it is possible to get. His grave in the Novodevichy cemetery. Paradoxically, though this is where Eisenstein's journey ended, it was the beginning of mine. I now had to start writing the postscript to his life. P.S. . . . .

PART I

ENTHUSIASM

1

The Childhood of Sergei Mikhailovich Eisenstein

I had no experience of poverty or deprivation in childhood, nor any of the horrors of struggling for existence. Further on you will encounter descriptions of my childhood – for the time being, take it on faith!

An orchestra was playing at the summer resort of Majorenhof, on the coast just outside Riga. Yulia Ivanovna Eisenstein was seven month's pregnant. The guests at the dacha had had far too much to drink that evening. A fight broke out and someone was killed. Yulia's husband, Mikhail Osipovich Eisenstein, grabbed his revolver in an attempt to restore order. Yulia Ivanovna was terrified and almost gave birth prematurely. As it was, back in Riga, Sergei Mikhailovich Eisenstein arrived three weeks early, on January 23, 1898, having absorbed, in the womb, a love of gunshots and orchestras.

A couple of years later, the family was again holidaying at Majorenhof. The child Sergei was lying in a small, white bed. A bough of white lilac spilled through the window of the room, its flowers and green foliage cutting across a ray of sunshine above his head. 'My first childhood impression was . . . a close-up,' he wrote towards the end of his life.[1]

It is easy to pass by 6 Valdemara Street in Riga without a second glance. Although large, it is an undistinguished, rectangular, off-white, four-storey building, the paint peeling off the facade. It

17

contains the offices of an established printing firm. On the wall beside a rather pretentiously tall doorway, a discreet, unpolished plaque is visible. It reads: 'Sergets Eisenstein, film artist, was born and lived here between 1898–1916.' Virtually no other evidence exists that Sergei Mikhailovich Eisenstein was born and brought up in this Baltic seaport, the capital of Latvia. There is an Eisenstein Street, but that is named after Sergei's father, the architect and civil engineer Mikhail Osipovich. It is true to say, that among the general population of Riga, Eisenstein Senior is better known than his film director son.

Now, as at the turn of the century, the house on Valdemara Street (Nicholas Street in Tsarist times) is in an expensive and fashionable part of town. A splendidly spacious and verdant park, a golden church dome and a meandering blue canal can be seen from the windows of the house. Apart from some modern high-rise buildings in the background, this would have been approximately the view that greeted the young Eisenstein through his bedroom window in Flat 7, on the third floor.

The picture of a privileged middle-class child, with his long, fair, shoulder-length hair and his sailor suit, Sergei would go for walks with his beloved nanny, Maria Elksne, in the parks off the pleasant boulevards. In a photograph taken in 1904, the six-year-old Eisenstein is standing in his sailor suit and laced-up boots, holding his large hat in his small right hand. His left hand seems even tinier because it is almost lost in the grip of his father, a portly, officious-looking man, with a trimmed handle-bar moustache. Mikhail Osipovich Eisenstein is proudly wearing the uniform of the senior city engineer in the roads department of the Livonian provincial government. (In most of the surviving photographs he is bedecked in some uniform or other.) The little Sergei, plainly ill at ease, stares tentatively out at the camera. He resembles the description he once gave of himself as an adult: 'When I look at myself in complete privacy, the image that most readily springs to mind is that of . . . David Copperfield. Delicate, thin, short, defenceless, and very timid.'[2]

Erwin Mednis, a former school classmate, recalled that 'physically he was slightly built and rather frail. There was something rather feminine about his appearance, so that he often looked more like a girl than a boy.'[3]

18

Much to his father's disgust, Eisenstein's mother kept her son's hair in a kind of medieval bob, rather like that of the effeminate Vladimir's in *Ivan the Terrible*. Eisenstein saw himself as a 'well-brought up boy from Riga with the Lord Fauntleroy ringlets and lace collar . . . Since my earliest years it was the shackles of cuffs and starched collar instead of torn trousers and ink blots . . .'[4] Eventually, when his mother left her husband and went to live in St Petersburg, his father had Sergei's head shaved bare.

Eisenstein was certainly a victim of incompatible parents, bullied and ignored by his father, flattered and pampered by his mother. Yulia Ivanovna was a snobbish woman who regarded her husband as vulgar and was determined that Sergei should grow up to be a man of culture. 'She was eccentric. I was eccentric. She was ridiculous. I was ridiculous,' her son remarked.[5] To him, his father represented philistinism and bourgeois values, his mother the arts and refinement. She provided him with a wide culture, while his father incited his rebellion.

Given this situation, it is all too easy for commentators to fall back on psychological commonplaces such as the Oedipus complex when explaining Eisenstein's actions, personality and sexuality – his antipathy towards his father, his ambivalent love for his mother – yet in his oblique writings about his emotional life, the self-perceptive Eisenstein encourages this view.

Mikhail Osipovich was a powerful, stocky man with a Kaiser Wilhelm moustache, who came from a family of German-Jewish origin which had been baptised and assimilated into Russian society. Not much is known about them. Although Mikhail Osipovich's grave in Berlin is marked 'Born St Petersburg', no record of his birth there has been found. It is possible that he was born somewhere close to the city or that he had no wish, for some political or social reason, to divulge his real birthplace. (The name of Eisenstein was quite common in Czechoslovakia and Austria.) Among Sergei Eisenstein's possessions was a souvenir glass on which there is a picture of a church in the town of Eisenstein, somewhere in Europe. Almost nothing is known of his paternal grandparents, though the wife of his cousin once remarked that her husband mentioned that the grandmother was thought to be Swedish.

For Eisenstein, his father exemplified all that was reprehensible in the bourgeois mentality and, it could be argued, that his father's persona informs the bourgeois characters he depicted in his films, such as the fat bosses in *The Strike* and the heartless double-chinned *kulak* in *The General Line*. With this in mind, it is difficult not to see Eisenstein's treatment of Alexander Kerensky in *October* as not only a political gesture, but a private one. In one visual metaphor, the caricatured Alexander Kerensky is compared, through montage, to a mechanical peacock spreading its metal feathers. The satirical effect is increased in the sequence where the 'dictator' Kerensky is made to ascend the same flight of steps several times with the inter-cutting titles denoting ever higher rank. In the same film, a uniformed general is meticulously presented button by button from his oiled-flat hair to his shiny boots. From Eisenstein's own, albeit subjective, testimony of his father, a grotesque Gogolian picture of a pompous, pedantic, rather preposterous man emerges.

'Father had 40 pairs of patent leather shoes . . . His valet Ozols, in his greatcoat, would give him the pair he requested with the aid of the list, taking them from what looked like a multi-tiered rabbit hutch which hung in the corridor . . . Papa would only wear shiny, black boots with square toes. He did not acknowledge any other sort. And he had a huge collection of them "for every occasion." He even listed them in a register, with any distinguishing feature indicated: "new", "old"; "a scratch". From time to time he held an inspection and roll-call. Then Ozols would slide up and down, opening wide the gates of this boot garage. Vainglorious, petty, too stout, industrious, unlucky, broken – but still he wore his white gloves (on weekdays!) and his collars were perfectly starched.'[6]

Writing in the last decade of his life, Eisenstein's aversion to his 'tyrannical' father was as strong as ever. However, many of his caustic reflections on a man who had died in 1920, could be seen as a transference of his unexpressed and inexpressible private views on 'Papa' Stalin. During the most repressive period of Stalin's 'paternalistic' rule, it was extremely dangerous to write down one's negative thoughts on the regime, even in one's personal diary, especially for Eisenstein who was always closely watched for any 'deviations'. Yet, in 1928, after the leader's interference with *October*, Eisenstein did confide to his diary his disgust at 'the barbarism of Stalin'. It was one of the very few pages destroyed by Eisenstein's widow, Pera Attasheva, out of fear for him, and she collected almost everything of his.

Eisenstein's mother, Yulia Ivanovna (née Konyetskaya), who had the simian features, big head and stocky body of her son, resembled Sergei in drag. The resemblance was so striking that the reminiscence of the pain Eisenstein recalled feeling as a child when his mother denied, during an angry exchange, that he was her son, seems hardly credible. If there had been any dispute as to his parentage, it would have been far more likely, given his mother's 'oversexed' nature – she had several affairs before, during and after her marriage – that his father was not his natural one, a far-fetched notion that Eisenstein enjoyed contemplating.

Yulia Ivanovna was independent-minded, and had travelled to Egypt alone, an unusual undertaking for a middle-class woman in the late 19th century. She was the daughter of a self-made merchant, Ivan Ivanovich Konyetsky, who established a flourishing barge-hauling firm in St Petersburg, which carried freight on the Marinsky canal system which linked the Baltic Sea and the River Neva to the River Volga. Her mother, Iraida Matveyevna Konyetskaya, ran the company after her husband died. Eisenstein, always fond of finding analogies in literature, saw his grandmother as the eponymous character in Maxim Gorky's 1910 play *Vassa Zheleznova*, a woman who rules her bourgeois family and its shipping empire with a rod of iron. Iraida died of a brain haemorrhage while praying vigorously in the Alexander Nevsky church in Riga. Perhaps she was in the throes of religious ecstasy, a state of mind that theoretically fascinated Eisenstein most of his life, linking it as he did with sexual ecstasy.

In addition, in keeping with a certain pattern of correspondences (some accidental, others predetermined) between Eisenstein's life and work, the 'family saint' of the Konyetskies happened to be Alexander Nevsky, the hero of the director's most acceptable film in the Soviet Union. As a child, he would often take walks in the Alexander Nevsky monastery, 'the silver shrine of the saint whom

I was destined to glorify in film after his country had made him a national hero.'[7]

If one is searching for further associations, the only mother who has a substantial role in his films is Euphrosinia, the monstrous mother in *Ivan the Terrible*. She smothers (almost literally at times) her weak, epicene son Vladimir, and is prepared to commit any crime to see him become Tsar, despite his reluctance. The mother of Vassili Bouslay, the axe-wielding blond warrior in *Alexander Nevsky*, tells him, 'I thought to see you wedded. You have brought disgrace,' when he gives up Olga to his friend Gavrilo.

At his parents' separation, after staying a short period with an aunt, Eisenstein remained with his father and only saw his mother on infrequent visits to St Petersburg, although he lived with her for two years at No. 9 Tauride Street while he was a student at the Engineering School. When he had embarked on his career as a director, after his father had become an exile in Germany, he was in constant touch, allowing her to share in his triumphs, and sending her cards from wherever he was travelling, later getting her to come to Moscow to be near him.

It was Yulia Ivanovna, who had written a number of unfinished and unpublished novels herself, who first indulged her son's love of books. Her great-uncle, General Botovsky, who was the president of the Russian Olympic Games committee, and had been responsible for Russia joining the Olympic movement, wrote stories for magazines. According to Eisenstein, 'He was extremely miserly. He was no less mean in his literary craft. He wasted no time, for example, describing nature. "It was one of those dawns that Turgenev describes so inimitably well . . ." This was but one of the literary pearls to roll off the General's pen.'[8]

'Books are attracted to me,' Eisenstein wrote. 'They make a bee-line for me, and stick to me. I have been so fond of them that at last they have begun to reciprocate. In my hands books burst like ripe fruit. Like magic flowers they unfold their petals to show me the vital thought, the suggestive word, the confirming quotation, the decisive illustration.'[9]

Director Mikhail Romm, visiting Eisenstein's apartment in the early 1930s, remarked, 'There were books everywhere. A huge table was covered in books. An entire wall was filled with bookshelves, and Eisenstein used to sit among the books, on the books, under the books.'[10]

His English friend Ivor Montagu had a similar impression when he visited him in 1933. 'The one-big-room flat he inhabited was everywhere knee-deep in books. He could, of course, never find a wanted one and, if something had to be looked up, he had each time to buy another copy.'[11]

By his early teens, Eisenstein had read most of the works of Alexander Dumas, Jean Racine, Pierre Corneille, Emile Zola and Stéphane Mallarmé in French, Edgar Allan Poe in English, and Leo Tolstoy and Fyodor Dostoevsky in Russian, making copious notes as he did so.

It was from books that Eisenstein derived his 'first impressions of sadism . . . the first situations to suggest themselves to me came not from live or personal experience but were "reflected" and "refracted."'[12] As if to contradict this, Eisenstein relates his earliest memories of thrashings he had received as a small boy. The first was from Ozols, his father's servant.

'My second thrashing came a little later, but before my school-days began and with much less ceremony. I remember here being half-naked – only my trousers were down. I remember the "weapon" – a strap folded three times . . . Mama was the executioner. And it had absolutely no effect whatsoever, I laughed cheekily the whole time, although my cheekiness alone deserved punishment. I had been thoroughly obnoxious to my French (or English?) governess on a walk in Strelkovy Park. It was worse for Eton schoolboys.'[13]

Eisenstein then goes on to describe, in some detail and with relish, the punishments at Eton. 'In the schoolroom . . . stands a small wooden step-ladder with three rungs. The victim kneels on it, bending over obediently. And as he does so, the ancient rule dictates, "there shall be nothing between the birch and the body."'[14]

The sado-masochistic streak in S. M. Eisenstein's character, and a morbid fascination with martyrdom, especially that of St Sebastian, so prevalent in gay iconography, dates back to his child-hood reading, later revealing itself in his drawings, films and in his memoirs, particularly in a chapter headed *To the Illustrious Memory of the Marquis.*

He remembered an article he read as a child in a copy of his father's *Petersburg Gazette*, which described how a group of drunken butchers took an apprentice into a back room, stripped him, and hung him by his legs from a hook in the ceiling. 'They then began to flay him with a double hook, the sort used for hanging carcasses up. Skin came off in chunks . . . I expect it was this image that gave rise to my predilection for St Sebastian . . . In my Mexican film, I named the peon who was martyred in the fields of agave, Sebastian; he died in excruciating agony, after suffering all manner of torture, being buried up to his shoulders and trampled beneath the hooves of the *haciendado's* horses.'[15]

At the age of twelve, while visiting his mother in St Petersburg, he came across a number of books which she had hidden under the seats of chairs and sofas. One of them, which he surreptitiously read and took delight in, was the Marquis de Sade's *Histoire de Juliette ou Les Prospérités du Vice (The Story of Juliette or Vice Amply Rewarded)*, which Eisenstein mistakenly remembered in his memoirs as being called *The Stages of Vice*. Other representatives of his mother's rather exotic taste were *The Torture Garden* by Octave Mirbeau and *Venus in Furs* by Leopold Sacher-Masoch, the latter being illustrated with 'the first pictures of an "unhealthy sensuality" that I found.'[16] He also felt that these books aroused 'an alarming streak of brutality' within him, and influenced 'the ocean of brutalities in which my pictures are steeped.'

The thirteen-year-old schoolboy Eisenstein would stare through the windows of a bookshop in Riga, where the lurid covers of penny dreadfuls were displayed. 'The covers had a terrifying, magnetic force. And I remember being unable to take my eyes off those horrors behind the glass, but standing there for ages.'[17] A cover that made a vivid impression was one which depicted detective Nick Carter, his hands and feet tied up, suspended above a sarcophagus filled with molten metal. 'On one side was a lady, her dress in disarray, wearing a short skirt, her bodice undone. She had one arm stretched out as she took aim. The caption read: "If Nick doesn't tell her what she wants to know, she'll shoot through the rope." The metal bubbled with hospitality, ready for the doomed Nick.'[18]

Without elaborating, Eisenstein admits that his first erotic dream came from a Nick Carter-inspired fantasy. One summer, at a dacha in Bullen, on the Riga coast, Eisenstein 'reconstructed' a Nick Carter cover, getting the young Baron Tusenhausen, the son of a friend of his parents, to strip to the waist and wear a cap, as the captive of a villain who was forcing him to print counterfeit notes.

Another book cover that attracted him was one which displayed various implements of torture, with the neck of a young man, who was stripped to the waist, gripped tightly by an iron collar. These, and other images of torture, were to find their way into some of his produced (and unproduced) screenplays and films. 'In fact, people in my films are gunned down in their hundreds; farm labourers have their skulls shattered by hoofs, or they are lassoed and buried in the ground up to their necks (*Qué Viva México!*); children are crushed on the Odessa steps (*The Battleship Potemkin*); thrown from rooftops (*The Strike*); are surrendered to their own parents who murder them (*Bezhin Meadow*); thrown onto flaming pyres (*Alexander Nevsky*); they stream with actual bulls' blood (*The Strike*) or with stage blood (*Potemkin*); in some films bulls are poisoned (*The Old and the New*); in others, tsars (*Ivan the Terrible*); a shot horse hangs from a raised bridge (*October*); and arrows pierce men lying spread-eagled on the ramparts outside a besieged Kazan (*Ivan the Terrible*). And it seems no coincidence that it was none other than Tsar Ivan Vasilyevich the Terrible who ruled my mind and was my hero for very many years.'[19]

He could have added the tower of Timur, in the unrealised *Ferghana Canal*, constructed from tortured human bodies, and the hundreds of sketches of the beheading of John the Baptist, the murder of King Duncan from *Macbeth*, and martyred bulls dying at the hands of a matador, that he drew in Mexico.

There is a particular homoerotic image in *The Battleship Potemkin* that appealed to Eisenstein. After the killing of the leader of the mutiny, 'a young lad tears his shirt in a paroxysm of fury' revealing his bare chest. (Actually, it could also be read as the ancient Jewish tradition of tearing one's clothing in mourning). This derived from Eisenstein's reading of reports about a young man who, during the 1917 revolution in St Petersburg, had his shirt torn off his back before being executed – his 'perforated body lay on the granite steps, half submerged in the Neva . . . the two halves of the boy's shirt lying on the granite steps near the sphinxes of the Egyptian Bridge.'[20] Revealingly, Eisenstein admits that he was more interested in the section with the boy tearing his shirt than in the hoisting of the red flag in *The Battleship Potemkin*. The motif reoccurs in *Ivan the Terrible*, when the Tsar's would-be assassin, a young monk, has his shirt torn off him.

Apart from literature and the forbidden delights of *serie noir*, Eisenstein found both his imagination and rebellion fuelled by history books, particularly Auguste Mignet's *History of the French Revolution*.

'The history of France was one of the first things to make an impression on me . . . By some miracle, "the impressionable little boy" stumbled upon more historical works in his father's bookcases. They seemed out of place there, in the library of this upright citizen who had successfully worked his way up the ranks. But I found 1871 and the Paris Commune there, in a handsomely illustrated French edition. It was kept next to albums about Napoleon Bonaparte, who was my father's ideal – as he was of any self-made man. (In *October*, the 'democrat' Kerensky, obsessed with power, gazes at a bust of Napoleon).

'My fascination with revolutions, especially French ones, dates from that tender age. First of all it was because of their romance. Their colour. Their rarity. I greedily devoured book after book. The guillotine enthralled my imagination . . . I was excited by figures like Marat and Robespierre. I could hear the crack of rifles – the Versailles firing squads – and the peal of the Paris tocsin . . . Living in Riga I spoke German better than Russian. But in my thoughts I lived French history.'[21]

After the uprising of February 1917, when Tsar Nicholas II had abdicated, Eisenstein expressed a regret, albeit ironically, that a guillotine had not been set up in Znamenskaya Square in St Petersburg, where stood the Alexander III memorial. 'I used to imagine that Doctor Guillotine's "widow" stood on top of the granite pedestal . . . I wanted so much to be part of history . . . but what sort of history was it, if there was no guillotine?'[22]

This romanticising of a bloody revolution imbues much of

October, particularly in the storming of the Winter Palace sequence. The film, designed to glorify the Bolsheviks and the revolution of 1917, owes a great deal to Eisenstein's childhood visions of French revolutions, derived as much from his reading of *Les Misérables* as from history books.

'The romance of the fighting on the barricades was informed with elements of the ideas being fought for. Naive though it may be as far as the profundity of its social programme is concerned, Hugo's sermon on social injustice is nevertheless expressed with passion and pitched at just the right level to inspire anyone young and just beginning to think about life, with similar ideas . . .'[23]

It must not be forgotten that Eisenstein spent his childhood in Riga 'during the heat of the events of 1905.' Eisenstein was only seven years old when the revolution broke out in St Petersburg, but he was steeped in the stories of the uprising. On January 9, a workers' group moved in a peaceful procession on the Winter Palace in order to claim redress of grievances from the Tsar himself, using revolutionary language. The procession was fired upon by order of one of the grand dukes (Nicholas II was absent from the Palace). The event was termed "Bloody Sunday" and may be considered the beginning of the Revolution of 1905.

Eisenstein remembered a detail of Bloody Sunday that a witness recounted to him. Little boys had sat in the trees of Alexandrovsky Park 'just like sparrows', and when the first volley was fired upon the crowd, they jumped. In February 1905, for the first time in the history of modern Russia, millions of people in the cities as well as the villages took part in a genuine mass movement. In late September and early October the movement swelled toward a dramatic climax. Strikes spread everywhere. The result of the struggle was paralysis throughout the economy and panic among the leaders of the government, including Baron Alexander Meller-Zakomelsky, known for his cruel suppression of mutinies during the Revolution of 1905.

'There are as many terrible and brutal impressions as you could wish from all around; the wild outburst of reaction and repression from men like Meller-Zakomelsky and his accomplices. Even more important, the brutality in my pictures is indissolubly tied up with the theme of social injustice, and revolt against it . . .'[24]

Yet, Eisenstein, an artist who claimed to be a Marxist all his life, makes an astonishing admission. 'The reason why I came to support social protest had little to do with the real miseries of social injustice, or material privations, or the zigzags of the struggle for life, but directly and completely from what is surely the prototype of every social tyranny – the father's despotism in a family, which is also a survival of the basic despotism of the head of the "tribe" in every primitive society.'[25]

Again, elsewhere, Eisenstein puts the origins of his rebellious or 'revolutionary' nature in art as much down to his father as to politics and philosophy. 'Father was a pillar of the church and the autocracy . . . Father who instilled in me the whole melting-pot of petit-bourgeois, petty passions for self improvement at the expense of others, but was not able to see that an *Oedipal* [author's italics] protest would make me hate them even though they were part of my baggage. And instead of being invisibly intoxicated by them, the cold eye of the analyst and tally clerk would break down whatever charm they might have held . . . I do not represent my late father – a typical bully about the house, and slave to Tolstoy's ideas of *comme il faut* – with a list of grievances. But it is interesting that my protest against what was "acceptable" in behaviour and in art, and my contempt of authority, was certainly linked to him.'[26]

In the second version of the aborted *Bezhin Meadow*, there is a reversal of the patricidal Oedipus story – the origin of the Freudian 'Kill the father'. It is the *kulak* father who kills his young son after declaring, 'If a son betray his own father, let him be slaughtered like a dog.'

Two months before his mother's death in 1946, and over two decades after his father's death, Eisenstein wrote: 'Perhaps to tell the truth, I never felt a particular love for Mikhail Osipovich according to the Biblical code. But one of the fundamental commands in the Bible is that we "honour" our parents: "Honour thy mother and thy father and thou shalt dwell long on the earth." A reward that was of dubious value. And anyway, why should one be grateful to one's parents.'[27]

Eisenstein's 'protest' against his father extended to Mikhail Osipovich's work as an architect. (Sergei also lived to see, but not comment on, the heavy post-war Stalin Gothic skyscrapers.) 'Father was one of the most flowery representatives of that architectural decadence – *style moderne*. Father was a reckless follower *de l'art pompier. Pompier* in his behaviour.'[28]

Eisenstein Senior built over fifty houses in Riga in the first decade of the century, three of which have become tourist attractions. These are numbers 2, 4 and 6 Albert Street designed in what Sergei called 'the crazy *art nouveau* style, which so transported my dear parent.' They show a surprising side to Eisenstein's father. The *Jugendstil* (as *art nouveau* is called in German) dominates much of the old city centre, most of it unremarkable, but those in Albert Street built by Mikhail Eisenstein have genuine style and imagination, especially the sinuous lines and phallic motifs of the interiors. The facades are encrusted with rather antic statuary – two nude women who seem to be making the Roman (fascist) 'heil' gesture, while two others hold up laurel wreaths. On another corner is the head of a bearded man who bears a resemblance to Nikolai Cherkassov as Ivan the Terrible, being harangued on either side by two shrews. A couple of sphinxes guard the entrance of number 2. Although *Jugendstil* was becoming fashionable, if not respectable, when these buildings were erected around the turn of the century, they were certainly not the work of the arch-conservative, shoe-obsessed, domineering, uniformed philistine and petty 'government inspector' described by his son. Sergei dismissed his father as 'a maker of cakes' urging all his friends to 'look at the cream on that house's face.'

'Father, who placed statues of human beings one and a half storeys high, stretched out as a decoration, on the corners of the houses. Father, who deployed women's arms, made from iron drainpipes and with gold rings in their hands, beneath the angle of the roof. In bad weather, it was fun watching the rain stream down between their tin legs. Father, who triumphantly entwined in the sky the tails of the plaster lions – *lions de plâtre* – which were piled up on the rooftops. Father himself was a *lion de plâtre*. And he bequeathed to me an unhealthy passion for winding layer upon layer – which I tried to sublimate into a fascination for Catholic baroque and the over-elaborate work of the Aztecs.'[29]

His father's (bad?) taste certainly imbues much of the aesthetics of Eisenstein's films, whether it is 'sublimated' or treated with mock reverence: the statues of lions (*'lions de plâtre'!*) leaping up in anger in *The Battleship Potemkin*; the succession of gods descending from a baroque Christ through a number of divine images down to a wooden idol in *October*; the death masks in *Qué Viva México!*, and the grotesque murals in *Ivan the Terrible*.

Eisenstein muses that his memory of his father's statues led him to dismember 'the giant statue of Alexander III which such mouth-watering excitement, in the opening episode of *October*.'[30] He also felt that if the 'dismembered and overturned hollow figure of the Tsar served as an image for the overthrow of Tsarism in February, then it is clear that this start to the film . . . was about my personal liberty from Papa's authority . . . A tyrannical Papa was common-place in the 19th century. But mine dragged on into the 20th! . . . How many times did little Sergei, the exemplary little boy, answer his Papa's questions – weren't his buildings marvellous? – in a stud-ied formula of delight like a learned parrot, even though it ran deeply counter to his ideas and convictions!'[31]

Until the October Revolution, which ignited his personal revolt, there was in Eisenstein what he called 'my irrational submissiveness and obedience.' Eisenstein's father was in the habit of asking his son to praise him when they had visitors and the boy duly obliged. Years later, when he discovered that Stalin liked to be praised, he repeated this technique, ritualistically rendering unto Caesar what was Caesar's 'even though it ran deeply counter to my ideas and convictions!' In both cases, though the penalty for silence ranged from mere disapproval to possible death, silence would have been a sign that he was being contrary.

One enthusiasm which Eisenstein did share with his father was a love of the circus, but with an important difference: 'I have adored clowns since I was in my cradle. My father also adored the circus, but what attracted him most of all was what he used to call "high class equestrianship". So I carefully concealed my passion for clowns and pretended to be wildly interested in horses.'[32] For Eisenstein, clowns represented freedom from official life. Later, when he no longer had to hide his fascination with circus clowns, they (or versions of them, such as Pierrot) would make their appearances throughout a variety of his work, from his early stage productions to the clowns acting out the 'fiery furnace' parable in *Ivan the Terrible: Part II*, his final film.

Apart from the great 19th-century French pantomimist Jean-Gaspard Deburau, whose picture he kept on his wall, he considered his friend Charlie Chaplin the finest clown of all. 'Reality is like the serious white clown. It seems earnest and logical. Circumspect and prudent. But in the final analysis it is reality that looks the fool, the object of derision. Its partner, Chaplin, guileless and childlike, comes out on top. He laughs carelessly without even noticing that his laugh slays reality,'[33] Eisenstein wrote in 1943, wishfully hoping to destroy the 'earnest and logical' reality with his own laughter.

The 'earnest and logical' side to Eisenstein was one of the few positive traits that he inherited from his father – the engineer's quality of preparedness, the belief in the need for pre-planning, and the merits of construction. He developed intricate, detailed blueprints for each project, as his scripts and sketches testify. As a teacher, he also liked to take a plot apart like a machine to see how it worked.

Erwin Mednis recalled, 'If things usually seemed easier for him than for the rest of us, it was largely because of this quality of preparedness. If few things went wrong it was because so few things were left to chance, and if genius is really, or at least partly, "the infinite capacity for taking pains," then Eisenstein was a genius indeed.'[34]

Aside from the combined influence, both positive and negative, of his parents, there were other components in Eisenstein's background that doubtless contributed to his 'difference' from many of his contemporaries.

Although he considered himself to have only an eighth of Jewish blood he has always been perceived as being of German-Jewish descent. Riga had a fairly large Jewish community, although there was (and is) only one synagogue. Both in Latvia and Lithuania, the Jews were treated as equals under the law. (It was only under the Nazi occupation that the persecution and killing of the Jews began.) In Odessa, however, whose population was 30% Jewish, countless Jews were slaughtered in the streets in 1905 in one of the most terrible pogroms in Russian history, the sort of pogrom that must have driven Eisenstein's paternal grandparents to give up their Jewish heritage. 'Down with Jews,' says the sneering bourgeois in Odessa in *The Battleship Potemkin*, suggesting that he was typical of the attitude held by his class during the Tsarist regime. Of course, the proletarian population react violently to this remark and attack the man. This sequence was obviously influenced by Eisenstein's friend, the Jewish writer Isaac Babel.

While Eisenstein was writing the script of *The Battleship Potemkin*, he was simultaneously working with Babel on a script of *The Career of Benya Krik* based on the latter's story in *Tales of Odessa*. In Babel's story *How It Was Done in Odessa* (1924), one character asks rhetorically, 'Wasn't it a mistake on God's part to settle Jews in Russia so they suffer in Hell?'. There is a further link with Babel (who also co-wrote the second version of *Bezhin Meadow* with Eisenstein). Babel wrote the intertitles for a Yiddish film called *Jewish Luck*, made the year before *Potemkin*, which has a dream sequence shot on the Odessa steps.

Eisenstein learned to use Yiddish slang and Yiddish humour. A Jewish student of his at the G.I.K. (State Cinema Institute) had an elementary English grammar book open on a page on kitchen utensils. As a joke, Eisenstein ringed the word 'pots' (*putz*) meaning penis in Yiddish.

There was also a risky and risqué Jewish joke that Eisenstein liked to tell. Stalin, who was receiving important visitors from Poland, decided to present them with a large painting entitled *Lenin in Poland*, which he wanted done in a few days by a Jewish artist he particularly admired. When he was informed that the artist had been deported to a labour camp in Siberia, Stalin demanded his immediate release. The poor emaciated man was flown to Moscow, given a good meal and accommodation, and instructed to paint the picture. Stalin and his Polish guests gathered on the great day of the unveiling of *Lenin in Poland*, but when the painting was uncovered, it revealed a man and a woman having sex. Even worse, the man was recognisable as Trotsky and the woman as Lenin's wife. A shocked Stalin turned on the little Jewish artist, demanding, 'But where is Lenin?' 'In Poland,' replied the man shrugging.

Eisenstein's semi-Jewishness is rarely mentioned in his own writings, nor in much that has been written about him. Nor did he ever seem a victim of overt anti-semitism in the Soviet Union – suspect comrades were often referred to pejoratively as 'cosmopolitans'. According to Herbert Marshall, the English film historian, 'All the Soviet Jewish directors had to keep silent in order to survive and this included all the leading directors – Roshal, Kozintsev, Trauberg, Zarkhi, Heifitz, Vertov, Room and Romm.'[35] It is doubtful whether Eisenstein's Jewish ancestry had anything to do with his detachment from the mainstream of Soviet artists, though his 'cosmopolitanism' in the objective sense, did cause him problems.

In July 1941, with the Soviet Union at war with Germany, Eisenstein was wheeled out as a Soviet Jew to speak on a radio programme to America, 'To Brother Jews of All the World.' But, as a child, it was because he was German-speaking that he was never wholly accepted as Russian, nor was (or is) he considered a Latvian by natives of the country of his birth. Almost half the population of Riga, at the time of his birth, was German, and Eisenstein spoke German better than he did Russian as a child.

'At school,' Eisenstein wrote, 'there was a blatant nationalist hatred amongst the different sections of the population to which the pupils' parents belonged. I belonged to the '"Colonists", the Russian civil-servant class, detested equally by the native Latvian population and by the descendants of the first German colonists who had enslaved them.'[36]

In addition, Eisenstein's name would forever make him sound foreign. His almost exact contemporary, Dziga Vertov, born Denis Kaufman in Bialystok in Poland, then annexed by Russia, changed his name both to assimilate more, and to give it a revolutionary ring; Dziga Vertov are Ukrainian words that evoke spinning and turning. In contrast, Eisenstein's father rejoiced in his surname.

'It was not only the fact that his name was to be found in the *Official Gazette*; any mention of his name tickled Papa's pride. For example, Papa never missed a production of the operetta *Die Fledermaus*. He always sat in the front row and when they came to the famous couplets: "Herr Eisenstein! Herr Eisenstein! Die Fledermaus!" he would close his eyes in bliss. Papa was an exemplary worker and stay-at-home, which probably explains

why the nocturnal adventures of his chance operatic namesake –
outwardly respectable but actually a profligate playboy – so
impressed Mr Eisenstein. Papa was flattered, even when it was
sung at home . . .'[37]

In 1907, the eight-year-old Sergei went on a trip with his mother to
Paris, a city that was to mean a great deal to him, not only because
of its revolutionary history. Mother and son stayed at the Du
Helder Hotel on Rue du Helder, and visited the Jardin des Plantes,
the Bois du Boulogne, where Eisenstein drank bitter mulled wine to
treat an attack of dysentery, and Napoleon's tomb at Les Invalides,
the drapery of which he reproduced in his drawings for the projected first production of Sergei Prokofiev's opera *War and Peace* in
1942. (Another example of the way little of what made an impression on him, even at such an early age, was ever wasted.) He
enviously watched children playing in the Tuileries gardens, and
was particularly impressed by the gargoyles on Notre Dame cathedral. At the Musée Grevin, he marvelled at the wax effigies of
Napoleon and Josephine, and other historical figures, but the section that attracted him most was the Chamber of Horrors. There,
Marie Antoinette and other aristocrats ascended the guillotine. (In
1924, Eisenstein saw Paul Leni's German Expressionistic film
Waxworks, in which one of the wax exhibits is Ivan the Terrible,
played by Conrad Veidt, whose appearance bears a striking likeness
to Eisenstein's Ivan.)

But his most vivid impression of that visit to Paris was seeing
'the famous coachman by that genius Méliès, who drove a carriage
pulled by the skeleton of a horse.'[38] Eisenstein is referring to
Georges Méliès' *400 Jokes of the Devil*, which his mother took him
to see at a cinema on the Boulevard des Italiens. The 20-minute
film starred Méliès himself in his favourite role, that of Satan, who
buys the soul of the English engineer William Crackford. In
exchange Satan must procure for him the pleasures of speed,
because Crackford has a passion for breaking records in horseless
carriages. It is then that the famous apocalyptic horse appears,
pulling a devilish coach carved in wood. There follows a wonderfully effective descent into Hell, and the film ends with a diabolic
ballet. Crackford is placed on a spit and roasted over a glowing

fire, while demons dance around him, an effect that obviously appealed to Eisenstein's developing sado-masochism.

The memory of the skeletal horse kicking at the spectral coach in the 1906 Méliès film could well have influenced the scene of the white horse caught on the drawbridge in *October* twenty years later, as well as the skeletons of horses on 'the field of death' in the prologue to *Alexander Nevsky*. 'I have been fascinated by bones and skeletons since childhood. (It was skeletons, for example, that made me go to Mexico)', Eisenstein explained.[39]

Despite the indelible visit to the Méliès film in Paris with his mother, the cinema, perhaps inevitably in the early years of the century, played a much smaller part in his life than the theatre or the circus, though he visited Riga's two cinemas, the Crystal and the Progress, from time to time, and always with Maria, his governess. One film he saw had an American spy as hero, of which the young Eisenstein commented, 'I hate stories about spies, and my nanny and I left before the end.'[40] (He must have changed his mind in adulthood, because there are a number of spies in *The Strike*.)

In 1913, he saw Louis Feuillade's serial, *Fantômas*, the adventures of the arch criminal and genius of disguise, the rooftop chase of which Eisenstein remembered when he made his first short film, *Glumov's Diary*. In the same year, he was 'much impressed' by the first French film version of *Les Misérables*.

Another French film he saw as a child whose title escaped him, but which stayed with him throughout his life, was set during the Napoleonic Wars. It included a sequence in which a cuckolded blacksmith catches the young sergeant with whom his wife has deceived him, ties him up, rips his coat, and brands him on his bare shoulder with a white-hot iron rod. 'The scene of the branding still remains ineradicable in my memory. It gave me nightmares when I was young . . . Once I was the sergeant. Another time, the smith. I grabbed hold of my own shoulder. Sometimes, I thought it was my own. And sometimes someone else's. And it became uncertain who was branding whom. For many years, I had only to see fair curly hair (the sergeant was blond) . . . for that scene to come to mind.'[41]

One of his closest friends in Riga was Andrei 'Alyosha' Bertels, who was blond, had a sweet disposition, and on whom Eisenstein had a crush. Years later, Eisenstein saw something of his childhood friend in the twelve-year-old Vitka Kartachov, the wondrous boy from the aborted *Bezhin Meadow*, whose hair he dyed blond for the role. Grigori Alexandrov, Eisenstein's companion from his earliest years in the theatre and films, also had the fair-haired good looks of young Bertels. In the darkest days of Stalinism, Bertels, who became a geneticist, was exiled to a work camp in Kazakhstan because of his suspected 'anti-Sovietism'. At the time, Eisenstein managed to send him money, books and foodstuffs, although their friendship had ended in adolescence. The break had come about because Alyosha's father, General Bertels, was having an affair with Eisenstein's mother, a contributing cause to his parent's divorce in 1909 which had a traumatic effect on him.

'These events poisoned the family atmosphere at a very early age. They corrupted both my belief in the foundations of the family and the charm of the family hearth, driving them from my imagination and emotions . . . My room and that of my parents were adjacent. All night long I heard the bitterest exchanges of insults. How many times did I run barefoot through the night to my governess's room, to fall asleep with my head rammed into a pillow. And no sooner had I dropped off than my parents would come rushing to wake me up to say how sorry they were for me. Another time, both parents believed it was their duty to open my eyes to the faults of the other. Mama cried that my father stole. Papa, that Mama was an immoral woman. Court Counsellor Eisenstein did not shrink from using more precise terminology. Yulia Ivanovna, the daughter of a merchant in the first guild, accused my father of worse yet . . . One day – and I remember it as if it happened yesterday – mother, in a beautiful red and green checked silk blouse ran hysterically through the flat to throw herself down the stairwell. I remember Papa carrying her back; she was writhing in her hysteria. Then there were a number of days when I was taken out to spend the whole day walking around town. Then Mama, her face red from crying, bade me farewell. Then Mama left. Then the removal men came. Then the furniture was taken (it had been Mama's trousseau).'[42]

In *Bezhin Meadow*, the cruel *kulak* father of Stepok, kills his wife, the boy's mother. 'Why did your father beat her so much?' asks an old peasant. 'Because she understood me,' Stepok replies.

So Eisenstein remained with his despised father in the constricted atmosphere of Riga, in fact relieved by the divorce because the unbearable nocturnal quarrels ceased. His mother had taken most of the furniture and, 'I had a whale of a time on my bicycle, racing up and down the empty dining-room and drawing-room.'[43] For warmth he turned to his governess, who was to look after him until her death in the 1930s. She called him Rorik, an affectionate form of Sergei which he used to sign his early sketches.

The boy visited his mother in St Petersburg from time to time during the year, and every Christmas. He would always take a bag of boiled sweets and books on the train journey to and from St Petersburg. For him, travelling and reading became indivisible. 'The rattle of wheels and the rhythm of prose are essential complements of each other.'[44]

From Riga, he would send her letters and postcards, many of them addressed to 'Ma chére Maman', often accompanied by a drawing or photo of himself with comments such as 'Look at the clever expression on my face.' His mother had sent him a camera for his birthday.

'Dear Mummy. Thank you ever so much for the camera. I wanted it so dearly . . . Daddy took pictures of me and I take pictures of Daddy and myself.' Other letters contained the following pieces of information: 'I went to the opera today. I was also at the zoo . . . My grades are pretty good. I draw a lot now and obey my Dad . . . Yesterday I went with Dad to the pictures again . . . They say the Tsar is coming to Riga. When the Tsar comes I'll stand in line with all our school. Is this fellow called the "King of the Universe"? . . . Kisses from your little boy to St Petersburg.'[45] Tsar Nicholas II did come to Riga, and Eisenstein saw him unveiling the memorial to Peter the Great.

It was in 1908, when Eisenstein was ten, and his parents were still together, that he entered the first class of the Riga city secondary school in Nikolayevsky Street.

'School was a hollow, unrewarding place,' he wrote. 'That was because I was a horribly exemplary little boy. I studied diligently . . . I did not form a single true friendship in those school rooms. Although if I try very hard, I can discern a certain supposed friendship, but it was very shortlived; a sentimental disposition towards a schoolmate who was younger and more delicate than I; and to one other – a stronger, older boy who was the best gymnast and a desperate hooligan.'[46]

The latter's name was Reichert, 'a muscular, dark-haired athlete' whom he was not allowed to invite home. Despite or because of this proscription, Eisenstein enjoyed the company of 'nasty boys' as a child, particularly delighting in the games of bandits that were played on Sunday mornings in the countryside around Riga. The boys divided themselves into two gangs, with members of one gang taking those of the other prisoner and 'hanging' them mercilessly. These games were played without the knowledge of his father, who strictly forbade his consorting with the 'lower element' in society.

In fact, Eisenstein did form some friendships with his peers, one of whom was Erwin Mednis. Mednis remarked that Sergei 'was always very sociable, and invariably good-natured, and there can be no doubt at all that intellectually he was extremely gifted. He spent a great deal of his time drawing caricatures of both his fellow pupils and, more dangerously, of his teachers, and he preferred to draw them during lessons in the classroom, with the natural consequence that drawing was one of the only two subjects in which he got less than top marks in his examinations. Russian language, ironically, was the other . . . When he came to school for the first time he could already speak two languages very well indeed: French and German. Later, but not much later, he learned English.'[47]

Mednis failed to mention that Eisenstein's best subject at school was religious education. 'I think that the religious element in my life was a considerable advantage,' Eisenstein wrote during his final years.[48] Indubitably Eisenstein was a Christian believer into his late teens – his last confession was around 1916 – and no evidence exists that he ever lost his faith, though he, rather uncomfortably, wore the robes of an 'atheist' director in an officially 'atheist' state. Marie Seton, in her biography of Eisenstein, recalled that he had once told her that he had spent sixteen years of his life striving to destroy the fascination that religion exerted over him.

Father Nikolai Pereshvalsky, the religious mentor of his childhood, impressed him deeply during that time by the overwhelming dramatic way he officiated at religious rituals. This, he thought, probably lay at the root of his attraction to church spectacle and ornate religious vestments. Neither did he ever forget the priest called Father Pavel at Suvorov Church in Tauride Street in St Petersburg who 'went through Holy Week as if suffering the Lord's Passion. I remember him in tears of torment at vigils of incessant prayer . . . [his] forehead exuded droplets of blood in the candle-light when he read the Acts of the Apostles . . . I practically left the domain of these emotions and ideas, while preserving them in my stock of useful memories. It was at Tsar Ivan's confession of course that this knot of personal experiences, which always flickered weakly in my memory like the dull glow of an icon lamp, burned at their strongest.'[49]

After 'a period of hysterical, puerile religiosity and juvenile sentiments of mysticism . . . I became an atheist.'[50] Yet, whatever ideological lens he looked through, he was forever in thrall aesthetically to churches, priests, and holy rites in his films.

Another boy around his own age and class was Maxim Strauch, whose family (the von Strauchs) lived in Moscow and spent the summer holidays on the Baltic Coast. Strauch, who was to become a leading Soviet actor (portraying Lenin a number of times) and an associate of Eisenstein's on several films, first met Sergei in the garden of Frau Koppitz's boarding house in Edinburg, on the seaside on the outskirts of Riga, where they were staying with their families.

'What I saw in that garden was a boy with a huge forehead and close-cropped hair, bent over a table and drawing something in a very fat exercise book,' Strauch remarked. 'I soon learnt that this unusual boy was never idle, but always busy creating something. He spent hour after hour sketching or writing, and the lumber room was filled to overflowing with his exercise books. Yet he never looked like some sort of child prodigy, pushed reluctantly beyond his strength, and even his appearance was in some way unchildlike.

'We were very close in those days, as indeed we remained for the rest of his life, and even in 1908 he was an unusual child. By nature he was never particularly frank except to a few of his dearest friends, and he was both lonely and shy, conditions of personality which probably owed a great deal to his parents' separation, and to the fact that his arrogant father was both too busy and too disinclined to spend much time with his only son. It was this very loneliness that both made him shy and yet at the same time forced him into forms of activity which were curiously conspicuous. Despite his personality, it was impossible for him not to do the things he could do so well.'[51]

Strauch recalled that Eisenstein already displayed talents as a director at the age of ten. This was manifested in the battles they fought with toy soldiers.

'Together we built fortresses and castles, but it was Eisenstein who designed the tiny sets, dressed the troops in battle dress, and directed miniature crowd scenes in that Riga garden which today I could easily connect with some of the sequences in *October* or *Alexander Nevsky* or *Ivan the Terrible*. His sense of drama, reflected by the way he manoeuvred our toy soldiers, increased every year.'[52]

Eisenstein's desire to direct grew out of his constant visits to the theatre. There were two leading theatres in Riga, the 'German' and the 'Russian', and he showed an early preference for the latter, considering it more realistic, less artificial and flowery than the German. At the Russian theatre, he saw not only most of the established 'classics' but several pieces that were less known such as *The Death of Ivan the Terrible*, part of the historical trilogy (the other two plays were *Tsar Fyodor Ivanovich* and *Tsar Boris*) which idealised old feudal Russia. Banned until 1898, they had been written between 1866 and 1870 by Alexei Konstantinovich Tolstoy – not to be confused with the Soviet writer Alexei Nikolaivich Tolstoy, who also wrote a historical trilogy on Ivan the Terrible, which was produced in 1943 starring Nikolai Cherkassov, Eisenstein's Ivan. To Strauch, Eisenstein wrote, 'I liked this tragedy very much indeed.'[53]

But the greatest theatrical experience of his early youth was a performance of Carlo Gozzi's *Turandot* under the direction of one of the greatest producers of the pre-Revolutionary Russian theatre, Fyodor Komisarjevsky, which toured Riga in 1913, when Eisenstein was fifteen. 'From this moment the theatre became the subject of my deepest attention, and my fascination with it was essentially an active one.'[54] What must have caught Eisenstein's imagination was the *commedia dell'arte* aspect of the 18th-century play, reproduced in the production.

Every summer, Eisenstein and Strauch would compare notes on all the plays, operas and circus performances they had each seen since their last meeting. Although Eisenstein sometimes visited his mother in St Petersburg, he never went to Moscow, where Strauch lived for most of the year. Eisenstein would be hypnotised by his friend's descriptions of productions he had seen in the capital. One summer, after hearing Strauch's enthusiastic account of Konstantin Stanislavsky's production of *The Blue Bird* by Maurice Maeterlinck at the Moscow Arts Theatre, Eisenstein insisted on their creating their own production of the play. This they did with and for the children at the resort, with Strauch directing and Eisenstein taking the role of Fire. Sometimes he presented plays at school, where one of his successes was Johann Schiller's *Wallenstein*, in which he played a woman's part that, according to Strauch, 'suited both his voice and his physical appearance.'[55]

The young Sergei was equally interested in opera. His first written notes about the theatre were concerned with opera, and the subjects of the wittiest of his series of youthful drawings were performances of *The Queen of Spades* and *Carmen*. Of the composers of operas his favourites were Tchaikovsky, Borodin, Suppé and Glinka, and he was even bold enough to stage a performance of Glinka's *Russlan and Ludmilla* in his own home.

The Russian Theatre was only a few yards from the school and, at the end of a performance, Eisenstein would usually run home to draw cartoons of the performers. He became especially interested in drawing when a friend of his father's, a Mr Afrosimov, an elderly railway engineer, drew pictures of animals for him. 'I remember particularly well what delighted me the most: a fat bow-legged frog . . . Here, before the eyes of the delighted beholder, this outline took form and started moving . . . Years later I still remember this acute sense of line as dynamic movement; a process, a path . . . The dynamics of line and the dynamics of "movement", rather than "repose", remain my abiding passion, whether in lines or in a system of phenomena and their transition from one into the other.'[56]

Mr Afrosimov suggested to the small boy that the animal world might be easier to draw for illustrated stories than human subjects. Thus Sergei would caricature the guests at his parents' dinner parties by drawing them as animals in human clothing. He filled his notebooks with 'In the World of Animals', a series of satirical observations, many in comic book form, unwittingly his first story boards and a preparation for his becoming a director, though he was unaware of it. In his children's world, people and animals were interchangeable, and the drawings exist as a sharp comment on the life around him. Throughout his life, his drawings offered him a self-liberating outlet.

An example was a comic strip he drew around the age of ten, just before his parent's estrangement. It depicted a day in the life of his Papa and Mama, in the shape of rather fat dogs. 'Papa wakes up. [Woken by a dog butler carrying a ringing alarm clock on a tray.] Mama wakes up in her separate bedroom. [Woken by a dog maid carrying a ringing alarm clock on a tray.] They take showers. They exercise. Papa leaves for his office. Mama shops for cloth. Papa receives messages. Callers visit Papa. Papa and Mama meet and take a carriage. They eat dinner. [Served by a bird waiter.] Indulge in sports. Visit an art gallery. Go to the theatre. [In a box is a dowager frog and various society birds.] Go home very tired.'[57]

These drawings were the first of an important element of Eisenstein's work, though neither they, nor his theoretical writings, teaching, or reading can be considered separately from an assessment or understanding of his films. In later years, he expressed his regard for Walt Disney, whom he met in Hollywood. 'I have always liked Disney and his heroes from Mickey Mouse to Willie the Whale . . . The moving lines of my childhood, outlining the shape and form of animals, animated the real lines of the cartoon drawing with real movement . . . Disney is the unique master of the cartoon film. Nobody else has managed to make the movement of a drawing's outline conform to the melody.'[58]

In an essay about his 1939 Bolshoi production of *Die Walküre* Eisenstein evoked Disney's *Snow White and the Seven Dwarfs* as an example of 'audiovisual cinema . . . creating an internal unity of sound and vision within the spectacle.'[59] Around the same time, on a sketch for a hoped-for production of *Das Rheingold*, he suggested the water of the Rhine be a 'Disney-like blue'. Indeed, the spirit of Disney's cartoons pervades (consciously or otherwise) much of Eisenstein's work: The animal dissolves in *The Strike*, the comic courting of the bull and the cow in *The General Line*, and Marfa's dream of an enormous bull filling the sky in the same film. 'Rivers of milk flow from the clouds, a rain of milk falls from the sky . . . cowsheds, pigsties and chicken-houses rise up from the ground . . .'[60] and isn't Euphrosinia in *Ivan the Terrible* an ugly sister of The Wicked Queen and some of the boyars brothers to the dwarfs in *Snow White and the Seven Dwarfs*? And doesn't the parade of swan-shaped platters, also in *Ivan*, remind one of 'The Dance of the Hours' in *Fantasia*?

By his late teens, Eisenstein had discovered the artists for whom he would have the deepest admiration throughout his life: Dürer, Hogarth, Goya and Daumier. But it was with Leonardo da Vinci that he modestly identified, calling Leonardo 'the creator of the montage sequence.'[61] He draws attention to Leonardo's catalogue or 'montage script' for an unrealised picture (like many or Eisenstein's 'unborn children') called *The Deluge*: 'some purely graphic (i.e. visual) elements, elements of human behaviour (i.e. dramatic acting), elements of noise, rumbling, crashing and screaming (i.e. in sound) are all in equal degree combined into a single, ultimate generalising image of the idea of a deluge . . . With what finesse he directs the overall shift of accentuation within the total picture, now veering off into sound, now plunging back again into depiction, as the orchestration of the audiovisual counterpoint is subtly built up.'[62]

Historian Herbert Marshall, who was one of his pupils at the Moscow Institute of Cinematography in the 1930s, recalled 'an Eisenstein cinémontage breakdown of Leonardo's *The Last Supper* which was part of an exercise he gave his class.' According to Marshall, Eisenstein noted that 'the objects on the table are shown in a perspective derived from a different viewpoint from that on which the perspective of the rest of the room is based.'[63] In other words, the use of multiple perspectives is one of the basic elements of the art of film.

Ivor Montagu, the British film-maker/writer, expressed a comparison between his friend and Leonardo. Eisenstein 'was one of those many-sided people of whom there are so few nowadays. He was a sort of Renaissance man, a Leonardo da Vinci, a scientist as well as an artist.'[64] Maxim Strauch thought: 'The historical figure closest to Eisenstein is, in my opinion, Leonardo da Vinci',[65] and film director Grigori Rostotsky declared: 'When a great man lives close to you, you often fail to appreciate his greatness. Now, so many years after his death, I am absolutely convinced that Eisenstein was a Leonardo da Vinci of the 20th century.'[66]

It would be some years into the future before Sergei Eisenstein could even begin to justify this rather hyperbolic analogy. But the pattern of his creative life was already taking shape at the age of seventeen: his mastery of languages, his talent as a visual artist, his extensive reading, the instinct for satire and the passion for the circus, opera and the theatre, all of which would finally be subsumed into his theory and practice of the art of the cinema.

2

Revolution!

The Revolution gave me the most precious thing in life – it made an artist out of me. If it had not been for the Revolution I would never have broken the tradition, handed down from father to son, of becoming an engineer . . . The Revolution introduced me to art, and art, in its own turn, brought me to the Revolution . . .

The summer of 1914, the last before Eisenstein finished school, was spent with his mother at a dacha in Staraya Russa. During that holiday two events made even more of an impact on him than the fact that war was declared in July. The first was a procession on a patron saint's day at a recently opened church, which informed the fanatical religious procession in *The General Line*. It is a sequence that Eisenstein later examined as an example of how his montage advanced uninterrupted, weaving 'diverse themes and motifs into a single, cumulative movement.'[1] In the manner in which he analysed Leonardo's catalogue for *The Deluge*, he itemised the motifs of the sequence, demonstrating how he would utilise and transmute vivid impressions from his life onto the screen, only slightly diluted by ideological prerequisites.

In *The General Line*, the motifs were those of progressive heat. They grew from sequence to sequence, matching the mounting intoxication of religious fanaticism which was illustrated by successive close-ups of the faces of peasant men and women, who were singing and carrying icons.

The second most memorable event of that summer, but with less direct significance than the procession, was Eisenstein's meeting with Anna Grigoryevna Dostoevskaya, Fyodor Dostoevsky's widow, 'my first ever literary encounter.'[2] His mother had invited her to the dacha, and in preparation for the meeting, he rapidly read *The Brothers Karamazov* for the first time 'so that I would have something to talk to the great lady about.'[3] But when Madam Dostoevskaya arrived, he had gone into the kitchen where he encountered a young girl called Nina, one of the servants' daughters, with whom he took large slices of blackberry pie to eat in the park. Eisenstein was so intrigued by this slender, dark girl, whom he thought looked like a young monk, that he was late for tea with the honoured guest, only managing to kiss her hand just before she was leaving.

No literary conversation took place, and he reproached himself for reading *The Brothers Karamazov* 'for nothing, instead of playing tennis the whole time.'[4] However, Dostoevsky was a novelist who would come to mean a great deal to Eisenstein, and among his final unrealised wishes was to follow *Ivan the Terrible* with a film of *The Brothers Karamazov*. One of the courses he gave in 1933 at the G.I.K., the Cinema Institute, where they had the cost-free luxury of imagining and acting out any film they desired, was getting the students to construct a scenario of Raskolnikov's murder of the money-lender from *Crime and Punishment*.

Vladimir Nizhny, a student at the Institute, quoted his teacher thus: 'The murder of the money-lender – this is the outer subject of the scene. The real, inner, subject – is the fall and dethroning of Raskolnikov. "Freedom and power – power above all. Power over all the trembling vermin, and over all the ant-hills." That is his motto. It is precisely in this passage we are treating that he himself becomes one of the "trembling vermin."' Nizhny adds: 'Carried away as he speaks of the task set by the scene, S.M. simultaneously portrays Raskolnikov's action.'[5]

In July 1914, while the sixteen-year-old Eisenstein was reading Dostoevsky, swimming and playing tennis, the Russian government had been drawn into the war with Germany – nothing but an 'imperialist war', according to the exiled Lenin – and a general mobilisation was ordered. At the holiday resort, people began panicking. 'In the Kursaal galleries, complete strangers threw themselves into each other's arms, sobbing,' Eisenstein recalled. 'A colonel sat weeping in his wheelchair, covered by a tartan rug; he wore dark glasses and had doffed his forage cap, showing a scanty head of hair . . .'[6]

The panic resulted in people being turned away from the station because it was so crowded. There were others who tried to sail across Lake Ilmen, down the River Volkhov, and then take the train to Tikhvin. Eisenstein and his mother took a steamer, which sailed from Staraya Russa to Lake Ilmen, and then on to St Petersburg.

'We sailed down the Volkhov, past Novgorod, bathed in moonlight. Dazzling white churches, too many to count, in the still night air. We glided silently past. A magical night! Where had these temples come from, that appeared to have come down to the stately river? Had they rolled, like white currents, to drink the water? Or had they come to moisten the hems of their white garments?'[7]

Eisenstein never forgot the image of the white mass of churches on the banks of the Volkhov, and returned to Novgorod in 1938 to film sequences for *Alexander Nevsky*. Captured on screen are the white domes of the Church of Soas-Nereditsa in front of which gather the merchants of Novgorod calling for Nevsky to save them from the Germans. Six years later, during the Second World War, the church that Eisenstein had seen as a boy, and filmed as a man, was destroyed by the Germans.

'Not a mummy's boy. Not an urchin. Just a boy. A boy aged twelve. Obedient, polite, clicking his heels. A typical boy from Riga. A boy from a good family,' was how the forty-eight-year-old Eisenstein remembered himself.[8] At seventeen, he was still 'obedient, polite, clicking his heels',[9] his revolution (both public and personal) was yet to come. Thus, despite his passion for the arts, there seemed no question that Eisenstein, on completing his secondary schooling in Riga, would go to the Institute of Civil Engineering in Petrograd (as St Petersburg was renamed in 1914). This was certainly the wish of his father who had once studied there, but the decision seems to have been taken without reluctance or resistance. At the time, Eisenstein could see no other future for himself than to become an engineer like his father.

In his ironic manner, Eisenstein later wrote: 'I do not smoke. Papa never smoked. I always followed my father's example. From the cradle I was destined to become an engineer and architect. Up to a certain age I competed with my father in everything I did. Papa went riding. He was very corpulent, and only one horse from the Riga Tattersall could carry him: it was a massive draught horse, with a bluish wall-eye. I had riding lessons too. I did not become an engineer and an architect. Nor a great horseman.'[10]

Erwin Mednis, Eisenstein's classmate at school, recalled that 'in those days it was his intention, if not exactly his ambition, to become a professional engineer like his father, and to pass from the school in Riga to the Institute of Civil Engineering in St Petersburg, where his precocious gift for drawing would be an enormous advantage.'[11] Eisenstein once declared, 'I approach the making of a motion picture in much the same way that I would approach the installation of a water system', the sort of remark that lent fuel to his detractors.[12]

Eisenstein's period as a student at the Petrograd Institute of Engineering on Furstadt Street in the old *Annenschüle* was, until the Revolution, uneventful. But his studies would influence him long after he abandoned engineering because it was during this period that he developed his 'leaning towards disciplined thinking' and his love of 'mathematical precision'. His mathematics professor at the Institute was Professor Sokhotsky, whom he was later to describe as 'one of those flaming old fanatics . . . who could by the hour and with the same fire of enthusiasm discourse on integral calculus and analyse in infinite detail how Camille Desmoulins, Danton, Gambetta or Volodarsky thundered against the enemies of the people and the revolution. The temperament of the lecturer absorbs you completely . . . And suddenly the mathematical abstraction has become flesh and blood.'[13] Thanks to his engineering training, Eisenstein 'eagerly delved . . . deeper and deeper into the fundamentals of creative art, instinctively seeking the same sphere of exact knowledge as had succeeded in captivating me during my short experience in engineering.'[14]

The urge to become an artist, and especially to work in the theatre, became more persistent during his time as a student in

Petrograd, where the opportunities were much greater than they had ever been in Riga. Now he was away from his father, living with his mother in the home city of so many of Russia's creative artists: Dostoevsky, Gogol, Turgenev, Pushkin. There were two Leonardos in the Art Gallery, there was the circus and, of course, the theatre.

Two figures in the theatre who had the most powerful effect on Eisenstein at the time were Vsevolod Meyerhold and Nikolai Yevreinov. The latter was a symbolist playwright who ran the Distorting Mirror Theatre on the Catherine Canal in Petrograd. There, Eisenstein saw *What They Think, What They Say*, which had characters speaking their thoughts long before Eugene O'Neill used the technique in a more 'ponderous, painstaking' manner in *Strange Interlude*.[15] (The possibility of using 'inner monologues' on film excited him when preparing his script for *An American Tragedy* in Hollywood.) There was also *In The Backstage of the Soul* (aka *The Theatre of the Soul*), a monodrama, in which various aspects of the same person appear as separate entities. This was something which Eisenstein personalised, seeing in his own psychology the struggle between his emotional (or 'romantic' ego) and the rational ego, which 'had been educated in the Institute of Civil Engineering on differential calculus and integrated differential equations.'[16]

In Yevreinov's three-volume theoretical work called *The Theatre for Oneself*, the author argued that every individual was capable of metamorphosis and role-playing, everyday life could therefore be metamorphosed in theatre so that every individual could simultaneously be actor and spectator. The books contained plays which had no audience, critics or auditorium. One of them, *The Trying on of Deaths*, described the sensations Petronius, who committed suicide for political reasons, felt as he died: 'his veins cut – a small incision of the auxiliary blood-vessels in his arm in a warm bath – monitored by a concealed accomplice (a doctor) to the strains of a distant harp.'[17]

Meyerhold, born in 1874, was an actor, producer, artistic director, pedagogue and theorist. In 1905 Konstantin Stanislavsky had invited Meyerhold to take charge of productions at the newly formed Studio which was to be an experimental laboratory for the

Moscow Arts Theatre along the lines of the Symbolists, but it soon closed. From 1906–1907, Meyerhold was at the Theatre of Vera Komisarjevskaya, where he was able to put into practice the symbolic or stylised method he had envisaged at the Moscow Arts Theatre Studio (Komisarjevskaya had played Nina in the first production of Chekhov's *The Seagull*, and was one of Stanislavsky's teachers.) In effect, this amounted to 'abstract' theatre, placing the human element, the actor, on a level with the other elements of the production, thus reducing to nothing the actor's individual contribution to the ensemble, and making him merely a super-marionette in the hands of the producer – in fact a realisation of Gordon Craig's one-time ideal. This treatment of the actor led inevitably to a break with Komisarjevskaya. Meyerhold then staged some brilliant productions at the Marinsky and Alexandrinsky Theatres in Petrograd, at the same time continuing his experimental work in his own Studio where, from 1913 to 1917, he continued, under the influence of the improvisation and stylised traditions of the *commedia dell'arte*, to work out his own methods.

At the Alexandrinsky Theatre, Eisenstein saw Meyerhold's productions of Calderon's *The Constant Prince* (aka *The Steadfast Prince*), Molière's *Don Juan* and Mikhail Lermontov's *Masquerade*, which Eisenstein claimed was one of the reasons why he chose the theatre as his profession. 'It actually defined my unspoken intention to abandon engineering and "give myself" to art.'[18]

Masquerade was Lermontov's greatest play and the only one for which he is now remembered. The climax, in which a man poisons his wife whom he loves, is not the result of intrigue, but of the psychological state of the husband, driven to crime by the corrupt society in which he lives. Meyerhold introduced the figure of the Blue Pierrot (played by himself) who, during the masquerade of the title, intrigues Nina, the heroine of the play, with the lost bracelet, the motive around which the plot is constructed. Thus a character from the *commedia dell'arte*, integrated into the romantic tragedy through the device of the masked ball, became one expression of the theme of Fate which lay at the base of Meyerhold's conception.

The profound effect of this production on Eisenstein cannot be underestimated. It distilled his early love of clowns into a life-long passion for *commedia dell'arte* allied to 'the comedy of masks', which, in turn, led to what he called – from the French – *typage* in his films. The latter has been defined by his American friend and former student Jay Leyda as 'type-casting (by non-actors) elevated by Eisenstein to the level of a conscious creative instrument.'[19] In other words, Eisenstein would choose people on the basis of their facial characteristics so that audiences would be immediately aware of their social and psychological characteristics, as theatre audiences recognised the masks of Harlequin, Pantaloon and Columbine, but in a wider spectrum.

So much has been made over the years of Eisenstein's *typage*, that it is sometimes forgotten how much Hollywood has always depended on it. Not only in the use of type-casting, but in such signifiers as platinum blonde = dumb and sexy; bespectacled woman = spinster; bespectacled man = weakling; pipe-smoking bespectacled man = earnest intellectual etc. etc.

Masquerade opened at the Alexandrinsky Theatre on February 25, 1917, literally on the eve of the February Revolution. It was in Petrograd that the February uprising began, spreading throughout Russia. The Duma (the Russian parliament) assumed real power and the Tsar was forced to abdicate a month later.

The chaotic situation led to the serious disruption, and even cancellation, of classes at the Engineering School. The building was soon converted into a centre for law and order and assigned to the Izmailov regiment. Eisenstein was caught up in the revolutionary fervour and, with many of his fellow-students, joined the city militia. After an intense training period at a camp, he was issued with a service card and an arm band, and sent on night picket duty.

That period, when General Kornilov attempted a monarchist *putsch*, was recreated in a visually symbolic manner in *October* as Kornilov's train moves closer and closer to the capital. Because, as Eisenstein argued, Kornilov tried to put an end to Kerensky's Bonapartist plans, he showed the General's tanks shattering a plaster figure of Napoleon that stands on Kerensky's desk.

It was about this time that Eisenstein's artistic interest in the fermenting public events was first aroused. With his characteristic keen-eyed and caustic powers of observation, he started sketching the scenes around him. His first attempt at selling his work was a caricature of the haloed head of Louis XVI above the bed of Nicholas II, which carried the caption: 'He got off lightly!' This he took to the editorial offices of the *Satirikhon* review, only to have it rejected by the editor, the writer Arkady Averchenko, with a scathing 'anyone could produce that.'[20]

Undaunted, Eisenstein continued to draw cartoons. His next effort depicted a fracas between a group of housewives and militia men above the caption: 'What's going on? Looting?' 'No, it's the militia keeping order.' For this he chose the *Petersburgskaya Gazeta*, a paper taken by his father and familiar to him since childhood. Now he was actually in the paper's editorial offices, seeing its staff reporters for the first time. Eventually, he was summoned to the editor Sergei Khudekov himself. The editor scrutinised the sketch, nodded, and tossed it into the in-tray on his desk. A few days later, it appeared in the paper under the pseudonym, Sir Gay (an English pun). For it, Eisenstein received his first payment as an artist – ten roubles.

In the first week of July 1917, he was on the corner of Nevsky Prospect and Sadovaya Street, moving towards a crowd of demonstrators brandishing banners, when the army opened fire with machine guns. People fled in all directions. 'I saw people quite unfit, even poorly built for running, in headlong flight. Watches on chains were jolted out of waistcoat pockets. Cigarette cases flew out of side pockets. And canes. Canes. Canes. Panama hats.'[21]

Eisenstein managed to dive under the arches of Gostiny Dvor, the city's largest department store. 'My legs carried me out of range of the machine guns. But it was not at all frightening . . . These days went down in history. History for which I so thirsted, which I so wanted to lay my hands on!'[22]

When filming *October* ten years later, he attempted to recreate this scene by stopping the traffic for half an hour at the same spot, the juncture of Nevsky and Sadovaya. 'But I was not able to film the street strewn with hats and canes, in the wake of the fleeing demonstrators. (Even though there were people in the crowd who were there for the purpose of strewing things.) Some economically minded old men who took part in the crowd scene diligently picked them all up as they ran, no matter where they had landed!'[23]

His first record of those July shootings took the form of sketches, among them a series of four, the last of which featured a man with a shell protruding from his back, carrying the laconic caption: 'Look out, citizen, you've been hit!' – 'What are you talking about? Really?'[24] When Alexander Kerensky became premier on July 12, 1917, Sir Gay's name appeared on vicious caricatures of Kerensky in the *Petersburgskaya Gazeta*.

At the same time, Eisenstein had formed an interest in the French 18th-century engraver Jean Moreau, and collected articles about him as well as a number of engravings, some of which he bought for ten roubles from an antiquarian dealer in the Alexandrovsky market. One evening, he was sorting them out with other 18th-century engravings, when 'there seemed to be more shooting than usual coming from one part of town. But it was quiet in our house in Tauride Street. Before going to bed, I pedantically wrote the date on the cuttings to show when they were put into order. October 25, 1917. By evening, that date was already part of history.'[25] Eisenstein was not present at the storming of the Winter Palace, but he was able to compensate for his absence by filming it for *October* ten years later.

As the Russians had yet to convert to the Gregorian calendar as used in the Western world, the October Revolution actually took place on November 7, 1917 i.e. October 25 in the Russian calendar. On that date, the provisional government under Kerensky was overthrown by the Bolsheviks led by Lenin, who had been allowed to return to Russia by the German government, and 'the dictatorship of the proletariat' was proclaimed.

Having been fascinated by stories of the 1905 revolt, of which he had vague and somewhat tantalising memories of the disruption of every day existence, as well as his reading of the French Revolution in childhood, and his hatred of the bourgeois, stoked by his father's tyranny, Eisenstein welcomed the Bolsheviks enthusiastically. It was the Revolution of 1917 that gave him that precious 'freedom to decide' his future.

With the Institute dissolved, Eisenstein joined his fellow students in enlisting in the Red Army as an engineer. When the civil war broke out in 1918, fifty-one-year-old Mikhail Osipovich Eisenstein joined the opposing White Army as an engineer. At the

Revolution, Eisenstein had sketched a caricature of his father horrified by the raising of the red flag, which was coloured in with red crayon, rather like the colouring of the flag in *The Battleship Potemkin*. To reverse the expression in *Bezhin Meadow*, 'If a father betray his own son, let him be slaughtered like a dog.' Now Eisenstein was literally at war with his father and defending Russia against any incursions made by Latvia, the country of his birth.

Petrograd, once the well-guarded capital of Imperial Russia, was left dangerously exposed to attack. In less than six months, five new independent states emerged in the Baltic lands that once had been part of the Russian Empire – Poland in the west, Finland in the east, Lithuania, Estonia and Latvia. Half a millennium of antagonism and conflict made it certain that all of these states would be anti-Russian, and there were trials and executions of Communist sympathisers in these countries. Further to the north, in the area centred on the White Sea ports of Murmansk and Archangel, Finnish, White Russian and British and American forces clashed with Bolsheviks. England had moved a fleet into the Finnish Gulf to threaten Petrograd's defences at the Bolshevik's naval base at Kronstadt. The greatest threat to Petrograd came from North Russia, where the Allies had increased their forces rapidly between July and October 1918, the Tsar and his family having been assassinated by firing squad at Ekaterinburg on July 17.

At the beginning of the Civil War, Eisenstein, as a member of the College of Ensigns of the Engineering Corps, was sent to build bridges over the Neva River and fortifications around Petrograd. In a chapter in his memoirs, headed 'Why I Became A Director', he describes a particular scene that also indicates one element of what made him the *kind* of director he was.

'An ant hill of raw fresh-faced recruits moved along measured out paths with precision and discipline and worked in harmony to build a steadily growing bridge which reached hungrily across the river. Somewhere in this ant hill I moved as well. Square pads of leather on my shoulders supporting a plank, resting edgeways. Like the parts of a clockwork contraption, the figures moved quickly, driving up to the pontoons and throwing girders and handrails festooned with cabling to one another – it was an easy and harmonious model of *perpetuum mobile*, reaching out from the bank in an ever-lengthening road to the constantly receding edge of the bridge . . . all this fused into a marvellous, orchestral, polyphonic experience of something being done, in all the variations of its harmony . . . Hell, it was good! . . . No: it was not patterns from classical productions, nor recordings of outstanding performances, nor complex orchestral scores, nor elaborate evolutions of *corps de ballet* in which I first sensed the rapture, the delight in the movement of bodies racing at different speeds and in different directions across the graph of an open expanse: it was the play of intersecting orbits, the ever-changing dynamic form that the combination of these paths took and their collisions in momentary patterns of intricacy, before flying apart forever. The pontoon bridge which extended across the immeasurable breadth of the Neva, towards the sandy shore of Izhora, opened my eyes for the first time to the delight of this fascination that was never to leave me.'[26]

This became a seminal image of Eisenstein's aesthetic. Something specific had been created out of the complex movements of man and material. Many things happening simultaneously with one effect; it was the polyphonic construction which fascinated him.

Eisenstein may have interjected 'Hell, it was good!' when watching (and participating) in the building of the bridge that so impinged upon his imagination, but it was hard work, even for a fit young man in his early twenties. Much more endurance was required on the Eastern Front on the White Sea, but the comradeship and shared passionate belief in the defence of the Revolution kept him going.

Although the subjects of each of Eisenstein's films, whether historical or modern, are ostensibly about significant collective events, the director's personal associations and reminiscences would not merely be integrated into the work, but often permeate them. A small specific incident at that period found its way into *The General Line*.

At a military work site close to Khom, seventy kilometres from the nearest railway in one direction and ninety-five kilometres in the other, where more fortifications were being built, Eisenstein acted as adjutant to the chief of works. A *kulak* (rich peasant) family named Pudyakov invited Eisenstein to dinner one night with the aim of getting him to ensure that their only son – a section leader at Eisenstein's site – would not be posted further away.

They supplied a hearty meal from a communal round bowl, the first Eisenstein had ever eaten at a peasant's house. (In a few years, the *kulaks*, who were opposed to collectivisation, would be liquidated as a class.) After the meal, as Eisenstein described it, 'there was an amazing sunset. And an unhealthy sleep at sunset lying on a very narrow bench . . . while the girls danced. And the accordion played uproariously . . . For some reason . . . I sensed this strange phenomenon, a marvellous farandole before my eyes – now a gigantic nose, the only one of its kind; now the peak of a cap, leading an independent life; now a whole line of dancing faces; now an exaggerated moustache, now just the little crosses embroidered on the collars of a Russian shirt, now the distant view of the village swallowed up by the twilight, now again the too large tassel of silk cord hanging around a waist, now an earring tangled in some hair, now a flushed cheek . . . Oddly, when I embarked upon the theme of peasants and collectivisation for the first time, just over five years later, I did not lose sight of this vivid impression. The *kulak*'s ear, and the fold of his neck filled the entire screen; another's massive nose was as big as a hut; a huge hand hung limply above a jug of kvass; a grasshopper, the size of a reaping machine – all of these were constantly being woven into a saraband of countryside and rural genre pictures, in the film *The Old and the New* [*The General Line*].'[27]

Eisenstein's first memory as a child was the close-up of white lilac swaying above his cot. A few years later, he would doze off while looking at a floral branch of a tree that stood out from a painted landscape on a Japanese folding screen near his bed. 'And so I was aware of foreground composition before I saw Hokusai or was entranced by Edgar Degas . . . For me it was two Edgars who encapsulated the tradition of foreground composition. Edgar Degas and Edgar Poe.'[28] The Poe story that particularly impressed him was one in which the author described looking out of a window and seeing a gigantic prehistoric monster crawling up the ridge of a distant mountain, only to discover that this supposed monster was a death's-head moth crawling upon the pane.

*

During the winter of 1918–1919, with howling winds dumping six feet of snow on Archangel on the Northern front, and with temperatures falling well below zero, the anti-Bolshevik forces suffered worse than their enemies. The Bolsheviks continued to spread propaganda everywhere. Now that the armistice with Germany had been signed and the fighting had ended in Europe, handbills nailed to trees and scattered along city streets asked, 'British soldiers, why don't you return home? What are you fighting for?' There were mutinies among the Russian soldiers under the Allies in North Russia, that spread from Lake Onega to the Dvina river, where Eisenstein had been sent in the spring of 1919. As the Bolsheviks organised Latvian, Lithuanian and Estonian people's armies on Soviet territory to 'liberate' the workers of their homelands, Stalin, the people's commissar for nationalities, vowed that 'proletarian revolution, awe-inspiring and mighty, is on the march through the world', and that 'petty kinglets' on the Baltic would be 'no exception'. Riga fell to the Reds at the beginning of January 1919. Eisenstein's father had escaped to Berlin, where he settled down and remarried Elisabeth Michelsohn, a much younger woman.

More fearful of an attack by the Finns than by the Northwestern White Army, the Bolsheviks had already begun to mobilise the workers of Petrograd for the city's defence. On May 17, Lenin had sent Stalin to take charge of the city's defences. 'Soviet Russia cannot give up Petrograd even for the briefest moment,' the Central Committee announced. 'The significance of this city, which first raised the banner of rebellion against the bourgeoisie, is too great.'

Although Petrograd was in a state of siege, the Whites were too weak and too disunited to launch an attack. At least the meagre army rations that Eisenstein had at the front were more than the daily ration of the population of Petrograd. A half-pound of bread and a bowl of watery soup comprised the basic meal for the adult citizen. Leon Trotsky, the minister of war, gave Petrograd's starving men and women a new belief in themselves and a certainty that a place in the revolutionary pantheon awaited each who did his or her duty. 'Happy is he,' proclaimed Trotsky, 'who in his mind and heart feels the electric current of our great epoch.'

Eisenstein, who was serving as a draftsman, technician and adjutant to the chief of works at Gatchina, felt the electric current.

'The melting pot of the Civil War and military engineering work at the front made me acutely aware of the fates of Russia and the Revolution and gave me a fascinating sense of history in the making, which had made a deep impression with the broad canvas of the fates of nations and epic ambitions, and was then realised in the thematics of future films of monumental scale.'[29] These 'epic ambitions' never left him as most of his projects testify. Unfortunately, his ideas were often too broad for the narrow minds that he had to confront in order to realise them.

On November 7, the second anniversary of the Bolshevik Revolution, and the day of his fortieth birthday, Trotsky stood before the Central Committee and announced, 'In the battle of Petrograd, Soviet power showed that it stands on its feet firmly and indestructibly.' Eisenstein, coming up to his twenty-second birthday, had been tempered in the fire of this victory, but his natural impulses as an artist were always to the fore.

Towards the end of 1919, as the Red Army drew ever closer to victory in the Civil War, the 15th Army's Military Construction Unit No. 18, to which Eisenstein was attached, was posted to Communist-controlled Velikie Lukie. Having more leisure time than was possible elsewhere, he and a number of young soldiers on his site decided that it might be diverting to form an amateur theatrical group. With this in mind, Eisenstein contacted the local House of Culture, which had a thriving theatre company run by the painter Konstantin Yeliseyev. Eisenstein asked Yeliseyev if he and his comrades could sit in on rehearsals to gain some knowledge of theatre. During the following weeks, Eisenstein, in his faded uniform, palely loitered around the theatre on every possible occasion. He was a shadowy presence at discussions between the actors and Yeliseyev, and sat in the dressing rooms staring at the actors making up.

Due to Eisenstein's conscientious study of the troupe, added to his earlier reading and absorption of theatre pre-war, his new amateur group was able to make its debut on February 9, 1920, with several short plays, including Gogol's *The Gamblers* and Arkady Averchenko's *The Double*, which he directed. In the latter, Eisenstein himself took the small role of 'the first passer-by'. But, according to witnesses, his words were barely intelligible because of a peculiar hoarseness of his voice which, the result of chronic laryngitis apparently, caused oscillations of pitch between high and low – 'the two voices of my mother and father', as he put it.[30] In later years when he had to communicate coherently as a director and lecturer, the condition was treated with some success by a doctor who advised him to speak loudly. However, any thoughts of his becoming an actor were immediately curbed by the quirky timbre of his voice.

The first productions at Velikie Lukie were followed by Romain Rolland's *Quartorze Juillet/The 14th of July*, about the first days of the French Revolution, which had the audience cheering the heroes and hissing the villains.

In the spring of 1920, the unit moved further south to Lepel, near Polotsk, not far from the Lithuanian border. Yeliseyev had been appointed director of two theatrical groups attached to the 15th Army and was planning a production of Victorien Sardou's *Madame Sans-Gêne* for which he needed a designer. While Yeliseyev was travelling the area in a search for talent, Eisenstein contacted him in Polotsk. At their meeting, Eisenstein declared how much he wanted to leave the construction unit and join the theatrical group in whatever capacity. Yeliseyev was willing to take him on, but had to gain the permission of the chief engineer Peyich, Eisenstein's superior. However, Peyich refused to grant Eisenstein a transfer, explaining that he was indispensable for the defence constructions. Yeliseyev, who obviously thought Eisenstein was worth fighting for, appealed to Peyich as a former actor – he had played leading roles in the amateur productions at Velikie Lukie – and eventually won him over. To celebrate his official entry into the theatre, the two colleagues drank a precious tin of condensed milk in Eisenstein's room.

The celebrations were premature. While in Polotsk, Yeliseyev was informed that his troupe had been incorporated into the PUZAP (Political Administration of the Western Front), and that he was to report immediately to Smolensk, further south. Eisenstein and Yeliseyev travelled together by goods train to Smolensk. During the slow journey, both men expounded their theories on theatre, which were still unrelated to the momentous changes that were taking place in Russia. On one issue, especially, did they find themselves at odds. Since Eisenstein's exposure to Meyerhold's production of Lermontov's *Masquerade* on the day before the February Revolution in 1917, he was predisposed forever towards *commedia dell'arte* and the 'comedy of masks'. Yeliseyev, on the other hand, to Eisenstein's disappointment, declared that he would never allow his actors to hide their faces with masks.

On arrival at Smolensk, they discovered that Dneprov, PUZAP's drama chief, had amalgamated the various theatrical groups and that all theatrical projects had been temporarily suspended. As Smolensk was so overcrowded, many of those on the lower levels of the Political Administration had to live in a goods train, so that Eisenstein spent several weeks of stupefying inaction in the cramped quarters of a wagon at Smolensk station.

It was at the station at Smolensk that Eisenstein had what he described as one of the most terrifying experiences of his life. 'When I was trying to find my way back to my freight wagon, making my way down between the rails and going under the wheels . . . How many times in the hours of my wanderings along the tracks did those night-time monsters of trains treacherously, with barely a rattle, steal up on me almost furtively, looming out of the darkness; and move past, dwarfing me and then retreating into darkness once more?

'I think it was that; their implacable, blind, pitiless movement which migrated into my films; now got up in soldiers' boots on the Odessa steps, now turning their blunt noses into the Knight's helmets in the "Battle on the Ice", now sliding in black robes along the stone flagging the cathedral, following the candle as it shook in the hands of the stumbling Vladimir Staritsky [in *Ivan the Terrible*] . . . This image of the night train migrated from film to film; it has become the symbol of fate.'[31]

The most obvious example is in a sequence of stills from *Bezhin Meadow*, showing a parade of tractors at night creating a sinister effect, the reverse side of the sunnier images of tractors in the earlier *The General Line*, when Eisenstein's fate seemed brighter.

The months of inactivity at Smolensk ended when the Political Administration for the Western Front was transferred to Minsk, just after the Red Army had 'liberated' it from Poland. However,

Eisenstein, with four other painters, was merely given the job of decorating the carriages of an agitprop train leaving for the front. Agit-prop was the Russian term coined from Agitatsiya-propaganda, a means of informing and educating the masses in political principles and ideas, often using mobile theatre troupes.

The term was used previously to apply to the sharp, folksy agitational poems of Demyan Bedny (pseudonym of E.A. Pridvorov), poet laureate of the Civil War period. It was one of Bedny's satirical *agitki* that the Cinema Committee filmed in the autumn of 1918. In November of that year, Lenin inaugurated the first Red Train, which toured the towns and villages of Soviet Russia. He declared: 'There is no form of science or art which cannot be linked with the great ideas of Communism and the diverse work of building a Communist economy.'

The first intense use of *agitka* came as a result of a general inventory of suitable film material for Red Army screenings – in training and at the front. The agit-train that had done duty on the Eastern Front at Kazan was now sent in the opposite direction – to the Western Front for a three-month tour. The chief film carried along was Dziga Vertov's first editing job, *The October Revolution*.

The particular train that Eisenstein was painting was called *The Red Army Soldier*, which would carry theatre productions around the country. It contained a collapsible stage, the sort which Eisenstein would design the following year for the Moscow Proletkult's Studio Theatre 'for shows either in the open air or in an enclosed space.' But it seemed then, as Eisenstein worked from dawn to dusk on the train, that his theatrical ambitions were being thwarted. Eventually a production of Gorky's *The Lower Depths* was planned, for which Eisenstein started painting the backdrop.

One evening, after his day's work, he attended a Rosicrucian service given by Bishop Bogori, whose 'worldly' name was Boris Zubakin, a professor of archaeology. It was held in the back room of a building that the Red Army had taken over for billeting the troops. While the sound of a balalaika and accordion could be heard in the background, the Rosicrucian bishop, wearing a cape and holding a mitre, began initiating the small group into the Cabbala and the Arcana. Eisenstein claimed to have dozed off through most of it and to have found it rather comical, though he was obviously fascinated by all forms of the occult, particularly with those forms of ecstasy of which Rasputin was the most famous follower.

One day in October 1920, rehearsals for *The Lower Depths* were suddenly interrupted by the announcement that armistice negotiations had been opened with the Poles. (A peace treaty would be signed in Riga the following March.) Although the Civil War was not yet over – there were still areas for the Red Army to win – Eisenstein was now free to return to his engineering studies on the resolution of the Council of People's Commissars. He was now faced with the painful choice between the Institute in Petrograd or moving on with PUZAP from whom he had permission to study Japanese at the Oriental Language Department of the General Staff Academy (Eastern Front) in Moscow. He spent a sleepless night rolling feverishly about on his bed, dishevelled, having to 'undertake the most unpleasant task' of his life, to take such a cardinal decision. 'There – the Institute. Here – the Department of Oriental Languages. A thousand Japanese words. A hundred characters. The Institute? A stable way of life? . . . Every branch of higher mathematics was on offer. Right up to integrated differential equations (how much did mathematics teach me about discipline!). But I felt it might be time to see some Japanese theatre. I was ready to cram and cram words. And those astonishing phrases from a different way of thinking. Before that I wanted to see the theatres in Moscow. The career that my father had so carefully sketched out for me had been lost. By morning my mind was made up . . . the Institute was abandoned.'[32]

A few days later, Eisenstein was in Moscow. It would be his home – except for the three-year period in the West, which he called an 'Épopée – for the rest of his life.

3

Agitka!

The first distant thundering of revolutionary art on the move
was audible all around, convulsing the heavens.

During the Civil War, while Eisenstein was a soldier, between oper-
ations and in the most uncomfortable circumstances, he would
snatch as much time as possible to read and study. In Novo-
Sokolniki, he read Schopenhauer 'in the shade of a freight wagon,
under the carriage awaiting the uncoupling of the train.' In similar
circumstances he read Heinrich von Kleist's and Gordon Craig's
essays on theatre, both of whose theories on the 'hypermarionette'
appealed to him. In *On the Marionette Theatre*, Kleist wrote: 'At
its purest grace is apparent in a human body whose consciousness
is either non-existent or unending i.e. in a marionette or god';
while Craig argued that the director's conception could only be
guaranteed by 'a larger-than-life-size doll like those used in cult
worship in the ancient Orient and Greece.' The widespread excitement of Craig's ideas had reached Russia when he visited the
country at Stanislavsky's invitation before the Revolution to stage
a production of *Hamlet*.

On a troop train, with a rucksack on his back, Eisenstein was
introduced to psychoanalysis by reading Freud's *Leonardo da
Vinci: A Psychosexual Study of Infallible Reminiscence* and its
application to the 'early erotic awakening of a child.' He became
absorbed in Maurice Maeterlinck's *Princess Maleine* while sitting
on a felled tree, shouting orders to his troops busy constructing
trenches. At night, at camp, he explored the works of Hogarth

and Goya by lamplight, as well as those of Jacques Callot, the 17th-century French etcher whose masterpiece was *Les Grands Miséres de la guerre*. Even more significantly, Eisenstein started teaching himself Japanese. (He later explained that these Japanese language studies, as had Leonardo's catalogues, helped him understand the principles of montage.) Japanese culture made a deep and lasting impression on him, particularly his discovery of Japanese graphics and writing. He also became passionately interested in the Kabuki Theatre, which he had not yet seen, and by oriental culture in general, which he felt held the secrets of the 'magic' of art.

In October 1920, Eisenstein came to Moscow directly from the front with two friends, Fyodor Nikitin, a young artist, and Arensky, the son of the composer Anton Arensky. On the first night, Arensky's ex-wife gave them the kitchen of her apartment to sleep in. Eisenstein then spent some nights sleeping on his trunk in a cold hotel room shared by Mikhail Chekhov, the nephew of the playwright, and Valeri Smishlayev, both of whom had already worked in pre-revolutionary theatre. Chekhov, who, as Michael Chekhov, would end up playing character roles in Hollywood, had already appeared in a few films, one of them being *Tercentenary of the Romanov Dynasty's Accession to the Throne* (1913), in which he played Nicholas II.

Their conversations, according to Eisenstein, 'took a rather Theosophical turn . . . Smishlayev was trying to accelerate the growth of his carrot seedlings by suggestion . . . [and] Chekhov alternated between fanatical proselytising and blasphemy . . . I remember one conversation we had about "the invisible lotus" which flowered unseen in the devotee's breast . . . I alone remained in possession of my wits. I was by then ready to die of boredom one minute, or to burst out laughing the next.'[1]

It wasn't long before Eisenstein was given a bed in a student hostel, prior to his taking up his studies in Japanese at the General Staff Academy. The hostel was in the building that would later be converted into the Kremlin Hospital, where Eisenstein would spend his last days, thus bringing his life in Moscow full circle, ending where it had begun. He never, in fact, became a formal student of oriental languages, and the reason was an accidental encounter in the entrance hall of a Moscow theatre with his childhood friend Maxim Strauch.

'In 1914, Eisenstein and I had been separated by the war, and for several years had completely lost sight of each other,' Strauch recalled. 'Then, in November 1920, we met in Moscow, on an occasion that was very strange, very funny, and full of importance for both of us. It happened at the entrance to the Kamerny Theatre, whose company was working at that time under the outstanding director Alexander Tairov [whose Expressionist style of acting was opposed to the naturalism of Stanislavsky]. I very much wanted to see his latest production, but in those days it was extremely hard to get tickets. I had begun to bargain for a seat with a middle-aged ticket-tout when I suddenly had the sensation that someone was watching me from behind. I turned round, and indeed there was a man staring at me, very intently too, and with great concentration. I said to the ticket-tout: "Let's move on, I think we've been spotted." So we walked to another part of the foyer, and continued our somewhat irregular negotiations. After a minute or so I turned round again, and the man was still there, and still watching me. In the end, he walked boldly up to me and said, very quietly, "Aren't you Strauch?" It was Eisenstein! I hadn't recognised him because he had just arrived in Moscow from the Front, and he still wore his service greatcoat. We both began to bargain for tickets, and we were both successful.'[2]

After the play, the two friends wandered the streets for hours talking about the performance and theatre in general. In the early hours, Strauch offered to put Eisenstein up at his home on Chysti Prudi, more comfortable than the students' hostel. On the same night that Eisenstein and Strauch met at the Kamerny Theatre, they pledged to make theatre their profession. Not for them, however, the theatres of the past such as the Moscow Arts, but the new theatrical movement.

They decided to join one of the new workers' theatres that were springing up around Moscow. At first they got nowhere, since these theatres were, by definition, restricted almost exclusively to the working classes. Only ten per cent of their personnel could come from other social strata, and this allocation had long since been filled. Undaunted, Eisenstein and Strauch continued to look for theatre work during the bitter winter of 1920.

Rationing was in place, but ration cards were only issued to those in work or to students. Having left the General Staff Academy, Eisenstein was not eligible for a card. One day, cold and hungry, he slipped into Meyerhold's unheated RSFSR (Russian Soviet Federation of Socialist Republics) Theatre, where the shivering actors were rehearsing the first Soviet play, Vladimir Mayakovsky's *Mystery-Bouffe*. The play, which showed the Bolshevik revolution spreading throughout the world, had already been produced in 1918, then as now directed by Meyerhold. Eisenstein watched the man, whose production of *Masquerade* had so profoundly impressed him in Petrograd, put the actor Igor Ilyinsky through his paces. Suddenly, the rehearsal was interrupted by Mayakovsky, who strode over to Meyerhold and launched into a furious tirade. At this point Eisenstein was discovered in the shadows and firmly asked to leave. This was his first glimpse of the two theatrical giants with whom he was soon to work.

Mayakovsky was only five years Eisenstein's senior. He has been described as 'over six foot tall and built like a boxer, he lowered over everyone like a storm cloud. A scruffy lock of dark hair tumbled over his deeply lined forehead. In manner, he appeared alternatively morose and exuberant, taciturn and witty, cruel and supremely gentle. But whatever his posture, his genius was unmistakable – a goad to some and an insult to others.'[3] Although they were very different physically and temperamentally, many of Mayakovsky's character traits could have been attributed to Eisenstein in his prime. At this period, Eisenstein idolised the older man, who had joined the Communist party in 1908, and was twice arrested and imprisoned for underground activities.

In 1920, Bolshevik Moscow was teeming with literary movements and artistic credos – Futurists, Cubists, Suprematists, Imaginists, Expressionists, Presentists, Accidentists, Anarchists and Nihilists. Every credo had a movement and every movement had its literary café. Painters, poets and playwrights gathered at their preferred cafés to celebrate their liberation by the Revolution, and to test this new freedom of artistic expression in every conceivable way.

Among the artists who gathered at the Poet's Café, which the Futurist artist-poet David Burliuk had opened with Mayakovsky and the poet Vassili Kamensky, were journalists, and Red Army soldiers and sailors laden with weapons and hand grenades. Anarchists dressed in black, with automatic pistols and daggers bristling from bandoliers that bore the slogan 'Death to Capital', mixed with an assortment of speculators, whom the management disparagingly referred to as 'bourgeoisie who hadn't had their throats cut yet.' Scrawled across one wall of the café was 'I love to watch children dying', a line from *A Few Words About Myself*, one of Mayakovsky's pre-revolutionary poems.

No matter who was there, Mayakovsky was always the centre of attraction. He declared in his *Left March*:

> *Deploy in marching ranks!*
> *There is no room for verbal tricks.*
> *Silence, you orators!*
> *Your turn to speak,*
> *Comrade Rifle.*
> *Enough of living by the law*
> *Given by Adam and Eve.*
> *We will ride the mare of history till she drops.*
> *Left!*
> *Left!*
> *Left!*

It was the beginning of an ideological struggle over what sort of art was proper to a Communist system. In Lenin's view, Art and nothing else could serve as a substitute for religion. Amid the heated debates and revolutionary intoxication of the first years of the Soviet regime, Lenin declared, 'Every artist, and everyone who regards himself as such, claims as his proper right the liberty to work freely according to his ideal, whether it is any good or not. There you have the ferment, the experiment, the chaos. Nevertheless, we are communists, and must not quietly fold our hands and let chaos bubble as it will. We must also try to guide this development consciously, clearly, and to shape and determine its results.'

Lenin recognised the fact that the artist required creative liberty, but he declared that the regime, not the artist, should and would determine the outcome of the arts. Although he was a reasonably cultured man, Lenin was far from being a cultural revolutionary. His preferred taste was for a kind of Russian Victorianism, as was Stalin's, the difference being that Lenin did not try to impose his preferences. He encouraged new developments in the arts, but he did not pretend to know exactly what these would be and he attacked what he regarded as 'unhealthy' schools of the arts without prohibiting any of them.

In the first flush of victory, many, including Meyerhold, would have swept away the Moscow Arts Theatre with other pre-Soviet organisations, but they were rebuked when Anatoli Lunacharsky, Soviet People's Commissar for Enlightenment (i.e. Education), gave it generous support. Lunacharsky, who had written film scripts, saw that the revolutionising of a delicate organism such as the Moscow Arts Theatre, could not be done by decree, or by external change, but only by its absorption into the general stream of Soviet activity, strengthening what was healthy and rejecting what was decadent. This plan was the seed of a malignant plant that would finally asphyxiate radical artists like Meyerhold and Mayakovsky. Unfortunately, it would not be the creative artists, exhilarated by the possibilities that the Revolution opened up for them, who would decide what a Communist aesthetic should be like; this would be defined by the politicians and ideologues.

Meyerhold was indisputably the greatest figure in the new Soviet theatre. At the outbreak of the Revolution, he was the first artist of the theatre to offer his services to the new government, and in 1918 he became a member of the Bolshevik Party. Two years later he was appointed head of the Theatre Section of the People's Commissariat for Education, where he began a campaign to reorganise the theatre on revolutionary lines, launching the slogan 'October in the Theatre!'

He advocated the principle of 'bio-mechanics', that is, translating dramatic emotion into archetypal gestures, the abolition of individual characterisation, and the emphasis on the 'class kernel' of the dramatic presentation. In some ways he anticipated Bertolt

Brecht in desiring the spectators never to forget that they were in the theatre, unlike Stanislavsky, who wanted them to forget. Meyerhold's 'constructivist' stage dispensed with curtains, utilised movable stage sets, and attempted to create a 'symphony of motion' using the audience as co-creators of the drama. 'Our artist must throw away the paint brush, and compasses, he must take in hand hammer and axe in order to reshape the stage in the image of our technical century,' Meyerhold asserted.

Naturally, Eisenstein would have liked to join Meyerhold's theatre company but, as it happened, he and Strauch were eventually both taken on by the Proletkult Theatre in January 1921. Proletkult (proletarian culture) had been set up during the February Revolution, but only during the Civil War and the immediate post-war years of reconstruction had it begun expanding into a union with almost two hundred local branches, dozens of theatres, and literary and musical circles.

The group around the magazine *Proletarskaia Kul'tura*, led by A.A. Bogdanov, declared that 'bourgeois' culture must be forced to give way to a new one of purely 'proletarian' character. It laid claim to express proletarian interests in the sphere of culture as the Party did in social and political matters and the trade unions in the realm of the economy. This amounted to a demand that Proletkult, free from Party control, should itself be allowed to act as collective dictator over the arts.

In the autumn of 1920, Lenin insisted on incorporating the movement into the People's Commissariat of Enlightenment, ostensibly to counteract Proletkult's continued 'damaging' attempts to set up a culture of its own, but in reality to curb Bogdanov's increasingly powerful influence. In Moscow the movement was broken up into the Central Proletkult with its headquarters in the old Hermitage Theatre and the Moscow Proletkult, which were in conflict with each other.

Moscow's Proletkult Theatre had its headquarters in a lush villa, formerly the home of a Tsarist millionaire called Morozov who had imported it stone by stone from Portugal, and it was here that Eisenstein was accepted as set designer. The town house became a centre for conferences, lectures and discussions attended by the young Muscovite workers. Among the lecturers were some of the leading figures of the theatre including Stanislavsky, Meyerhold, and Foregger.

On joining the Proletkult Theatre, then headed by the writer and revolutionary Valeri Pletnyov, Eisenstein had no very original ideas of the theatre. It was without conscious intent, almost by accident, that, searching for an approach to entertainment in general, he hit upon techniques more appropriately associated with cinematography.

Sergei Yutkevitch, a seventeen-year-old student of Meyerhold's, who was working at Proletkult, explained: 'Eisenstein's first job as a designer for the Proletkult was for two plays . . . which went largely unnoticed. Then, and surprisingly early in his career, came the production that made him famous overnight – though still within a fairly narrow artistic circle – an adaptation of Jack London's story *The Mexican*. The producer was a member of the famous Moscow Arts Theatre, Valeri Smishlayev, and Eisenstein was officially the designer of the sets and the costumes. But it was Eisenstein who really created the entire production. It was typical of him not to be satisfied with a subsidiary function, and it was impossible for him to do anything less than think out the production in its entirety; by which I mean that he worked out the director's interpretation and applied it in a manner wholly typical of that extraordinary young man named Eisenstein.'[4]

The plot of *The Mexican* concerned a young revolutionary's efforts to make enough money as a boxer in order to buy guns for the Mexican Revolution in 1910. Eisenstein's visual treatment of the two rival boxing managers was to make the office of one circular and the other square. This stylisation applied to the actors as well; those on stage left had square heads and wore square checked costumes, and on stage right they were all circular. The make-up was also grotesquely caricatured, with only the boxer hero appearing without make-up as a sympathetic human figure.

Eisenstein based the advertising on the on-stage billboards to greet the boxer on those that greeted the arrival of Oscar Wilde in New York; 'Who Is Coming? Who Is Coming? Who Is Coming? He Is Coming! He Is Coming! He Is Coming! Oscar Wilde!" Oscar Wilde! Oscar Wilde! The Great Aesthete! The Great Aesthete! The

Great Aesthete!' He substituted the name of the boxer for Wilde, and 'great boxer' for 'great aesthete', a subtle in-joke which, by definition, only a few people were able to enjoy.

In the interlude between Acts One and Two, fairy lights lit up the proscenium arch and the revolutionary leaders came forward to harangue the audience about the evils of capitalism, especially as manifested in Mexico. The speech ended with a policeman arresting the speaker as an agitator. Two clowns rushed out and knocked the policeman down.

In the text, the climactic boxing match took place off-stage while the cast on stage merely reacted to it. Eisenstein, however, placed a boxing ring downstage, as close to the audience as possible, with 'real fighting, bodies crashing to the ring floor, panting, the shine of sweat on torsos and finally, the unforgettable smacking of gloves against taut skin and strained muscles.'[5] (This was a few years before Brecht used a boxing match in *The Rise and Fall of the City of Mahagonny*.) Eisenstein had wanted to stage the fight in the middle of the auditorium, but the Fire Commission forbade it.

Because of his lean and muscular figure and explosive temperament, the future film director, twenty-year-old Ivan Alexandrovich Pyriev, was ideally suited to the role of the young victor, the Mexican revolutionary, Filipe Rivera. One of the other boxers was played by an athletic eighteen-year-old boy called Grigori V. Alexandrov.

Eisenstein and Alexandrov met for the first time during that bitter winter of 1920. Eisenstein had arrived for a rehearsal with only one piece of black bread, which he left on the lighting switchboard. Driven by hunger, Alexandrov leapt on the board and was wolfing it down when Eisenstein spotted him. A fierce argument ensued. Only when Alexandrov explained that he had not eaten for two days did Eisenstein, who had eaten the day before, allow the younger man to consume the rest of the bread.

'Grisha' Alexandrov's life in the theatre began in his home town of Ekaterinburg (later Sverdlovsk), where he worked as a wardrobe assistant, scene painter and electrician at the Opera House. In 1918, he enrolled in the production course at the Workers and Peasants' Theatre, and had just arrived in Moscow to become an actor with the Proletkult. Grisha captivated Eisenstein, and they were to become very close friends for over a decade. Ivor Montagu described Alexandrov as 'that slim, strong, handsome, fair-haired and golden-skinned athlete – an Adonis.'[6] If there was anyone who would have led Eisenstein to take 'the road to perversion', as he once admitted to a friend, it would have been Grisha. They once shared a bed, but Eisenstein resisted anything more than an affectionate kiss. Fortunately (in one sense) for Eisenstein, given the homophobic legal restraints that were to come, Alexandrov seemed to be implacably heterosexual.

The production of *The Mexican* demonstrated Eisenstein's childhood love of the circus and his passion for the *commedia dell'arte*, but it was also plainly a first step on the road towards film direction. By unfolding the action on two planes simultaneously – thereby exposing the audience to a dual emotional shock – Eisenstein not only completely disregarded the conventional unity of action, but at the same time foreshadowed a film-making technique – the audience was, in effect, witnessing a sort of montage in embryo. As Eisenstein later recognised, bringing the events onto the stage was 'a specifically cinematographic technique' as distinct from the purely theatrical element of 'reacting to events'. (*The Mexican* was filmed as *The Fighter* in 1952 starring Richard Conte and directed by the left-wing American documentarist Herbert Kline.)

According to Eisenstein, exactly concurrent with the triumphant first night of *The Mexican*, his father died in Berlin where he had been living as an exile, although Eisenstein only learnt of the death three years later. This dramatically ironic occurrence would have fitted neatly into Eisenstein's Freudian interpretation of his relationship with his father – the father is dead, long live the son.

Although *The Mexican* was a popular success, Eisenstein was more concerned with how Meyerhold, whom he would later refer to as 'my spiritual father', would react to it. On the evening Meyerhold came to see the production, Eisenstein sat in the front stalls in nervous apprehension, watching Meyerhold's reactions. Much to his relief, Meyerhold liked the show and invited Eisenstein to join him and Lunacharsky at the futuristic coffee house known as Sopo (*Soyuz Poetov* i.e. Poet's Union). Eisenstein could only listen as his elders discussed Isadora Duncan's dancing and the controversy raging round her ideas on plastic movement. He had not yet seen the American dancer, who had just married the 'peasant poet' Sergei Esenin and settled in Moscow.

Despite this approval from Meyerhold and others in the theatre, Eisenstein, like most of the population of Moscow, was poor, often hungry and badly clothed. At the end of the Civil War the city was on the verge of starvation but, despite the crippling shortage of both food and heating in Moscow that winter, creative warmth and fire pervaded the artistic circles.

'No one bothered about cold or hunger,' wrote the film director Lev Kuleshov. 'Life seemed marvellously interesting, and there was no doubt at all that this moment marked the coming of a new era, the era of art. This art had to be as bold as the workers' power itself, as pitiless towards the past as the Revolution . . . The extent to which we were crazed about art in those difficult years now seems quite astonishing . . . All were ready, at once and with no reckoning the cost, to carry out the "Order of the Army of Art" given by Mayakovsky.'[7]

Eisenstein was next asked to design the sets and costumes for Valeri Pletnyov's *Precipice* (aka *On the Abyss*), but a clash of opinion with Smishlayev, who was again to be the nominal director, brought the production to an abrupt halt. Had the play been staged, it would have shown how Eisenstein's ideas were moving further towards cinematic solutions, though he only later recognised 'a film element that tried to fit itself into the stubborn stage.' For one scene in which an inventor, staggered by his latest discovery, has to rush wildly through the town, Eisenstein devised the use of mobile props, pulled by actors on roller skates.

Of the scene, Eisenstein remembered 'the four legs of two bankers, supporting the facade of the stock exchange, with two top-hats crowning the whole. There was also a policeman, spliced and quartered with traffic. Costumes blazing with perspectives of twirling lights, with only great rouged lips visible above.'[8]

In the spring of 1921, Eisenstein saw an advertisement announcing the opening of the State School for Stage Direction, to be run by Meyerhold. It was situated in a former lycée where Meyerhold himself had a small flat, and boasted a tiny classroom and an adjoining hall with a stage. Meyerhold, dressed in a faded sweater, trousers drawn in tightly at the ankles by gaiters, gigantic slippers, a woollen scarf and a red fez, presided over the Examining Board. Its other members included the poet Ivan Aksyonov, a member of the Centrifugal literary circle and author of a monograph on Picasso, the mysterious Valeri Bebyutov and the actor Valeri Inkhizhinov, later to star as the Mongolian fur-trapper in Pudovkin's *Storm Over Asia* (1928).

First came questions to test general cultural knowledge, followed by the setting of a practical problem. Eisenstein was asked to draw on the blackboard a stage setting for the subject 'six men in pursuit of a seventh.' With swift strokes, he executed an ingenious and complicated *mise-en-scène*. For the final test, in expressiveness of movement, the candidates had to draw an imaginary bow. The next day, Eisenstein, who had also presented his huge portfolio of sketches to the Board, heard that he had been accepted. Thus began a two-year association with Meyerhold that was to prove decisively important for his development as a film director.

On the first day of lectures, Eisenstein and Sergei Yutkevich, who had been accepted at the same time, rushed to take up two front seats, in order to be close to Meyerhold during the course he ran on stage direction and bio-mechanics. His lectures on stage direction incorporated formulae for the calculated planning of each separate step in stage production, though allowing for improvisation. It was through Meyerhold's influence that Eisenstein developed that mixture of spontaneous improvisation and scientifically calculated planning that he later used in his films.

The parallel course in bio-mechanics included training in acrobatics, in which Eisenstein participated enthusiastically. Meyerhold insisted on his students gaining direct, practical experience of the stage and, when the season opened, arranged for them all to take part in the ball scene from Ibsen's *The League of Youth* at his own RSFSR theatre.

At the end of the first term Eisenstein was asked to design the sets for Ludwig Tieck's *Puss in Boots*. Again he displayed his originality by constructing a stage within a stage, the imitation stage being viewed as if from the wings so that the actors were shown in two distinct roles: as actors addressing an imaginary audience from the imitation stage as well as playing to the real audience.

Throughout Eisenstein's period at the School, scholarships were non-existent and he lived a tough hand-to-mouth existence. He still lodged with Strauch, while Yutkevich, whose mother regularly baked him potato pies, saw to it that he never starved.

Aside from their work with Meyerhold and the Proletkult Theatre, Eisenstein and Yutkevich worked for MASTFOR (*Masterskaya Foreggera*), the Workshop Theatre run by Nikolai Foregger, the former Baron Foregger von Greiffenturn, who shared Eisenstein's passion for the circus and the *commedia dell'arte*. Foregger, who transferred to the stage many of his observations of real life, was experimenting in the use of masks, though he refused to stylise them in the manner of the *commedia dell'arte*. Instead he chose his masks from contemporary life, depicting a young woman Communist, a poet, an intellectual philosopher, a city merchant and so on. In a sense it was the kind of *typage* that Eisenstein would use in his films.

Yutkevich and Eisenstein's first joint venture at Foregger's theatre was designing the settings for a triple bill of parodies satirising Vladimir Nemirovich-Danchenko's penchant for operetta, the propaganda style of certain contemporary plays and Alexander Tairov's excessively stylised performances at the Kamerny Theatre, especially his production of Racine's *Phèdre*.

The next play was by the poet Vladimir Mass, an associate of Foregger, entitled, after Mayakovsky's poem, *A Human Attitude to Horses* (*Good Relations with Horses*) which opened on New Year's Eve, 1921. It was divided into two parts, the first having a bitingly satirical content, highlighted by the use of *typage* masks, while the second was a music hall parody. Eisenstein designed a series of strange and fantastic costumes; instead of skirts, the chorus wore thin and revealing, wide, bell-shaped wire frameworks bedecked with multi-coloured ribbons. (Not unlike those Busby Berkeley chorines would wear in Warner Bros. musicals in the early 1930s.) The Poet's costume was made up of half peasant dress half evening clothes.

Eisenstein also designed the sets and costumes for another of Foregger's productions, *The Kidnapper* (aka *Child-Thieves*), based on *Les Deux Orphelines*, the old melodrama by Adolphe d'Ennery which D.W. Griffith had adapted as *Orphans of the Storm*, released in America almost at the same time. This time, Eisenstein took his inspiration from Honoré Daumier, whose caricatures of the middle classes and their pretensions delighted him.

In April 1922, Yutkevich and Eisenstein designed the sets of *Macbeth* for another group – the Central Theatre of Enlightenment. On a single set with no curtain was a throne and a huge cage that was used, among other things, as the entrance to a castle, a rampart, and the porter's closet. The set was in grey and black, the costumes in red and gold. Even at this early stage of his career, Eisenstein was interested in the dramatic function of colour, which, alas, he was only able to test in the cinema in the colour sequence from *Ivan the Terrible Part II*. The helmets of the Scottish warriors covered their faces with slits for the eyes, a design which Eisenstein was to reproduce for the helmets worn by the Teutonic Knights in *Alexander Nevsky*.

Eisenstein spent the summer of 1922 with Foregger's company in Petrograd, where he met Grigori Kozintsev and Leonid Trauberg, founders of FEKS (Factory of the Eccentric Actor). The group's aim was to reform socialist theatre along the lines of circus and vaudeville. (*Ekstsentrik* is one of the Russian words for clown.) Trauberg and Kozintsev proclaimed 'art without a capital letter, a pedestal or a fig leaf,' and that 'the streets bring revolution to art. Our street mud now is circus, cinema, music-hall!'

Among FEKS' first presentations was an unconventional staging of Gogol's *Marriage*, less an enactment of the play than of 'the product of their own imagination', and a play written by the group called *Foreign Trade at the Eiffel Tower*, both of which used some film sequences. This led to Trauberg and Kozintsev embarking on a remarkable twenty-year co-directing film partnership.

Under the influence of FEKS, Eisenstein and Yutkevich wrote a three-act satirical pantomime for Foregger called *Columbine's Garter*, to music by Ernst von Dohnanyi. It was an extremely free adaptation of Arthur Schnitzler's play *Beatrice's Veil*, which had been produced by Meyerhold in 1910 as *Columbine's Scarf*, and by Tairov in 1916 as *Pierette's Shawl*. Eisenstein and Yutkevich's play, updated to a contemporary setting, was divided into two parts:

Mama the Automatic Café and *Papa the Watercloset*, with Pierrot turned into a bohemian and the exploiting Harlequin into a parvenu banker, who would enter on a tightrope. The authors wanted to call the work 'stage attractions', foreshadowing Eisenstein's theory of the 'montage of attractions'.

Another, less obvious, influence on the piece was Jean Cocteau. Eisenstein had read about the 'scandalous' play, *Les Marieés de la Tour Eiffel*, which had opened at the Théatre des Champs Elysées the year before, and was struck by the use of radio announcers standing on either side of the stage, dressed, as he wrongly remembered, 'in Cubist costumes designed by Picasso'.[9] (They were, in fact, Jean Hugo's costumes, and they were not Cubist.) Eisenstein even cut out a photograph of Cocteau from the magazine *Je Sais Tout*, and pinned it to the wall of his flat.

The play, dedicated 'to Vsevolod Meyerhold, the maestro of the *Scarf*, from the apprentices of the *Garter*,' failed to be put on by Foregger and was never performed. Piqued at this rebuff, Eisenstein left to work as an assistant to Meyerhold, whom he 'loved, revered and respected' more than any other man.

Meyerhold later claimed, 'All Eisenstein's work has its origins in the laboratory where we once worked together as teacher and pupil. But our relationship was not so much the relationship of teacher and pupil as of two artists in revolt, up to our necks and afraid to swallow for fear of the disgusting slime in which we found the theatre wallowing . . . The theatre was sinking in a swamp of naturalism, feeble imitation and eclecticism'.

Grigori Kozintsev asserted that the cinema learnt more from Meyerhold than did the theatre. In 1925, Proletkult, knowing of Meyerhold's interest in cinematographic problems, tried to get him to make a film of John Reed's *Ten Days That Shook The World*, two years before Eisenstein made *October*.

Eisenstein worked at the GVYTM, the State Higher Theatre Workshops at 23 Novinsky Boulevard. 'These two floors, with a mezzanine, were packed with life . . . The master lived in the attic with his family . . . The master had the rare facility of dressing up in the most *outré* clothing. Contriving not to let his slippers drop off his feet, he hopped round the edges of the steps of the tiny spiral staircase and flew downwards. I could barely keep up with his youthful speed. I caught him up in the kitchen . . . Shaking, the hapless old man [Meyerhold was forty-eight] lay on the stove. Who could have said that this same old man, playing Lord Henry in *Dorian Gray*, would embody the irreproachable dandy, rocking in his armchair and staring at his parrot, beak to beak? He huddled up. Frowned. His collar reached above his ears. His jaw was bound in a cloth. His long fingers were just showing out of his overcoat's cuffs.'[10]

Meyerhold had, in fact, played Lord Henry Wotton in a lost film of Oscar Wilde's *The Picture of Dorian Gray*, which he directed in 1915. Of course, Eisenstein remembered him as the tall and thin Blue Pierrot in *Masquerade* in St Petersburg in 1917. When Eisenstein joined the group, Meyerhold was rehearsing *The Magnificent Cuckold* by the Belgian dramatist Fernand Crommelynck. It was his intention that 'against the bare constructions of the set surfaces, young actors in blue linen overalls would demonstrate their mastery without make-up, in pure form, as it were, without theatrical illusions.'[11]

At the workshop, Eisenstein made a model set for a production of *Heartbreak House*, which Meyerhold was planning for his own theatre. Eisenstein, taking his cue from George Bernard Shaw's suggestion that the house in the play should resemble a ship, designed the set as a modern ship in which the actors, who would never leave the stage, moved to a large striped semi-circular divan at the back, where they would rest whenever they had finished each particular sequence in their performance. The play was never produced, but the model survived.

In September 1922, a painful rupture between Eisenstein and 'the grand old man of my youth, my leader in drama, my teacher . . . a combination of creative genius and treacherous personality.' Apparently, Meyerhold was rather offended by a question Eisenstein asked him during a lecture. 'I suddenly saw Mikhail Osipovich in his aquiline face, with its penetrating gaze and the striking set of the mouth beneath the bent, predatory nose. A glassy stare which darted left and right and was then utterly transformed, assuming an air of official politeness, a slightly derisive sympathy, before showing ironic surprise at the question.'[12]

Subsequently, Eisenstein was surprised to receive a note via the actress Zinaida Raikh (also Reich), Meyerhold's assistant and soon-to-be second wife: 'When the pupil is not merely equal, but superior to the teacher, then it is best for him to go!' Eisenstein was devastated. 'The countless agonies of those like myself who self-lessly loved him. The countless moments of triumph as we witnessed the magical creativity of this unique wizard of the the-atre . . . What purgatory . . . I was expelled from the Gates of Heaven . . . My heart was heavy with great sadness . . . I was, beyond all argument, unlucky with my fathers.'[13]

Whenever Eisenstein was rebuffed or reprimanded by an older man, he would see his father in them. 'Perhaps that was why I so hated all those features in Upton Sinclair, because I have known them since I was a babe in arms?,' Eisenstein wrote after the American novelist had withdrawn his financial backing for *Qué Viva México!*[14]

In June 1936, while Eisenstein was struggling to make *Bezhin Meadow*, about a father who kills the son he feels has betrayed him, Meyerhold sent him a photograph of himself, with a dedica-tion written in ink on his shirt collar. 'I am proud of my pupil who has now become a master. I love the master who has now founded a school. I bow to this pupil and master, S. Eisenstein.' There is cer-tainly something of Meyerhold's demeanour and personality in the manner in which Nikolai Cherkassov portrays the Tsar in *Ivan the Terrible*.

In the event, the rift with Meyerhold proved to Eisenstein's advan-tage. He was almost immediately appointed artistic director of Proletkult's Touring Theatre known as *Pere Tru* (*Peredvizhaniya* – The Strolling Players), a group of fifteen members of the Central Proletkult Theatre, who had founded an independent group.

Eisenstein now had a theatre of his own, which he could use to destroy the traditional theatre. 'In a few words, Proletkult's the-atrical programme consists not in "using the treasures of the past" or "in discovering new forms of theatre" but in abolishing the very institution of theatre as such and replacing it by a showplace for achievements in the field at the *level of the everyday skills of the masses*. The organisation of workshops and the elaboration of a scientific system to raise this level are the immediate tasks of the

Scientific Department of Proletkult in the theatrical field,' he explained.

One of his first actions was to establish a systematic study programme that included conferences, serious study sessions on circus art, and practical training in acrobatics, his aim being to imbue his actors with an attitude to precise application to their work. The day began at nine in the morning and continued until the evening with sports, boxing, athletics, team games, fencing and special voice training.

Eisenstein's debut production for Proletkult's Touring Troupe was *Enough Folly in a Wise Man* (*Enough Simplicity for Every Wise Man/Even a Wise Man Stumbles*) by Alexander Ostrovsky. He had seen the play at the Moscow Arts Theatre in the cold and hungry days when he had cajoled the usherette to let him in without a ticket. It was while watching this performance that he conceived the idea of taking the bare bones of the plot and adapting them to a contemporary context.

For Eisenstein, it was not a matter of 'revealing the playwright's purpose' or 'correctly interpreting the author' or 'faithfully reflecting an epoch'. In what he called his 'theory of focal points', the aim was to 'attract' the audience, and then to smash an artistic fist in its face by a carefully planned sequence of 'focal points', of which the boxing match in *The Mexican* was an obvious example.

'Its stylistic premise derived from a very simple starting point: the proposition that every action by an actor should expand in intensity to pass beyond the bounds of that activity itself,' Eisenstein explained. 'Roughly speaking, it meant that in registering "astonishment" the actor should not limit himself to "starting back" . . . it had to be a backward somersault in the air.'[15] Among many other tricks were 'visual puns': when Kurchayev, the dim hussar, says to Mamayeva (Vera Yanukova), 'It's enough to drive one up the pole!', she immediately thrusts a long pole into a socket attached to his belt, and climbs up it. To demonstrate Kurchayev's commonplace character, he was played by three men, all dressed alike, moving together and speaking in chorus, an effect used for three shareholders in *The Strike*.

The production took place in a circus arena in which clowns (among them Ivan Pyriev and Maxim Strauch) juggled, performed acrobatics, threw water onto each other and placed explosions under their seats. There was a woman who had lamps for breasts which lit up from time to time when she got excited. The characters included the French General Joffre, the British Foreign Secretary Lord Curzon and Pavel Milyukov, a prominent counter-revolutionary and white emigré, depicted as white clowns. Naturally, the red clowns were the goodies. One of them, Grigori Alexandrov, who had been a boxer in *The Mexican*, was required to walk a tightrope while holding a conversation with a girl walking beneath the wire. At this point in the play Eisenstein always hid in terror in the wings until the applause indicated it was over safely.

At one performance, Alexandrov was making his way across the tightrope when it suddenly snapped. He was almost killed and the metal support crashed down onto an empty seat in the auditorium, pulverising it. Had it fallen a few centimetres to the right, it would presumably have fatally crushed Edouard Tisse, thus altering the course of cinema history. Reputedly, Tisse, the future cinematographer of all Eisenstein's films, hardly batted an eyelid.

The show was a great success, and among the first to congratulate Eisenstein backstage with a bottle of champagne was Mayakovsky. Though critical of Eisenstein's textual adaptation of the original, he was sorry that 'he himself had not thought of collaborating in this gay and lively show.' So successful was the production at deconstructing (to use a contemporary expression) Ostrovsky's play, that Anatoli Lunacharsky was worried that he might be forced to close down the Maly Theatre, which had become known as the House of Ostrovsky, whose statue stands at the entrance. (Despite Eisenstein, the Maly, meaning 'small' as opposed to *bolshoi* – big, has survived to the present day.)

Eisenstein presented an excerpt from *Enough Folly in a Wise Man* to a select audience at the Bolshoi Theatre. When the performance ended to applause, he was so overwhelmed that he failed to notice that he had ripped his expensive (for him) brand new suit on a nail.

Eisenstein's next production was called *Can You Hear Me, Moscow?* by Sergei Tretyakov, one of the earliest of Soviet playwrights. The play, which opened on November 7, 1923, dealt with the recent revolutionary events in Germany. A few months before, the Communists thought their time had come in Germany. Inflation had reached an extent unparalleled in any other industrial country in modern times, there was popular discontent and many strikers were gaining in militancy. Hitler seized the occasion to launch his beer-hall putsch in Munich, invoking the Communist danger.

The title of the play echoed the dissension in Moscow on how to take advantage of Germany's unrest. Zinoviev, Radek and Trotsky were in different ways inclined to hope for great things from a German uprising, while Stalin believed insurrection foolhardy at the moment. A 'formalist', Eisenstein seemed less involved in the content than the form. Throughout his life, politics was never an interest in itself, but only insofar as they affected his ability to function as an artist.

During the play, the cast addressed the audience, demanding 'Are you listening?', and they responded (with prompting), 'I'm listening!' A massive portrait of Lenin was unveiled in Act Three. Eisenstein described a scene from the play thus: 'In the epilogue at the opening ceremony to the sovereign of the small German duchy, the official court poet recites a celebratory poem on the German defeat of the semi-cultured, naive population by German armour. He is himself wearing armour. He is also on stilts (his poetry is stilted too). And his knight's costume covers his body and his stilts, so he appears as an iron giant. At the critical moment the straps break and the empty armour falls away from him with a crash of empty buckets.'[16]

This anticipated the hollow echo of the bucket helmet of the Livonian knight in *Alexander Nevsky* after being hit by a Russian harness, and the empty armour in the tent of the traitor prince in *Ivan the Terrible*.

Moving from the highly artificial atmosphere of his last two plays, Eisenstein's final theatre production before embarking on his film career, was staged in the realist setting of the Moscow Gas Works during working hours in March 1924. For *Gas Masks*, also by Tretyakov, the audience sat on rows of wooden benches placed on the factory floor, while the machines kept on working. The actors wore no make-up, and the final scene was timed to coincide with the nightshift workers, who took over from the actors and set about lighting their fires.

It was not a success, owing to the mutual disruption of factory and theatre, and the noxious smell of gas, and the production ran for four nights only. However, Eisenstein realised that its failure lay deeper.

'*Gas Masks* with its general aims . . . was the last possible attempt within the confines of theatre to overcome its sense of illusion . . . in fact that was already almost cinema, which builds its effects on precisely that kind of theatrical "material" through montage juxtaposition . . .'[17]

The theatre had become too confined for his imagination. As he explained, 'the cart dropped to pieces, and its driver dropped into the cinema.'[18]

4

Ciné-Fist!

Soviet cinema must cut through to the skull! . . . We must cut with our ciné-fist through to skulls, cut through to final victory and now, under the threat of an influx of 'real life' and philistinism into the Revolution we must cut through as never before! Make way for the ciné-fist!

In November 1922, Eisenstein and Sergei Yutkevitch published an article in praise of 'The Eighth Art' (i.e. the cinema) and, especially, of Charlie Chaplin, who had 'taken the eighth seat in the council of muses.'[1] While criticising the 'corrupting influences of naturalism' on some directors, such as Louis Delluc, films like *The Cabinet of Dr Caligari*, animated films and the detective adventure comedy film, gained their approval. 'Everyone is aware of the enormous influence that cinema now exerts on the other arts . . . Thus the happy infant (as Ilya Ehrenburg called it) grows bigger and prettier and the directors, artists, poets and technicians of the whole world who are interested in the victory of the new art must devote all their efforts to ensuring that their favourite infant does not fall into the obliging clutches of the "heliotrope auntie" and the sanctimonious watchdogs of morality.'[2]

In the near future, there would be more menacing 'watchdogs of morality' than these heliotrope aunties or Mrs Grundys presenting themselves in various forms during Eisenstein's life. While researching *An American Tragedy* in the USA, he came across a photo of three Daughters of the American Revolution, archetypically prim and proper looking (bespectacled, hair in buns etc), on which he could have drawn for the censorious women in the courtroom, a *typage* not unknown in Hollywood films. He was also to suffer from the prudish disapproval of a group of Pasadena women who had invested in *Qué Viva México!*

Eisenstein's first practical experience with the eighth art was the five-minute film interlude used in his production of *Enough Folly in a Wise Man*. It shows the actors, including Grigori Alexandrov, Maxim Strauch, Mikhail Gomorov and Eisenstein himself in masks or highly stylised make-up.

The play opened with the hero Glumov, played by Alexandrov, in top hat, white face, white smock and tights, recounting how his diary has been stolen and that he has been threatened with exposure. Curtains parted at the back of the stage to reveal a screen on which a film was projected. The film showed Glumov's acts and thoughts over a period of a week. It begins with the theft of his diary by a man in a black mask – a pastiche of the American detective film, especially Pearl White's cliffhanging serials such as *The Exploits of Elaine*(1915). The depiction of the contents of the diary parodied a Pathé newsreel and took a dig at the *Kino-Pravda* newsreels then being made by Dziga Vertov.

The film goes on to reveal Glumov's flattery of his patrons. By the use of dissolves, he transforms himself into whatever object is desired by each person; with General Joffre he becomes a machine gun, with his scolding uncle he turns into an obedient ass, with his doting aunt he becomes a babe in arms . . . (it was an unintentionally prescient reminder of how Soviet artists had to take whatever shape the regime demanded, when their spring changed instantaneously into winter.)

Glumov then wanders over the rooftops, climbs a steeple, waves at an aeroplane flying above, hangs his top-hat on the steeple, loses his footing and falls into a motorcar that takes him to the very theatre (the Proletkult) where the show is taking place. As the film ended, Alexandrov burst through the screen onto the stage, triumphantly holding up a reel of film. This final idea had been used several years earlier by Max Linder in Moscow, which Eisenstein had probably heard about but not seen.

'Thus the theatre took a leap into cinema, expanding metaphors to degrees of literalness unattainable in the theatre itself,' recalled

Eisenstein. 'And this culminated in the final stroke: when the audience called for me, I did not come on stage to take any curtain-calls – instead I appeared on the screen bowing like a peculiar version of the Pathé cockerel, with the shock of hair I affected in those days that was worthy of the Metro-Goldwyn-Mayer lion!'[3]

Glumov's Diary, as the segment is often referred to, was shot at Goskino (State Cinema Enterprise) on a Thursday, and was ready for the show's first night the following Saturday. 'As the Goskino people thought that I might be too mischievous, so they gave me as a teacher . . . Dziga Vertov! After watching us take our first two or three shots, Vertov gave us up as a hopeless case and left us to our own fate.'[4]

As the untrained Proletkult group had been warned about wasting precious raw film, each shot was filmed exactly as it was to be cut, none of the hundred and twenty meters was wasted. The conclusion of Eisenstein's first shooting script reads: 'Baby/Head of Strauch/Strauch (long shot)/Mashenka (close-up)/ Legs/Mashenka and Glumov (close-up)/Cheque paid to organisation (long shot)/Thumb/Trio [Pyriev, Antonov, Strauch]/Thumb/Trio/Grisha/I bow.'

By this time the cinema was no revelation to Eisenstein. Several years earlier, as a penniless student, he had wormed his way free into a St Petersburg cinema and seen the repertory of American films showing there. At the same time he had seen the first German expressionist films such as Robert Wiene's *The Cabinet of Dr Caligari* with its weird and distorted sets and grotesquely angled photography. Most important was his encounter with the films of D.W. Griffith and, through them, with the principal of montage. *Intolerance*, which had found its way through the blockade early in 1919, was an exciting discovery of the possibilities of cinematic expression and proved a seminal influence.

In 1920, a copy of *The Birth of a Nation* reached Moscow. According to Eisenstein, Griffith, 'The Great Old Man of all of us', had 'played a massive role in the development of montage in the Soviet film.'[5] (In 1923, Griffith was invited to make a film in the Soviet Union, but declined the offer.) Some years later, however,

Eisenstein felt that Griffith was unable to take the possibilities of cross-cutting and parallel action any further. It was, of course, Eisenstein who realised its full potential.

Yet several years before Eisenstein, Lev Kuleshov, one of the first theorists of the cinema, was advocating the study of American films, especially Westerns and the work of Griffith. 'I was the first in Russia to speak the word "montage", to speak of the action, of the dynamic of the cinema, of realism in the art of film,' Kuleshov claimed.[6] He articulated what seems basic to us today, that the arrangement of individual shots in the cutting room (montage) is central to the specificity of cinema. He arrived at montage almost by accident because the shortage of film during the Civil War years led him to experiment with making new movies by cutting up and rearranging parts of old ones.

'We make films, Kuleshov made cinema,' declared Pudovkin.[7] In 1924, Kuleshov put his researches at the services of his first fiction feature, the gag-filled satire *The Extraordinary Adventures of Mr West in the Land of the Bolsheviks*, made with members of his workshop, including Pudovkin, who played one of the criminals. Using mobile cameras, quick cutting and sequences derived from American chase films, the picture managed to deride the West's stereotyped view of 'mad, savage, Russians,' while creating its own stereotyped Americans – the Harold Lloyd-type Mr West, clutching an American flag, and his faithful cowboy aide Jed, firing his six-guns and lassoing motor cyclists in like steers from the top of a Moscow taxi.

The first meeting between Eisenstein and Kuleshov took place at the time of *Enough Simplicity for a Wise Man*, which had impressed the latter. 'Here was a theatre director who used new methods,' Kuleshov recalled, 'and who seemed to be speaking to us with those new words for which we were all waiting, and not always patiently, in those stormy and passionate years.'[8] Kuleshov was then only twenty-four, one year Eisenstein's junior, but had made his first short film, *The Project of Engineer Prite*, when he was eighteen.

Kuleshov was running 'films without film' workshops in the first Soviet State School of Cinematography, preparing film-makers for the day when they could obtain raw stock to put in their empty cameras. He and Eisenstein made a 'business arrangement.'

'Our intentions were entirely admirable, but our accommodation was totally inadequate, whereas Eisenstein had superb accommodation in the building of the Proletkult. Hence our business agreement, whereby Eisenstein gave my own students the use of his floor-space for their gymnastics, sport, acrobatics, and so forth, and in return I gave lectures on the cinema to his actors. We both gained from our collaboration, and in Eisenstein's case the gain was largely due to his ignorance of the cinema. Yet he had already developed a great interest in it, and his appetite had been increased by his experience in making that short sequence for *A Wise Man*. So he decided to study the cinema in earnest, and he asked if he might join my laboratory as an observer. I agreed at once, with the consequence that for three months, and regularly each evening, he worked with me on the technique of film editing and especially the editing of the subject matter that attracted him most of all – mass movement and mass action . . . Eisenstein proved to be the most extraordinary student, and I can say in all sincerity that in those three months he completely mastered all that was known at that time about the arts and techniques of the cinema. He began as my pupil, but very soon he became my teacher, thereby proving the truth of one of his favourite sayings: that anyone in the world could learn to become a film director, but some people needed three years' training and others at least three hundred . . . For Sergei Eisenstein the time required was exactly three months – part-time!'[9]

Eisenstein and Grigori Alexandrov attended the workshops held in the attic of Meyerhold's theatre. It was not long before Eisenstein was formulating his theories on montage, which would later veer away from those of Kuleshov. But he had to wait a little longer to be able to put any of his theories into practice. He came closer with his work with Esther Shub, which marked the real beginning of his cinematic apprenticeship.

The Ukrainian-born Esther Shub studied literature in Moscow in the years before the Revolution. With the Revolution she enrolled in classes at the Institute for Women's Higher Education, and became 'theatre officer' at the State Commissariat of Education.

Shub began work at Goskino in 1922, editing and titling foreign and pre-revolutionary films, some of which had to be adjusted to accord with revolutionary principles. All films from abroad were closely censored to eliminate any 'unhealthy tendencies' before their general release to the public. In this censoring process the entire sense of the film could be radically altered. There was a case when excerpts from two completely separate films were edited into a single film so as to point out the contrast between the life of leisure enjoyed by the passengers of a luxury liner and the sweat and toil of the stokers below deck. She also completely re-edited *Carmen* (1916), Charlie Chaplin's first film to be seen in Russia.

Eisenstein frequently visited Shub in her cutting room, observing her at this questionable practice, and watching the run-through of films she had edited. At the end of March 1924, assisted by Eisenstein, she was cutting the two parts of Fritz Lang's *Dr Mabuse, The Gambler* (1922), which she reduced to one film under the title *Golden Putrefaction* for Soviet distribution. Then, at her home, where she had a small cutting table and projector, she would put together pieces of film with often startling results. It was at Shub's cutting table that the mysteries of montage were revealed to Eisenstein.

Shortly after working with Shub, Eisenstein left Proletkult, following a clash of opinions. One reason was the feeling that their co-operative mentality did not permit him the recognition he felt he deserved as a director. He turned for help to his old friend from the Civil War days, the painter Konstantin Yeliseyev, who was now editing the review *Red Pepper*. Yeliseyev readily accepted Eisenstein's suggestion that he should join the review as a cartoonist. The very next day, however, Eisenstein apologetically explained to Yeliseyev that he had changed his mind overnight, having been given the chance to make his first full-length film. Although there was a constant shortage of film stock throughout the 1920s, Soviet film production was gradually increasing, and Goskino's director, Boris Mikhin, was keen to shoot a projected cycle of seven films to be called *Towards the Dictatorship of the Proletariat*,intended as an historical panorama of the Party and the working class movement before 1917.

They were to be: 1) *Geneva-Russia*: the work of the Tsarist secret police 2) *Underground*: underground political activity 3) *The First of May*: the organising of illegal May Day meetings 4) *1905*: the conclusion of the first stage of the Russian Revolution 5) *The Strike*: revolutionary responses by the proletariat 6) *Prisons, Revolts, Escapes* 7) *October*: the seizing of power and the establishment of the dictatorship of the proletariat.

Valeri Pletnyov, the head of Proletkult, was given the job of writing the script for one of the films, *The Strike*, and invited Eisenstein to direct this joint production of Proletkult and Goskino. Though planned as the fifth film in the cycle, it was to be the first to start shooting. Boris Mikhin was determined to draw Eisenstein into filming despite his unconcealed dislike of his theatre work. But, as he later claimed, he intuitively recognised Eisenstein's potential as a great film director.

Before shooting began in the summer of 1924, the cautious Mikhin began breaking Eisenstein in on the technical aspects of the film studio, and chose the people to work with him. He introduced Eisenstein to twenty-seven-year-old Edouard Tisse, a cameraman who had distinguished himself in newsreel work during the Civil War. In 1918, Tisse shot the first Soviet feature, *Signal*, and a film about Soviet Latvia the following year for Vertov's *Kino-Glaz* group.

There is so much mystery surrounding Tisse's origins that many false statements about them have been printed. He was said to have been born in Latvia of a Swedish father and Russian mother (or vice versa). Because of his name, people presumed him to be French, putting an acute accent on the final 'e'. Even more confusing was the fact that Eisenstein referred to him as 'The German'.

Tisse was born Kazimirovich Nikolaitis in Lithuania of Catholic Lithuanian parents; his father was Kazimir Nikolaitis, and his mother was of Swedish extraction. For some reason, the son took the name Edouard, changed his surname to Tisse, and claimed to be German. (Later, in the early 1930s, when it was extremely unpopular to be German, he explained that a mistake had been made, and that he was really Lithuanian.)

Eisenstein and Tisse met for the first time in the garden of the Morozov mansion, the headquarters of the Proletkult Theatre.

Eisenstein showed Tisse the treatment for *The Strike*, which Tisse went through carefully, calmly correcting several technical terms such as substituting 'double exposure' for what Eisenstein had imaginatively called 'profusion upon profusion'.

Though very different physically and temperamentally – the volcanic Eisenstein with massive head, wild hair and boyish face; Tisse, tall, blue-eyed, blond, calm, modest and temperate – they were well suited in their daring and eagerness to experiment. Tisse was probably the person with whom Eisenstein talked least about filming. There was no need. Nor did they even address each other by the familiar form of address, bound though they were by a deep aesthetic affinity.

Mikhin explained to Eisenstein why he chose Tisse as photographer. 'In the theatre you get carried away by your passion for acrobatics. You'll probably be just as rash when it comes to filming. Edouard has an outstanding record as a news reporter and he's also still an excellent athlete. You'll doubtless get on well together.'[10]

However, it was touch and go as to whether Eisenstein would make his first film at all. Mikhin made Eisenstein do some test filming, but when the first two tests were rejected, Goskino were on the verge of dropping the tyro director. He then made a third test, and due to the persistent efforts of Mikhin and Tisse, including their willingness to give a written guarantee of the film's successful completion, Eisenstein was given the go-ahead.

Certain principles formed the foundation of *The Strike*. It would present a generalised picture of a strike, and not an actual historical event, a synthesis of many such clashes between the workers and the owners. Also, instead of individual heroes the workers should be portrayed as collective heroes in their clash with the capitalists.

Eisenstein spent some months researching the subject prior to shooting, meeting a number of formerly outlawed Party activists and strikers; he visited factories, assembled a prodigious amount of documentation, and read books such as Emile Zola's *Germinal*, the novel of hunger and misery during a 19th-century coal strike. He worked day and night, as he was always to do, and since he was still dealing in an unfamiliar medium, he asked the experienced Esther Shub to collaborate with him.

For two months they worked on the script at her house, but after its official acceptance, he left her out of the filming team – an action which she never understood and which wounded her deeply. The reason is hinted at in a characteristically teasing paragraph from Eisenstein's memoirs.

'In her relationship with me in the 1920s, Esfir Ilyinichna Shub probably saw herself as some kind of enigmatic George Sand. Although it would be difficult to find anyone bearing a fainter resemblance to Chopin or de Musset than me, short-legged and corpulent as I am. But why else would she have advised me to read Tynyanov's *A Nameless Love* . . . a picture of such a love. A love hidden and illicit. But illicit rather than hidden. But of such strength. And inspired. A love which strove to immerse its unattainability in the flourishes of the endless Don Juan catalogue.'[11]

Esther Shub, four years Eisenstein's senior, wanted to get closer to him than he wished, and he was always ironic about her from the beginning of their relationship. In the passage quoted, Eisenstein equivocally implies that Shub was in love with him, but failed to declare it, as well as making an underlying reference to 'the love that dare not speak its name'.

On *The Strike*, Eisenstein's object of desire, Grigori Alexandrov, was credited three times, as assistant director, as co-screenwriter, and as actor in the role of the foreman. Mikhail Gomorov and Alexander Antonov from the Proletkult played workers, and Maxim Strauch a police spy. Strauch's wife, Judith Glizer, was one of the leading female workers. Other parts were filled by actors and students of the Proletkult studio, joined by Moscow factory workers for the later crowd scenes.

The first scenes were filmed at the studio in Zhitnaya Street, which for that time was relatively well equipped. Every evening, after filming, the team would discuss the work they had done and decide on a programme for the following day. At these discussions, which Mikhin also attended, Eisenstein almost invariably made demands considered excessive by the management, as when he insisted on using a thousand extras for the episode in which the police and firemen drive away the workers with jets of water. Mikhin pointed out the impossibility of such a demand, but Eisenstein refused any concession. After a fierce quarrel, Mikhin resorted to the stratagem of pretending to agree, while secretly giving orders for only five hundred extras to be called in.

Eisenstein wanted to shoot the clash between the workers and the boiler-house mechanics opposed to them as a 'series of complicated circuses' with men leaping and vaulting about, brawling, throwing each other into barrels. When a stool had to be smashed over the head of one of the fighters, he insisted on the splinters of wood being clearly visible. Everything was rehearsed to perfection, but repeatedly failed to work out during shooting. Once Tisse found he had run out of film and the whole process had to be repeated.

On one occasion, while filming on location at the Simonov Monastery, Eisenstein wanted to liken the factory manager to a grinning frog – shades of his earliest sketches – whereupon filming came to a standstill while everyone went off to the lake in a desperate search for a frog. On a freezing October day, one of the property men had to wade into the water up to his waist, but to no avail since the director rejected every frog produced as being too small, or unsuitable in some other way. At long last the right frog was found. Too late, however, as it was already getting dark and the frog had to be thrown back. Eisenstein was unaware of the resentment this incurred among the crew, because his mind was set only on the realisation of his ideas, irrespective of the difficulties involved. (He did, however, get a gruesome close-up of a magnificent frog in *The General Line*, a few years later).

The film's method of construction was based on what Eisenstein called 'The Montage of Film Attractions' set out in an article he wrote after *The Strike* was completed. 'An attraction is in our understanding any demonstrable fact (an action, an object, a phenomenon, a conscious combination and so on) that is known and proven to exercise a definite effect on the attention and emotions of the audience and that, combined with others, possesses the characteristic of concentrating the audience's emotions in any direction dictated by the production's purpose. From this point of view a film cannot be a simple presentation or demonstration of events; rather it must be a tendentious selection of, and comparison between, events, free from narrowly plot-related plans and moulding the audience in accordance with its purpose.'[12]

In what could be called Eisenstein's Theory of Relativity, he demonstrated that cinema is 'the art of comparisons . . . montage is fundamental to cinema . . .' These theories become clear in practice when one is watching *The Strike*.

The Strike was a logical extension of Eisenstein's energetic approach to the theatre, showing the same enthusiasms and the same fundamental principles of entertaining and shocking the audience. Although the workers are handled for the most part naturalistically, and several sequences, such as the scene in which the factory workers are beaten up by the mounted forces of the Tsar, are totally realistic, the capitalist bosses and their stooges are extreme caricatures, realised through the techniques of the circus and American slapstick film comedy. Other influences seem to have been German Expressionism, remembering that Eisenstein had worked with Shub on the cutting of *Dr Mabuse, the Gambler*, and he knew George Grosz's savage portraits of the bourgeois of the Weimar Republic.

The director of the factory is so gross (Grosz) that he can hardly sit behind his desk. A couple of dwarfs do a tango on a table laden with caviar and champagne, and another pays court to 'The King', the leader of a gang of thieves, vagabonds and beggars, in a parody of upper-class manners.

There are also images that foreshadow the films of Jean Vigo and Luis Buñuel. Dead cats hang upside down on ropes in a junk yard. (In *The Battleship Potemkin*, sailors imagine themselves hanging from the yardarm in a similar manner.) There are two tight close-ups of an eye. (Even more Buñuelian is the scrutiny by the doctor through his pince-nez of the maggots in the meat in *The Battleship Potemkin*.)

In an extraordinary surreal dissolve, a 'cemetery' of empty barrels suddenly comes alive with hundreds of low-lifes crawling out of them. Police agents nicknamed The Monkey, The Fox, The Owl and The Bulldog, are revealed by means of dissolves behind the animals in the same postures and expression, in a manner used by Vigo in *À Propos de Nice* (1930).

Visual jokes and tricks abound: three of the stockholders are identical fat men in top hats, while others resemble Chaplin heavies

Eric Campbell and Mack Swain. A foreman gets stuck upside down in cement, and another is put in a wheelbarrow and thrown into a muddy pool, leaving his boater floating on the surface; a silhouette of Sherlock Holmes discloses an ordinary detective with a pipe, and photographs come alive, with one of the subjects hanging his hat outside the frame.

Diverting as these effects are, they are used for a dialectical purpose in a film which opens with a quote from Lenin: 'The strength of the working class lies in organisation. Without organisation of the masses the proletariat is nothing. Organised, it is everything. Organisation means unity of action. Unity of practical operation.'

The causes and results of the strike are powerfully exposed, the brutal suppression of the workers living up to Eisenstein's ambition to 'never make films in which the camera is an objective witness, to be watched by an impassive eye of glass. I prefer to hit people hard on the nose . . . I don't produce films to please the eye but to make a point.'[13] (This was Eisenstein's unflattering reference to Dziga Vertov's *Ciné-Eye/Kinoglaz* documentaries.)

As in the Odessa Steps sequence from *The Battleship Potemkin*, there are scenes of people desperately trying to escape advancing soldiers, the dynamic, rhythmic cutting almost coinciding with the more rapid beating of the spectator's heart. In fact, *The Strike* has a number of sequences that were further developed in Eisenstein's following film.

Despite the attempt to make a film not about individuals but types, the hero being the mass of collective actions, certain individuals stand out: the bald-headed worker who hangs himself when accused by the management of being a thief, the father who cannot feed his child but throws him his empty tobacco pouch to chew on, the children imitating their elders by putting a young goat in a wheelbarrow, and two of them playing with dolls as the mounted police enter the tenement building, and two brave young leaders of the strike, played by the blond Mikhail Gomorov and the dark, curly-haired Alexander Levshin, two of Eisenstein's closest collaborators.

Although *The Strike* was a silent film, it contained what Eisenstein considered his first experiment with sound in the cinema, in a sequence of a workers' picnic in the countryside with 'singing', accompanied by an accordion. 'The sequence attracted attention, of course, because the method was not used for purely graphic purposes but as a means of conveying, through one exposure, a picture, and through the second, a sound; through the realistic, objective long shot, a depiction of the event and the source of the sound; through the close-up, the idea of the sound itself, the sound of an accordion . . . At the edge of the frame the distant view disappeared, allowing the keyboard of the accordion and the fingers moving over it to emerge sharply and solidly into the foreground. The rhythm of the moving metal strips corresponded to the walking rhythm of the approaching group, and the sound, conveyed by graphic means, embraced the whole landscape in song, thus embodying a generalisation of the entire scene.'[14]

But what was most innovatory in the film was the use of visual metaphors such as the shock-cuts between the police moving into action against the strikers, and a lemon-squeezer being manipulated by one of the factory bosses. Or again: the final sequence in which the workers are massacred inter-cut with documentary shots of a bull being butchered in a slaughterhouse. (An influence on Georges Franju's *Le Sang des Bêtes/Blood of the Beast* in 1949).

Eisenstein described his reasons for choosing these images in his tongue-in-cheek manner. 'I did this, on the one hand, to avoid over-acting of the extras from the labour exchange "in the business of dying" but mainly to excise from such a serious scene the falseness that the screen will not tolerate but that is unavoidable in even the most brilliant death scene and, on the other hand, to extract the maximum effect of bloody horror. The massacre is shown only in establishing long and medium shots of eighteen hundred workers falling over a precipice, the crowd fleeing, gunfire etc, and all the close-ups are provided by a demonstration of the real horrors of the slaughterhouse where cattle are slaughtered and skinned.'[15]

It was obviously more than a practical solution to 'the business of dying' on screen, a metaphor of a 'human slaughterhouse', a juxtaposition of images that strove to transcend the literal shooting of workers. The final scenes are described in the script thus: (Close-up) People roll over a cliff. The bull's throat is slit – the blood gushes out. (Medium close-up) People lift themselves into the frame, arms outstretched. The butcher moves past the camera (panning) swinging his bloody rope. A crowd runs to a fence, breaks through it, and hides behind it. Arms fall into the frame. The head of the bull is severed from the trunk. A volley. The crowd rolls down a slope into the water. A volley. (Close-up) The bullets can be seen leaving the gun-barrels. Soldier's feet walk away from the camera. Blood floats on the water, discolouring it. (Close-up) Blood gushes from the slit throat of the bull. Blood is poured from a basin (held by hands) into a pail. Dissolve from a truck loaded with pails of blood – to a passing truck loaded with scrap-iron. The bull's tongue is pulled through the slit throat (to prevent the convulsions from damaging the teeth). The soldiers' feet walk away from the camera (seen at a further distance than previously). The bull's skin is stripped off. 1,500 bodies at the foot of the cliff. Two skinned bulls' heads. A hand lying in a pool of blood. (Close-up) Filling the entire screen: the eye of the dead bull. THE END.

The Strike was completed at the end of 1924, premiered in Leningrad on February 1, 1925, and shown to the general public in March. *Pravda* considered it 'the first revolutionary creation of our cinema', and *Izvestia* 'an immense and interesting triumph in the development of our cinematographic art.' However, puzzled by the satirical and grotesque elements, public reaction, on the whole, was unfavourable. The film's strong passages of naturalism seem to have been easier for audiences to digest than those sequences whose origins were the circus and the theatre of satire. There were also those in authority who criticised the film's eccentricity and lack of harmony between ideological content and form.

The execution of Eisenstein's theory of the 'Montage of Film Attractions' was greeted by modernists as an exciting advance. In *The Birth of a Nation* and *Intolerance*, Griffith used parallel montage for dramatic purposes – two different, distant actions, shown alternately, used mainly to create suspense. But when Eisenstein used juxtaposition and parallel montage, he did so with a clear dialectical purpose.

In the mid-1930s, Eisenstein told his students at the State Cinema Institute in Moscow, 'It is noteworthy that Griffith, first to put into practice . . . parallel and cross-cutting, could take its possibilities no further. For him there existed only the plot cross-cutting of the action, he did not realise that such parallel presentation of action contained further possibilities. Look at his film *Orphans of the Storm* – he made it in 1923 [actually 1921] that is, the year before *The Strike*. Notice the crowd scenes. You will see his work lacks particular plastic development of given content, and the crowd scenes are extremely chaotic.'[16]

It was at this time as well that Eisenstein diverged from Kuleshov, who favoured a cinema of fiction and a style of continuity, with characters related in a plot. Five years later, Eisenstein wrote: 'The old film-makers, including the theoretically quite outmoded Lev Kuleshov, regarded montage as a means of producing something by describing it, adding individual shots to one another like building blocks . . . but in my view montage is not an idea composed of successive shots stuck together but an idea that *derives* from the collision between two shots that are independent of one another.'[17]

Surprisingly, there is virtually no comment by Eisenstein anywhere on the style of the films of Abel Gance, although he later met the French director in Paris. Gance's rapid cutting and montage techniques, particularly as used in *La Roue*, preceded *The Strike* by two years.

Writing a little over two decades later, Eisenstein called his first feature 'a typical "beginner's piece" . . . the picture was as tousled and pugnacious as I was in those far-off years.'[18] This was not only a mature artist's normal affectionate but condescending view of a work of his green years but, in a climate of apprehension and suspicion, every utterance he made had to be circumspect. In 1946, at the height of the stultifying Soviet Socialist Realism, the portrayals of great national heroes, and the 'cult of personality', especially that of the leader of the 'united' nation, both the modernist form and the 'collective' content were frowned upon.

'*The Strike* brought collective and mass action onto the screen, in contrast to individualism and the "triangle" drama of the bourgeois cinema,' Eisenstein explained. 'No screen had ever before reflected an image of collective action . . . But our enthusiasm produced a "one-sided" representation of the masses and the "collective"; one-sided because "collectivism" means the maximum development of the individual within the "collective", a conception irreconcilably opposed to bourgeois individualism. Our first mass films missed this deeper meaning . . .'[19]

Today, though the potent ideological content seems no less relevant to the continuing exploitation of workers throughout the world, *The Strike* stands high among the modernist masterpieces of the cinema, and is indicative of what was to come. In addition to demonstrating the 'montage of film attractions', in which normal action is interrupted by shots that do not contribute to the action but comment on it, the film contains most of the themes, motifs, stylistic effects and personality of Eisenstein, which he was to deepen, develop, and transmute in all his work, whether written, drawn, filmed or dreamt. Although *The Strike* met with mixed reactions, and was not shown much outside ciné clubs abroad, it gave Eisenstein the confidence and desire to make more films. 'For my part I was rather like an impetuous tiger-cub, not quite sure of its legs, reared on the milk of theatre, but who had been allowed a small taste of the blood of freedom as a film-maker!'[20]

5

Fire!

As I approached the tennis court, Chaplin's exclamation greeted me: 'Just seen Potemkin. *You know it hasn't aged a bit these last five years? Same as ever!' And all this was the result of just three months (!) work on a film. (That includes two weeks spent on the montage!) It is easy now, twenty years later, to cast my mind over the withered laurels. To laugh off the three months' work – a record.*

After *The Strike* was released, Eisenstein finally left the Proletkult Theatre after a five-year stint. He and the theatre were in dispute over the ownership of the script and whether or not Eisenstein should get a percentage of the film's profits. 'My stance was absurd, dangerous, and not at all advisable for someone who wished to make any progress in his work and creativity,' Eisenstein subsequently declared.[1]

Although the film credits the screenplay to Valeri Pletnyov, Sergei Eisenstein, I. Kravtchunovsky, Grigori Alexandrov and the Proletkult Collective, Eisenstein felt he was entitled to some money. Two years later, largely because of Eisenstein's campaign, the scriptwriters and directors in Soviet cinema began to receive a legally determined percentage of the takings from every showing of their work.

Lenin died on January 21, 1924 after a series of strokes, and left a power vacuum behind him. The Revolution was in its seventh year, and most of the existing film companies were merged into a state trust called Sovkino. With the slogan 'The Proletarianisation of the Screen!' a drive was organised to form workers' film groups in order to attract and encourage a wider class-conscious audience. A Central Council was set up to which all scenarios had to be submitted in advance of filming, and which functioned as a censor and ideological guide. Many features were Civil War melodramas, such as *The Red Devils, In the Service of the People* and *The Commander of the Ivanov Brigade*.

A handful of more ambitious productions were made under the supervision of Anatole Lunacharsky, Commissar of Education. Cultured, Europeanised, and tolerant of radical experiments in art, Lunacharsky nevertheless saw the cinema mainly as a means of bringing the classics to the workers. Under his influence, the Moscow Arts Theatre acted out before the camera such works as Pushkin's *The Station Master*, Tolstoy's *Polikushka*, and Gogol's *Taras Bulba*. These films were 'artistically' designed and lit, but their only interest today is in the acting.

However, even while Lunacharsky was laboriously reproducing literary works on the screen, new tendencies were developing. The FEKS group (Factory of the Eccentric Actor) shifted its activities from the stage to the cinema in 1924. With only an old Pathé camera, Leonid Trauberg and Grigori Kozintsev made *The Adventures of Oktyabrina*, an experimental comedy about an attempted bank robbery. At the opposite extreme was Dziga Vertov, the recently appointed head of a new studio, Kultkino, who continued to assert: 'Only documentary facts! No illusions! Down with the actor and scenery! Long live the film of actuality!'

In an essay written in April 1925, a cocksure Eisenstein distanced himself from Vertov's *Ciné-Eye (Kinoglaz)*, an 'exploration of life caught unawares.' Eisenstein stated: 'My starting point is that *The Strike* has no pretensions to being an escape from art and in that lies its strength . . . Vertov takes from his surroundings the things that impress *him* rather than the things with which, by impressing the *audience*, he will plough its psyche . . . The *Ciné-Eye* is not just a symbol of vision: it is also a symbol of contemplation. But we need not contemplation but action.'[2]

After *The Strike*, Eisenstein began work on two screen projects, Alexander Serafimovich's Civil War novel, *The Iron Flood*, and

Isaac Babel's *Red Cavalry*, based on a collection of short stories which depicted the savagery of the Civil War along with its nobler aspirations. However, both projects were interrupted because of the elaborate plans for the anniversary of the 1905 Revolution, and the Jubilee Committee set up to co-ordinate them decided that several films should be made in honour of the event.

The director of one of the main films in the series, entitled *Year 1905*, had yet to be appointed. Then came the preview of *The Strike* and, almost immediately afterwards, the Jubilee Committee, on March 19, 1925, decided to assign the film to Eisenstein.

They set only two conditions: that the film should not have a pessimistic ending (like *The Strike*) and that one of the major episodes must be completed by December 20 of the same year.

Eisenstein at once started work on the scenario, together with Nina Ferdinandovna Agadzhanova-Shutko. She was not only a reputable screenwriter, but someone who had herself played a very active part in the events of 1905 as a member of the Bolshevik Party. Eisenstein, who called her Nuné, the Armenian form of Nina, described her as 'short, blue-eyed, shy and infinitely modest . . . the one human being who extended a helping hand to me at a very critical period of my creative life.' Eisenstein claimed that 'Nuné was the first Bolshevik civilian I had met – all the others had sat on military committees or they were "senior staff". She was quite simply a human being . . . Nuné instilled in me a true sense of the historical revolutionary past.'[3]

Once, after a quarrel, Eisenstein presented her with a live dove as a peace offering. But the dove escaped, and managed 'during its panicky flights from sideboard to screen, from chandelier to telephone, and from the cornice of the tiled stove to the shelf with the complete Byron – so utterly to befoul both rooms that it was almost banished in disgrace.'[4]

At soirees held in her apartment, Nina was a calming influence on people seated around her samovar. 'The most important thing was that here each could derive strength from the realisation that the revolution needed everyone. And everyone exactly as he was, in his unique pointed individual way. And what you should definitely not attempt was to take a plane to your idiosyncrasies and smooth them off – which was what the RAPP (Russian Association of Proletarian Writers) bandwagon was making such a song and dance about. No, you had to find the proper way of applying your own particular idiosyncrasy to the task of building the Revolution . . .'[5]

Unfortunately, the reality, even in those early, heady days of experimental art, was beginning to clash with Eisenstein's idealism. It was at Nina's apartment that Eisenstein first met Kazimir Malevich, whose abstract paintings such as *White Square on White*, were out of favour in the 1920s, and the artist was forbidden to exhibit. (He left Russia for Germany in 1926.) *The Year 1905* was conceived by Nina and Eisenstein as a vast fresco in eight episodes, beginning with the end of the Russo-Japanese war and Bloody Sunday (when a peaceful crowd was fired on before the Tsar's palace at St Petersburg on January 9), and ending with the crushing in December of the insurrection in Krasnopresnia, a working-class district of Moscow. Eisenstein's epic vision of the film was extremely complicated from the technical and organisational point of view, entailing full-scale battles, night-time fires and mass movements of peasants.

Shooting started on *The Year 1905* in Leningrad (as St Petersburg/Petrograd was now officially known) in March 1925 at the Nevsky Prospect, lit, as it had been during the 1905 strike at the electricity generating plant, by the Admiralty searchlight. Filming was already well under way when bad weather made it impossible to carry on. Mikhail Kapchinsky, director of the first Goskino studio in Moscow, advised the unit to go south for a time and work on another sequence until the weather in Leningrad improved. They never returned.

Alexander A. Levitsky, one of the most senior Soviet cameramen, had begun filming with Eisenstein in Leningrad when differences led to their rupture. Eisenstein noted: 'Lost a month and a half because of a personality clash with Levitsky . . . It is difficult to make a contemporary revolutionary piece when your cameraman nurtures a philistine antipathy and enmity towards cranes, wharves and locomotives, and his ideal is represented by Catholic churches made out of cardboard.'[6] To Eisenstein's great satisfaction, Levitsky was replaced by Tisse.

For much of the summer of 1925, Eisenstein and Nina worked on the screenplay of *The Year 1905* on the upper floor of her dacha in the village of Nemchinov Post. On the lower floor was Isaac Babel with whom Eisenstein was working simultaneously on a script for *The Career of Benya Krik*, based on the Babel story. Eisenstein did not, however, have the time to continue it, and it was directed by V. Vilner the following year.

Eisenstein described these rather hectic months in letters to his mother, who had now moved to Moscow. Judging from the correspondence, he obviously thought he had more time to make the film than he was given.

On May 3, he wrote, 'I'm about to go mad with work. I think I'll be travelling a lot this summer – to the south where I'll film a mutiny in the fleet . . .' Then, on July 2, 'I'm making *1905*. Will start to film in a few days. July – in the country (outside Moscow – farms – and in the Tambov district.) August, September (and perhaps October) in the south (Odessa and Sebastopol). The film is to be ready in a year (we're to give it in in August 1926.) At the same time I'll be making *Benya Krik*, a scenario by Babel. (Do you remember reading those *Odessa Tales* in LEF? Both very interesting. But the work is hellish . . .'[7]

Given the time and money available, the decision was finally taken to reduce the overambitious film to one episode, the mutiny on board the *Battleship Potemkin* and its consequences. The title of the film was changed accordingly.

Grigori Alexandrov recalled: 'We had very little time in which to make the film, and by modern standards the timetable given to us was alarmingly short. It was also unavoidable, for a film designed to celebrate the twentieth anniversary of a particular series of historical events should clearly be completed before the end of the anniversary year. That year was 1925, and so in principle we had until December 31 to finish it, or nine months from the day when Eisenstein and Nina first began work on the script. Nor should we forget that the film was originally intended to cover a great many incidents in 1905, and indeed the *Potemkin* affair was a tiny part of the original conception, occupying only two pages of the first scenario.'[8] Actually, the *Potemkin* mutiny took up half a page, or just 44 shots out of the 800 envisaged for the entire film.

Maxim Strauch, who was one of Eisenstein's assistants on the film, recalled: 'Although the *Potemkin* mutiny was originally planned as a short sequence in the long film of *1905* . . . there is no doubt that Eisenstein would have found a place for it in his film. I can state this with certainty because I remember very well the night when he came back in enormous excitement from the Lenin Library in Moscow to the flat we shared together at that time. He carried a copy of a magazine published in Paris called *L'Illustration*, which contained an article about the mutiny, and included a drawing of the famous scene on the steps of Odessa. What happened on those steps – or rather what did not happen, for historically the scene is extremely dubious – seemed to Eisenstein to have all the potentialities of a sequence that on a single location could summarise so much of what he wanted to say in his film.'[9]

Eisenstein wrote: 'In my memory was a vague recollection of a picture from the magazine *L'Illustration* in 1905, where a horseman, shrouded in smoke, slashed at someone with his sabre, on a flight of steps . . . In the same French magazine is another illustration bearing the caption, "Omelchuk's body lying in state on June 23 on the new dyke at Odessa" which is strikingly similar to the scene in the film of the meeting around Vakulinchuk's dead body . . .'[10]

One of the very first things Eisenstein did when the unit moved to Odessa was to go out and see the steps for himself. There were one hundred and twenty in all, not as many as he makes them appear in the film. If timed, the soldiers' descent would be found to be three or four times slower than what would have actually happened. Eisenstein climbed up and down them again and again, getting the feel of them.

'The very flight of the stairs suggested the idea of the scene – this flight set the director's imagination soaring on a new "flight" of its own. The panicky flight of the crowd sweeping down the stairs is nothing more than the material embodiment of the first impressions ensuing from the encounter with the stairway itself.'[11] Elsewhere, Eisenstein mentioned that he got the idea of the 'flight' from watching the way a cherry stone bounced when spat out from the top of the stairs.

Actually, so immense does Eisenstein make the steps seem in the film – as endless as the stairway to heaven in Powell and Pressburger's *A Matter of Life and Death* – that they are bound to be a disappointment in reality. In 1995, Neal Ascherson, the Scots historian, described them thus: 'To see them, for anyone who cannot forget how Eisenstein in *The Battleship Potemkin* made them into the most famous flight of stairs in the world, is like seeing a famous actress : smaller, drabber, less purposeful than in the movie. The Steps seem to go nowhere in particular. Once they leapt straight down from the city to the harbour, a triumphal strut towards the sea and the southern horizon. Now the main dock highway cuts across the foot of the steps and the view is blocked off by walls of stained cement . . . And from the top, the Steps seem short and neglected.'[12]

Eisenstein relied greatly on his assistants, Grigori Alexandrov, Mikhail Gomorov, Alexander Levshin, Alexander Antonov and Maxim Strauch, the five actors who left the theatre with him in 1924. They became known as 'The Iron Five' – a phrase coined by a newspaper reporter who saw them working together and was impressed by their image of 'corporate toughness'. Strauch recalled: 'We walked about in striped football gear looking like a pack of zebras, which was Eisenstein's way of making sure that we were conspicuous enough to be easily located in a crowd scene.'[13]

Alexander Levshin told of the working routine in Odessa. 'After each day's filming, we rehearsed the next day's scenes before dinner. Alexandrov stayed near the camera, Strauch watched over the foreground, and the mass scenes were divided up among Antonov, Gomorov, and me, each being in charge of a hundred people. Antonov's group was to walk or run from one point to another, Gomorov's to move across them, and mine to move at an angle established by the camera's position that day. Each of us, representing our hundred, walked or ran through the rehearsed *mise-en-scéne* while Eisenstein made corrections in the working script. Although seventy-five per cent of the shooting script was ready in advance, most of the remainder was determined in these rehearsals. We were then ready to solve the balance during the next day's work. Our "Five" would now know what their tasks would be during the actual shooting.'[14]

The first task was to find a battleship to represent the *Potemkin*. Warships had changed their appearance in twenty years and the real ship had been dismantled. Luckily, Lyosha Kryukov, one of Eisenstein's assistant directors, came across a surviving sister ship, *The Twelve Apostles*, moored to rocks in the Gulf of Sebastopol. Although the entire superstructure of the ship was missing it could be successfully reconstructed in wood from plans preserved in the naval archives.

'This is almost a symbol of the film itself: recreating the past through the medium of art, and on a factually accurate basis,' Eisenstein concluded. Then it was discovered that the seabed around the ship was strewn with mines. And worse still, the hold of the vessel had been used as a mine-store. To remove the mines would have been time-consuming, so the decision was taken to film on the reconstructed deathtrap with the mines rolling around in the hold. Consequently, all the episodes on board *The Twelve Apostles* (for those sequences which necessitated a fully operational ship, the battleship *Komintern* was used) – episodes depicting a violent mutiny – had to be made under the most restrictive conditions, with smoking and excessive movement strictly forbidden. There was a further obstacle: the ship was so positioned that no matter from what angle the deck was filmed, rocks appeared in the frame. Since the mutiny had taken place out at sea, a solution had to be found. In the end, the ship was rotated through ninety degrees, which eliminated the rocks – but only if the camera was kept absolutely static. The unit was thus forced to work under constant pressures of time and space. 'Try filming a mutiny in those conditions!' Eisenstein exclaimed.[15]

During the filming, Eisenstein was summoned to Moscow by Mikhail Kalinin, the Soviet Head of State, who wished to see those parts of the film that had so far been made. While there he sought the permission of the Red Army Commander, General Frunze, to use a flotilla of the Black Sea Fleet for filming the scenes of the flotilla's meeting with the *Potemkin* and its guns firing in salute. Back in Odessa, however, the carefully made plans for filming this sequence went awry. Everything was ready, with Tisse and his camera installed on the battleship's turret, when some officers arrived on board and asked Eisenstein how he was going to get the ships all firing simultaneously. 'Oh, quite simple; I'll take my hand-kerchief from my pocket and wave it three times,' he answered, giving them a demonstration. Seen through binoculars from the ships, his gesture was mistaken for the real thing, and the guns opened up far beyond the range of Tisse's camera, which in any case, was not yet running. After this mishap, Eisenstein didn't dare ask for a repeat performance, and the episode was omitted.

Maxim Strauch was delegated to scour the town for the right faces for the film, in line with Eisenstein's *typage* doctrine. The character that presented the greatest difficulty was that of the doctor, and Eisenstein was not satisfied with the eventual compromise choice. In the boat on the way to the filming, however, he noticed a boil-erman from the hotel who had been taken on as an electrician for the unit. He wondered, 'Why do they take on such weaklings to hold heavy mirror reflectors? This one's in just about a fit state to drop the mirror in the sea and break it – a sure sign of bad luck.' But looking at the man's face more intently he suddenly saw him in a different light, picturing him with a moustache, goatee and pince-nez. The man took on the features of Dr Smirnov. 'I mentally swapped his oil-stained cap for the hat of an army medic . . .'[16]

An aged gardener from one of the orchards around Sebastopol was taken on to play the priest. The white beard was his own, although it was slightly combed to one side, and he wore a wig of thick white hair. (Eisenstein actually doubled for the priest for the rear shots of him falling down the steps.) Olga Ivanovna (Grisha Alexandrov's first wife) is seen in close-up nodding at the funeral, and Konstantin Isidorovich Feldman, who had been one of the actual delegates from the ship in Odessa to the ship in 1905, and became a critic and playwright, played the student who comes aboard the ship in order to establish a link with the shore.

Pavel Alexandrovich Glaubermann, later Professor of Physics at the University of Odessa, played the small boy who is shot on the steps and trampled underfoot. In 1970, he looked back on how he came to be cast.

'Had I known that this charming man with hair like an electric shock, and who discovered me on the school football field, would one day be described as the greatest film director of his age, then possibly today I might remember a great deal more. I was goal-keeper, and Eisenstein chose me because he wanted a boy of my age who could fall convincingly. Perhaps, so it seems to me now, he was really looking for a boy who positively relished the idea of falling. But to play on a playing field is one thing, and to fall on the hard Odessa Steps is quite another. Anyway, he chose me, this man with the bristling hair, and he made me fall for five or six days. I had to fall "well" so they kept telling me. I remember those five or six days, and I remember the little cigarette packet that lay on the particular step where I had to fall. I am not a film man, and I know literally nothing of the techniques of film-making, but at least I now know that in order to end my fall at the proper place in the shot I had to finish on that wretched empty cigarette packet . . .

'I had no idea that I had taken part in one of the greatest film sequences ever to be made, or that my falling would be shown all over the world, and is indeed being shown to this day. Nothing that I might achieve in my chosen profession can ever count as much in the eyes of the world as a faller on cigarette packets.'[17]

In those days, so-called 'iron-clad' screenplays were encouraged by some in the film industry. This meant that a screenplay should encompass every detail of a film before it went into production, and that in production the screenplay should be strictly adhered to. This was supposed to ensure political reliability and to encourage economy. Eisenstein counterposed his own notion of an 'emotional' screenplay or 'libretto', which would confine itself to the broad outlines of the film and permit the director a very considerable degree of scope for innovation and creative freedom. 'More than simply an array of typical facts and episodes; it was an attempt to get to grips with the dynamism of the epoch, to feel its pulse, the sinews within that connected the different events . . . without being deflected from the sense of truth, we were able to indulge any whim or fancy, bringing it into any event or scene we wished, even if it were not in the original libretto (like the Odessa Steps!) and any unforeseeable detail (such as the mist at the funeral scene!).'

One day, in Odessa, while Eisenstein, Tisse and Alexandrov were crossing in the boat in the mist ('*Three Men in a Boat*, the subtitle being *To Say Nothing Of the Dog*; in our case it was to say nothing of the camera'), Alexander Levitsky, *Potemkin*'s ex-cameraman, who was filming Vladimir Gardin's *Cross and Mauser* from another boat shouted 'You must be nuts!' across the water.

Eisenstein recalled: 'This encounter with the mist which chance threw our way, and which my mind developed emotionally as we sailed – this assortment of details, the outline of shots taken on the move – were gathered into material for plastic funereal chords. Only later did the interacting intricacies of montage, at the cutting stage become evident . . . This turned out to be the cheapest sequence in the film: hiring a boat to sail across the bay cost us three roubles fifty.'[18]

The day of filming in the mist in the Black Sea was described by Strauch: 'One morning in Odessa, during the shooting of the film, we all woke up in the Hotel London, which is not very far from the top of the steps and looks out over the harbour, and could see nothing but fog. The Black Sea, a few hundred yards away, was invisible. To film in such weather, with such minimal visibility, was ludicrous. Clearly the only sensible thing to do was to go back to bed and catch up on all our lost sleep. But Edouard Tisse disagreed absolutely and insisted on shooting. He persuaded a reluctant Eisenstein that he was right, and they went together down to the harbour, where they made that splendid sequence of the sailors of the *Potemkin* mourning their dead comrade. It would have been a fine scene anyway, but it was made infinitely more emotive by the very fact of the fog, adding its own comment to the tragic mood of the mourning.'[19] The ghostly ships in the mist are also reminiscent of the images from F.W. Murnau's *Nosferatu*, made in 1921.

The idea for the stone lions rising from their slumber in anger at the savagery of the Tsarist forces occurred to Eisenstein when, by pure chance, he saw several statues of lions, each in a different physical attitude, in the gardens of the Alupka Palace in Odessa. The filming of them was like a scene from a Charlie Chaplin movie. A park-keeper 'in down-at-heel boots and baggy trousers' at the Alupka Palace tried to prevent the team from photographing the lions there. 'We ran from lion to lion with our cameras and so confused this severe and abiding guardian of the peace that he finally shook his fist at us and left us to take close-ups of three of the marble beasts.'[20]

When the filming at Odessa was almost completed, Eisenstein left the finishing touches to Alexandrov, Antonov and Gomorov and returned to Moscow to start on the editing and to direct the scenes that had been impossible to shoot aboard *The Twelve Apostles*. These were filmed partly in a ridiculously small studio fitted up with rudimentary decor and partly at the Sandunovsky Baths where a model battleship (unfortunately, rather discernible as such) was used for some of the scenes set at sea.

Eisenstein worked day and night with a single assistant on the editing for less than three weeks in time for the first-cut preview of the film. This had been organised by the studio for a select audience including Lunacharsky, writers, journalists and naval leaders. As the lights went up at the end, Lunacharsky jumped on his chair and made an enthusiastic speech. 'We've been witnesses at an historic cultural event. A new art has been born . . . an art with a truly great future . . .'[21]

But Eisenstein was still not fully satisfied, and tried further montage combinations. He worked at a phenomenal pace in order to have the film ready for the special evening devoted to the celebration of the twentieth anniversary of the 1905 Revolution at the Bolshoi Theatre on December 21, in advance of its first public showing.

Alexandrov recalled: 'We spent most of the final days with the man who helped us to arrange the titles, which were always very important in any silent film by Eisenstein – not only the wording, but also the size and style of the lettering, the use of exclamation marks and so on. We were still working on this on the night of the first screening, which was in the Bolshoi Theatre, and I spent the evening riding on a motorcycle between the cutting room and the theatre, carrying the reels one at a time. When Eisenstein was finally happy with the last reel, he sat on the back of my motorcycle with the can of film under his arm. We had no time to lose because we both knew perfectly well that the performance must have started, but when we were in the middle of Red Square, and about a quarter of a mile from the Bolshoi, the motorcycle broke down. So we ran the rest of the way! Of course such a situation would be disastrous nowadays, but in 1925 every film was shown on a single projector with a break between each reel – and incidentally we constructed our films with those breaks in mind, a fact sometimes forgotten by modern critics. So all was well, except that the break between the last two reels was nearly twenty minutes long!'[22]

Eisenstein's theory of montage is one of collision, conflict and contrast, with the emphasis on a dynamic juxtaposition of individual shots that forces the audience consciously to come to conclusions about the interplay of images while they are also emotionally and psychologically affected. The theory was developed further in *The Battleship Potemkin*. The eighty-minute film contained 1,346 shots while *The Birth of a Nation* at 195 minutes had 1,375 shots. The average film of 1925 ran ninety minutes and had around 600 shots.

But these dry statistics fail to convey the impact of the shots and what they contain. It is also forgotten, mainly because emphasis has been placed on the film's revolutionary style (in both senses), that *The Battleship Potemkin* presents flesh-and-blood characters and tells an exciting story: the mutiny of the crew of the battleship brought about by their refusal to eat rotting food. The leader of the mutiny, Seaman Vakulinchuk (Alexander Antonov) is fatally shot by an officer, and hundreds of civilians on shore come to pay homage to the dead man and give their support to the mutiny. However, many of them are mown down by government troops. The *Potemkin* then goes out to sea to confront the Tsar's navy. Tension mounts as the enemy ships approach them. At the last moment, a sailor on board the *Potemkin* signals the other crews of the squadron, 'JOIN US!'. The opposing ships get closer and closer, their great guns trained on each other. Then the mutineers realise that the Admiralty's sailors have refused to fire on their brothers, and they sail past the cheering crew of the *Potemkin* who raise the red flag. This flag, hand-painted frame by frame by Eisenstein, must be the reddest flag ever seen in cinema, its effect intensified by its optimistic political significance, a vivid splash of colour in a black-and-white world in which red blood has been spilt.

The film starts below deck in the humid sleeping quarters, with its labyrinth of hammocks, heavy with bodies, gently swinging. This oscillating motion is later repeated by the pendulous metal tables in the empty mess laden with uneaten bowls of soup. The scene transmits a faint but unmistakable echo of Charlie Chaplin struggling to eat on a similar table in *The Immigrant*, the kind of analogy to which Eisenstein was never averse. 'In the encounter with the squadron, the machines were almost like the heart of Harold Lloyd, jumping out of his waistcoat because it was so agitated,' he wrote of the film's final sequence.

Of the characterisations, the only trace of the exaggerated Proletkult style is seen in the hypocritical priest with his white hair and beard lit as if they are on fire. He sadistically strikes a crucifix on the palm of his hand as he watches the mutineers rounded up to be shot, and pretends to have been killed during the revolt, opening one eye to see if the coast is clear. (A gesture repeated by the sinister monk in *Alexander Nevsky*.) But the repressive naval officers (replacing the callous bosses in *The Strike*) and the tiny doctor with the pince-nez, observing the maggots in the meat in close-up, avoid caricature.

The sailors (replacing the workers in *The Strike*) have the ring of truth; the youngest, gently weeping in his hammock, receives a fatherly pat of consolation from an older comrade, and later angrily breaks a plate on which he haltingly reads 'Give Us This Day Our Daily Bread.' The powerful Vakulinchuk, who 'Died for a spoonful of soup', is a true working-class hero, and it is entirely credible that streams of people – forming a line similar to that which forms under Tsar Ivan's beard at the end of *Ivan the Terrible Part I* – would pay him homage. (Vakulinchuk eerily resembles the dead Stalin, past whose tomb thousands of people filed in 1953.)

Nevertheless, everything in *The Battleship Potemkin* seems to swirl around the central maelstrom that is universally known as 'The Odessa Steps' sequence, against which the whole of cinema can be defined, before and since. The sequence, for which Tisse devised effects by using a trolley and a camera strapped to the waist of an acrobat, shows soldiers advancing on the fleeing citizens down a seemingly endless flight of steps. It is surprising that the sequence, having probably been anatomised more than any other, is still as robust as ever.

Part of Eisenstein's analysis ran thus: 'Formal tension through acceleration is here achieved by shortening the shots, not just with the basic scheme's formula of repetition, but also in violation of this canon . . . The drum-beat of the soldiers' feet descending the steps destroys all metrical conventions . . . The final build-up of tension is produced by switching from the rhythm of the soldiers' tread as they descend the steps to another, new form of movement – the next stage in the intensification of the same action – the pram rolling down the steps . . . The descent of the feet becomes the 'rolling down' of the pram . . . Consider how many people would have been left on the steps after the first volley from the soldiers? Bang – and nobody . . . How much time does this scene occupy in the film? Almost six minutes. In film this is an enormous period. But the feeling that the stream of people does not flow for all that time, but with interruptions, or that the action stops, never arises in the spectator. The separate episodes are so edited into the general stream of fugitives that the impression of the general action is strengthened. This is achieved by maintaining a steady increase in tempo and rhythm, every incident woven into the general plan and general action.'[23]

The sequence works on so many levels: the formalistic, as expounded above, linked to Marxist dialectics – force (thesis) colliding with counterforce (antithesis) to produce unity (synthesis) – filmic suspense, and the humanistic. Here are human beings – a legless man rushing to escape, an elderly woman teacher shot in the face, a nursemaid shot in the stomach and leaving her charge in the pram unattended (the suspense of this moment, the pram poised to topple, is positively Hitchcockian), a doctor administering to the wounded, a young bespectacled student helplessly regarding the scene in horror, civilians cowering in terror beneath the steps, and a mother carrying her dead child towards the advancing soldiers in a plea for mercy in a sudden, poignant counterpoint to the main flow of the crowd. It has even more impact because we have already seen these people in a euphoric state before the massacre. As a graphic illustration of state brutality The Odessa Steps sequence is worthy of comparison with *Desastros de la Guerra* by Goya, one of Eisenstein's favourite artists, and Picasso's *Guernica* . . .

*

Eisenstein often professed his agreement with Goethe's belief that 'in order to be truthful you can risk an occasional defiance of truth itself.' This is well illustrated by the fact that, since *The Battleship Potemkin* was first shown, audiences have believed that the scenes on the Odessa Steps is a faithful reconstruction of an actual event. There was no massacre on the Odessa Steps.

When *The Battleship Potemkin* was shown in Atlantic City, an elderly Jew came out of the cinema distraught and weeping. The manager of the theatre, concerned, asked the Jew if he had been in Odessa in 1905 or had lost family in the massacre. The man admitted that he had been on the steps, not as a victim but as a volunteer Cossack in the Tsar's army. He explained that it had taken twenty years and one Soviet film to open his eyes to the tragedy in which he had participated. Such was the power of Eisenstein's invention.

Eisenstein also invented the compassion of the common people, whom he depicted providing food for the mutineers, when this was only fellow revolutionaries ashore doing their duty by sending out food to the battleship. Moreover, the *Potemkin* was not greeted by the other ships as portrayed in the finale; rather the mutineers 'sailed away when other ships of the Black Sea failed to follow their example.'[24]

When *The Battleship Potemkin* was finally shown in Odessa, after its release elsewhere in the USSR, Eisenstein was accused of plagiarism by a man who claimed to have been a participant in the mutiny. It was a curious charge, because he had never even written about his experiences, but as he 'had taken part directly in the events', he felt he 'had the right to claim a portion of the royalties . . .' His assertion was that he had 'stood beneath the tarpaulin during the execution on deck.' The case actually came to court, where Eisenstein proved that 'nobody stood beneath the tarpaulin', as it was 'pure invention on the director's part!'[25] At the time, the naval consultant on the picture advised against covering the sailors with a tarpaulin when they were threatened with execution. 'People will laugh,' he said. 'It wasn't like that.' Eisenstein retorted, 'If they laugh, that's what we shall have deserved: it'll mean we didn't do it properly.' As it turned out, 'The image of a huge blindfold over the eyes of those condemned, the image of a shroud wound round a living body of men proved sufficiently convincing emotionally to cover up any technical "inaccuracy" which only a handful of experts and specialists knew of anyway.'[26] As Cocteau was to say, 'Alexandre Dumas, Michelet, Eisenstein, the only true historians.'

The Battleship Potemkin was given a festive public premiere on January 18, 1926, when the First Sovkino Theatre on Arbat Square was decorated with a display representing a ship, while the ushers and members of the film unit were dressed in naval uniforms. But there were soon criticisms that it was not an artistic achievement but merely didactic material, and others thought that it was a poor presentation of the subject. As late as 1933, Mikhail Kalotozov and S. Bartenev wrote that it was little more than a glorified documentary.

Neither did audiences respond warmly to the film – like almost everywhere else, the public preferred the products from Hollywood – and it played to half-empty theatres. Attendance figures were exaggerated by the authorities to demonstrate to the rest of the world that there was a large Soviet audience for Soviet films. Mayakovsky indicted the Sovkino executives for the fact that 'on its first showing, Potemkin was relegated to second-rate theatres only, and it was only after the enthusiastic reaction of the foreign press that it was shown at the best theatres.' Mayakovsky demanded of Konstantin Shvedshikov, Sovkino's President and a Soviet bureaucrat with pronounced bourgeois tastes, that he immediately export Potemkin otherwise he would 'go down in history as a villain'. Pounding his fists on the desk, Mayakovsky exclaimed, 'Remember that Shvedshikovs come and go, but art remains!' (Shvedshikov was anti-Semitic and, in private, called Eisenstein 'The Nobleman of Jerusalem.')[27]

A short while later, under pressure from a group of artists and journalists, Sovkino finally agreed to send Potemkin to Berlin where, though initially censored, it became an enormous success. It was first shown in a small cinema on the Friedrichstrasse, but it soon moved to the city's centre in the Kurfurstendamm, and then on to twelve cinemas around Berlin.

'The German censors cut out the scene where the officer is thrown into the water but it was all right for the doctor to be thrown into the water because he was, after all, the original cause of the mutiny by the Black Sea Fleet,' Eisenstein explained. 'He committed the sin of lying and vice must be punished. A close-up of a Cossack was also cut. The motive behind this was that the brutality of the Tsar's Cossacks was so well known in Germany that showing them once more than necessary would only harden the public.'[28]

In the final scene the number and shape of the ships in the flotilla bore no resemblance to German intelligence estimates of Soviet naval strength and led to questions in the Reichstag. The War Ministry forbade the armed forces to see the film, perhaps for fear of mutiny. Among those who praised *The Battleship Potemkin* publicly were the celebrated writers Lion Feuchtwanger and Ernst Toller, and the great star of the screen, Asta Nielsen. Max Reinhardt, the most renowned stage producer in Germany, claimed, 'I am willing to admit the stage will have to give way to the cinema.' Douglas Fairbanks and Mary Pickford, en route to Moscow during their grand tour of Europe in 1926, saw it in Berlin at a special showing. Fairbanks said that it 'is the most intense and profoundest experience of my life.' When 'America's Sweethearts' met Eisenstein in Moscow, they promised to bring him to the USA in the hope that he would make a film for their company, United Artists.

Meeting two of the biggest stars in the world left a deep impression on Eisenstein, and the prospect of going to America certainly excited him. He wrote: 'At twenty-seven, the boy from Riga became a celebrity. Doug and Mary travelled to Moscow to shake the hand of the boy from Riga – he had made *Potemkin*.'[29]

The Battleship Potemkin's depiction of a successful rebellion against political authority disturbed the world's censors. The French, banning it for general showing, burned every copy they could find, but it was seen at Paris film clubs including Les Amis de Spartacus, founded by Léon Moussinac, the critic and theoretician. It was also shown at film clubs in London, another city where it had been banned. In Pennsylvania it was forbidden on the grounds that it 'gives American sailors a blueprint as to how to conduct a mutiny,' but in December 1926 *Potemkin* made its American debut, following a severe censorship survey that lasted three weeks. Chaplin proclaimed it 'the best film in the world' and even the conservative *New York Sun* recommended it as an object lesson for all American film directors.

On October 15, 1926, David O. Selznick, then an associate producer of MGM, wrote to Harry Rapf, the no-nonsense supervisor of bread-and-butter movies at the studio:

'It was my privilege a few months ago to be present at two private screenings of what is unquestionably one of the greatest of motion pictures ever made, *The Armoured Cruiser Potemkin*, made in Russia under the supervision of the Soviet Government. I shall not here discuss the commercial or political aspects of the picture, but simply say that regardless of what they may be, the film is a superb piece of craftsmanship. It possesses a technique entirely new to the screen, and I therefore suggest that it might be very advantageous to have the organisation view it in the same way that a group of artists might view or study a Rubens or a Raphael. The film has no characters in an individual sense; it has not one studio set; yet it is gripping beyond words – its vivid and realistic reproduction of a bit of history being far more interesting than any film of fiction; and this simply because of the genius of its production and direction. (The firm might well consider the man responsible for it, a young Russian director called Eisenstein.) Notable, incidentally, are its types and their lack of make-up, and the exquisite pieces of photography.'[30]

A few days after *The Battleship Potemkin* opened in Berlin, Eisenstein strode into VOKS demanding the German reviews. Pera (Pearl) Fogelman, who used the professional name of Attasheva, was working there. The twenty-six-year-old had been a comic actress on stage, an English interpreter and a journalist. She was a small, rather dumpy woman, with rich dark hair and black eyes, and a wonderfully explosive laugh. At the time, the Russian director Boris Barnet was in love with her. Pera thought Eisenstein the most arrogant man she had ever met, but they soon struck up a friendship, she became his secretary, assistant, confidante and later his wife in an unconsummated marriage of convenience. It was generally thought, by people who knew that the couple lived apart, that Eisenstein was heterosexual but chaste.

It was said that the cause of Eisenstein's chastity derived from the time that a prostitute came to his room in Chysti Prudi. The encounter filled him with such fear and revulsion at the sex act, that he gave it up for ever. Another story, with a different gender twist, originated from the same period. It told of how Eisenstein went to see a psychiatrist in Moscow because he was worried about his attraction to men. The doctor told him that if he wanted to satisfy his homosexual desires, he knew of a young man who worked in Gosplan, the state planning agency, who would, for a small sum, help him out. However, the psychiatrist fatuously warned Eisenstein that he might lose his creativity if he did so. Apparently, Eisenstein went home, had a sleepless night, and decided in favour of art over sex, thus sublimating his physical passions to retain the passion of the intellect. He therefore never visited the boy, and lived a chaste life ever after.

Given Eisenstein's objective sophistication on sexual matters, and his understanding of himself, it seems highly unlikely that a prostitute would have turned him against heterosexual sex in general, or that he could ever have believed that homosexual gratification would destroy his creativity. According to biographer Marie Seton, Eisenstein's preoccupation with homosexuality was an 'intellectual' one. A few years later, when in the USA, he told Joseph Freeman that 'had it not been for Leonardo, Freud, Marx, Lenin and the movies, I would, in all probability, have been another Oscar Wilde.'

It seems likely that Eisenstein experimented with homosexual sex – mainly with young men for money in Western Europe and Mexico – as well as occasionally sleeping with women, something he was pleased to hint at in his memoirs. He did have a number of intimate relationships with women, and many, such as Esther Shub and Pera Attasheva, were attracted to him.

Apparently, during the cutting of *The Battleship Potemkin* an assistant of his became pregnant and tried to have a paternity order served on him, producing as 'circumstantial evidence' a photograph he had given her in recognition of her help, inscribed 'in memory of those nights spent together'. Flattered as he was, Eisenstein claimed that the note merely referred to the nights in the cutting room working on the film.

As evidence of Eisenstein's homosexuality, many critics (not all of them gay) have cited the homo-erotic images in his films. The gay American film writer, Parker Tyler, wrote 'Eisenstein has a great personal eye for human beauty, and more especially for male beauty.'[31] Predictably, *The Battleship Potemkin*, with its sailors (regular figures in gay iconography) has provided much material for this speculation. In the late 1980s, Nestor Almendros, the exiled Cuban cinematographer, claimed it was his favourite film.

'*Potemkin* has been considered a revolutionary film not only because of its subject, but for its treatment, and because it departed in its structure from conventional bourgeois drama – the eternal love affair between a man and a woman. Its absence from *Potemkin* was attributed solely to Eisenstein's pristine concentration on the social forces governing society according to Marx. Yet there is evidence to support another hypothesis. The absence of a conventional love affair (as in all Eisenstein's work) could result from the fact that there was very little space for women in his world. Sexuality as an added theme would only cloud the main issues. The trouble is that *Potemkin* is not asexual but very sexual – homo-erotic. From its very beginning, with the sailor's dormitory prologue, we see an "all-male cast" resting shirtless in their hammocks. The camera lingers on the rough, splendidly built men, in a series of shots that anticipate the sensuality of Mapplethorpe. Then appears the leader of the revolt, Vakulinchuk, who is also, for no apparent reason, naked to the waist, flashing his broad torso while he demands the beginning of action. Later in the film, the sailors' revolt and their action reaches what Eisenstein used to refer as "the collective extasis". At the great moment when the cannons are raised to fire, a sort of visual ballet of multiple slow and pulsating erections can easily be discerned.'[32]

Although subjective, Almendros, and other committed homosexual commentators, cannot be accused of special gay pleading. Eisenstein was 'out' as a phallic obsessive. Knowing this, it is not unlikely that Eisenstein was slyly playing with the slowly rising guns, as well as the scenes of sailors polishing pistons in a masturbatory manner. His most overtly sexual symbol in films was the 'coming' of the cream separator in *The General Line*, the sort of visual metaphor taken to its comic extreme in a *Naked Gun* movie, where a sex act is cross-cut with a phallic vase being modelled on a potter's wheel, cannons and rockets are fired, trains go through tunnels etc.

It was in the sketches that Eisenstein drew in Mexico in 1931 that his often regressive phallophilia reached its peak. It was also from Mexico that he sent his English friend Ivor Montagu the well-known photograph of himself perched on a gigantic bulbous cactus plant seemingly protruding from between his legs with the words 'Speaks for itself and makes people jealous!' Andrei Konchalovsky remembers being told by his mother, who was a friend of Eisenstein's, that he had shown her drawings he had made of a number of penises, in different postures, with faces drawn on them – a giant, a fat bourgeois, a sportsman, a dwarf – happy and erect or sad and drooping, small or large, in fact many of the characters from his films were all there in synecdochic form.

Then there is the phallic and ejaculatory exclamation mark that appears at the tail of so many of his sentences and intertitles. Given Eisenstein's explosive, revolutionary nature in those early days, he could have been one of the few people to put an exclamation mark after his name. This is not as fanciful a notion as it sounds. Eisenstein never missed an opportunity to make such analogies no matter how bizarre. During a lecture on the shape of the screen, given to the Technicians Branch of the Academy of Motion Picture Arts and Sciences in Hollywood in 1930, Eisenstein declared, 'It is my desire to intone the hymn of the male, the strong, the virile, active, *vertical* composition! I am not anxious to enter into the dark phallic and sexual ancestry of the vertical shape as a symbol of growth, strength or power. It would be too easy and possibly too offensive for many a sensitive listener! But I do want to point out that the movement towards a vertical perception launched our hirsute ancestors on their way to a higher level.'[33]

Among his intellectual circle in Moscow in the comparatively liberal mid-1920s, Eisenstein's attraction to Alexandrov was an open secret. Waclaw Solski, the Polish writer, first met Eisenstein in 1925, when he came to Moscow as an advisor to Sovkino on movie production for the foreign market. Eisenstein visited Solski's office with Tisse and Alexandrov.

Solski described Eisenstein as 'short, plump, with lively, piercing eyes, an unusually high forehead, and a great shock of hair. A strange semi-sarcastic smile never left his face. His voice had an unpleasantly squeaky quality to it. Everything about him was roundish – his head, face, body, and even his arms and legs . . . "I understand that you're to pass on our films chosen for showing to the rotten bourgeoisie of the West," Eisenstein said, chuckling ironically. "What about my *Potemkin*? They won't understand it but they may like it. People sometimes like what they don't understand."

"Why do you think they won't understand it," I asked.

"Because the Sovkino didn't understand it either . . . Sovkino did everything to kill my film . . . It is true that the public didn't like it much, but that was because of the NEP [New Economic Policy]. The NEP-men would rather see half-naked girls on the screen than a serious film. But I'm not a NEP-man and I'm not interested in girls." Grigori Alexandrov suddenly burst into a short laugh, but quickly stopped and turned red. I couldn't see what he was laughing about. Not until later, when I learned what everyone in Moscow knew, did Alexandrov's odd behaviour become understandable to me.'[34]

In March and April 1926, Eisenstein and Tisse were sent by Soyuzkino to Berlin to become acquainted with Western cinematography. It was Eisenstein's first trip abroad since he had gone to Paris as a child with his mother. They stayed at the Hotel Hessler, a modern glass structure which got Eisenstein first thinking of a typically over-ambitious film project he was to develop as *The Glass House* for Paramount four years later.

In Berlin, he became friendly with the left-wing novelist Lion Feuchtwanger, who had gained much fame for *Jew Süss*, the year before. Feuchtwanger saw Soviet films such as *Potemkin* as revolutionary bombs that could be flung again and again into the various centres of the bourgeois world. He later wrote in *Pravda* that *Potemkin* 'had a great deal of influence on my subsequent work: it revealed to me the technical means used in film-making and the possibility of transferring them into the art of epic prose.' In his 1930 novel *Success*, there is a chapter in which the reactionary

Otto Klenk, the former Minister of Justice of Bavaria, is extremely offended by the showing in Berlin of a film called *The Battleship Orloff*.

At UFA studios, Eisenstein and Tisse met F.W. Murnau and Emil Jannings on the set of *Faust*. Eisenstein remembered seeing Jannings, who played Mephistopheles, 'posing magnificently on a cliff, in the grey cloak of the Prince of the Underworld.'[35] Also in the film, in the role of Marthe Schwerdtlein, was one of his idols, cabaret singer Yvette Guilbert, whom he was to meet personally in Paris four years later.

The two Russians also visited the UFA studios at Neubabelsberg to watch the shooting of *Metropolis* with the director Fritz Lang, his wife, the scriptwriter Thea von Harbou, and the two cinematographers on the picture, Günther Rittau and Karl Freund. They were particularly interested by Eugen Shüfftan's new special effects process combining life-size action with models, which eliminated the need for huge, cumbersome sets. (Nevertheless, *Metropolis* ended up costing an unprecedented five million marks, almost ruining UFA).

Eisenstein asked Thea von Harbou what the idea behind the film was, 'because there are rumours in Germany that *Metropolis* is a revolutionary film and that it will be a great success in Russia but will scarcely be shown at all in America.' Von Harbou, who later joined the Nazi Party, replied, 'It is, of course, difficult to say in two words, but the message of the picture is that there must be some kind of compromise between the men who work with their hands and the creative brain of the factory owner'. Eisenstein, presumably comparing it with *The Strike*, concluded, 'I leave the reader to judge how "revolutionary" this is.'[36]

Eisenstein described Lang as facially resembling Lev Kuleshov 'if the latter had been well fed over a period of time. This similarity extends to the sphere of taste. The style and spirit of *Metropolis* are extremely close to what Kuleshov was endeavouring to do, and in part did, in *The Death Ray* . . . If you gave Kuleshov six million marks he would do just as well.'[37]

The success of *Potemkin* encouraged its German distributor to commission Edmund Meisel, the Austrian-born composer, to write a score for the theatre orchestra. (Prokofiev had already been considered earlier in the Soviet Union.) By the time of Eisenstein's arrival, Meisel had reached the last reel. Eisenstein's advice to him was, 'the music for this reel should be rhythm, rhythm and, before all else, rhythm.'[38] He dissuaded him from composing purely illustrative music and got him to accentuate certain effects. This came off well in 'the music for machines' in the final sequence of the *Potemkin*'s meeting with the flotilla.

It was not customary during the 'silent' period for a composer to work closely with the director on the score as became the case during the sound era, although D.W. Griffith had collaborated with J.C. Breil on constructing an elaborately cued score of *The Birth of a Nation*.

Eisenstein was offered work in Germany, but as he wrote in the *Berliner Tageblatt*: 'I am positive that the cinema collaboration of Germany and Russia could have great results . . . But for me personally to work in Germany is extremely doubtful. I could not forsake my native soil, which gives me the strength to create . . . and so for the present, I'll stay at home.'[39]

The visit and the offer made him question the whole notion of a film industry in a capitalist country. 'The resources we had for *Potemkin* "slayed" the Germans: the fact, for instance, that we were given command of the streets, that we were allowed to cordon off the Odessa Steps for six days and film there. These conditions are quite unthinkable in Germany. If we had had to film a city street in Germany we should have had to pay more money in bribes alone than the cost of the whole picture . . . In Germany a director is very rarely able to display the breadth of his initiative and skill. This usually happens if he can exploit the competition between two firms. For example, the transfer of the major part of the shares of UFA to the Deutsche Bank was marked by the fact that the Deutsche Bank embarked on a production like *Metropolis* to show how much richer it was, and how much greater its potential, than the bank it was competing with . . . German film production has been cut by seventy per cent and is gradually falling into American hands.'[40]

Before Eisenstein left Berlin, he paid a visit to his father's quiet grave in the Russian cemetery near Tegel, in the centre of which is a little Orthodox church with a bright blue onion dome. Mikhail

Eisenstein's gravestone, marked with an *art nouveau* cross seems to be growing out of a tree-trunk, as if he had requested it that way. The inscription (in Russian) reads: 'Mikhail Osipovich Eisenstein born St Petersburg 17 September 1867; died 18 June – 1 July [old calendar] 1920.'

Perhaps Eisenstein felt some guilt or pity for the man whose character he was to lampoon so in his memoirs, but he went to a florist and ordered that flowers should be placed on the grave at regular intervals until the time of his own death. Although there is hardly one positive word used by Eisenstein about Mikhail Osipovich in his writings, this act demonstrates the ambivalent nature of the son's relationship to his father, and adds more weight to the theory that his anger towards him was, in part, fuelled by his inability to express his anger towards that other 'fearsome and strict' father who was to control his life from then on.

6

Forward, Comrades!

October speaks with two voices. Falsetto and bass . . . The voice has a habit of breaking at transitional age. At an age when you are growing. The transition to adulthood. October appears at a similar turning point for cinema.

Immediately after *The Battleship Potemkin* Eisenstein planned a three-part film about China, based on a scenario by Sergei Tretyakov, to be called *Zhunguo*. The Chinese political question was then a topical one to which Eisenstein hoped to make a contribution. By 1926, the Russian Communists were already deeply embroiled in Chinese events. Stalin's ideological programme for China was to secure 'the hegemony of the proletariat', but he believed in collaborating with the Kuomintang, the Chinese Nationalists. He asserted that the Chinese situation was in important respects parallel to that in Russia on the eve of 1905. Trotsky dissented sharply from this view, arguing that it was necessary to strike for Communist power and a socialist economy. Trotsky and his colleagues attacked the Politburo for 'Thermidorism, degeneration, Menshevism, betrayal, treachery, *kulak*-NEP-man policy against the workers, against the poor peasants, against the Chinese revolution.' This opened up a further gap between Stalin and Trotsky as they struggled for power.

Naturally, Eisenstein, under cover of the political topicality, thought it might give him the opportunity to probe further into the oriental culture that intrigued him. But, in the spring of 1926, he was asked to make a film on a more crucial, domestic political issue: the collectivisation of agriculture, which was intensifying.

With characteristic enthusiasm, and after the usual massive documentary research, including the reading of Zola's *La Terre*, a depiction of the harsh life of the peasant in 19th-century France, he set off with a team to tour the villages of the Moscow region. By May 23, he and Alexandrov had outlined the scenario for the film called *The General Line*, and the following day he presented it at the Centre for Agriculture and Forestry. The complete shooting script, written between June 23 and 30, was discussed by the cinema's Artistic Council on July 7, after which filming commenced.

Filming continued for a month in a succession of villages and farms. The team shot old peasant huts, the death of a bull, a religious procession, the repair of a tractor, and a cow pulling a plough. After a month, however, filming was broken off by Sovkino, which had to produce a film in honour of the tenth anniversary of the October Revolution. Vsevolod Pudovkin had already started work in Leningrad on *The End of St Petersburg*, a film on the same subject in the same location for the same occasion, and Boris Barnet was completing *Moscow in October*.

Such was the nature of state patronage that, at the State's command, Eisenstein had to turn his mind from collectivisation to the event that made it possible. His meticulous research covered hundreds of historical memoirs and papers, newspaper reports and old newsreels. A further source was John Reed's *Ten Days That Shook The World*, the title under which *October* was released in America. There were also Eisenstein's personal memoirs of the events he had witnessed in 1917 (the dispersal of the demonstration on the Nevsky Prospect).

Unlike *Potemkin*, the scenario, written with Alexandrov, was 'iron-clad' in that it was worked out in minute detail that, in principle, left little room for improvisation when it came to filming. But, as with the earlier film, they intended to cover a broader spectrum. The first versions of the screenplay of *October* encompassed the stages of the Revolution from the overthrow of the monarchy to the end of the Civil War and the transition to peace-time construction.

At first, Eisenstein had the idea of showing the events through the eyes of an officer and a few other characters caught up in the Revolution, but he felt it ran counter to his theoretical aims to focus on the historical not the personal. Pudovkin, on the other hand, used an uneducated peasant boy, arriving in St Petersburg in time to witness the Revolution, as a central figure with whom audiences could identify, which may have helped make it the more popular film.

One of the leading consultants on Eisenstein's film was N.I. Podvoysky, an elderly man who was also cast as the revolutionary Chief of Staff, the post he himself had held in November 1917. When the reading of the script was taking place before the Artistic Council, Maxim Strauch observed that 'Podvoysky was taking notes so energetically, that I got scared. I sent a note to Eisenstein: "It looks as though we'll have to spend an evening with Podvoysky discussing things." . . . Podvoysky agreed to go to Leningrad with Eisenstein to look for locations. Then added, "You know how stubborn I am, you'd better not argue with me! Better listen to me, and then later don't do it. But make a note of everything I say so that I have the impression I'm being listened to." Leaving, he yelled across the hall: "Eisenstein! Be prepared!"'[1]

Time and money again imposed limits on the film's scope, and the final version of the script concentrated on the year 1917, from the February uprising to Lenin's assumption of power when, at the Congress of Soviets, he announced, 'The working-class and peasant revolution has been accomplished.'

In an article in *Kino-Front* in December 1927, Eisenstein, freely arguing for a State Plan for cinema, wrote: 'The surrender of the material was carried out with unusual cruelty and with the routine sighs about the State Plan. The damage done to the material did unprecedented violence to the nature of the film. Time compressed and nullified things that could never have been called superfluous. The script for *October* was compressed, not according to principle, but according to area: the front, as envisaged, went. Moscow in October went; the Civil War, the partisans went, as did a great deal of integral material . . .'[2]

Shooting on *October* started on April 13, 1926 with Leningrad becoming a vast film set. The Tsar's palace, the streets, and the populace were put at the disposal of Eisenstein and of Pudovkin, who was filming simultaneously. Eisenstein again insisted on the film's entire cast conforming to his *typage* theory, and a search for suitable types began. Maxim Strauch scoured the streets and the doss houses, going unshaven among the jobless. The outcome was a detailed dossier, complete with photographs, of a huge selection of possibles, from which Eisenstein selected for closer personal inspection those approaching his ideal. One of the first questions asked was 'How is Lenin to be depicted?' A wide search turned up a worker called V. Nikandrov, who was a near double of Lenin, and could play the late leader with a minimum of make-up. Nikandrov, however, was of limited intellect, though he did manage to imitate Lenin's way of walking and gesturing after being thoroughly drilled by Eisenstein.

The tall, blond Tisse, the cinematographer once more, played a German officer; a student, N. Popov, got to play Kerensky, whom he resembled, and Boris Livanov portrayed a cabinet minister. The rest of the cast was almost entirely drawn from the citizens of Leningrad. Strauch, evidently wearing rose-coloured spectacles, noted: 'Tomorrow we're filming the hunger queue at the bread shop. But no gaunt faces! We even went to the T.B. clinics. We must have thin children. There aren't any! Whenever we find a thin child, his expression is too happy – the inside shows! – no sad eyes.'[3]

For the opening scene, the toppling of the statue of Tsar Alexander III, Strauch observed that pieces of the original were stored in the cellars of Christ Saviour. 'Padlocked, and inscribed "People's Commission to Preserve Monuments of Art." Dust. Wires rusted. Had to saw our way through . . . two hundred pieces of the monument . . . Found Alexander's head in another cellar. They had torn down the monument with "prehistoric methods" – ropes and clubs.'[4]

For the storming of the Winter Palace, there were gathered thousands of sailors, soldiers and workers. 'I always say that the masses can only be used like this in our country because there are not many countries where you can lead two or three thousand armed workers onto the streets with impunity!' Eisenstein claimed. 'Everyone wanted to play the Bolsheviks and no-one wanted to play the Mensheviks. In that case we used a very simple process: we gave the actors the text of an inflammatory speech and they spoke it with great fervour. After this we added titles that said the exact opposite.'[5]

Before shooting the attack on the Winter Palace, Eisenstein

explored the interior exhaustively, having himself photographed mischievously lounging on the Tsar's throne, just like the little boy in *October* who curls up on the throne.

Grigori Alexandrov, the assistant director, recalled: 'When we filmed the storming of the Winter Palace, the headquarters of our unit was underneath the big bronze horses on top of the arch that leads into the square from the main part of the city, and exactly opposite the Palace itself. It was from this position that Eisenstein shouted his orders through a megaphone to the vast crowd that stormed the Palace on our behalf. There were more than five thousand of them altogether, armed with rifles and blank ammunition, and nearly all of them came from the factories of Leningrad. Many had taken part in the October Revolution of 1917, and had attacked the Winter Palace in reality ten years before. Their job was to do once again what they had done then. So, at the agreed time, our orders went out from beneath those bronze horses, and three thousand people went into action from the various sides of the square. The rest came running from beneath us, under the arch, heading straight for the Palace.

'In 1917, the real attack had taken place at night and in the dark, and so we filmed at night. But in those days it was very difficult to light a large area, even though we chose to shoot the sequence in June during the so-called White Nights. But the film stock available to us in 1927 was by no means "fast" enough, and for much of the time we were forced to crank the camera more slowly than usual to increase the exposure; which in turn had the effect of unnaturally speeding up the tempo of the crowd movements. This was a problem we could anticipate and allow for. Other hazards were totally unexpected. For instance, some of those who took part in the sequence had returned from various fronts of the Civil War, bringing some of their live cartridges, and decided to add to the realism by using them for the filming, so that when it was all over we had difficulty in accounting for some of the windows in the Palace that had been smashed by bullets, and a few of the rare sculptures outside the building that had been clipped by the same cause. We had arranged to explode dummy grenades during our shooting to help the realism of the atmosphere, but compared with the live bullets they were innocence itself. Not surprisingly, we had our own genuine casualties, and most of them were caused by badly handled bayonets. Indeed, it has long been a joke in the Soviet film industry that more casualties were caused by Eisenstein's storming of the Winter Palace in June 1927 than by the attack of the original Bolsheviks in October 1917.' After this exploit, Eisenstein recalled being told by an elderly porter who had been sweeping up the broken glass, 'Your people were much more careful the first time they took the palace.'[6]

Eisenstein also bombarded the Winter Palace from the *Aurora*, which he had towed from the naval port of Kronstadt into the Neva, where it was stationed in 1917. Once again fixated on conveying the idea of sound through visual images, he wrote, 'In the palace rooms I achieved a plastic recreation of the impressions made by a salvo from the *Aurora*'s guns. The echo rolled through the rooms and reached a room where everything had been covered by white sheeting and where members of the Provisional Government were awaiting the fateful moment – the establishment of Soviet Power. The crystal chandeliers tinkling in reply to the rattle of machine-gun fire on the square was more successful and remained in the audience's memory.'[7]

However, the single image that most impressed itself on the audience's memory is that of the dead white horse being caught at the top of an opening drawbridge, and then plunging into the river below. This was one of those inspirational, improvisational moments that came to Eisenstein during shooting.

'God knows why I should wake up one morning in the Nicholas Library after filming interior shots for the storming of the Winter Palace and see through a window the giant arms of the Palace Bridge, raised heavenwards like the arms of a dying man. I saw the arms of the bridge almost as a vision; then the broken cab and the shot horse appeared, and then the golden rays of the sun played upon them before turning into the fair curls of the dying girl. The bridge evolved into a symbol; a symbol of the city's split, between its centre and the workers' dormitories during the July days . . . Thus a chance glimpse at dawn, the silhouette of the raised bridge, evolved into an image which in turn branched out into a complex of images, ultimately the symbol of two outstretched arms, reaching out to each other in a firm grip.

This was of structural importance in my conception of the whole film.'[8]

But the filming of the scene of the palace bridge was more complicated than Eisenstein could have imagined. He spoke to the bridge operators about the best way to raise the bridge repeatedly for half an hour, from six o'clock when the bridge was due to be raised, until six-thirty. Otherwise the trams would be late arriving at Finland Station, and the passengers, streaming in from the dormitory suburbs to the factories and plants, would be delayed.

'On our last day of work we dodged the vigilant mechanics, who were so engrossed in what they saw going on above that we were able to hold the bridge's maw open for a further ten minutes. And the rows, the disruption of work, the hold-ups and irritation! But you can't blame us for heaven's sake! We only had twenty minutes a day. And in those twenty minutes we had to kill a white horse, as it galloped madly pulling a cab; let drop a golden-haired girl, let the two halves of the bridge open up, let the golden hair stretch across the bottomless abyss, let the dead horse and the cab swing from the raised edge of the bridge, let the cab fall . . . On screen this takes a lot less than twenty minutes. But to film it takes hours!'[9]

October was completed in a phenomenally short time, thanks to having two film crews shooting simultaneously (and to the pep pills they took to keep them going day and night). '*October* is ready. Ready and not ready,' wrote Eisenstein in *Kino*, a week before its first public showing on March 14, 1928. 'A year of quite back-breaking toil. A year in which coping with thirty to forty hours' shooting was regarded as the easy part of our job and most of our energy was expended on a fight with the slow, sluggish and malevolent machinery in the Leningrad studio. Towards the end of the year this flattened us. We had no teeth left to bite out another ten days from the inexorable deadlines . . . All we needed was a clear head and a little time. We did not manage, as it were, to redeem our new-born infant. So the film is tainted with a certain hint of negligence which in places hinders perception and everywhere provides "dilettanti" with ammunition for their derision.'[10]

Eisenstein edited most of the lengthy footage by himself, occasionally asking Esther Shub's opinion about certain montage effects. During the editing, he claimed that his head was 'so full of celluloid' that the mere mention of the 'utterly detested' word 'film' was enough to send it 'spinning dizzily . . . And perhaps something of this dizziness, this chaotic confusion of kilometres of film transferred itself to the film's composition.'[11]

In the midst of the editing, Edmund Meisel arrived in Moscow to compose the music. For the scene when the collapse of the statue of Alexander III is shot in reverse, Meisel wrote the music in reverse, the same music that had been played 'normally' at the start. Eisenstein recalled 'the trick with the "palindromic" music . . . Filming in reverse is always diverting and I remember how the first old comic films made use of this device . . . But I do not suppose anyone noticed this musical trick.'[12]

The French film scholar Léon Moussinac visited Eisenstein in November 1927, when he was cutting *October*: 'Eisenstein was aware that side by side with the overpowering sequences . . . there were other sequences of considerably lesser quality, and he foresaw that his film could never be "complete" in the way he would have liked. He knew perfectly well that it would have to undergo certain revisions and cuts, and that even under the best circumstances only fragments would be shown abroad.'[13]

The first cut of 3,800 metres was ready for the anniversary of the Revolution on November 7, 1927, but only a few selected reels were shown at the anniversary celebrations. By the time the film was re-edited, it had lost 1,000 metres. The reason for this was clear. In an article submitted to *Pravda*, Trotsky called on his adherents to follow the example of Clemenceau (who had opened the way to take over from his predecessor's failures in World War I) in case war engulfed the USSR. Stalin promptly engineered the expulsion of Trotsky and Zinoviev from the Central Committee. After the two men led street demonstrations on the tenth anniversary of the October Revolution (i.e. November 7, 1927) while Eisenstein was still cutting *October*, they were expelled from the Party. The way was now clear for Stalin to oust the opposition from the Party en masse. The XV Congress in December 1927 decreed as much. Trotsky refused to accept the Congress's decision and was thereupon exiled to Alma Ata in Central Asia, where Eisenstein would film *Ivan the Terrible* years later. Zinoviev and Kamenev soon recanted and were permitted to crawl back into the Party.

Late one night, according to Alexandrov, when Eisenstein was working on the film, Stalin unexpectedly dropped in at the studios. He did not meet Eisenstein, but was shown several sequences. He ordered Trotsky, who figured prominently, to be expunged from the film altogether, and those scenes that showed Lenin in 'an unsatisfactory light . . . Lenin's liberalism is no longer valid today', as Stalin remarked. Therefore numerous changes had to be made for political reasons, the first experience Eisenstein had of direct state interference. He would never again enjoy untrammelled freedom to create.

An advantage of being a film-maker in the Soviet Union has always been the financial support and the positive encouragement of all ideas which are not regarded as politically 'mistaken'. So Eisenstein was relatively happy in the 1920s, and seems quietly to have accepted political 'advice' during the editing of *October*. If he complained, then few of his complaints, other than the occasional moan about technical facilities in Leningrad, have been recorded. Alexandrov's attitude is that in 1927, at the peak of the Trotskyite dispute, some degree of political interference was generally regarded as a fact of life.

There were rumours alleging Eisenstein's adherence to Trotsky – rumours which he felt compelled to repudiate publicly in a press article – explaining at the same time his reasons for the film's delay. Eisenstein must have thought the allegations pretty serious to have broken off in the midst of work to write an article purely to clear his name.

In December 1927, two Harvard graduates, Alfred Barr and Jere Abbott, arrived in Moscow for a visit. Barr noted in his diary of January 1928: 'He [Eisenstein] was extremely affable – humorous in talk, almost a clown in appearance . . . We saw four reels of *October* – his revolutionary film which was supposed to be finished three months ago – and may be ready by February. His mastery of cutting and camera placement was clearly shown, especially in the

July riot scenes. We didn't see the storming of the winter palace, which is the high point of the film. Certain faults appeared – he seemed to yield to the temptation of the fine shot – viz. the drawbridge scene. At times the tempo was too fast. The film seemed, however, a magnificent accomplishment . . . We asked whether much of the excellence of Eisenstein's films did not develop in the cutting rather than the shooting. He laughed, and answered that the critics wrote of his filming as "always carefully premeditated."' A few weeks later, Barr wrote: 'Found him very weary. "Will you go on vacation after *October* is finished?" "No, I'll probably die!"'[14]

The premiere of the full and final version of *October* was held in Leningrad on January 28, 1928, two months after Pudovkin's *The End of St Petersburg* was applauded at the Bolshoi on the precise day of the anniversary. Pudovkin's film, as Eisenstein was swift to recognise, was 'the first epic from an individual psychological theme of the past.'[15]

Audiences were disoriented by *October* with its dynamic montage, the constantly contrasting images, its visual metaphors, everything that makes the film such a rich experience today. It was perhaps unwise of Eisenstein to allow himself to experiment with a film whose subject matter was as sensitive as that of the Russian Revolution. Everyone from Lunacharsky down to the selected 'representative' workers had their say about the film in the press. Unlike Lunacharsky, who hailed *October* as 'an enormous triumph' and a 'symphony after the étude of *Potemkin*,' both Mayerhold and Mayakovsky tended towards the negative. Mayakovsky's main criticism was the portrayal of Lenin. 'For all the outward similarity, there is no hiding the inner emptiness. How right the comrade was who said that Nikandrov doesn't resemble Lenin, but a statue of Lenin.'[16] Lenin's widow, Krupskaya, expressed the same opinion in an article on *October*, although she qualified her criticism by saying that it represented a 'landmark on the road towards a new art, towards the art of the future.'[17]

The film historian Nikolai Lebedev, looking back in 1947, dismissed *October* as one of the 'conspicuous failures of the experimental cinema . . . Eisenstein considered that the basic facts of the October days were generally known, so that he presented not these, but, by his own admission, "my own associations, my visual puns" that those facts called to mind.'[18]

Eisenstein tried to answer his critics in an article in *Kino* in March 1928 called 'Our *October*: Beyond the Played and the Non-Played'. 'It would be a very great mistake to judge *October* by the criteria generated by the appearance of *Potemkin* . . . In some reels, *October* is trying to take the next step, trying to seek out *speech* that in its construction will wholly correspond to a similar vocabulary . . .'[19]

In a letter to Moussinac in December 1928, Eisenstein wrote: 'From the point of view of construction, *October* is by no means flawless. It is just that in this film that is so much of "the people", of the "masses", I allowed myself to experiment. Despite the fact that my experiments are seldom appreciated . . . they were enough to break the composition of the work as a unity. But on the other hand they were also enough to allow me to make deductions which are very, very far-reaching.'[20]

Eisenstein's 'montage of film attractions' reached its apotheosis in *October*. It developed his theory of 'intellectual montage', at which the audience must not only be shocked, but shocked into thinking. The number of shots – 3,200 – was more than double those in *The Battleship Potemkin* and more than in any of his other films. *October* also took the idea of the visual metaphor to its extreme, spreading layer upon layer of meaning over almost every image. The Latvian film writer Yuri Tsivian has revealed numerous connections between many of the film's images and Russian symbolist culture that the general viewer could not be expected to make. For example, the white horse falling from the bridge (which seems to be a white horse falling from a bridge) is explained by Tsivian thus: 'For Eisenstein and the Russian symbolists, the Russian Revolution was connected with the Apocalypse. One of the images in Russian symbolist poetry was a white horse in the sky. Andrei Bely wrote that film is the end of art, an apocalypse of art. A falling white horse represents the end of culture.'[21] *October*, among all of Eisenstein's films, lends itself to endless interpretations of this sort.

The film opens with the toppling of the statue of Alexander III, the autocratic father of the newly-ousted Tsar Nicholas II, an emblem of the overthrow of the monarchy. It is later reconstructed (by reverse photography) to represent the reactionary measures of the Kerensky government. Other symbols abound, some obvious, some arcane. A strutting Alexander Kerensky, who embodies all of Eisenstein's hatred for his father's bourgeois mentality, is rapidly cross-cut with a gilded mechanical peacock. As Kerensky enters the Winter Palace as leader, the peacock turns and the doors close behind him, implying that power has trapped him into the notion of vanity. Both Kerensky and the advancing monarchist General Kornilov, are seen as twin Napoleons, represented by busts. A girl in the Women's Death Battalion guarding the palace from the Bolsheviks, poses wistfully against Rodin's statue of *Spring*, a variation on *The Kiss*, which reminds the audience that, under her uniform, she is just a young woman after all.

During the protracted Menshevik speeches, Eisenstein inter-cuts hands playing harps (a Busby Berkeleyesque moment) until a Bolshevik (to the relief of the audience) reacts by saying, 'The time for words is past.' The most puzzling of all the symbolic sequences is that which follows General Kornilov's declaration that his anti-Bolshevik crusade was taken in the 'name of God and Country!' Here, a baroque Christ gives way to a many-armed Indian deity, and subsequently Japanese and African masks as well as voodoo idols, a sacred Chinese statue and Buddhas, exploding the myth of monotheism.

Because of the advanced style of the film as 'slogan', the characters, more than in any of Eisenstein's other works, have little intrinsic personality beyond the strict *typage* imposed on them. Rather like Christ in Hollywood movies Lenin is treated hagiographically, depicted in historic leadership poses, while his audience glows in his presence.

But *October* is a magnificent constructivist propaganda poster brought to life. (While working on the picture, Eisenstein wrote, 'The time has come to make films directly from a slogan.'[22]) It captures the sweep of revolution, and the political comings and goings, leading up to the spectacular climax (equal in scale to many a Hollywood epic of the period). Because of the absence of newsreel footage of the event, this replication, obviously imbued by

Eisenstein's reading of the French Revolution, has long been taken as truth – the classic image of the Revolution – and is still frequently used in documentaries of the Russian Revolution; stills from *October* have appeared in school history books. (The following year, a similar mutation from fiction to fact happened with Lewis Milestone's *All Quiet On The Western Front*, the battle scenes of which were so realistic that they have often been incorporated into documentaries about World War I.)

October completed Eisenstein's trilogy of the Revolution through which certain motifs reappear – especially that of turning wheels representing change which eventually, in *October*, become clocks showing different times from various cities around the world, implying the cataclysmic moment when 'Workers of the World Unite.' The factory bosses in *The Strike* become the naval officers in *The Battleship Potemkin* who reappear as the bourgeois leaders of the provisional government in *October*, while in all three films the workers/sailors/Bolshevik activists fight nobly for their liberation, each time having to submit to government repression by police or soldiers; in the first case ending in defeat, the second in partial triumph, the third in ultimate victory.

7

Poet and Peasant

After The General Line, *when I began thinking of the development of my work in the future, I took a creative approach towards characterisation and depiction. Introducing Marfa Lapkina into* The General Line *could be seen as an 'embryonic' demand for a 'hero' in future works.*

In the same month as the general release of *October*, while Eisenstein was defending it and blithely planning to experiment further in the art of film, The All-Union Party Conference on Cinema assembled on March 15, 1928, under the sponsorship of the Department of Propaganda and Agitation. On the eve of the conference, and unaware of its agenda, Eisenstein published a short exhortatory piece entitled What We Are Expecting from the Party Conference on Cinema. The last line resounds with a particularly piquant irony: 'The dictatorship of the proletariat, at last, and in the cinema sector: socialist construction . . . The merger of film-producing organisations and the transfer to the merged enterprise of all cinemas . . . a rod of iron now for all those who bring disgrace on the cinema.'[1]

At the Conference itself, the resolutions were full of references to 'remnants of bourgeois influence' and warnings against 'formalistic' tendencies by directors, without any names named. The conference resolved that 'the basic criterion for evaluating the art qualities of a film is the requirement that it be presented in a form which can be understood by the millions.' Thus the tone was set for the doctrine of socialist realism that would dominate the Soviet cinema, as well as the other arts, until Stalin's death and beyond – proving so severely restrictive to 'formalists' like Eisenstein.

Stalin's first Five-Year Plan was implemented in 1928. By that time he had substantially taken over the secret police, the trade-unions, and the army, via adroit use of the Party machine. Some of the critics within the Party he had won over; others he had not, but he was able to keep watch on what they were saying and doing.

Even after the Stalin clique liquidated the opposition and seized complete control of the state apparatus in 1928, the effects were not immediately felt in the cinema. The great directors were in the middle of some of their most important films and their international prestige was so enormous that even the bureaucracy trod warily – at first. Although literature was handed over to RAPP (Russian Association of Proletarian Writers) in 1928, it was not until the spring of 1930 that systematic attempts were made to bring the cinema to heel.

The year 1928 saw the golden era of silent Soviet films draw to a close with Dovzhenko's *Zvenigora*, Pudovkin's *Storm Over Asia*, Shub's *The Russia of Nicholas II and Leo Tolstoy*, Yutkevich's *Lace*, Fedor Ozep's *Earth in Chains*, Nikolai Okhlopkov's *The Solid Appetite*, Yakov Bliokh's *The Shanghai Document*, and Nikolai Shengalaya's *Eliso*, most of which were made in total freedom.

In the same year, Eisenstein, Alexandrov and Pudovkin issued a manifesto denouncing the realistic use of sound in the cinema and outlining a new 'contrapuntal' approach, based on montage, which promised to revolutionise the sound film as their theories had already reinvented the silent cinema. They predicted that the capitalist cinema would use sound 'according to the laws of least resistance' and that the commercial sound film would enter into 'a terrible . . . epoch of automatic utilisation for "high cultural dramas", and other photographic performances of a theatrical nature . . .

'The first experiments in sound must aim at a sharp discord with the visual images. Sound, treated as a new element of montage, cannot fail to provide new and enormously powerful means of expressing and resolving the most complex problems, which have been depressing us with their insurmountability using the imperfect methods of a cinema operating only in visual images.'[2]

Although the Russians claimed to have developed sound-on-film recording systems as early as 1926, it wasn't until late in 1930 – three years after *The Jazz Singer* – that the country's first synchronous sound movie, Yuli Raizman's *The Earth Thirsts*, was made. Late in 1931, a hitherto unknown director, Nikolai Ekk, a student of Eisenstein's, produced *The Road to Life*, the first Soviet film to be conceived and made as a talkie.

While completing the lengthy process of montage for *October*, Eisenstein, through his experiments in the filming of abstract ideas, came to believe that cinema could go even further into uncharted territory. Had the cinema been less dependent on finance and the will and ideology of others, who knows how far Eisenstein might have taken it!

In his article, Beyond the Played and Unplayed, in *Kino* in 1928, Eisenstein announced his new film project, Karl Marx's *Das Kapital*. 'Since we recognise the immensity of this theme as a whole we shall shortly proceed to delimit in the first instance which of its aspects can be cinefied. This work will be carried out with the historian A. Efimov (Alexei V. Efimov), our consultant in the preparation of the script for *October*.'[3]

As he told the audience at the Sorbonne in 1930, 'It will not be a story that unfolds but an essay to make the illiterate and ignorant audience understand and learn the dialectical way of thinking.' In this direction, he believed, lay the theme for the film of the future. 'A purely intellectual film which, freed from traditional limitations, will achieve direct forms for thoughts, systems and concepts without any transitions or paraphrases. And which can therefore become a SYNTHESIS OF ART AND SCIENCE.

'I think that only cinema is capable of achieving this grand synthesis, of providing the intellectual element with its life-giving sources, both concrete and emotional. That is our task and that is the path that we should follow.'[4]

In a letter to Léon Moussinac, Eisenstein wrote: 'The "proclamation" that I'm going to make a movie on Marx's *Das Kapital* is not a publicity stunt. I believe that the films of the future will be found going in this direction.'[5]

In connection with this project, Eisenstein wrote on a postcard of the Aga Khan: 'On deity. Aga Khan – irreplaceable material – cynicism of shamanism carried to the extreme. God – a graduate of Oxford University. Playing rugby and ping-pong and accepting the prayers of the faithful. And in the background, adding machines click away in "divine" bookkeeping, entering sacrifices and donations. Best exposure of the theme of clergy and cult.'[6]

Meanwhile Eisenstein was in conflict with *Novy LEF* (the New Left Front of the Arts). At a meeting at Sergei Tretyakov's home in March 1928, Mayakovsky tried to persuade Eisenstein against breaking with them, but Eisenstein insisted that there was no future in remaining. As he wrote to Léon Moussinac at the time:

'I have the impression that the enormous breath of 1917 which gave birth to our cinema is blowing itself out . . . We're getting classical – "artistic"! The bleeding wounds have healed – no more chances to scream loud and rip old film traditions apart . . . Cream puffs instead of naked hate . . . We're losing our teeth. We aren't fighters any more . . . We're losing our teeth because we don't need them now . . . I am horrified to see gradually creeping into our "avant-garde" a stultified manneristic academy, dressed in magistrate's cap, which, while still red, is whimsically crumpled above the traditional aesthetic robes of perfect and impeccable cut . . . It's stifling! . . . We are evolving – effortlessly evolving to a point where it will again be necessary to revolutionise to the roots what has become sterile stylisation instead of palpitating life and true passion . . . To arms, citizens! Butt the stomach of anyone opposed to what we *must* do!'[7]

In the meanwhile, Eisenstein was interested in making any international contacts he could. During a conference celebrating the centenary of Leo Tolstoy's birth in 1928, he met and became friendly with the Austrian writer Stefan Zweig. The latter dined with Eisenstein at his small flat in Chysti Prudi in his 'book-filled room, at the table with its waxed tablecloth.'[8] Eisenstein knowing that Zweig was close to Sigmund Freud, asked him about 'the great man from Vienna'.[9] Eisenstein, an avid reader of Freud, listened as Zweig described the meetings of the Wednesday

Psychological Society, which grouped Freud around a table with his followers, among them Adler and Jung.

'There was mutual suspicion and jealousy between the disciples . . . And there was Freud's even greater suspicion of them. The suspicion and jealousy of a tyrant. Merciless towards anyone who was not steadfast in the doctrine. Especially to anyone who tried to follow his own deviations, in the context of his own ideas which did not coincide with those of the teacher in every respect. The surge of rebellion against the Patriarch-Father . . . The Oedipus Complex . . . is discernible in the strife within the school itself: the sons who encroach upon their father.'[10]

Though his own father had been dead some eight years, Eisenstein never ceased to be fascinated by interpretations of the Oedipus complex and father-son conflicts, which he suffered in various forms, not only with Mikhail Osipovich, but with surrogates like Vsevolod Meyerhold and Josef Stalin.

Zweig offered to introduce Eisenstein to Freud if he came to Vienna, 'an almost unthinkable meeting with this tragic Wotan who stood in the gloaming of bourgeois psychology.' Eisenstein never met Freud, but Zweig later sent him a small volume signed by 'the great Doctor of Vienna . . . It had his characteristic signature – the capital F of his surname.'[11]

Eisenstein once said that he believed that any one of Freud's volumes contained thousands of revolutionary film ideas, and considered that it was impossible in the twentieth century for anyone who wanted to make films or write plays of poetry to do so without reading Freud. Certainly, there is as much of Freud as of Marx in his films.

In May 1928, for the first time since his theatre classes at Proletkult, Eisenstein resumed formal teaching at GTK (State Cinema Technicum, later GIK and VGIK). It was then housed in the former premises of Yar, the notorious restaurant on the Leningrad Chausee, once the haunt of Rasputin and gypsy dancers. The old mirror room of the Yar provided the lecture theatre, its mirrors stretching almost the whole length of the room, and reaching to the ceiling, with tall white columns hiding the narrow piers between them. Vladimir Nizhny, one of the students, described his first lesson.

'Keyed up, the students await the arrival of their teacher. His name is already famous both in our country and abroad, his face is familiar from photographs. Yet not one of us has so far met the man himself. Today he is due to give us his first lecture. A noise at the door, it swings open, and he enters the lecture theatre. We rise in respect and stare intently, but we see neither his figure nor the people who come in with him. All we see, and it registers so that it becomes fixed in our memories forever, is a close-up – the vast dome of forehead crowned with the tangled wreath of hair and, shining from beneath the dome, the shrewd and penetrating eyes. This close-up is endlessly repeated in the mirrors lining the walls of the lecture theatre. A mischievous glint in his eyes. We hear his voice. "Good day, be seated." He gestures towards the reflections in the mirrors and goes on, "One thing at least is obvious – as you perceive, you're going to have not one but a whole bunch of teachers." At once our tension vanished. This was my first meeting with Sergei Mikhailovich Eisenstein. And this is how I always remembered him, no matter how swiftly the years passed, how thin grew the wreath of hair, or how the wrinkles inexorably lined the forehead and set circles round the eyes. The image registered, because throughout the many years that passed afterwards, he stamped it exactly likewise on every generation of students – the enthusiast always striving for something better, always searching for new creative ways and means. You could never tell those eyes a lie, or find anywhere to hide from them with your little creative blunder, which you might have even thought something to be proud of a few moments before.'[12]

As Yutkevich confirmed, 'Eisenstein was an outstanding teacher, not only the possessor of a truly encyclopaedic knowledge, but an artist-teacher, who brought to the task of training new directors not less talent and enthusiasm than to his films and stage productions. He himself never distinguished his scientific, theoretical and teaching activities from his creative work.'[13]

Future director Mikhail Schweitzer, another student, said, 'He was a teacher to everybody. Everybody learned from him whether they wanted to or not. Some learned even by quarrelling with him, for the influence of his work, the way it broke new ground, was so great that he obliged everybody – the most diverse sorts of people – as long as they had a spark of talent burning in them somewhere and weren't complacent – to learn something from his art.'[14]

According to the American Jay Leyda, who became Eisenstein's student in 1933, his lessons 'took the form of explorations, wherein lecturer and pupils together embarked on a voyage of joint discovery of truths, whose logical inevitability, once arrived at, stamped them in the pupil's mind . . . He never simply paraded his knowledge . . . he never condescended; he never looked bored, excepting only if a pupil had not properly prepared his material.'[15]

In August 1928, the Japanese Kabuki theatre visited Moscow, giving Eisenstein his first, exciting experience of Japanese theatre and enhancing his theoretical and experimental progress. Eisenstein invited both the leader of the troupe, Ichikawa Sadanji – 'the Stanislavsky of Tokyo' – and one of the younger artists, Kawarazaki Tsiojuro, to demonstrate some of the methods of the Kabuki actor.

'The extreme precision and measured treatment of every movement that characterises the classical work of Japanese theatre have enormous educational significance for our actors and this is even more true of the film actor than the stage actor,' Eisenstein explained. 'The Japanese have shown us a different and extremely interesting form of ensemble, the *monistic ensemble*. Sound, movement, space and voice *do not accompany* (or even parallel) one another but are treated as *equivalent elements*. The first association that occurs to us in our perception of the Kabuki is football, the most collective ensemble sport. Voice, rattle, mime, the narrator's cries, the folding sets, seem like innumerable backs, half-backs, goal-keepers, forwards passing the dramatic ball to one another and scoring a goal against the astonished audience. It is impossible to speak of "accompaniments" in the Kabuki, just as we would not say that, when we walk or run, the left leg "accompanies" the right, and that they both "accompany" the diaphragm! . . . We actually "hear movement" and "see sound" . . . We too, crossing the successive Rubicons that flow between theatre and cinema and cinema and sound cinema, must also develop it! We must learn this necessary new sense from the Japanese.'[16]

According to Eisenstein, it was the Kabuki method that lay at the basis of the montage for his next film, *The General Line*, already begun before *October*. 'This montage is not constructed on the *individual dominant* but takes the sum of *stimuli* of all the stimulants as the dominant. That distinctive montage *complex within the shot* that arises from the collisions and combinations of the individual stimulants inherent within it.'[17] It was what Eisenstein called 'the fourth dimension in cinema.'

Coming back to *The General Line* after nearly two years, Eisenstein realised that circumstances had changed and that the original scenario no longer corresponded to the contemporary reality of collectivisation at the beginning of Stalin's first Five-Year Plan. He and Alexandrov, who was given a co-director credit, wrote a new, less theoretical scenario, more closely inspired by village life and its continuing problems.

The shooting was dogged by bad weather conditions, so to escape the ice and snow of Rostov-on-Don, the unit first moved to Baku, then to the Kura Lowland and on towards the Persian frontier. There, torrential rain and thick mud again stopped work, and the unit had to move on, this time to the province of Ryazan, then east again to Penza.

Now the film had at its centre a popular heroine, a peasant woman who protests against the general ignorance and apathy of her own district, and with the help of the official representatives of the new policy, inspires her neighbours to form a co-operative.

Pera Attasheva recalled: 'The filming went on but the heroine had not been found. For two months the directors of *The General Line* combed railway stations, night-lodgings, factories. They rode through the country. They summoned women for inspection by ringing church bells. They looked at thousands of faces and tested some of them. No heroine. In this extremity, Eisenstein even decided on a step directly contrary to all his principles originally formulated on beginning this film – he decided to test actresses for the role. Interviews of actresses began. Nothing came of this. Actresses looked insulted when they were asked whether they could milk a cow, or plough, or drive a tractor. They would proudly answer, No! and that would end the interview.'[18] At last, quite by chance, the right person was found: Marfa Lapkina, an illiterate peasant from Konstantinovka, who needed much persuasion to leave her farm work for the filming.

There were further problems in Eisenstein's search for the right faces among the peasantry. 'There was one woman who only agreed to be photographed on condition that she had her mother-in-law beside her because her husband was in another town and she was afraid that people would say bad things about her!!! In this case, there is a device you can use: you arrange the shot so that you can cut out the person you do not want and leave them outside the frame. We had to shoot a wedding scene. The first day we had gathered about twenty girls who were to act in this wedding. Everything was going well and we had started shooting but on the second day not one girl turned up to be filmed. We could not discover why and we made enquiries to find out what could have happened. We were then told that the old women who are always opposed to progress had persuaded the girls that the cameras were able to photograph through their clothes, and the girls who were quite decent when they were being filmed would when projected be as naked as nymphs!!! Naturally nobody wanted us to film them any more and we had to explain to them afterwards that their fears were unfounded. But the interesting thing to note is the premonition of X-rays in this village which imagined that you could photograph through something.'[19] (There is an extraordinary moment in Alexander Medvedkin's *Happiness*, released in 1935, and much admired by Eisenstein, when a priest imagines he sees the breasts of a nun through her habit.)

Shooting went on twelve hours a day, sometimes with as many as five cameras working simultaneously. After the location scenes were completed, the unit returned to Moscow for studio shooting, and the film was ready for showing in April 1929. Suddenly, however, Stalin himself, having seen a rough cut, summoned Eisenstein, Alexandrov and Tisse to the Kremlin to discuss the 'weaknesses' of *The General Line*. It was the first time Eisenstein and Stalin had come face to face. Also present was Nina Agadzhanova-Shutko's husband, who was on the Central Committee and a friend of Eisenstein's since his wife co-wrote the script of *The Battleship Potemkin*.

In his office, two of the leader's cohorts criticised the film while Stalin played the understanding father. He said it could have been worse, and that maybe some peasants were as the film had depicted. This was the kind of ostensibly conciliatory role Stalin liked to play. A possibly apocryphal story was told to illustrate this. Once, after midnight, during a party held at the Kremlin, Stalin demanded that the leading tenor at the Bolshoi be summoned to entertain the guests. The poor man was dragged out of bed, and taken to the Kremlin. 'Sing a Ukrainian song!' shouted one drunken partygoer. 'Sing 'Vesti la giubba'! screamed another. Stalin held up his hand magisterially. 'How dare you!' he said. 'This man is an artist! He has the right to sing what he wishes. Don't you know that he wants to sing Lensky's aria from *Eugene Onegin*!'

Suggestions were made by Stalin to Eisenstein and his two comrades as to how to change the focus of *The General Line*. They were in no position to disagree. Eisenstein then asked Stalin for permission for him, Alexandrov and Tisse to go abroad, ostensibly to study Western sound methods. Eisenstein also added that he would like to make a film of *Das Kapital* there. Stalin replied, 'You're crazy,' and that was the end of that, although he said he would think about giving them permission to travel. (In fact, unbeknownst to Stalin, Joseph Schenck, the president of United Artists, while in Moscow in August 1928, had already been in touch with Eisenstein about the possibility of his working in Hollywood.)

After Shutko had seen the three film-makers out of the Kremlin building and was on the second floor on his way back up the stairs, he was summoned by a soldier to come to the telephone. Shutko took the call. It was Stalin, phoning from his office two floors above. He asked Shutko if Eisenstein had said anything about him. 'Oh yes, you made a very good impression on him, Comrade Stalin. They all liked you very much.' Apparently, Stalin could not wait for Shutko to come back to ask what they had thought of him. Stalin respected Eisenstein as an artist, and probably had him in mind for an eventual biopic of himself. Eisenstein was aware of this need of Stalin's to be praised, and played on it when absolutely necessary.[20]

Following the meeting, Eisenstein spent a further two months of the spring in 1929 chasing from village to village in the Northern Caucasus filming the changes and substitute ending, which he caustically termed 'a kind of emotional semi-epilogue'. Yet even the new ending did not satisfy the official pundits, though the only further alteration they demanded was to change the title, at Stalin's suggestion, from *The General Line* to *The Old and the New*, thus dissociating it from the official policy on agriculture.

Although in May 1928, Stalin had declared that the 'expropriation of the kulaks would be folly', in the summer of 1929 he ordered Party workers to 'liquidate the *kulaks* as a class.' The Party's definition of a *kulak* was a peasant who had more property than his neighbours and therefore might exploit them in some way, a deviation from the Marxist definition of exploiters as those who own the means of production but do not work it themselves.

The decrees of June-July 1929 ended the NEP in the village, and the following year a decree insisted that one-third of the *kulaks* were sent to a concentration camp, one-third were deported to other areas, and one-third was given the worst land. Collectivisation also affected the ordinary poor peasant. Those who resisted inclusion in collective farms were uprooted and transported away from their homes, often to the far north in unheated freight cars. Many times whole villages were simply surrounded and attacked. During this period, a colonel confided to a foreign journalist, 'I am an old Bolshevik. I worked in the underground against the Tsar and then I fought in the Civil War. Did I do all that in order that I should now surround villages with machine-guns and order my men to fire indiscriminately into crowds of peasants? Oh, no, no, no!'

Of course, the negative side of collectivisation could not ever have been depicted in any work of art at the time, let alone in *The General Line* whose didactic purpose was to convince a mass audience, especially the backward peasantry, to accept technical progress and the 'new' form of agricultural organisation. In his copious writings on the film, Eisenstein utters few words on the subject of collectivisation, not out of political timidity, but from a greater interest in the 'methods of montage'; the means not the end. It was parallel with his work on *The General Line* that he began to concentrate more intensely on his theoretical writings which he was to continue throughout his life.

*

More than any of his films, *The General Line* can be seen to have a direct didactic purpose, rather like Brecht's *Lehrstück*, the goals of which were to 'arouse collective feeling and collective consciousness.' Brecht also claimed, 'Bourgeois philosophers make a distinction between the active man and the reflective man. The thinking man draws no such distinction.'

The General Line is a transparent parable and the, sometimes obvious, visual metaphors are much easier to read than in *October*. It opens with Mack Sennett-like twin brothers absurdly dividing their property exactly into two sections, putting up fences and even sawing their house in half. When collectivisation is triumphant, these barriers are knocked down by the tractor, driven by a man in an aviator's cap and goggles – the tractor being as exciting an invention as the aeroplane.

As in the later film of peasant life, *Bezhin Meadow*, Eisenstein used religious imagery in a paradoxical way. The opening shots of a peasant mother with a baby in her arms is meant to evoke a Leonardo *Madonna and Child*. As if to emphasise its pictorial origins, a copy of the *Mona Lisa* is seen in the primitive hut. Eisenstein later makes the contrast between this 'Holy Family' and the religious procession with its fanatical followers ceaselessly crossing themselves and praying, who are, in turn, compared to bleating sheep. Unlike the farm co-operative, the church disappoints its congregation by failing to produce results.

The shiny new cream-separator and tractor are used as symbols of the modern, mechanical age. The model collective farm producing gallons of milk, stacks of grain and tons of meat is first introduced in Marfa's dream. When she wakes up, we are told that it is not a dream but reality, though the farm continues to be filmed in such an idealised way that it seems more like a futuristic projection.

The obstacles on the way to collectivisation are the priests promising salvation in after life, the resistant *kulaks*, superstitious peasants hanging up cattle skulls on trees (a foretaste of the Mexican film), a Macbethian witch brewing up poison to kill the co-operative's animals, and government bureaucracy (portrayed in a Proletkult satiric vein using fast motion). The up-beat ending is Eisenstein's homage to the ironic one in Chaplin's *A Woman of*

Paris (1923). In the latter film, Edna Purviance is sitting at the back of a cart on the road while her former sugar-daddy passes her in his Rolls. In *The General Line*, Marfa, riding her tractor, passes her boyfriend, who is at the back of a cart.

The mock marriage of the cow and the bull is a kitsch Disneyesque parody of a traditional wedding ceremony. As the bovine couple mate, a tremendous rush of water rises orgasmically. The other memorable orgasmic sequence is the moment when the milk hovers for a moment in the spout of the cream-separator before it gushes out producing fountains of thick, white substance, splattering Marfa's face and almost filling the screen. For John Grierson, the 'father' of the British documentary movement, 'the most moving scene in all Eisenstein's work is the sequence . . . where the peasant woman, Marfa (surely the most beautiful face in film history), gets a milk separator to work. In that marvellous passage Eisenstein used the art of montage, and the assembling of images, to express untold joy, and this achievement is pure poetry.'

Marfa herself blossoms from a down-trodden barefoot peasant woman seeking help from a couple of lazy, double-chinned *kulaks*, into an active party worker and, finally, a strong, independent woman (with lipstick!) in her pilot's cap, driving a tractor better than any man. Before that, Marfa, in a semi strip-tease, coquettishly tears off part of her skirt for the use of the mechanic repairing his tractor.

Marfa's role and performance alone is the vociferous response to those critics who have complained Eisenstein shows little interest in women. Although there is less place for them in the male-dominated spheres that inhabit his films – the factory, the navy, the government, the mediaeval soldiery, and the Kremlin in the 16th century – one of the leading organisers of *The Strike* is a vigorous woman; women are the focal point of our sympathy during the massacre on the Odessa Steps; there is the Women's Death Battalion in *October*, and the sensuously filmed bare-breasted girl drifting along the river in a canoe, combing her long black hair, and giving herself to her lover in a hammock in the sun in *Qué Viva México!*; an independently-minded woman is not only the bone of contention between the two brave soldiers in *Alexander Nevsky*, but another female warrior outdoes them in valour. In *Ivan the*

Terrible, besides the lovely Tsarina Anastasia whom the Tsar loves and whose death almost unbalances him, there is the monstrous and manipulative Euphrosinia, dominating every scene in which she appears. Then there are the scenes that Eisenstein was never able to film: the Soldadera episode from *Qué Viva México!*, in which the *soldadera* or soldier's wife would have embodied 'no less than the image of her heroic fighting country'; and in both *The Glass House* and *An American Tragedy*, women would have played prominent roles. As Ian Christie commented, 'If we could see the films Eisenstein didn't make alongside the films he did get made, I think we would have a very different picture of him.'[21]

While immersed in the 'creative ecstasy' of editing *The General Line*, Eisenstein attended the premiere of *Arsenal*, Dovzhenko's highly symbolic and lyrical account of the Ukraine's emergence from feudalism. After the showing, Eisenstein, with Pudovkin and Dovzhenko, the three greatest Soviet directors, held a party over some sandwiches and mineral water, launching into high-spirited impersonations of Leonardo (Eisenstein), Michelangelo (Dovzhenko) and Raphael (Pudovkin). It was a riotous game, in and out of upturned tables and chairs, that went on till dawn. Subsequently, the relationship between the three became more strained as did the relationship between the State and themselves.

Eisenstein and Pudovkin, who had written theoretical pamphlets on the cinema (published later as *Film Technique*), clashed on the theory of montage. As Eisenstein explained, Pudovkin as 'a graduate of the Kuleshov school . . . zealously defends the concepts of montage as a series of fragments. In a chain. Bricks. Bricks that expound an idea serially. I opposed him with my view of montage as *collision*, my view that the collision of two factors gives rise to an idea . . . We already got into the habit: at regular intervals he comes to see me late at night and, behind closed doors, we wrangle over matters of principle.'[22]

All this, however, was on the eve of Eisenstein's extremely consequential three-year absence from the USSR, during which collision came to mean a lot more than an aesthetic credo.

PART II

Mr Eisenstein in the Land of the Capitalists

8

Western Approaches

To go abroad – it presents the ultimate test that one can set a Soviet citizen whose life has been inseparable from the October Revolution: the test of a free choice. Going abroad offers the final challenge to the creative worker: to prove whether he can really create outside the Revolution; whether he can even exist outside it.

The Moscow premiere of *The General Line*, retitled *The Old and the New*, the last film Eisenstein would complete for nearly ten years, took place on the anniversary of the Revolution, November 7, 1929. Yet, for once, Eisenstein was not present, and neither were Alexandrov and Tisse. They had already left for Berlin, preparing to tour Western Europe and thereafter embark for the United States of America.

A couple of years after Douglas Fairbanks and Mary Pickford's visit to Moscow in July 1926, during which they promised to invite Eisenstein to work for United Artists in Hollywood, Joseph Schenck, the president of UA, when in Moscow, reiterated the invitation. Schenck, who was born in Russia but who had lived in the USA from early childhood, had produced a number of films starring his brother-in-law, Buster Keaton.

When Schenck was touring the new Potylikha studio and criticising its layout, people were derogatory about Hollywood in front of him in Russian, until he shocked them by suddenly asking them questions in their own language, adding that on his way back he might visit his grandfather in Minsk.

Sovkino joined in the negotiations with Schenck, but at the

beginning of 1929 Eisenstein commented wryly, 'I won't really be sure whether I'm going until I'm on my way back home from there.'[1] On June 4, 1929, Eisenstein wrote to Léon Moussinac outlining his immediate plans and ambitions.

'My personal future is gradually taking shape. It is my obsession to add sound to *The Old and the New*, and to do that I must go abroad . . . Then after the European premiere I want to go to the USA. The Hollywood side of the USA doesn't interest me at all; I want to see the country! And the techniques of sound films. For I am absolutely certain that the entire future of the cinema lies with sound.'[2]

The reason for the trip was to study the use of synchronised sound, which at that time had not yet been developed in the Soviet cinema. But such a journey presented problems that were more than just technical; they were also political and philosophical, and Eisenstein himself was well aware of them.

In August 1929, Eisenstein left for Western Europe with Alexandrov and Tisse. Everywhere the three Russians were greeted with delight by film enthusiasts and harassed by government agencies who, with the increasing political isolation of the Soviet Union, treated them as undesirable visitors. The first stop was Berlin, where they attended the European premiere of *The Old and the New* on which Eisenstein wanted to collaborate with Edmund Meisel on the music.

The magnificent reception given to the film was marred by the news that Schenck's offer of a Hollywood contract had fallen through. Nevertheless, the three of them determined to continue on their way to America, although they had arrived in Germany with only $25 apiece that Soyuzkino had given them for expenses. For a while, they boarded with Eisenstein's widowed stepmother Elizabeth Michelsohn, and had to live on the charity of friends while trying to earn their way. With this in mind, Eisenstein had brought some of his writings to sell (the scenario of *The Old and the New* had just been published).

From Berlin, the trio left for Switzerland where they had been invited to the First International Congress of Independent

Cinematography. At the frontier, however, the party was refused permission to enter the country. The refusal was rescinded twenty-four hours later, but only after their hostess had intervened. It was the first of a trail of difficulties that they would come up against on their travels.

The Congress was held between September 3 and 7 at the Chateau of La Sarraz near Lausanne, which the owner, Madame de Mandrot, had offered as a meeting-place for a group of avant-garde film-makers. (She had already hosted congresses for leftist architects and musicians.)

'La belle chatelaine', as the delegates addressed her, was a cinema enthusiast, as well as having a weakness for Russians on whose departure she was to sigh, 'Oh! Those Bolsheviks! . . . The only true gentlemen!'[3]

The Congress was organised on the initiative of Robert Aron and Janine Bouissounouse, and was intended to bring together film-makers from all over the world who were eager to establish an independent industry, unfettered by commercial interests, and to lay the foundations for an International Film-making Co-operative with its headquarters in Paris. Among the sponsors were André Gide, Luigi Pirandello and Stefan Zweig, and included in the cosmopolitan gathering who attended were the experimental film-makers Walter Ruttmann, Alberto Cavalcanti and Hans Richter; Jack Isaacs, a British professor of English literature and one of the leading members of the London Film Society; the Hungarian film theorist Béla Balázs, Jean-Georges Auriol, the editor and founder of the *Revue du Cinéma* (the forerunner of *Cahiers du Cinéma*), Léon Moussinac, Enrico Prampolini, a fascist member of the Italian Futurist movement and co-author with Filippo Marinetti of the Futurist Manifesto, and twenty-five-year-old Ivor Montagu, a film-maker, writer and table-tennis champion, whom Eisenstein recalled as 'a particularly outspoken Englishman from Cambridge.'

The third son of the second Baron Swaythling, the Jewish Montagu developed a lifelong commitment to left-wing politics at Cambridge. In 1925, with Sidney Bernstein, he founded the Film Society in London with the main aim of showing the German and Russian films which were excluded from distribution. Among the

Society's patrons were Bertrand Russell, Julian Huxley, Maynard Keynes and H.G. Wells.

'The biggest star' attending, according to *Le Cinéma Suisse*, was Eisenstein. Ivor Montagu recollected: 'Before they [Eisenstein, Alexandrov and Tisse] arrived we had all been sitting and chatting together in this gorgeous chateau, with its superb tapestry and its medieval walls, admiring each other's films, and saying how wonderful and imaginative and important was everything we had done. Then, suddenly, as though through outer space, there came these three characters from the Soviet Union. As far as we were concerned they were already magnificent before they spoke a single word or performed a single action. We all knew and admired *The Battleship Potemkin*, and we regarded Eisenstein as an almost divine figure. And now here they were, three men in boiler suits; Eisenstein himself was short and squat, with the huge head that we already recognised from photographs, and a gigantic quiff, and eyes that sparkled with an amiable malice. The other two, Alexandrov and Tisse, were extremely good-looking, one younger than the other, but each with golden hair and golden skin, and both of them full of boundless energy.'[4]

At the chateau they showed, among other films, *The Old and the New*, Luis Buñuel's startling first film, *Un Chien Andalou*, Carl Dreyer's *The Passion of Joan of Arc*, considered by Eisenstein to be 'one of the most beautiful pictures in the entire history of the cinema', Man Ray's *L'Étoile de Mer*, three of Richter's 'absolute' films, in which he also acted with the composers Paul Hindemith and Darius Milhaud; Walter Ruttmann's *Berlin – Die Symphonie einer Grosstadt* (*Berlin: Symphony of a Great City*), Joris Ivens' *The Bridge* and *Rain*, and Alberto Cavalcanti's *Rien que les heures* and *Le Petit Chaperon Rouge* (*Little Red Riding Hood*), which featured Jean Renoir as the wolf, and his wife Catherine Hessling in the title role. In other words, an impressive panorama of the best avant-garde films of the day.

'For three or four hours our Soviet visitors behaved impeccably', wrote Montagu, 'and then they suggested that we should all stop talking and make a film. The immediate consequence of this proposal – which of course the rest of us accepted at once – was total annihilation of poor Mme de Mandrot. Her precious shields, the costumes and helmets and rare old weapons . . . everything was dragged from the walls. We were then all enlisted by Eisenstein and his two friends into a film that was really a dramatic simile of the commercial cinema, in which the art of film was at first imprisoned and rescued by the assembled intellectuals of La Sarraz. We all wore costumes of various shapes and colours and periods of history, but Eisenstein was careful not to make himself the director. He just ran about as a general dog's body. It was my first introduction to him, and what I remember most about it all are his boyish spirits.'[5]

The film, *The Storming of La Sarraz*, was shot in one day and never edited. Janine Bouissounouse, personifying The Spirit of the Artistic Film, dressed in white with her bosoms stuffed with two film reels, was fastened with chains to the chateau's chimney stack by the villainous Béla Balázs, the Commander of the Army of the Commercial Cinema, and had to be rescued by The Army of Independents led by Eisenstein. Jack Isaacs, who played a big business tycoon of Balázs' Commercial Army, sweated under a heavy suit of medieval armour decked with ostrich feathers. Several ghosts appeared, one of whom was Léon Moussinac, swathed in a white sheet as d'Artagnan. Jean-Georges Auriol, brandishing a copy of the *Revue du Cinéma* as a banner, joined in the fray with his typewriter-turned-machine-gun. In the culminating sequence a Japanese member of the Congress, symbolising the 'commercial film', committed hari-kiri.

This inconsequential allegory of the conflict between the exigencies of commercial cinema and those of art was obviously close to the heart (and reality) of the celebrated participants. Although this little film could not possibly be considered in the same hemisphere as *Bezhin Meadow*, it is a pity that it too has been lost. One theory was that Hans Richter, in the process of taking the film to London after the congress, left it on the train. Another was that a Japanese member at the chateau took it back to Japan, where it might have been destroyed during the bombing of 1945. Luckily, a number of still photographs were taken of many of the participants in their costumes and attitudes.

Although Eisenstein was enraptured by the company of his peers at La Sarraz and enjoyed their admiration, he was conscious of the necessity to earn some money. While he was in Switzerland, a young Swiss producer, Lazar Wechsler, suggested to Eisenstein that he might direct a short documentary on the subject of abortion in Zurich. Eisenstein refused, saying, 'Let me abort all Zurich, then I'm interested; but one woman, definitely no! After all, I am a director of mass spectacles.'[6] Tisse, however, took up the offer to direct, with advice from Eisenstein. Called *Frauennot-Frauenglück* (*Woman's Joy is Woman's Woe*), it portrayed a slum family expecting yet another child; the mother has an illegal abortion and suffers serious physical damage as a result of the incompetence of the doctor who performs it. (In 1935, Wechsler added new sequences with synchronised sound, which is the only version available.) On the strength of *The General Line*, a Swiss dairy firm offered Eisenstein the chance to make an advertising film. Turning it down, he hoped to give a series of lectures in Switzerland before the Swiss authorities again raised objections and asked him to leave the country.

Back in Berlin, Eisenstein helped on an advertising film for beer, with the American screen actor George Bancroft and Emil Jannings, who had only recently returned from America, and had begun filming *The Blue Angel* under Josef von Sternberg's direction. At the coming of sound, Jannings' thick German accent had put an end to his short Hollywood career, during which he became the first star to win the Best Actor Oscar (for *The Way of All Flesh* and Sternberg's *The Last Command*). Jannings, who three years earlier, had been cool to Eisenstein during the making of *Faust*, insisted that the Russian director make a film on Prince Potemkin, the lover of Catherine the Great, with him in the title role. 'Potemkin had only one eye. If you were to do the film I would gouge out one of mine,' Jannings told Eisenstein.[7]

Sternberg showed Eisenstein the rushes of *The Blue Angel*. 'He took each scene about twenty times,' Eisenstein recalled. 'He had a most pronounced inferiority complex . . . Snobbery could not hide Sternberg's trauma about his own inadequacy . . . A predilection for well-built males probably brought Sternberg some compensation. In Berlin, he even stayed at the Hercules Hotel, across the Hercules Bridge, opposite the Hercules Fountain with its huge grey statue of Hercules . . .'[8]

This curious statement by Eisenstein seems to be completely unfounded, unless the heady atmosphere of the last days of the Weimar Republic was penetrating everybody's psyche. The sexual licence in Berlin at the time highlighted the conflicts in Eisenstein's own sexuality. Certainly, codified notes in his diaries hint at wet daydreams, many of them involving Grigori Alexandrov.

Much concerned about these desires, he visited the psychoanalyst Dr Hanns Sachs, a disciple of Freud, 'a shrewd old salamander with the horn-rimmed glasses.' Eisenstein remembered that 'he had a terrifying African mask – "a symbol of complexes" – which hung above his small, low, patient's couch. We became great friends. He gave me a most interesting book about psychoanalysis. *Essay in Genital Theory* by Sandor Ferenczi, which explained a great deal of things (admittedly post factum!) which I had come across on my obsessive quest to penetrate the secrets of ecstasy.'[9]

Eisenstein also visited the *Institut für Geschlechts Wissenschaft* (The Institute of Sexual Science) under the directorship of Magnus Hirschfeld, where sexual 'abnormality' was analysed. The following year, in his notes for the death-cell scene for the screenplay of *An American Tragedy*, Eisenstein has Clyde Griffiths visited by a psychiatrist modelled on Magnus Hirschfeld.

He was particularly engrossed in the study of homosexuality, but, as he told Hans Feld, a friend, 'My observations led me to the conclusion that homosexuality is in all ways a retrogression – a going back to the state where procreation came with the dividing of the cells. It's a dead end!'[10] This may have accounted for his interest in pre-natal experience. Ian Christie believes, 'He was a figure that felt outside of sexuality. Something the grown-ups did.'[11] In a sense, his erotic drawings, puns and jokes do have the element of a little boy giggling at 'rude' words. Eisenstein confided to Marie Seton, 'A lot of people say I'm homosexual. I never have been, and I'd tell you if it were true. I've never felt any such desire, not even towards Grisha [Alexandrov] though I think I must, in some way, have bisexual tendencies – like Zola and Balzac – in an *intellectual* [author's italics] way.'[12]

Presumably what he meant in reference to the two 19th-century French novelists was their ability to enter all their characters' psyches, regardless of gender. His meaning was less clear in his own case. Anyway, Eisenstein was given plenty of opportunity to satisfy these tendencies in both an 'intellectual' and a carnal way in the notoriously decadent night-life of Berlin in the late 1920s.

Apart from visiting homosexual clubs, both male and female, the lionised Eisenstein was able to meet many of the great artists and intellectuals of the day, who found themselves in Berlin in 1929. Under the influence of the Soviets, working class theatrical groups, the German counterparts of the Proletkult, calling themselves Red Shirts and Red Rockets, had sprung up around the city. Between 1928 and 1930, there were about three hundred such groups in Germany. Alongside them were the more professional agit-prop associations, many inspired by Erwin Piscator, originator of the 'epic' theatre.

At the time of Eisenstein's visit, Piscator, who married Vera Yanukova, the actress in *Every Wise Man* and *The Strike*, had reached the peak of his achievements. Writers and artists such as Bertolt Brecht, Georg Grosz and John Heartfield had joined him at the Theater am Nollendorfplatz. One of the first directors to employ films and animated cartoons on stage, Piscator introduced a background film of Red soldiers on the march in his production of Alexei Tolstoy's *Rasputin*, and the sardonic drawings of Grosz illuminated his staging of *The Good Soldier Schweik*.

Piscator had opened his first season with Ernst Toller's expressionist drama *Hoppla! wir leben*. Eisenstein described a visit he paid to Toller's 'two small clean rooms which were a little effeminate in their floral decorations.' At the end of the visit, the thirty-six-year-old Toller, who had been imprisoned for his part in the Communist uprising of 1919, told Eisenstein he could take whatever he liked from his apartment as a memento. 'What should I take? Taking nothing might have caused offence. On the wall hung two early Daumier lithographs. Not particularly good ones. They were in narrow gilt frames. A cup, perhaps? One of the little vases? . . . There *was* something! A Mexican horseman made of wickerwork – a toy which, in its style and method of weaving looked like Russian bast-work. I took that. A little later – terrible embarrassment. The horseman had belonged to Elisabeth Bergner.'[13] Bergner, one of the most popular actresses at the time, had been Toller's lover for a short period.

Fortunately, considering his financial situation, Eisenstein hardly paid for a meal during his stay in Berlin. One evening he was at a Japanese restaurant dining with two Japanese film executives returning the courtesy after a visit to Moscow, the next at an Indian restaurant where Rabindranath Tagore's nephew was repaying his hosts for a reception in Moscow.

Eisenstein had a meal with Luigi Pirandello in a small Italian restaurant in Charlottenburg, on one of the less frequented Berlin side-streets. At the lunch was a gentleman who was a good friend of Otto H. Kahn, the American banker and patron of the arts. Eisenstein saw him as a potential patron who would somehow get him a contract in America. In fact, Paramount had invited Pirandello to Hollywood. But Eisenstein admitted that his 'interest in the business side of the meeting was slight.' What preoccupied him most was the delicious *zabaglione* and Pirandello sitting in front of him, despite his lack of appreciation of the Italian play-wright's work. 'If I were "in search of an author", I would hardly turn to him. He is too *fin-de-siécle* somehow.'[14]

Eisenstein remembered another business dinner, at the Hotel Adlon, during which he felt most uncomfortable. 'I experienced for the first time how inconvenient a butler can be if he stands behind your high-backed chair . . . These men walked up and down in their light blue coats and whipped the unfinished plates of steak away, shoving a salad before you, suddenly covering a dish that you were barely familiar with, with a dressing you weren't expect-ing. They seemed irritated, annoyed. Here, appearing out of nowhere, these hands paralysed your oesophagus.'[15]

There was talk of his making a film of Albert Londres' book, *Le Chemin de Buenos Aires* (the English edition had an introduction by Theodore Dreiser) about white slave traffic to Brazil. He also discussed a film *for* dogs with Jascha Schatzow, a representative of Debrie, the ciné camera manufacturers.

'He was interested by this, bearing in mind that Berliners of both sexes were very fond of their dogs – and there was a colossal number of dogs in Berlin. If one of the most picturesque graveyards in Paris is the one for dogs in Auteuil, then why should Berlin not have its own charmingly appointed dogs' cinema? This thought occupied me, of course, purely from the point of view of a reflex testing of a series of filmic elements (the degree of suggestiveness, questions of rhythm, "form", which would all be different from our customary system of thinking and imagery, and so on.) The project, of course, remained just that, going no further than two conversations: one in Schatzow's amazing billiard room in his house, and one in a nightclub in Berlin.'[16]

Eisenstein had formulated many of his theories before becoming acquainted with the physiologist Ivan Pavlov's work on the 'conditioned reflex'. Seven years later, in his 'Teaching Programme for the Theory and Practice of Direction' at the State Film School, Eisenstein included the study of Pavlov 'as an adjunct to the question of expressiveness.' In an interview, Eisenstein once claimed that his three gods were Marx, Pavlov and Freud.

At the invitation of the workers' cinema club, Volksfilmverband, he left Berlin for a three-day visit to Hamburg. Ten cinemas had been hired for a Sunday morning showing of *October*, but still crowds had to be turned away. At one of the cinemas, he gave a short introduction and met the audience afterwards. The rest of the time he spent touring Hamburg and meeting cinema enthusiasts.

On his return he felt unwell. He mentioned cardiac weakness – the phragma behind the left and right ventricles had never grown properly – which had troubled him earlier, and which was clearly linked to the infarct which was to kill him less than twenty years later. Some years before, in Moscow, he had visited a doctor who recommended that he take a break from his usual activities and mental pursuits. 'Take up photography!' advised the doctor. This was reminiscent of the story of the great French pantomimist Jean-Gaspard Deburau, who went to a doctor complaining of depression. The doctor's advice? 'If you want cheering up, go and see Deburau.'

The director Friedrich Ermler arrived in Berlin where he shared the furnished room which Eisenstein had at the Pension Marie-Luise in Martin Lutherstrasse. Ermler, born in Latvia in the same year as Eisenstein, was the director of *Fragment of an Empire*, just released in Russia, a film which combined political parable with social satire. He had organised KEM (the Experimental Film Workshop), which advocated revolution through content rather than form. Ermler and Eisenstein had little in common.

One night, while the two of them were lying on their two king-size beds, Ermler mentioned that 'No word of you has reached Moscow . . . in Moscow they feel that your travels lack impact . . .' Eisenstein mused that 'nobody in Moscow understood, obviously, that to go to Hollywood – the aim of the trip – was a problem fraught with difficulties. Negotiations took up a great deal of time. Still, in Moscow, in Moscow cinema circles, they felt that my travels – what was the phrase he used – lacked impact? "Now, if you would cause a bit of a stir, politically, somewhere . . ." "Cause a bit of a stir? Lacking impact? Wait let me find a way. Give me time. Moscow will be happy." What form would it take? For the present nobody knew . . . The light went out. We both fell asleep.'[17]

In November 1929, a month after the Wall Street Crash, the consequences of which were becoming evident, Eisenstein collected Tisse and Alexandrov in Zurich and together they all went to Paris where the editing of *Woman's Joy is Woman's Woe* would be completed.

At the end of the month, Eisenstein crossed to England where he had been invited by Ivor Montagu and Jack Isaacs as a guest of the London Film Society, for which he would give a series of lectures and attend a showing of *The Battleship Potemkin*, still forbidden to the general public. Sir William Joynson-Hicks, the anti-Semitic Home Secretary who disliked films in general and radical films in particular, was responsible for the banning. H.G. Wells, protesting about the censors, declared, 'We cannot be allowed to be ruled by a gang of mystery men.' In a letter to the socialist M.P. Fenner Brockway, George Bernard Shaw wrote, '*Potemkin* was exhibited to me privately. It is, artistically, one of the very best films in existence. Its suppression is an undisguised stroke of class censorship, utterly indefensible and inexplicable on any other ground. Simply an incident in the class war, as waged by our governing classes. Remind them of it when they next wax indignant against Soviet censorship.'[18]

In Britain, the provocative film could not have arrived at a worse time. The General Strike had collapsed earlier in the year and fear of a working class insurrection dominated the newly-elected Conservative government under Stanley Baldwin. Eisenstein visited the Houses of Parliament to watch Lloyd George argue for the recognition of the Soviet Union by the United Kingdom.

Potemkin was kept out of British cinemas until 1954. Eisenstein later commented: 'One censor was blind: for silent films? Another was deaf: for talkies? and, while I was there, the third one actually died! True, none of this was enough to ensure that my films were shown in London although the Board of Censors is not even a governmental body.'[19]

Many years later, in 1946, the British censor writing a note on the Boulting Brothers' social drama *Fame is the Spur*, scribbled 'Very reminiscent of the famous Montague [*sic*] in the Russian films, *Potemkin* and *Odessa* [*sic*] many shots of which the Board cut.' Someone then drew a pencil line through 'Montague' and inserted 'montage'.[20]

Among the films first shown at the Sunday performances at the New Gallery Kinema were *Nosferatu*, *Greed*, and *The Passion of Joan of Arc*. On this Sunday in November 1929, the Film Society gave a double bill of John Grierson's *Drifters* (a study of herring fishing in the North Sea) and *The Battleship Potemkin*. However, after the screening, Eisenstein, never one to mince words, said that the Film Society's version of his film, with music by Edmund Meisel, had transformed a fine work into a 'mediocre opera'. For this he blamed Meisel for having run 'the speed of the projector to suit the music, without my consent, slightly more slowly than it should have been! This destroyed the dynamism of the rhythmic correlation to such an extent that people laughed at the "flying lions" for the first time in the film's existence. The time allowed for the three different lions to merge into one, was crucial: if it took any longer than that the artifice would be spotted.'[21]

This caused a split with Meisel, although Eisenstein later added another reason. According to Eisenstein, Meisel's wife, Elisabeth, 'was unable to hide – indeed in an inexplicable outburst, confessed to her husband – a certain liaison that had existed between her and the director of the film for which he had written the music.'[22]

There seems no other evidence of this so-called 'liaison' between Eisenstein and Meisel's wife other than this statement from someone who once wrote about his own 'Donjuanism.' This was defined as 'a fear for one's own potency. It sees each successive conquest as yet further proof of one's potency. But why admit Donjuanism only in sex? It is a much stronger impulse in other areas, especially those where the important questions are to do with "success", "recognition" and "winning", which are no less important than sexual conquest.'[23]

Eisenstein's lectures in London, where 'I found the authentic atmosphere of Oscar Wilde',[24] were presented as part of a course of film studies that also included a lesson in practical film-making under the direction of Hans Richter. Richter gave film-directing classes in his studio over Foyle's bookshop in Charing Cross Road. A short film was made, of which only a brief sequence remains. This shows Eisenstein miming the part of a London bobby complete with uniform and helmet. At first he looks stern, then makes funny faces, blows a whistle and does a little can-can, kicking his legs up in the air. Perhaps he would have satisfied his own criteria for *typage* as a British policeman. It was characteristic of his sense of satirical observation and also, typically, was never in the original script.

Eisenstein's actual lectures, delivered at Foyle's in excellent English, were a tremendous success, and had a profound influence on the British documentary movement. John Grierson, the leading force behind the movement, never hesitated to acknowledge his personal debt to Eisenstein. 'All of us in the British documentary movement were influenced by Eisenstein's "montage", but in its poetic possibilities rather than its intellectual ambition . . . if you want to know where the courage of *Song of Ceylon* came from, or the courage of poetry in *Night Mail*, then you must go to the poetic rather than the violent sequences in Eisenstein.'[25]

Basil Wright, the future director of *Song of Ceylon* (1934) and *Night Mail* (1936) was then an enthusiastic twenty-two-year-old student at Eisenstein's lectures, of which he gave the following description: 'There we were, with notebooks and pencils, thinking passionately about films, the great new art form; and there was Eisenstein, chubbily built, plump in face; a pliable and expressive nose; a shock of dark hazel-coloured curly hair rising briskly from an imposing brow. There he was, with blackboard and chalk, about to expose us to the inner Eisenstein mysteries of film art. But what happened? He talked instead of Japanese Kabuki plays, about William James and Charles Darwin, Toulouse-Lautrec and Daumier; about Kenyon's proposition that "two opposite reactions can be provoked by the same stimulus"; about Duchenne's studies of muscular movements, and his conclusion that "L'action musculaire isolé n'existe pas dans l'expression humaine", about Stefan Zweig, Zola and James Joyce. As the lectures progressed we began to understand and appreciate all these surprising references. Eisenstein never forgot that film is a synthetic art. He made it clear that the approach to film theory, and in particular to montage, was not something in a vacuum. He claimed, in fact, that film montage was the cinematic aspect of a particular form of expression used by artists in other media – and in particular in poetry, painting, drama and the novel.'[26]

Others, still in their twenties, who attended the lectures, were Anthony Asquith, Thorold Dickinson, Ian Dalrymple and Herbert Marshall, later to become Eisenstein' student in Moscow. Ivor Montagu commented: 'How live he was! How one could laugh with him!'[27] Jack Isaacs thought Eisenstein was 'the most intelligent man I ever knew, and one of the nicest, with a sense of humour both robust and Rabelaisian.'[28]

The ginger-haired, myopic bald-headed Jack Isaacs, who had been at La Sarraz, showed Eisenstein around Oxford, Hampton Court, Windsor, Eton and the Tower of London. Eisenstein concluded, 'Properly speaking, you will understand nothing about the composition of a Briton – and a Briton as a civil servant above all – without a visit to the Penates of his logical development – Eton, Cambridge (or Oxford), London with the Tower, Westminster, the gentlemen's clubs and Whitehall.'[29]

Of Isaacs Eisenstein wrote, 'He was like something out of a Dickens novel, with his black gloves, inevitable black umbrella and galoshes all day long, all year round.'[30] At Windsor, Eisenstein admired Rubens' *The Rape of Ganymede*, 'who was here portrayed as a chubby little boy of six or seven. His mortal fear burst out in a stream he could not contain.'[31] One picture at the National

Gallery affected him profoundly, El Greco's *Agony In the Garden*, which he saw as 'a scream of colours.' It 'stood out sharply in the dull rooms . . . The dark red of the garment cuts like a razor through the greenery . . . It was as if I had already *known* it, seen it somewhere.' What the painting reminded him of was a priest from his childhood, who 'went through Holy Week as if suffering the Lord's Passion.'[32]

At Cambridge University, according to Professor Maurice Dobb, Eisenstein 'talked magnificently and . . . the audience listened to him spellbound . . . When he started to talk (and at that time he knew English reasonably well) he talked with great animation and force, using words with great deliberation and the sense of their import and meaning.'[33]

Pyotr Kapitsa, the Soviet physicist who worked with Ernest Rutherford at Cambridge, invited Eisenstein to high table at Trinity 'with the professors and the Master, beneath the high Gothic vaulting of the naves which vanished into the gloom . . . the antiphonic prayers sung in Latin by two voices before the food was served . . . the general setting and atmosphere of the whole scene remained so powerful that after many years it could still "surface", first on the screen of my memories and then in the screen images of *Ivan the Terrible* in the antiphonic reading of the psalter and the report of the boyar's treachery with the overlying voices of Pimen and Malyuta in the scene with Ivan and Anastasia's coffin.'[34] Even knowing of Eisenstein's extensive spectrum of allusions, it is surprising that so quintessential an English ritual and setting should have influenced such quintessentially Russian ones.

What interested Eisenstein at Madame Tussaud's, given his fascination with the French Revolution, was the chamber of horrors and the fact that the waxworks were founded when Monsieur Tussaud brought two wax models of the severed heads of Louis XVI and Marie Antoinette to London. He visited the British Museum where he pored over a letter written by Elizabeth I, the contemporary of Ivan the Terrible, to Mary Stuart in her dungeon. Much more exciting was, as he put it, a letter 'written by a young, dark-skinned French Commander-in-Chief, of Corsican extraction.' In the letter to his brother from the battlefields of Africa, Napoleon wrote: 'I am bored with human nature. I need solitude and isolation.

Greatness bores me. My feelings are dried up. Glory is insipid at twenty-nine-years-old. I have done everything. Only one thing is left: to become a true egotist.'

Thirty-one-year-old Eisenstein left London towards the end of December 1929, concluding that England was 'hidebound, petrified and conservative. It is difficult to say what gives rise to this physical sensation that you feel again when your foot touches its soil . . . The why and wherefore of this image is not important, but only half an hour from the moment you've begun to get to know London, Cambridge, Oxford or Windsor, this image is inevitably implanted in you causing you an almost physical pain.'[35]

He had hoped to spend Christmas in Switzerland, but once again he was refused entry and so stayed in Paris, revising the manuscript of some theoretical studies, until the middle of January, when he set off on another lecture tour.

The first stop was Antwerp, followed by Seraing-la-Rouge, a suburb of Liège where workers, who had seen a clandestine showing of *The Battleship Potemkin*, welcomed him warmly. He intended visiting Ostend and the ageing artist James Ensor, whose works he much admired, but repeated pestering from police enforced his hurried departure for Holland. His arrival in Rotterdam was greeted by a battery of journalists and photographers who thought they were meeting Albert Einstein.

'Ever since my childhood I had been unable to dissociate Van Houten's cocoa, the pointed caps of the ladies, and of course huge wooden clogs, from my idea of Holland. My first question when I got off the train was, "Where are the clogs, then?" The next day all the papers carried the banner headline, "Where are the clogs, then?" Eisenstein asks.'[36]

Following a lecture in Rotterdam, Eisenstein left for the Hague, where he went to the Van Gogh museum and enjoyed 'the whirlwind of colour produced in Arles by the great madman with the missing ear.'[37] In an essay on montage in 1937, Eisenstein wrote of Van Gogh's 'unity between drawing as gesture and the power of colour as the basis of representation . . . It is a mistake to take the crazy, wriggling outline of what he is depicting as *drawing* in our sense of the word. Drawing and contour in our sense burst out of these limitations and surge into the heart of the colour background itself, solidified by means not only of a new dimension but of a new expressive environment and material: *by the movement of the brushstrokes*, which simultaneously both create and define the picture's areas of colour.'[38]

During these travels he wrote several articles on the adventures of 'Eisenstein's team' which were published in the Moscow *Kino* under the pseudonym of R. Orick, echoing Rorick, the nickname his nanny had given him as a child. After spending his birthday in Berlin, Eisenstein was back in Paris in February 1930, where he was to satisfy Moscow's call for him to 'cause a bit of a stir, politically . . .'

9

A Russian in Paris

I am a Westerner. I feel at home in Paris. I feel as though I'm walking across the pages of books when I am there. There is Victor Hugo, there the Three Musketeers . . . And so I stood there in that Paris, whose ancient masonry appealed to the best in mankind, and at the same time I was in the grip of reactionaries who permitted the nearest sign of freedom to vanish without trace!

During his second, longer visit to Paris, Eisenstein stayed at the tiny Hotel des États Unis at 135 Avenue Montparnasse. 'I was preoccupied with the United States. Which was why out of all the possible small hotels I might have taken – and of which there were dozens in that area! – I chose the one with the sign announcing the aim of my wanderings.'[1] But he was no closer to getting a contract in Hollywood, and had to earn more money than was provided either by friends or by lectures in the meantime.

Luckily, Grigori Alexandrov's charm had persuaded Leonard Rosenthal, a millionaire Parisian jeweller, owner of the Maison de Perles, to sponsor a short film whose main purpose was to indulge his Russian mistress, Mara Gris, who could sing *chansons* reasonably well, and longed to act in a film.

With Tisse as his cinematographer, Alexandrov was permitted by the police to motor across France, shooting forests, landscapes, seascapes in Brittany and flowers in bloom in Provence. The film was called *Romance Sentimentale*, and Mara Gris was seen 'singing a sentimental song while gazing tearfully at the rain' as Eisenstein told his friends, taking off her actions as he did so.[2]

It is a strangely quirky twenty-minute film that opens with a four-minute montage sequence of the billowing sea (almost the same as the opening shot of *The Battleship Potemkin*), and a storm in which trees are blown down. What these rather arbitrary nature scenes have to do with what follows is unclear unless they represent the torment within Mademoiselle. She sings the sad Russian song at a grand piano, while her greyhound looks dolefully on. Then, suddenly, she is spirited up into the sky, playing a white piano in the clouds, before returning to her drawing room. At the happy ending, she is back in the clouds, smiling for the first time as the sun comes up.

Although Eisenstein's name appears on the credits as co-director (the producer insisted on it), his participation in it was peripheral, and it was largely the work of Alexandrov. But the opening sequence bears his mark. Edited to a mixed track of music and natural sounds, it gave Eisenstein the first opportunity to experiment with some of the ways in which images and sound might be used together both creatively and emotively.

Eisenstein himself later wrote a fair summary of *Romance Sentimentale* in a letter to Léon Moussinac. 'You know very well that there's not a lot of me in it (to say the least), except for the principles and possibilities of sound utilisation that are popularised in it . . . In any case we got what we wanted from it; we made some very valuable montage experiments, and it gave us enough money to stay in Paris.'[3]

One of the first among the roster of luminaries that Eisenstein met during his four-month sojourn in Paris was the cosmopolitan composer Darius Milhaud. Together they 'strutted along in our broad overcoats, headed for the Galeries Rosenberg. A "house" which dealt exclusively in Picasso and Braque.'[4] Eisenstein adored Milhaud's Brazilian-inspired orchestral piece, *Le Boeuf sur le Toit*, to which Jean Cocteau later wrote a choreographic scenario that is enacted in an American bar during the Prohibition period.

In the nightclub named after the piece, Eisenstein watched Kiki (the stage name of the cabaret artist Alice Irine) doing a bellydance in Spanish shawls on top of a grand piano played by Georges-Henri Rivière, curator of the Trocadéro Museum and father-in-law to Paul Cézanne's son. Kiki gave Eisenstein a copy of her memoirs suggestively signed: '*Car moi aussi j'aime les gros bateaux et les matelots.*' ('Because I also love big boats and sailors.')[5] In the estimation of the Cuban cinematographer Nestor Almendros, 'Kiki was no dummy, and might have owed her great popularity not only to her good looks but to her wit. That *clin d'oeil* (wink) to the Soviet film director proved that she had a better insight into *The Battleship Potemkin*, otherwise considered an austere film, than most of her contemporary critics and scholars with their Marxist analysis.'[6]

Besides modelling for most of the leading artists of Montparnasse, Kiki was a painter in her own right, and got Eisenstein to sit for a portrait. During the second sitting, Alexandrov walked in. According to Eisenstein, 'She squinted her large almond eyes like a well-disposed filly in the direction of Alexandrov.'[7] As a result, Eisenstein's portrait ended up with Grisha's lips, which was, supposedly, one way of Eisenstein actually possessing them.

With Ivor Montagu, he visited a brothel in the Rue Blondel where, as described by Montagu, 'the hostesses, all middle-aged and plain but with a special talent, sat beside us on the red plush sofas but without any clothes, chatting calmly of their husbands and children and kitchens and how much they earned in their working day, until the time came to display this talent, which was an ability to pick up coins from the edge of the table with an organ not usually so employed.'[8]

Eisenstein's first meeting with Jean Cocteau was at the French poet-playwright-novelist-painter-cinéaste's apartment behind the Madeleine church. 'I had been warned. Cocteau had two ways of receiving guests. He would either pose as the condescending Maestro. Or he would play the "slightly afflicted", admitting visitors [while] lying down, holding forth on his health in a plaintive voice, his huge hands lying across the counterpane. I was received in the latter way. I was even accorded the highest token of recognition. In the middle of our conversation there was an unexpected and expressive pause. And he spake unto me: "I see you now suddenly filled with blood . . ."'[9]

A few days later, Cocteau sent Eisenstein an invitation for two for a private dress rehearsal (*une répétition intime*) matinée of his new play, the monodrama, *La Voix Humaine*, at the Comédie Française on Saturday, February 15 at 2.15 p.m. Eisenstein dined the evening before with four antique dealers and two surrealist poets, Louis Aragon and Paul Eluard. The dealers had a little shop in the Rue des Saints-Péres which contained gilt-carved madonnas and Peruvian pitchers shaped like dogs, that appealed to Eisenstein.

At that time, Aragon and Eluard, both in their early thirties were still followers of André Breton, with whom Eisenstein had a cool association. 'I think that Breton, whose Marxist pose was fairly unconvincing, took offence somewhat when I failed to announce myself to him on my arrival in Paris,' explained Eisenstein. 'I find it an unrewarding experience mixing with draw-ing-room snobs who play at Marxism . . . What made Breton still more angry was my close association with a splinter group, young people of a more democratic outlook. Its headquarters was in a café which has two Chinese idols above the doorway – hence its name Les Deux Magots. This group had none of the arrogance, posiness or snobbery of the "elders"'.[10] (It was at Les Deux Magots, in St Germain des Prés, a favourite haunt of Eisenstein's, that he met the surrealist painters Max Ernst and André Derain.) The autocratic Breton might also have been envious of Eisenstein's reputation as a great radical left-wing artist who hailed from the country believed to provide the paradigm framework for radical left-wing art.

After the dinner with the antique dealers, Eisenstein invited Eluard to accompany him the following day to the theatre although he knew that the Surrealists of both groups detested Cocteau for what they considered his misbegotten attempts at surrealism, his dandyism and his bourgeois tastes and friends. In addition, Breton, like most of his group, was anti-homosexual – '*Ce n'est pas serieuse*,' was one of their declarations – though it is unlikely that Breton considered Eisenstein to be homosexual. Thus, on accepting the invitation to the Cocteau play, Eluard said ominously, 'But I warn you, I shall cause a scandal.'

'Whether I did not fully believe his words, or I was curious to witness a scandal – and there was every chance of one – I had to ignore what he said,' Eisenstein remarked. 'So there we were in the dress circle of the Comédie Française. Starched shirt fronts. Cuffs. Gold pince-nez. Sleek beards. The women in severe dresses. Society so respectable is was nauseating . . . A decorous drowsiness settled on all the propriety. There was only one actor in the play – a woman [the actress Berthe Bovy]. With an imaginary partner . . . at the other end of a telephone. An endless monologue. The endlessness slowly drained the scene of any fragments of possible drama. But my view of the stage was suddenly blocked by the towering four-square figure of Eluard. A piercing voice. "Who are you talking to? Monsieur Desbordes!?" [The twenty-four-year-old Jean Desbordes was Cocteau's current boyfriend.] The actress dried. The audience, unable to believe their ears, turned round to look at Eluard. An unheard of insult! A two-pronged one at that. First, insulting the tradition of the sacred walls of France's leading theatre. And second, a direct attack on the author – a hint at his all-too-well-known proclivities; in this case his name was linked with a young Monseiur Desbordes, a rising novelist. But Eluard gave the audience no time to come to its senses. He hammered out with percussive rhythm the classic: "*Merde! Merde! Merde!*" . . . This word fell like a hammer blow on the heads of the audience . . . "*Merde! Merde! Merde!*"'

[The audience reacted to this by rushing up to Eluard and attacking him.] 'Eluard stood still, like St Sebastian with the self-consciousness of Gulliver in Lilliput. But flecked with saliva, the Lilliputians dragged him downwards. The jacket ripped. Dinner jackets also ripped. The poet's pallid face sank like a frigate in the unequal combat, then it lunged upwards once more, jaws tightly clenched, before rolling down the massive staircase of the dress-circle, with a heap of other bodies.'

[After the intercession of Cocteau, the play continued, and was greeted with tumultuous applause at the end.] 'The success of Cocteau's work was assured . . . But for the incident would there have been such an ovation? If it comes to that, could Cocteau have much reason to complain? Perhaps he should even have been grateful. Anyway, I tried to slip out of the theatre without meeting him.'[11] Although Cocteau never blamed him, Eisenstein felt, that

Portrait of Eisenstein, 1925 *(Novosti)*.

Yulia Ivanova Konetskaya,
Eisenstein's mother *(Novosti)*.

Six-year-old Sergei with his father, Mikhail
Osipovich Eisenstein, Riga 1904 *(Novosti)*.

A studious seven-year-old Eisenstein *(David King Collection)*.

Caricatures, signed Sir Gay in 1917, for a projected 'pantomime', *Le Million de Pierrot*, written by Eisenstein *(Novosti)*.

A scene from Eisenstein's production of Ostrovsky's *Enough Simplicity in Every Wise Man* for the Proletkult Theatre in 1922. The sign on the effigy of Glumov reads: 'Hurrah! The bride is in my pocket!' *(Novosti)*.

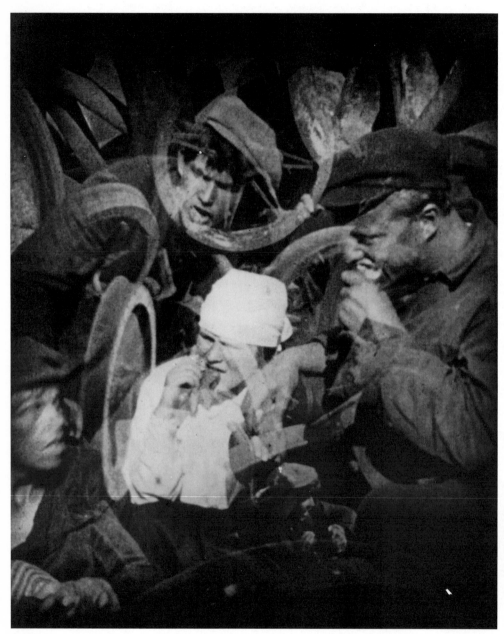

A workers' meeting in *The Strike* (1924) *(Ronald Grant Archive)*.

One of the police spies, known as The Monkey, in *The Strike (Kobal Collection)*.

The Tsar's mounted troops pursue the workers into the tenements in *The Strike (David King Collection)*.

Soldiers attacking the protesting workers in *The Strike (David King Collection)*.

The massacre on the Odessa Steps in *The Battleship Potemkin* (1925) *(Ronald Grant Archive)*.

One of the original posters for *The Battleship Potemkin*, reused for a screening at the London Film Festival in November 1987 *(Ronald Grant Archive)*.

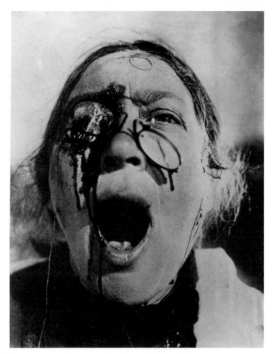

The woman shot in the face during the massacre on the
Odessa Steps in *The Battleship Potemkin (Kobal Collection)*.

The mother carrying her dead child (Pavel Glaubermann), facing the advancing soldiers
in *The Battleship Potemkin (Novosti)*.

Nikandrov as Lenin in *October* (1928) *(Kobal Collection)*.

The filming of the dead white horse dangling from
the drawbridge in *October (David King Collection)*.

The pregnant peasant woman in *The General Line (Kobal Collection)*.

Eisenstein during the shooting of
The General Line (1929) *(SOA)*.

Eisenstein posing with the peasant Marfa
Lapkina, the heroine of *The General Line*
(Hulton Deutsch Collection).

Douglas Fairbanks (centre), signing portraits on a visit to Moscow in 1926 with Edouard Tisse (left) and Eisenstein *(Novosti)*.

'Red dog meets Hollywood movie star', Eisenstein and Rin-Tin-Tin in Boston in 1930 *(Novosti)*.

Eisenstein with Josef von Sternberg and Marlene Dietrich in Hollywood in 1930 *(Ronald Grant Collection)*.

Eisenstein and Grigori Alexandrov at home in the Spanish-style villa in the Hollywood hills in 1930 *(Novosti)*.

Eisenstein meeting Paul Robeson in Moscow in 1934 with the English film historian Herbert Marshall (centre) *(SCRSC)*.

A portrait of Vsevolod Meyerhold, with the dedication written to Eisenstein on his collar: 'I am proud of my pupil who has now become a master. I love the master who has now founded a school. I bow to this pupil and master, S. Eisenstein. Moscow, 22 June 1936.' *(Novosti)*.

The three young peons awaiting execution in the Maguey episode from
Qué Viva México! (1931) *(Ronald Grant Archive)*.

A group of penitent monks leading a procession in the Conquest episode from *Qué Viva México!*
(Kobal Collection).

Stepok breaks the tension between the angry peasants and the saboteurs, one of the surviving stills from the lost or destroyed *Bezhin Meadow,* shot between 1935 and 1936 *(Kobal Collection)*.

The death of Stepok (Vitka Kartachov) in *Bezhin Meadow (Kobal Collection)*.

The Teutonic knights prepare for battle against the
Russian forces in *Alexander Nevsky* (1938)
(Kobal Collection).

An Italian poster for *Alexander Nevsky*
(Ronald Grant Archive).

A panoramic scene during the Battle on the Ice sequence from *Alexander Nevsky*
(Ronald Grant Archive).

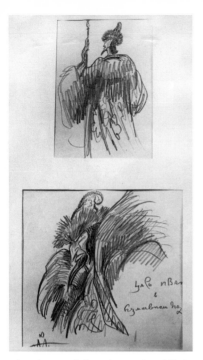

Sketches made by Eisenstein while in Alma Ata in 1941 for the title role in *Ivan the Terrible (Novosti)*.

Nikolai Cherkassov as the Tsar, plotting while praying in *Ivan the Terrible Part II (Kobal Collection)*.

Ivan and Vladimir (Pavel Kadochnikov), the pretender to the throne, in *Ivan the Terrible Part II (Kobal Collection)*.

The masses arriving at the mountain retreat of Ivan (Nikolai Cherkassov) at the end of *Ivan the Terrible Part I* (1944) *(Ronald Grant Archive)*.

by inviting Eluard to the performance, he had been the indirect cause of the scandal. Two days after the incident at the Comédie Française, Eisenstein was at the centre of an even bigger scandal.

At the invitation of Léon Moussinac, and under the aegis of the Social Research Department, Eisenstein was to give a lecture in the Salle Richelieu at the Sorbonne following a showing of *The General Line* there. Arriving with thirty minutes to spare, he was greeted at the large lecture theatre by Moussinac and Dr René Allendy, the psychoanalyst and art collector. The projector had been set up and the hall was filling rapidly. An estimated three thousand people – many of them French Communists – finally crammed into the amphitheatre with a seating capacity of a thousand. But the hall was also crowded with right-wing *agents provocateurs*, including members of the *Camelots de Roi* organisation of young monarchists, who were there to make trouble.

It all took place against an atmosphere of anti-Soviet feeling in France, especially among burgeoning right-wing groups including White Russian emigré organisations. One of the leaders of the latter, General Kutepov, had disappeared under mysterious circumstances for which the Soviet government was widely held to be responsible.

Shortly before the appointed time of the screening, a policeman in *képi* and white gloves took up a stand beside the projector, and the organisers were informed that the showing had been banned on the orders of Jean Chiappe, the Paris Prefect of Police, for reasons of 'security'. Although *The General Line* had not been passed by the Board of Censors, it had been thought that a screening inside the Sorbonne would count as a private one. Chiappe, who had already created difficulties for Eisenstein over his French residence permit, was the man who, in December of the same year, would suppress Buñuel's *L'Age d'Or* after the screen was splattered with ink by a fascist group.

There were thoughts of contravening the ban but that was just what the police were waiting for. There were police divisions in the courtyard, and the situation looked nasty. To catcalls and boos, Dr Allendy announced that the police had banned the film, adding that Eisenstein would nevertheless give an impromptu lecture on 'the intellectual film' and answer any questions afterwards. Eisenstein had prepared a mere twenty-minute introduction, but said he would try to stretch it out to forty minutes and then open up the talk for questions from the floor.

'I suddenly felt acute resentment and anger,' he recollected some years later. 'You – in the very heart of French scholarship and thought, the France of Descartes and Voltaire, the France of the Rights of Man and the Communards, the France of age-old struggles for freedom. And now some dirty *flic* dared to sit (now he was even sitting by the projector!) at the foot of the great cardinal! . . . Paris whose corridors of power impudently refused to recognise Soviet cinema . . . Paris which dared in its reactionary blindness to turn its back on the country which had taken the torch of the ideals of freedom from France and raced onwards with it to new horizons.'[12]

He kept these feelings about France to himself as he delivered his lecture on The Principles of the New Russian Cinema. 'I'm sorry that you cannot see my film . . . This makes my task much harder as I will have to make up what you cannot see with my limited French. When I am through speaking you may throw questions at me and I will try to answer. A sort of friendly ping-pong game. But I beg you not to ask me the whereabouts of General Kutepov or what salary I earn in the USSR, for if you do I am certain that my replies will not satisfy you.'[13]

Much of the speech was a celebratory description of the way the Soviets had organised the cinema, going on to praise the successes of the collectivist movement, its relation to the way films were produced and as the subject of *The General Line*.

'When the script is finished, we discuss it collectively in the factories or places with a special interest in the issue that is being dealt with. If it is a peasant film, like *The General Line* that I am unable to show you, we discuss the script with peasants, and every peasant, knowing that it is a film made for his benefit, shows an interest, gives his opinion, says what he thinks of the subject, assists and contributes to it through his familiarity with the background, and the interests involved and thus fulfils the role that we want him to fulfil . . . When the film is finished, and before it is shown in cinemas, we send it to factories and villages, and the

classes represented in the film subject it to very severe criticism . . .
You have to take it to the factory, listen to what people say about
it, change your film when required, add what is necessary to ensure
that it faithfully expresses what you intend.'[14]

It sounded so simple and practical, though it is doubtful whether
one single film made in the Soviet Union was ever altered because
of views expressed by the peasants or workers. Eisenstein gave not
an inkling that there was ever any criticism or censorship from
above, especially not for *The General Line*. A few months later, the
Soviet authorities censored a number of scenes from Dovzhenko's
Earth, a story of collectivisation in the Ukraine. The particular
scenes that displeased them were when a dead man's betrothed
mourns him, naked and hysterical, and when a peasant urinates
into the radiator of a tractor.

After his talk, Eisenstein answered questions from the audience,
scoring 'bull's-eyes', as he put it, on the Board of Censors, the
Ministry for Foreign Affairs and the Prefecture, producing 'great
hilarity from the auditorium.'

Floor: Could an independent artist with anarchic tendencies
develop freely in Russia?

Eisenstein: I think that the most fertile ground for that is France.

Floor: Do you really think that the Russian peasant is capable of
making useful criticisms of your film?

Eisenstein: Of course I must say that the best criticisms come
either from critics who understand art, but these are unfortunately very rare, or from primitive peasants, genuinely sincere
and direct people. Most people who fall between these cate-
gories are of no use to us in films. They are people who have
been deprived of their spontaneous *élan* and who know
absolutely nothing of what might interest us.

Floor: French reporters who have been there tell us that laughter
is dead in Russia. Is this true?

('My reply was an outburst of laughter. In those days I had
very strong, healthy white teeth.')

Eisenstein: There are so many things to make fun of that you can
be sure that people still laugh at them. When I tell them the tale
of my evening here I think they will laugh a lot![15]

Le Matin the next morning wrote, 'Don't worry about Bolsheviks with daggers between their teeth – look out for those with laughter on their lips!' Five years later, when Eisenstein had very little to laugh about, he wrote an article, devoid of humour and in his exigent sycophantic mode, entitled Bolsheviks Do Laugh (Thoughts on Soviet Comedy), in which he retold the story of that evening at the Sorbonne. What he now demanded was 'a new kind of humour, filling in a new page in the world history of humour and laughter, just as the very fact of the existence of the Soviet Union has inscribed a new page in the history and diversity of social forms. It is early days yet for us to chuckle idly. The task of building socialism is not yet finished. There is no place for random frivolity . . . It is only possible to rise above the constraints of crude slapstick and schoolboy humour by aspiring to understand perfectly the social significance of the ugly mug you direct your laughter at. The comedy of social mask, and the force of social mockery, must and do lie at the basis of the forms of that militant humour that our laughter must constitute. And that, I think, is what laughter, when we have reached the last decisive battles for *socialism in one country* [echoing Stalin's slogan associated with the Five-Year Plan], must and will be.'[16] How different from the spontaneous laughter that Eisenstein engendered that evening in the Salle Richelieu five years previously!

After that lecture, flanked by Dr Allendy and Léon Moussinac, he left the Sorbonne in triumph, through cordons of police. 'We could not believe what we saw! Lorries full of police were parked in alleys and courtyards. They were obviously expecting a regular battle.'[17]

At nine the next morning, the police descended upon Eisenstein's hotel in Montparnasse. In fact, they had arrived three hours earlier, but the hotel proprietor, an ex-diamond cutter, stopped them from going up to his room. The proprietor declared: 'Monsieur Eisenstein got back late last night . . . Monsieur Eisenstein is still asleep . . . I will not allow anyone to see Monsieur Eisenstein before nine o'clock.'[18]

Eisenstein spent the whole day being dragged around the security forces, the police, and the Prefecture, after which he was given twenty-four hours to leave the country. In desperation, he had no choice but to approach the Soviet Plenipotentiary in the Rue de Grenelle.

'Posters and slogans, posted along the walls right up to the very gate of the building, shrieked inaudibly, "Throw the Soviets out of Paris!" "Run them out of town!" The papers were filled with anti-Soviet shrieks. "Of course it took some doing to find the very worst time for this case of yours," our plenipotentiary, Dovgalensky, said to me . . . I felt sorry for Dovgalensky. The "mysterious matter" of General Kutepov's disappearance had come crashing down on his head. The reactionary yellow press was accusing the Soviets of kidnapping him. "It would be useless to send a communiqué to Tardieu [André Tardieu, the French prime minister] about you. You yourself must understand that."'[19] However, Eisenstein discovered another way of getting Tardieu to lend him a sympathetic ear.

When he learned of Eisenstein's predicament, Jean Cocteau immediately sent a note asking him to come to his apartment. 'Cocteau met me with his usual affectation . . . He excitedly held out his hands to me . . . He entreated me to "Forgive France" for the insult she had borne me. He wanted to help me. He was in despair. He could not now use his contacts in the police force.'[20]

Cocteau explained that his 'rascal' valet, a young Vietnamese had just been caught in possession of opium. But, he explained, there was another possibility. Mary Marquet, the actress, who was in *The Carriage of Holy Gifts* by Clara Gazul (the pseudonym of Prosper Merimée), currently at the Comédie Française in a double bill with *La Voix Humaine*, was the Prime Minister's mistress. 'She is making a lot of money because of me,' Cocteau explained. 'She won't object to talking to Tardieu in bed . . . In France, women are the key to everything.'[21]

Another friend of Eisenstein's who came to his aid was Jean Painlevé, the twenty-nine-year-old director of short scientific films, many of them on sea creatures. Having dinner with Painlevé, Eisenstein noted, 'He tucked into a crab or some other variety of crustacean which, had it been alive, would have found itself on his screen.' He was the son of Paul Painlevé, a former socialist member of the War Cabinet, and a renowned mathematician. 'My father has already written his letter of protest to the Prefecture,' he told Eisenstein.[22]

Renaud de Jouvenal, a motor car fanatic who took Eisenstein wherever he wanted to go in his sky-blue Bugatti, was the son of the statesman Henri de Jouvenal. 'I've heard all about it. Papa has already sent a letter of protest to the Prefecture.'[23] This might have had some effect as Senator de Jouvenal had no communist sympathies; he was ambassador to Rome at the time, and was trying to reach an *entente cordiale* with Mussolini. Jouvenal had been married to the novelist Colette for twelve years, but she had been unfaithful to him with her eldest stepson, Bertrand, Renaud's brother. Because of this, Renaud felt awkward about meeting Colette, who also had pull in high places. However, Léon Moussinac took Eisenstein to see her.

'Colette had a few tiny rooms above the arcade, with windows facing inwards on to the gardens of the Palais Royal.' Eisenstein remembered that, 'Colette arrived in a man's jacket, and her fringe tousled. Dark eyeliner. She will do everything . . . She would have a word with Philippe [Berthelot, director of the Ministry of Foreign Affairs]. The way I bowed and kissed her hand had something of the Regency period about it.'[24] Thanks to both Colette and Cocteau, Eisenstein got to see Berthelot.

Georges Henri Rivière, the curator of the Trocadéro Museum, introduced Eisenstein to the Museum's director, who had influence with the Foreign Ministry. Roland Tual, founder of the *Revue du cinéma* (with Jean-Georges Auriol) took Eisenstein to meet Anatole de Monzi, a former French minister who sympathised with the Soviet Union. With a phone call, he managed to extend Eisenstein's stay by a further seven days.

However, on March 4, despite all these powerful advocates, Eisenstein received a final police notification of his extradition from France. The *Refus de Séjour* gave him two weeks to leave the country. The reason for the extradition was given as 'décision ministérielle'.

In the meantime, Eisenstein took a trip to the south of France. In Cannes, he visited the pro-Soviet author Henri Barbousse; spent a few days writing at Léon Moussinac's cottage in Toulon, went dancing in a bar for sailors in Saint Tropez, and was invited to the villa of the Vicomte de Noailles at Hyéres. In Paris, Eisenstein had already entered the artistic salon of the Vicomte's wife, Marie-Laure de Noailles, who fascinated him because she was a direct descendant of the Marquis de Sade, and her house was crammed with editions of *Justine, The Philosophy of the Boudoir* and the *120 Days of Sodom*. Her husband had given financial backing to Cocteau's first film, *Le Sang d'un Poete* and Buñuel's *Un Chien Andalou*, which got him black-balled from the Jockey Club. Cocteau suggested that Eisenstein make a film in Marseilles with the backing of the Vicomte. But Eisenstein never even got to meet him.

On his return to Paris, Eisenstein's itinerary was as crowded as ever. He visited Abel Gance, the director of *Napoléon*, at his house at 27 Avenue Kléber, filled with both mock and genuine Gothic arte-facts, and sat on one of the uncomfortable straight-backed chairs. What intrigued him was a life-size plaster copy of the 'Androgyne of Naples', which took up a great deal of the room.

He accompanied Gance to the Studio de Joinville where the director was in the middle of shooting *The End of the World*, in which he himself took the role of the carpenter who played Christ in the Oberammergau passion play. Gance presented Eisenstein with a photograph of himself in the guise of a weeping, bloodied Christ with a crown of thorns upon his head. 'Gance tried to per-suade me that he was so overcome by an ecstasy that he began speaking in ancient Hebrew.'[25]

In Paris, Eisenstein, who 'had been examining the question of religious ecstasy as a particular aspect of pathos', spent much time browsing in the Catholic bookshops, where he bought the works of St John of the Cross, St Theresa and St Ignatius Loyola, in pursuit of the theory, if not the practice, of states of ecstasy – ex-stasis, 'stepping outside oneself.' This had preoccupied him since he had begun trying to rationalise the effects *The Battleship Potemkin* had on audiences.

'Pathos is what makes a viewer leap from his seat. It is what makes him jump. It is what makes him throw up his arms and shout. It is what makes his eyes sparkle in delight, before that same feeling makes him cry. In a word, it is everything that makes the viewer "come out of himself."'[26]

He also paid visits to the cathedrals of Reims, Chartres, Amiens and Lisieux, though, above all, he really longed to go to Lourdes, which had captivated him ever since his childhood reading of Emile Zola's novel *Lourdes*. 'I was fascinated by the onset of mass hysteria as crowd psychosis during "miracle cures."'[27] He did not make it to Lourdes because his stay in France did not co-incide with the dates of the pilgrimages, but he did see a copy of the grotto – with life-size models of the Madonna and the little Bernadette – in Marseilles in a side street full of brothels, a perfect symbol of Eisenstein's sacred and profane temperament lying side by side.

Marie Seton explained: 'It seems to me a little fallacious for critics in the West, who are probably rationalists, to assume that individuals in a society based upon a materialist philosophy can eliminate religious influences and interests at will simply because they desire to be thoroughgoing materialists. Having no predilection towards religion myself, I was considerably jolted to discover Eisenstein's conflict between his intellectual desire to be rationalist and his emotional pull towards mysticism. I was also exceedingly aware of Eisenstein's "horsing around", for no-one could be more double-edged than Eisenstein . . . Allowing for the fact that a conflict between rationalism and mysticism is not an uncommon phenomenon, it is easy to understand that Eisenstein would keep his problem to himself during that period 1918 to 1929 when a policy of active anti-religious activity was carried on by the League of the Godless . . .'[28]

However, Seton suggested that when Eisenstein arrived in France, no longer in the environment of anti-religious activity, in the different intellectual climate where belief in religion or adherence to atheism was solely a matter of personal disposition, Eisenstein, for the first time in his adult life, was able more openly to express this side of himself. Perhaps, even more so than Buñuel, Eisenstein could say, 'Thank God, I'm an atheist.'

On the secular side, Eisenstein was frequently seen at Shakespeare & Co, Sylvia Beach's celebrated bookshop on the Left Bank. 'I greatly loved this modest quiet bookshop and the grey-haired

Sylvia Beach. I often dropped in on her. Sat in her back room. And gazed at the walls for ages; they were hung with innumerable faded photographs. An idiosyncratic pantheon of literature.' At her shop he was delighted to find Paul Verlaine's *Hombres*, banned for its homo-eroticism and 'sold under the counter quite openly.'[29]

It was through Sylvia Beach that he got to meet James Joyce, whose *Ulysses* she had first published. He received a first edition of *Ulysses*, one of his favourite novels, signed by the author, and a recording Joyce had made of readings from *Finnegans Wake*. Eisenstein's first impression of Joyce, whose glaucoma had brought him to the brink of blindness, was of a modest and jocular man totally dedicated to his work. They spent hours together at subsequent meetings during which Joyce sometimes read from his works or discussed examples of interior monologue from *Ulysses*. He fired Eisenstein with enthusiasm for his technique of 'unfolding the display of events simultaneously with the particular manner in which these events pass through the consciousness and feelings, the associations and emotions' of Leopold Bloom. So much so that Eisenstein yearned to adapt *Ulysses*, 'the Bible of the new cinema', to the screen. Joyce for his part was fascinated by ideas Eisenstein had evolved over the previous five years for conveying the interior monologue on the screen, where, he was convinced, it would find even fuller expression. Though almost completely blind, and the films were silent, Joyce wanted to 'see' *The Battleship Potemkin* and *October*. So impressed was he by his talks with Eisenstein that he commented to a friend that if *Ulysses* were ever filmed, only two people were capable of directing it – Walter Ruttmann or Eisenstein.

Ulysses certainly helped Eisenstein master 'the obvious tangibility of the technique of musical counterpoint . . . the multiple passages of regular, intricate constructions from the chapters of this novel's exceptionally musical prose whispered the secrets of these melodic structures in my ear one by one.'[30]

Between the completion of *October* and the resumption of *The General Line* in 1928, Eisenstein had spent a short holiday at Gagri in the Crimea, taking *Ulysses* with him to study. A few months later, unable to try out an interior monologue in a sound film, he wrote some 'stream of consciousness' pages, mostly in English.

At Shakespeare & Co, Eisenstein made the acquaintance of 'a

young man with a fringe and slightly powdered cheeks – Georges Anteuil . . . He had just become famous.'[31] Anteuil, the American composer and pianist, who, at thirty, was only three years younger than Eisenstein, had recently had a great success with his jazz-influenced first opera *Transatlantic*. Someone else Eisenstein met at the bookshop was the poet Léon-Paul Fargue, who signed a copy of his verses for him, with the dedication 'A Eisenstein poète. Jean-Paul Fargue poète. Paris 1930.

At the Dadaist poet Tristan Tzara's house, he met 'the close-cropped' Gertrude Stein, who gave him advice about his trip to America. Tzara, 'never to be seen without his monocle . . .' had a superb collection of masks and early Picassos. ' Dadaism,' Eisenstein noted, was 'the latest stage of artistic notions in disintegration, and the retreat not merely to the nursery but to the cradle itself.'[32]

Enrico Prampolini, the Futurist artist whom Eisenstein had met (and disliked) at the conference at La Sarraz, took him off to an exhibition and party largely attended by other Italian Futurist painters and poets. 'The limping figure of Prampolini . . . belonged to the belligerent camp of followers and minions of the then fairly active Marinetti, in whom the Italians found a figure of authority,' Eisenstein wrote. 'Italian Fascism was increasingly spurring on that herald of militant Futurism, which in those years had long outlived itself . . . The painting may have been bad but the poetry was atrocious. I found myself quite unexpectedly shaking hands with Marinetti. For my part such a meeting could give me no pleasure at all. As one newspaper put it, in its account of the exhibition's opening, it was only "piquant to watch one of the prophets of Fascism in the same room as one of Communism's angry disciples."'[33]

More to his taste was twenty-nine-year-old André Malraux, with whom he had long discussions on literature and who told Eisenstein that he could quote from memory any passage from any Dostoevsky novel he could name. They talked about *Lady Chatterley's Lover* for which Malraux was writing the preface to the French translation. As it had been banned in America and England, Eisenstein quickly obtained a copy in English, which he took with him to the United States, 'not to read it, but out of snobbery.' But when he did get round to the novel, it 'completely bowled me over.'[34] He later bought every D.H. Lawrence book he could find. What he found attractive in Lawrence's work was his ability to 'step outside the boundaries of sex and into (inaccessible for a limited being) a cosmic, universal confluence. Which is why I find pre-logic so attractive: it grants the subconscious sensuality but does not subordinate it to sex.'[35] Among the other books he bought in Paris was Lucien Lévy-Bruell's *La Mentalité Primitive* (*Primitive Thought*), which dealt with just such pre-logic theories, which he would draw upon in his teachings.

Apart from writers and painters, Eisenstein also formed friendships with the photographers Germaine Krull, Eli Lotar and André Kertesz. Krull specialised in documentary 'photo-novels' and she, Joris Ivens and Eisenstein filmed some counters in cafés in the suburbs. Ivens, the Dutch director of left-wing documentaries, recalled his short time with Eisenstein in Paris.

'Often when we walked together in Paris, he would take his camera with him, but the subjects he chose to photograph were never conventional "sights" of the city, but human beings in comical situations. I suspect that this highly developed and very conspicuous sense of fun might have been a form of compensation for his basic shyness. For although he was undoubtedly a very good friend to many people in many countries, he was far less emotional in his personal friendships than most others I have known. With Eisenstein, and especially at the beginning of a relationship, there was a feeling of reserve. He must have been conscious of this, and might even have been ashamed of it, trying to compensate for it by an excessively extroverted sense of humour.'[36]

As the Hollywood contract had still failed to materialise – Eisenstein was upset to hear that Douglas Fairbanks had been in London and not bothered to contact him – Eisenstein felt insecure even though he had had his *carte de séjour* extended slightly, and he continued to discuss the possibilities of making a film in France. But he was unable to agree with producers who proposed that he should make 'mass-appeal' films, using certain young actresses in alluring roles. Eisenstein was dumbfounded and managed to blurt out, 'But I don't use actors . . . Actors are too artificial! . . . How could you suppose for one moment that I would give up my ideas? Doesn't my success in France rest entirely on their realisation? Why do you think the showings of *Potemkin* are packed out?'[37]

However, he was approached with a proposal to make a film of *Don Quixote*, starring Fyodor Chaliapin. The great Russian bass had only once appeared on screen, as Ivan the Terrible, in a disastrous silent film version of Rimsky-Korsakov's *The Maid of Pskov*, made in 1915. Eisenstein had seen the film in which 'his [Chaliapin's] nobility, his statuesque bearing and dramatic performances all survived the ridiculous breakneck speed of the 16 frames per second film running through the projector at 20 frames a second.' Chaliapin had since avoided films, but the prospect of a 'talkie' intrigued (and terrified) him. The proposal, however, was left hanging in mid-air when Eisenstein left for the USA. Three years later *Don Quixote*, starring Chaliapin, was made by G. W. Pabst in France, a film which Eisenstein, 'to my shame', found he could not sit through.[38]

Finally, towards the end of April, Paramount's Vice-President, Jesse L. Lasky, turned up in Paris with a proposition from his studio. This was largely due to the diplomacy of Ivor Montagu, who had gone to Hollywood a few months earlier to use his contacts to get Eisenstein work there. Eisenstein's first meeting with Lasky took place at Lasky's hotel, the George V, in the Champs Elysées. Eisenstein described Lasky as 'one of the real characters of the film business. One of the first to tread on the fertile soil of golden California . . . Mr Lasky gave me paternal encouragement.'[39] The fifty-year-old Lasky, showman and co-founder of Paramount, who wore a pince-nez, was accompanied by a couple of other big guns, Albert Kaufman, general manager of the studio, and Richard Blumenthal, an executive producer.

Negotiations commenced on the basis that Eisenstein would spend six months in the USA making a film for Paramount, after which it would be open for him to return to Moscow to direct a Sovkino production. The subsequent plan was for alternate work on American and Russian films until he had completed three or four films for Paramount. The contract would be terminated only if he failed to settle on a subject for a film and conditions of work by the end of three months in the USA.

Several possible subjects were suggested by Lasky including the Dreyfus affair, a film on Emile Zola, and Vicki Baum's bestseller *Menschen in Hotel* (*Grand Hotel*), none of which held much appeal for Eisenstein. He countered with three works, each of which had the advantage of having been offered to him personally by their respective authors: H.G. Wells' *The War of the Worlds*, James Joyce's *Ulysses* and George Bernard Shaw's *The Devil's Disciple*. (All of these subjects would eventually be filmed, but not by Eisenstein.) As Lasky was taking a huge enough risk in inviting a 'dangerous' Bolshevik to Hollywood in the first place, Eisenstein wisely resisted expressing his desire to make a film of *Das Kapital*.

While he awaited confirmation from Sovkino and the official extension to his leave of absence from the Soviet Union, the financial side of the contract was discussed. Lasky offered him a weekly sum of $500 until a subject was decided, and $3,000 weekly once filming began. But Eisenstein categorically refused to sign any contract that failed to include Tisse and Alexandrov – in whose services Lasky was not interested. Because of this condition negotiations were almost broken off. But Paramount, who obviously thought Eisenstein worth courting, came up with an offer of $900 a week from the beginning, out of which Eisenstein himself could pay his colleagues.

The general terms were spelt out by Eisenstein in an article that he sent to Moussinac for publication. 'After a movie at Paramount – to be completed in about six months – our team will return to Moscow for our next Soviet production. After that we shall return to Hollywood for a second film. We foresee a third and fourth film under the same conditions, our team travelling to and fro between the USSR and America. If during the first three months of our stay in the USA we are unable to agree on a subject for the movie, or on working conditions, our relationship can be terminated, in which case we will return at once to Moscow.'[40]

That version of the contract reads more optimistically than the account given by Ivor Montagu, whose recollection is that the arrangement was not so much 'a contract of service' as 'an agreement of Paramount to allow expenses for a period of six months.'[41] Those expenses, given the riches of Hollywood, seem surprisingly small: $500 for Eisenstein, and a hundred each for Alexandrov, Tisse, Montagu and Montagu's wife, Helle. It was hoped that this would be increased on acceptance of a script.

The contract was finally signed on May 3. Three days later Eisenstein received his visa and prepared to sail immediately for America.

10

Hollywood and Bust

When anybody first arrives in Hollywood he is automatically the white-haired boy. Everything is laid out for him, and he is told, 'Don't hurry, just take your time, sit down, absorb everything, enjoy the fleshpots, be entertained, meet all these wonderful people.'

On May 8, 1930, Eisenstein and Tisse sailed for New York on the *Europa* which 'carried us across the benign serenity of the Atlantic Ocean like a magic carpet.'[1] (Alexandrov, who was completing *Romance Sentimentale*, followed a short while later.) While on board, Eisenstein received a cable from George Bernard Shaw giving him permission to film *Arms and the Man* 'on condition that the entire text be altered not one jot.' A condition which Eisenstein would have been glad to accept, as Shaw had never yet sold anyone the right to film one of his works.

Eisenstein's arrival in New York was welcomed by a fanfare of studio publicity, as well as an anti-Communist and anti-Semitic campaign to have him deported. 'This internationally notorious communist agitator is now here, undoubtedly preparing to let loose upon America more of that destruction which has flooded the rivers of Bolshevik Russia with the blood of the murdered. And that aims at shedding more blood throughout the world wherever communism can plant its agents,' was how one Hollywood journalist expressed it.

Major Frank Pease, self-styled 'professional American patriot', led the campaign against Eisenstein's presence in America, denouncing him as part of a 'Jewish-Bolshevik conspiracy to turn the American cinema into a Communist cesspool. Why allow Eisenstein in, this red dog and sadist?' At Major Pease's instigation, the Fish Committee, the forerunner of the post-war UnAmerican Activities Committee, visited Hollywood later in the year in order to investigate Communist infiltration of American cinema.

Eisenstein, secure in the backing of his liberal and left-wing friends and supporters in America, and feeling confident that his Paramount contract would act as a safeguard, took the attacks with a certain amount of equanimity.

'Almost since my actual entry into the USA, the reactionary press and particularly the Fascist-orientated movement of "shirt-wearers" under Major Pease, had raised a maddening howl against my invitation, and demanded that I be removed from the American continent. Apparently, my visit was "more terrible than the landing of a thousand armed men."'[2]

Because of Jesse Lasky's insistence that 'We have a reputation to keep up you and I,' Eisenstein was booked in at the Savoy Palace. Although he enjoyed the noisy vigour of New York, he found difficulty in memorising the streets of Manhattan, 'because of their unfamiliar designation by numbers, which, in contrast with names, conjured up for me no pictorial associations . . . To produce these images, I had to fix in my memory a set of objects characteristic of one or another street, a set of objects aroused in my consciousness in answer to the signal "Forty-Second" and quite distinct from those aroused by the signal "Forty-Fifth."'[3] This not only illustrated how Eisenstein's mind worked, but was another demonstration of the way montage was 'the associative chain between a certain depiction and the image which it should evoke in our minds . . . a chain of intermediate depictions which coalesce into an image.'[4]

The day after arriving in New York, Eisenstein was whisked off by special train to give a lecture to Paramount licensees at a convention in Atlantic City, one of the most 'terrifying' he ever gave. 'You'll need to make a presentation to the people who'll be selling your films in the future.' Lasky informed him. 'Personal impressions count for a great deal . . . Just don't be too serious . . . On the whole Americans like their lectures to be funny.'[5]

Eisenstein remembered little of the speech, only that it seemed a success because as he descended the platform he felt a heavy slap on the back – 'the highest sign of affection from the natives, delivered by the towering, thin figure of Sam Katz, the head of world film distribution for Paramount-Publix as it then was. "I don't know what sort of director you are (this was a typical remark from the trade division of large companies!) but I could use you as a salesman right away!" There could be no higher praise.'[6]

Back in New York, he had lunch with Otto H. Kahn, the millionaire and financial director of Paramount, at his Italianate palazzo on Fifth Avenue. Kahn pointed out a portrait of a bearded man above the fireplace. 'Recognise the brushwork?' he asked Eisenstein, who replied he did not. 'Only a Jew can paint a face with such subtlety,' he proudly exclaimed, adding, as if as an afterthought, 'Rembrandt'.[7]

Also present at the lunch was Kahn's daughter and Horace B. Liveright, the publisher who had promoted the careers of younger writers, including Theodore Dreiser, and had produced a stage version of *An American Tragedy* in 1926, another subject Eisenstein was already considering filming. Just as artichokes were being served, a vegetable with which Eisenstein was unfamiliar, he was called to the phone. It was Alexandrov phoning from Ellis Island. He had just arrived on the *Ile de France* but there was something amiss with his visa, and he was not allowed ashore. Eisenstein promised to sort matters out for his friend immediately after lunch (which he did). When he returned to the table, he found the others had finished their artichokes and were now 'waiting to see how this Russian barbarian would extricate himself from this difficult situation. My embarrassment derived from not knowing how to eat this strange vegetable, whose leaves form a cupola and end in a small spike that sticks maliciously upwards . . . To make matters worse, there was an endless array of countless forks and smaller forks, spoons and teaspoons, knives, breadknives and smaller knives still!'[8]

The next day, Eisenstein attended a prestige luncheon at the Astor Hotel where he was to meet the press. Arriving with three days growth of stubble on his chin and a worker's cloth cap on his head, he astounded the conformist audience with sarcastic remarks.

'I think you picture all Russians with beards. I didn't want to disappoint you.' He then announced that he had come to make 'a truly American film'.[9]

Already at the back of his mind was the possibility of filming Theodore Dreiser's *An American Tragedy*, something that may have prompted him to go 'up river' to visit Sing-Sing, where the novel's hero, Clyde Griffiths, is sent to the electric chair. The memory of the details of the execution room reappeared in his screenplay for *An American Tragedy*.

'I had the honour to sit in the electric chair, only, of course, after I had made sure it was disconnected. A monstrous experience! But the most depressing sensation was evoked by various details near the chair. Beside it, for example stood a spittoon. Gleaming, brightly polished, the sort you usually find beside you at the dentist's . . . There was nothing fantastic about the place, no freakish lights or shadows such as people love to show in films . . . It's just this primitive practicality that is so sinister.'[10]

It was in the lobby of the Astor Hotel, D.W. Griffith's home for many years, that Eisenstein's first meeting with 'the Great Old Man of all of us' took place. Griffith, the 'old man', was only fifty-five but drink, poor health, and the 'nightmare of the mind and nerves' – his description of the recent making of his penultimate film and first talkie, *Abraham Lincoln* – had aged him far beyond his years. (Griffith and Eisenstein were to die in the same year, the younger man preceding the older by six months.) Griffith gave Eisenstein the customary litany of his woes – especially his battles to finance his films, a situation the Russian had yet to experience. At the time Griffith was cultivating a rich widow, among others, who would put money into his next and last film, *The Struggle*, an adaptation of Emile Zola's *L'Assommoir* (*The Drunkard*), updated and relocated to 1920s New York.

Eisenstein also renewed his acquaintance with Douglas Fairbanks, who took him to a speakeasy and informed him that both his marriage to Mary Pickford and his career were reaching breaking point. For Eisenstein, just arrived in the New World, certainly a new world to him, with Hollywood expectantly awaiting his arrival, he could only feel that he was ascending as his idols were descending.

Aside from film people, Eisenstein was feted by the academic community: the philosopher John Dewey at Columbia University; while at Harvard, where he spoke about the new possibilities of presenting abstract ideas through film, he was the guest of Professor Henry Wadsworth Longfellow Dana, grandson of the poet. Dana's house had previously belonged to his grandfather, and had earlier been George Washington's residence during the War of Independence. This prompted Eisenstein to express a desire to make a film about American history centred on this house. He might have had in mind one of his favourite short stories, Ambrose Bierce's *The Affair at Coulter's Notch*, which had had some influence on the battle scenes in *Alexander Nevsky*.

At a luncheon given at the Hotel Vendôme in Boston, 'Harry' Dana was among the assembled company of the wise and the wealthy, which included such illustrious society names as Mrs Ralph Adams Cram, Mrs Felix Frankfurter, Mrs Cornelia Stratton Parker and Courtney Crocker. The famous canine star Rin-Tin-Tin trotted over from the Keith Albee Theatre to greet Eisenstein, with whom he was photographed. Man and dog are seen on a sofa staring bemusedly into each other's eyes as if to gain mastery. On the back of the photograph he sent to Pera Attasheva he wrote, 'Red dog meets Hollywood movie star.'[11] He then answered approximately a hundred questions about Russia, Russian movies, and the Russian soul.

The *Boston Herald* of May 27 reported: 'Mr Eisenstein . . . is a young man apparently in his early 30s. His hair is light brown and bushy, receding slightly from his temples. He spoke fluently and well, taking the occasion a little less seriously than his hosts . . . He seemed, likewise, less worried than his hosts about the possible effect of Hollywood on his art . . . He is confident that an "artistic success" can be a commercial success – even in the movies – if the subject is wisely chosen. He does not know just what he will do here; that is, he says, a Paramount business secret. He has had no experience with sound pictures, but he does not fear the new technique; his four years with the legitimate stage plus his six years with the movies are enough training, so he thinks, for his direction of the talkies.

"You destroy illusions about Russia," one woman told him.

"Illusions ought always to be destroyed," he said. "The truth is better." What director does he think is best in America? "The man who directs the Mickey Mouse films, animated cartoons with sound. Eisenstein likes them . . .""

With Alexandrov and Tisse, he finally left New York for Hollywood, having meantime enjoyed a spending spree, buying clothes and the best film equipment available. The journey west was broken in Chicago, where the trio spent some days exploring the city, including its Mexican slums and black ghetto. In a cafeteria one day, Eisenstein suddenly pretended to be a waiter, serving an imaginary customer at an empty table with appropriate Chaplinesque flourishes and gestures, even down to leaving himself a ten cent tip.

In Los Angeles, Ivor Montagu had rented a Spanish-style villa at 9481 Readcrest Drive in Coldwater Canyon. It came complete with the requisite swimming pool, a well-used De Soto car and a black cook. The three Russians enjoyed a completely new way of life in the 'incomparably picturesque' Californian surroundings. 'We bathed, played tennis, saw the sights, and made more friends,' Eisenstein recalled.[12]

Paramount required him to attend innumerable meetings, banquets and other social occasions, where, in the studio's eyes, he committed several social blunders. At a banquet given by a multimillionaire he offered to change places with the butler on the grounds that he disliked being waited on.

Eisenstein found J.G. Bachman, one of Paramount's supervisors and associate producers, 'a kind man and a specialist in "Europeans". When a picture is being made, the supervisor has to work like stink; when it is ready for release, he worries himself sick that the film will bring in less money than was budgeted.'[13] Bachman was desperately worried at the time about *Playboy in Paris*, directed by German-born Ludwig Berger and starring Maurice Chevalier, which flopped, and resulted in Berger returning to Europe soon after.

Eisenstein met Greta Garbo at Ludwig Berger's house. He had first been introduced to the Swedish star, who had just made her sound debut in *Anna Christie*, through Salka Viertel (née Steuermann), the bisexual Polish-born actress and writer and former manager of Garbo for whom she had co-written a number of screenplays. Eisenstein remembered Garbo sprawled across a billiard table talking intimately to her friend Friedrich Murnau.

'I called her Garbelle (by analogy with beau-bel, Gar-beau, Gar-bel). She called me Eisenbahn (railway in German) . . . She never permitted anyone to see her while she was being filmed in the studio, because she acted – brilliantly! – purely by intuition without any formal training. And as is known, intuition is not wholly reliable . . . For Garbo, acting was a hard way of making a living.'[14]

He also watched Marlene Dietrich being directed by Josef von Sternberg on a set at Paramount in *Morocco*, her first American film. 'There was deathly silence. A crowd scene: a packed Moroccan café and not a sound. Sternberg was on a platform wearing a black velvet jacket. A hand supported his head. He was thinking. Everyone was silent, holding their breath . . . ten minutes . . . fifteen. It didn't work.' Eisenstein also observed that Sternberg was not accepted into the higher circle of Hollywood society. 'He tried to humble "this Hollywood" by a Europeanism. He collected leftist art. But it was not quite the thing. The names weren't "right", the pictures were of the wrong periods . . . He was short, greying with a slightly artistic haircut. He sported a greyish moustache which drooped unevenly on either side. He had a passion for jackets and short, square cut coats.'[15]

Of Sternberg, Chaplin remarked to Eisenstein, 'I've never met a more disagreeable layabout in all my life.' Sternberg was much more generous to Eisenstein in his memoirs. 'We had met in Berlin while I was at work on *The Blue Angel* and we became good friends . . . Eisenstein was a fluidly expressive commentator, and we frequently discussed all our common interests. He barred none, not even one of such potential danger to him as the subject of government control of the arts. When I asked him how his country rewarded good films he told me jokingly, though he might well have been serious, that when a director made a good film in Russia he was rewarded by having a window added to his room and if a film was bad he was shot for treason. I enquired as to the numbers of windows in his room and he answered, one. We discussed modern painting and related subjects (to commemorate our first meeting he had given me a book by Malevich on his abstract work) . . . He always had pencil and paper with him and his sketches showed extraordinary talent. The sketches he made in my presence were probably destroyed for they could have been shown in only a very understanding circle. Had he lived longer he may have given them to Professor Kinsey.'[16]

When visiting the Paramount studio, Eisenstein also watched the filming of *Tom Sawyer*, starring sixteen-year-old Jackie Coogan, 'an overgrown lad [who] had long since lost the unique charm of the "kid" . . . I cannot imagine Tom round-faced, brown-eyed, plump and well fed.'[17] Of course, Eisenstein remembered the six-year-old Coogan from Chaplin's *The Kid* (1921), elements of whose performance he had imposed on the hungry blond child in *The Strike*.

It was (and is) customary for European intellectuals in Hollywood to take a lofty view of its film celebrities, and Eisenstein found most of them 'stupid and mediocre'. Apparently he received this message, sent to Paramount, from Samuel Goldwyn: 'Please tell Mr Eisenstein that I have seen his film *Potemkin* and admire it very much. What we should like would be for him to do something of the same kind, but rather cheaper, for Ronald Colman.' Eisenstein described Jean Harlow as 'the platinum beauty queen, full of airs, gracing the marble surround of the Ambassador Hotel's sky-blue bathing pool.'[18]

He wrote to Léon Moussinac that 'on the intellectual level Hollywood is in the same class as Soissons or Brive.'[19] However, neither Soissons nor Brive could have boasted the number of extraordinary people that Eisenstein met, admired and liked in Hollywood. There is a photograph that he sent to Pera Attasheva in September 1930 with the inscription (in English), 'To my best friend in the USSR together with my best friend in the USA.'[20] The photograph was of himself, smiling at the camera, one hand on his hip and the other holding the four-fingered hand of a small model of Mickey Mouse. It must be remembered that this meeting took place when Mickey was only two years old, and Walt Disney was some years away from working in colour and making his first feature. What fascinated Eisenstein, who adored Disney's work throughout his life (although he later had certain qualms about his colour films) was the way Disney used sound, a subject uppermost in his mind.

'Disney's most interesting – most valuable – contribution has been his skill at superimposing the "drawing" of a melody on top of a graphic drawing . . . He has an incomparable feel for an intonational gesture in music, and he can weave this gesture into the outline of his figures. Disney is a genius at doing this. No one can do this apart from him.'[21] It was Disney's ability to match these 'gestures' that he and Prokofiev attempted to emulate in *Alexander Nevsky* and *Ivan the Terrible*.

It was not with Eisenstein that the American critic Jonathan Rosenbaum, in the 1970s, suggested a parallel with Disney, but with Leni Riefenstahl, seeing 'a dream of perfection and simplicity which makes every detail on the screen an expressive part of a continuous animistic whole, implicitly turning the entire cosmos into a single idea . . . a particularly aesthetic attitude that is usually *open* to ideology because of its childlike innocence and its predilection for primal myths of unity and perfection.'[22] Rosenbaum's comparison could be applied to much of Eisenstein's work, particularly *The General Line* and *Bezhin Meadow*.

As late as 1946, Eisenstein noted Disney 'as an example of the art of absolute influence – absolute appeal for each and everyone, and hence a particularly rich treasure trove of the most basic means of influence.'[23] In the same year, in an essay called How I Learned to Draw, he wrote: 'I have always liked Disney and his heroes, from Mickey Mouse to Willie the Whale [*Make Mine Music*, 1946]. Because of their moving figures – again animals and again linear. The best examples had neither shading nor depth (similar to early Chinese and Japanese art) and were made up of outlines that really did move.'[24]

Eisenstein and the twenty-nine-year-old Disney seemed to have got on well, and they corresponded for some time afterwards. (There is another photo taken at the same time, with Eisenstein standing, his arm around Disney's shoulders, staring down at the figure of Mickey Mouse.) Eisenstein did not live long enough to discover that Disney later became an anti-Semitic, racist, union-bashing, anti-Communist right-winger.

Eisenstein also met another idol, Mack Sennett, the 'King of Comedy', whose rapid, irreverent, crazy slapstick comedy influenced many of the early Soviet comedies such as Lev Kuleshov's *The Extraordinary Adventures of Mr West in the Land of the Bolsheviks* and Pudovkin's *Chess Fever* as well as, to a certain extent, *The Strike*. Sennett was then struggling to come to terms with sound.

Eisenstein had seen King Vidor's *The Crowd* in New York and was intrigued by some of the technical devices used in it. Vidor, who showed him round MGM studios and several of the location sites, recalled, 'I remember his particular interest in what I can best describe as the first use of the "zoom", though it was really nothing of the kind but a camera that could move forward and descend at the same time. He was also intrigued by another device we were using, which allowed us to take travelling shots up the side of a tall building. It was very soon clear to me that he and I, despite our national and political differences, really spoke the same language.'[25]

Eisenstein, accompanied by Alexandrov and Tisse, went to dinner with Vidor, and after the meal they screened *The General Line*, with Tisse working the projector. As Vidor told it, 'He got along fine until the third or fourth reel at which point Eisenstein jumped up, went to the booth, and told him that he had put on the wrong reel. Tisse quietly assured him that he had done nothing of the kind, and that the reel was undoubtedly the correct one. So they stopped the film altogether, came back into the room and began to argue about whether it was the right reel or the wrong one. So here was one of the greatest directors in the world disagreeing with one of the greatest cameramen the cinema has ever known, about the order of reels of a film they had both made together. I can no longer remember which of them was right . . . I believe that story to have an important moral for film directors. It proves that film has its own form, and that this form, is so dynamic that it has no need of a First Act, a Second Act, or a Third Act. You don't have to follow the traditional forms of the theatre or the novel, because the form you are working in is an art form in its own right. Which is why Eisenstein could argue in all seriousness about the correct reel being on or not being on. In a play, or at any rate in the conventional plays of the 1930s, you soon got lost if you skipped from Scene 2 to Scene 5. You also knew it soon enough if you began a novel with Chapter 6 and then went back to Chapter 1 . . . Eisenstein and I shared a faith in the unique and dynamic power of the camera and the cutting-room.'[26]

Above all, there was Charles Chaplin. 'Of course, Chaplin is the most interesting person in Hollywood,' Eisenstein wrote.[27] Eisenstein was invited to United Artists by Douglas Fairbanks where he was shown Fairbanks' gigantic office, with his own personal Turkish bath adjoining it.

'Sitting on a crimson pouffe in the middle was "The Thief of Bagdad" himself, surrounded by what looked like ancient Rome: the monumental pink body of Joseph Schenck, the President of United Artists, draped in a sheet.' In came Chaplin, who greeted Eisenstein in broken Russian. '*Gaida, troika, sneg pushistyi* . . . (Hey there, troika, snow's like powder . . .') Schenck commented, 'Charlie and Pola Negri were close for a year, so he reckons his Russian's fluent.'[28]

Despite vast differences in background, upbringing and culture, Chaplin and Eisenstein had much in common – not only in their shared taste for clowning and the type of comedy they responded to, but also in their intrinsically melancholy natures. Of course, Eisenstein valued Chaplin's art highly.[29]

'What makes Chaplin so remarkable? What puts Chaplin above all the poetics of comic film? Chaplin's profound lyricism. The fact that each of his films makes you shed, at a certain point, tears of genuine, warm humanity. Chaplin is a queer fish. An adult who behaves like a child.'

Chaplin took the Russian trio on a three-day trip on his yacht to Catalina Island, 'surrounded by sea lions, flying fish and underwater gardens, which you could look at through the glass hull of special steamboats.' It was on this trip that Chaplin confessed that he disliked children. Eisenstein commented, 'The director of *The Kid*, which made five-sixths of the world weep at the fate of an abandoned child, does not like children. He must be a monster! But who does not like children *normally*? Only . . . children themselves.'[30]

The Russians would also play tennis at Chaplin's mansion in Beverly Hills. 'They used to play very bad tennis on my court,' wrote Chaplin. 'At least, Alexandrov did . . . Even Sergei Mikhailovich, who bought ducks and tried pursuing the ball with a sort of savage spite, spoiled it all by wearing braces and scarlet ones at that, as well as a belt for security. When I told him this was improper he was downcast, but reassured when I added that braces for tennis were a practice of the late Lord Birkenhead . . . Discussing Communism with Eisenstein one day, I asked if he thought the educated proletariat was mentally equal to the aristocrat with his generations of cultural background. I think he was surprised at my ignorance. Eisenstein said, "If educated, the cerebral strength of the masses is like rich, new soil."'[31]

Eisenstein described 'a terrible evening' spent at Chaplin's home. Apart from the three Russians, there were also two Spaniards – Luis Buñuel and the writer Eduardo Ugarto – and Ivor Montagu. The Spaniards were communicated with in sign language until it was discovered that Buñuel spoke fluent French. 'Chaplin was trying his best to keep his end up in a highbrow English conversation. Then he started clowning around. That day he was especially animated and mischievous . . . When you are with him he is not still for one moment . . . One moment he dances to the radio, parodying oriental dances. And the next he impersonates the King of Siam, whose nose would barely reach the table top . . . Chaplin is afraid of solitude. He grabbed his guests. He was like a child scared of being alone in the dark. He asked us to stay to dinner.'

The evening turned into a melancholy occasion, with Chaplin reminiscing about his bitter marriage and divorce from Lita Grey, and his love for Marion Davies, 'his one and only real, long-lasting love.' But Marion belonged to William Randolph Hearst, who did everything he could to crush Charlie.

'Chaplin slid off his chair. Ran upstairs. We waited a little while. Then we left. We didn't see Chaplin again that evening. We saw him then as few people see him. Pale, suffering, his face crumpled. He remembered a lot that was difficult and painful. But it takes even more pain and hardship to forget about something . . .'

Eisenstein ends this heartfelt empathetic anecdote (written in the twilight of his life in June 1946) by adding, in parenthesis,

'Now around me is the dazzling gold of the midday sun. Yet I am burdened by melancholy. We all have our Marion Davieses . . .'[32]

If we take this literally to mean that Eisenstein, too, was in love with someone he could not possess, then we can only speculate as to who that was. In two fragments written in 1946, which he admitted were meant to 'fictionalise one's tragic romantic experience,' he expressed this experience obliquely through the means of a fairy story entitled The Little Princess and the Great Cathedral Builder Who Swallowed His Tongue. The only clues given are that The Little Princess was a millionaire's daughter ('a dollar princess'), who might have been called Catherine (or another form of that name) and the Great Cathedral Builder was Eisenstein himself.

'Once upon a time there lived the richest little princess in the world. Never married, afraid, and so she whored around . . . On the other end of the great big world there lived the famous Cathedral Builder, who had swallowed his tongue and talked through the edifices he built. At high table were the greatest Grands of the world at that time . . . Earl Venceslas with his fair-haired spouse – Pearl of the East . . . Then the Princess asked him to deliver her of a drunken beastly baron trying to seduce her by his love proposals . . . When somebody looked at him [the architect], he thought they looked at his cathedrals [films]. When somebody looked at her, she thought they were hunting for her millions. So he ran to her and wanted to tell her – sister, don't we suffer of the same? And shouldn't we go together? . . . But never, never could he get in touch with her. Fate was against them . . .'

Eisenstein remarked that 'this meeting quite unexpectedly opened my eyes to the cause of the age-long trauma of the ugly duckling . . . And it certainly went a little way to overcoming this trauma.'[33] Many have tried to decipher this fairy story, which bears a resemblance to the one that Count Danilo sings about in Franz Lehar's The Merry Widow, though few have succeeded.

Naum Kleiman suggests that Earl Venceslas was the foreign minister Wenceslas Molotov, who had a fair-haired wife, though Pearl is the name of Eisenstein's own wife, Pera. As Eisenstein was often invited to official receptions given by the Molotovs during 1944 and 1945, Kleiman feels that he might have fallen for someone at their house, perhaps a maid.[34] Because Eisenstein went to such extremes to bury his secret in the story, it seems more likely to have been a far more hopeless and forbidden love.

While enjoying the social life of Hollywood, and living in comfort in the pleasant house in Coldwater Canyon, a subject for a film that would be acceptable to Paramount had to be found. Though Eisenstein still harboured a desire to film *Das Kapital* and felt that an American experience was necessary to the understanding of its subject, he knew it was obviously not suitable for an American studio. The fact that he was still thinking about it, and about Joyce's *Ulysses*, shows how far his preoccupations were from those of the film industry in which he found himself.

Without considering Eisenstein's particular skills or tastes, Paramount suggested an eclectic range of subjects. Lasky proposed *The Criminal* (*Die Verbrecher*) by Ferdinand Bruckner; J.G. Bachman suggested *The Criminal Profession* by Albert Londres, and Rudyard Kipling's *Kim*. Another was *The Hairy Ape* to be adapted from Eugene O'Neill's raw and symbolic play about a ship's stoker who lusts after the rich bitch who visits his boiler room. One would have thought the latter, with its proletarian theme and powerful emotions, would have appealed to Eisenstein, but he dismissed it mischievously as 'one hundred percent propagandist.'

The first project Eisenstein suggested to Paramount was *The Glass House*, another idea that he had carried around with him for some time.

He had made the first notes and sketches for it after his 1926 trip to Berlin, where he and Tisse stayed at the Hotel Hessler in Kantstrasse, an example of new Berlin architecture employing a quantity of glass. It started him thinking about the contradictions of a society that was able to see through all walls but maintained a code of morals that prevented it from doing so.

In 1927, while editing *The General Line*, he wrote, 'America seen through Hollywood clichés. Reality to be an element of parody, as if Hollywood clichés were factual element . . . Do it as farce, as grotesque, as nightmarish tragedy. Loneliness while constantly being "among people" and being seen from all sides . . . Introduce a series of episodes with typically American stars playing various characters – and "kill" them with reality . . . Indifference to each other is established by showing that the characters do not see each other through the glass doors and walls because they do not *look* – a developed "non-seeing". Against this background, one person goes crazy, because he alone pays attention and looks. All live as though there are real walls, each for himself.'[35]

Eisenstein went on to suggest some of the inhabitants of the building – a suicide, a blackmailer, 'moral police', a woman dying in a fire – leading to the destruction of the glass house. He added: 'Perhaps for the premiere worth trying a monster screen – four times the usual screen size? Why not???' For this vast enterprise he suggested the help of the left-wing novelist Upton Sinclair. 'Only Upton can help this . . . And perhaps later it could be accepted by the Douglas Fairbanks Corporation.'[36]

By the time he got to Hollywood, Fairbanks was a has-been, and the studio system was growing ever more powerful. While searching for an idea acceptable to Paramount, *The Glass House* resurfaced when Eisenstein saw an illustrated article in the *New York Times* magazine on Frank Lloyd Wright's project for a glass tower. The story might also have been suggested by Eugene Zamiatin's novel *We*, as well as by the futuristic aspects of *Metropolis* and the social ones in *The Crowd*.

Eisenstein wrote a synopsis of *The Glass House*, which included a number of sketches, for Paramount. Montagu explained its theme. 'People live, work and have their being in a glass house. In this great building it is possible to see all around you; above, below, sideways, slanting, in any direction, unless, of course, a carpet, a desk, a picture or something like that should interrupt your line of sight . . . People do not see, because it never occurs to them to look . . . Then suddenly, something occurs to make them look, to make them conscious of their exposure. They become furtive, suspicious, inquisitive, terrified. Fantastic, you would say? Even silly? But it was not at all in this manner that Eisenstein saw it. He did not see it as a fantasy. He wanted to embody his idea on the most mundane possible plane. A serious, down-to-earth ordinary story.'[37]

In a letter to Pera dated July 7, 1930, Eisenstein wrote: 'Chaplin considers the idea wonderful and demands that we make only this! (And the authorities say he is envious because he isn't doing it! We've enjoyed talking a lot about it.)'[38]

Among the characters living in the building are two young lovers, a laundress, a clerk in a shoe store, a wife and her husband who beats her, a policeman, a poet, 'Christ or a technician', a leading nudist, bootleggers, and a parade of robots. From the incoherent, fragmentary, plotless, episodic synopsis, it would be difficult to blame Paramount for rejecting it. Though Eisenstein was worldly in many ways, he was a babe in Hollywood, and Montagu does not seem to have understood the mentality of the studio bosses any better.

A different case was *Sutter's Gold*, based on Blaise Cendras' novel *L'Or*, which Eisenstein had acquired the novelist's permission to film. It was the story of John August Sutter, a Swiss immigrant who founded his New Helvetia settlement in California in 1839 and discovered gold there in 1848. Eisenstein wanted to show 'the destruction caused by the discovery of gold on his Californian estates; it led to his prosperous farms being ravaged and to his own death . . . Mountains of spoilage still stand where they were flung up from the half-excavated mines . . . Beneath the soulless layer of stones lay once-verdant orchards, fields, pastures and meadows . . . the feet of thousands of madmen trampled over Sutter's land; thousands of hands ran through it and turned it over; thousands of people raced towards this spot, coming from all corners of the globe and ready to tear each others' throats out for the sake of a tiny clod of this earth which bears so strange a crop in its core. The flourishing paradise of Captain Sutter's Californian groves and pastures were trampled underfoot and crushed by filthy crowds lusting for gold. Sutter was ruined.'[39]

In order to build up the atmosphere of the America of the first gold rush, Eisenstein travelled extensively in California. He visited Sutter's fort in Sacramento, and in a San Francisco factory he was shown the saw-blade from Sutter's wood mill, where the first grain of gold was found. 'These comings and goings took us from the porches of small provincial houses, with the customary rocking-chair and old ladies sunk in their reminiscences, to harsh landscapes, where soil had been turned over by the dredges to resemble grey hills and mountains, burying the green fields and meadows. The scenery spoke eloquently of the lust for gold, devouring the organic joy of nature.'[40]

Eisenstein produced the preliminary scenario after three days of non-stop work. He outlined the action to Alexandrov who wrote it down in Russian. Paramount translators, standing by, immediately made a literal translation. Montagu took the translation to Eisenstein. They discussed it, changed it and made notes on it. Montagu wrote out in longhand an exact copy of the corrected and noted translation which then became the final script. Eisenstein then made his production sketches and costings.

In 1928, Eisenstein, Alexandrov and Pudovkin had published a manifesto on the sound film, stating that, 'Only the contra-puntal use of sound *vis-à-vis* the visual fragment of montage will open up new possibilities for the development and perfection of montage. The first experiments in sound must aim at a sharp discord with the visual images . . . Sound treated as a new element of montage . . . cannot fail to provide new and enormously pow-erful means of expressing and resolving the most complex problems . . .'[41]

Eisenstein, like René Clair, who made the musical *Sous les Toits de Paris* in 1930, realised that sound which simply accompanied action on the screen was tautological. Here is how Eisenstein imag-ined the use of sound as a metaphor in a sequence from *Sutter's Gold*.

'GOLD. The word rings through the forests, and echoes through the hills and canyons. and then from the depths of these canyons a new theme of the noise symphony can be heard. The sound of thousands of feet trampling over stones. The sound of endless trails of creaking wagons. The mixed sounds of horses' hoofs and screeching wagon wheels. And the murmur of limitless crowds . . . The sound of the approaching procession grows louder and nearer . . . Through these sounds can be heard the chopping of axes, falling trees, the whispering of saws, crashing trees. Pigs are screaming and frightened ducks quack frantically as they are pur-sued by the invaders. Sutter is driven wild by these sounds. The picks grow louder, and now the sound of stone striking stone – stone piled high from out of the river-bed, stones burying the fertile fields. Stones growing into mountains that crush all the fertility that preceded this terrible symphony of sounds . . .'[42]

Initially, Paramount objected that the film 'would cost too much'. Eisenstein then broke down each page of the script to prove that it could be done in '57 and a half days (two and a half days in reserve) = 60 days.' Yet, it was turned down. As Ivor Montagu wrote: 'This extraordinary tale, full of moral lessons, was turned by Eisenstein – with some help from the rest of us – into what I still regard as a marvellous script. We took it to Paramount, who simply pointed out to us that nobody in America was interested in history, and it was very old-fashioned of us to think otherwise. It would be as dull, so they politely explained, as if we tried to make a film about Henry VIII in England. [Three years later Alexander Korda made a hit film on exactly that subject.] It was hard to take seriously such naive reasons for rejection, and I believe that the true reason lay among the conflicts that undoubtedly existed within the Paramount company. Those who were jealous of the others who'd signed us up were trying to discredit the ones that supported us . . .'[43]

Although its theme was the kind to appeal to a committed socialist, its moral and social messages were indirect and oblique. Eisenstein thought, however, that 'not for nothing were my American hosts perturbed when I chose *L'Or* as the subject for a screenplay . . . "What? Let the Bolsheviks get at the subject of gold?"'[44]

Initially the synopsis of *Sutter's Gold* reveals that Eisenstein made few concessions in either style or subject to the more conventionally minded American producers. Curiously, only the musical (a genre born with sound) was given the creative scope within the commercial structure of Hollywood to experiment in colour, overhead shots, *trompe l'oeil*, split-screen techniques, superimposition, trick photography, surreal settings, animation and juggling with time and space. The musical would become an important force in imaginative film-making, without ever being accused of 'avant-gardism' by cautious studio moguls. Perhaps, if the plots were not so frivolous, the musical might have been the genre in which Eisenstein could have spread his wings in Hollywood. (It was Alexandrov who eventually made his name with Hollywood-style musicals in the Soviet Union.)

Sutter's Gold would have sat uncomfortably among Paramount's releases in 1930. These included *The Royal Family of Broadway*, Edna Ferber and George S. Kaufman's sophisticated comedy based on the Barrymores; Sternberg's *Morocco*, the Marx Brothers in *Animal Crackers*, and two 'naughty' Maurice Chevalier musicals. *The Spoilers*, from the Rex Beach novel about the Alaskan gold rush, starring Gary Cooper and filmed twice previously, was nearest in subject matter to *Sutter's Gold*, but worlds away in conception.

In 1936, Universal Pictures made *Sutter's Gold*, a conventional film directed by James Cruze, starring Edward Arnold. It cost $2 million, was a terrible flop, and almost sank Universal. In the same year as the American version, the Austrian Luis Trenker directed and starred in *The Emperor of California* (*Das Kaiser von Kalifornien*) in Nazi Germany after Universal had turned him down. Trenker portrayed Sutter as a visionary German nationalist who heroically rejects 'degenerate' American capitalism.

Theodore Dreiser was a visitor to Eisenstein's apartment in Chysti Prudi in Moscow in November 1927. Eisenstein called Dreiser 'the living Himalaya of an old man', although he was only fifty-six at the time. In his notes on his trip, the author of *An American Tragedy* wrote: 'On entering, I remarked that he had the largest and most comfortable looking bed I had seen in Russia, and I envied him the same, I having thus far only seen narrow and most uncomfortable looking ones. He smiled and said he had bought this magnificent thing from an American farming commune near Moscow where he had been taking pictures.'[45]

Paramount had secured the rights of *An American Tragedy* in 1925 (the year of its publication) and several directors, among them D.W. Griffith and Ernst Lubitsch, had considered the subject, but taken it no further. Lasky, therefore, offered it to Eisenstein.

The novel, based on an actual New York murder case, told of a charming but weak drifter, fatally torn between a drab factory girl whom he has made pregnant, and a rich society beauty. In order to free himself from his obligations and raise himself socially and economically, he takes the pregnant girl out in a rowing boat with the intention of drowning her . . .

According to Ivor Montagu, 'We embarked on the script with a sense of doom, knowing very well that as a group of foreigners, led by a Soviet director with two Soviet associates, we would never be permitted to make a film whose theme was essentially a criticism of American society.'[46] During the course of writing the script, Paramount boss B.P. Schulberg asked Eisenstein, 'Is Clyde Griffiths guilty or not guilty in your treatment?' The director replied, 'Not guilty.' 'Then your script is a monstrous challenge to American society!', Schulberg retorted. Eisenstein explained that he thought the crime committed by Griffiths was the summary result of the social relationships whose influence he had been subjected to at every stage of the development of his life. The main point in the treatment – conditions of education, upbringing, work, surroundings, and social conditions drove the characterless boy to crime. He explained that nothing was added to Dreiser's novel, and that the important sociological points were all in the book. The characters in the book were 'creatures of circumstance.' Schulberg suggested they complete the script 'as you feel it' and then they would see[47] – a directive similar to that which Stalin would give to Eisenstein many years later on *Ivan the Terrible Part II*.

So they went ahead, working round the clock at Coldwater Canyon. Montagu described it thus: 'Eisenstein would be closeted with Grisha, narrating verbally the treatment he had planned. Grisha would go off and write it. As soon as it was written it would be typed and translated. I would take an English text, read it, and go to Eisenstein. Now he and I would go through it, discussing and making emendations. Then I would go off and rewrite it. Helle [Montagu's wife] would receive my manuscript . . . to type fair copies. The Paramount staff would make more copies of this final state.

'This process meant, of course, that Grisha would always be two or three reels ahead of me. While he was on, say, the draft of reel four, I would still be discussing with Eisenstein the revision of reel two. Eisenstein would have to keep the whole in his head and switch from one to the other, like a chessmaster giving a simultaneous display.'[48]

On October 5, 1930, Eisenstein sent the finished scenario to Paramount with an accompanying letter.

'Gentlemen, So here we see the miracle accomplished – *An American Tragedy* presented in only 14 reels! Still we think the final treatment must not be over 12. But we withdraw from the final "shrinking" leaving it for the present "in extenso", so as to have the possibility of making this unpleasant operation after receiving the benefit of notes and advice from 1) The West Coast Magnates 2) The East Coast Magnates 3) Theodore Dreiser 4) The Hays Organization. Accordingly, gentlemen, we have the honour to submit to your "discriminating kindness" The Enclosed Manuscript and . . . Honi soit quit mal y pense. The AUTHORS' Among the notes attached to the first draft was 'Inner monologue. Why not??! Joyce in literature. O'Neill in drama, we in cinema. In literature – good, in drama – bad, in cinema – best.'[49]

Almost everybody who read the scenario was impressed, and Eisenstein, confident that it would be accepted, set off to New York to meet Dreiser and the leaders of Paramount with whom the final decision rested. Dreiser, especially, was full of praise for the adaptation. Eisenstein stayed at Dreiser's villa on the banks of the Hudson, and 'the old grey lion' showed him the lesser known parts of New York City, including speakeasies. (It was the era of Prohibition.) Schulberg said it was the best scenario Paramount had ever had. Then came the memo to Schulberg dated October 9, from David O. Selznick, associate producer at Paramount, that probably sealed the screenplay's fate.

'I have just finished reading the Eisenstein adaptation of *An American Tragedy*. It was for me a memorable experience; the most moving script I have ever read. It was so effective that it was positively torturing. When I had finished it, I was so depressed I wanted to reach for the bourbon bottle. As entertainment, I don't think it has one chance in a hundred . . . Is it too late to persuade the enthusiasts of the picture from making it? . . . I think it an inexcusable gamble on the part of this department to put into a subject as depressing as is this one, anything like the cost that an Eisenstein production must necessarily entail. If we want to make *An American Tragedy* as a glorious experiment, and purely for the advancement of the art (which I certainly don't think is the business of this organization), then let's do it with a [John] Cromwell directing, and chop three or four hundred thousand dollars off the loss.

If the cry of "Courage!" be raised against this protest, I should like to suggest that we have the courage not to make the picture, but to take whatever rap is coming to us for not supporting Eisenstein the artist (as he proves himself to be with this script) with a million or more of the stockholders' cash. Let's try new things by all means but let's keep these gambles within the bounds of those that would be indulged in by rational businessmen; and let's not put more money than we have into any one picture . . . into a subject that will appeal to our vanity through the critical acclaim that must necessarily attach to its production, but that cannot possibly offer anything but a most miserable two hours to millions of happy-minded young Americans.'[50]

So *An American Tragedy*, directed by Eisenstein, remains one of the great might-have-beens of cinema. Why was it rejected and why was Eisenstein's contract terminated so abruptly? King Vidor thought: 'Because Eisenstein knew he was handling a new art form, and because in personality he was the man he was, he refused in Hollywood to compromise his ideals or be talked out of the way he himself saw things. Anybody who behaved like that in the California of the 1930s was bound to be heading for a pile of trouble, and in my view this was why he failed . . . the pattern in all our studios at that time was the conventional one of telling a story, and going through the normal routine . . . and Eisenstein was already seeing far beyond that . . . But of course Eisenstein was not the only artist in the history of the world to suffer by being ahead of his time.'[51]

Montagu, Alexandrov and Eisenstein should have sensed it was clear from the beginning that a sociological approach to the theme would not correspond to the studio's demands. 'The Paramount bosses aspired to make of the "sensational" novel a run-of-the-mill (just another) albeit dramatic tale of "boy meets girl" without conceding on any of the "superfluous" issues,' Eisenstein remarked. 'These issues as I saw them were much weightier.'[52] He wondered why they bothered to take Dreiser's novel when they could just as easily have paid less for a story out of the newspaper.

'Some people have said the reasons were political, a basic fear of a Bolshevik who represented Bolshevism,' wrote Montagu. 'This factor undoubtedly existed, and there were various elements of the lunatic fringe who ran around writing letters to the papers and making demonstrations as to how Paramount had betrayed America by signing up this notorious Red Dog, and a great deal of angry correspondence arrived in the company's offices. All this must inevitably have carried some weight when it came to making the final decision but to claim that this was the only reason for Eisenstein's failure in Hollywood is to make a great over-simplification. If this had been the only problem, I doubt whether Paramount would have surrendered to it . . . Lastly, but of considerable importance, was the general fear that existed in Hollywood in those days . . . of anybody with intellectual pretensions; and the brutal fact is that not only did we have intellectual pretensions, but we had them written all over us.'[53]

Perhaps if Eisenstein had delivered the sort of script Paramount could sanction then the political pressure might have been discounted. Though it must be remembered that the three Russians were practically the first Soviets in California, and the relations between the two countries were strained, existing purely on a commercial footing. In fact, both Paramount and Eisenstein had been visited by the police. The new Code of Production had also come into practice in 1930, so the screenplay could have been used as an excuse to escape from an embarrassing contract. Whatever the studio's private views on its quality, they must have realised after *The Glass House*, *Sutter's Gold* and now *An American Tragedy*, that Eisenstein could never adapt to the house style as even such independent personalities as Sternberg or Lubitsch had.

Looking at the Hollywood studio system in the 1930s, where each of the majors developed its own characteristic style and philosophy, one could have foreseen that Paramount, though the most European of studios, would not have been the most suitable company in which the radical Eisenstein would have been able to work. If MGM encapsulated middle-class values, then Paramount's decorative opulence, with its mountain logo symbolising the upper crust, was the studio with aristocratic, even Tsarist, pretensions. Hans Dreier was the supervisory art director whose set designs established the lustrous surface that dictated the feel of the films. Ernst Lubitsch, the *bon viveur* with the inappropriate forename, embodied the Paramount spirit of elegance, sensuality, wit and cynicism in opulent surroundings, and Austrian-born Josef von Sternberg was just beginning his erotic-exotic cycle of films with Marlene Dietrich. In sharp contrast to Paramount's sheen, and MGM's *nouveau-riche* glitter, Warner Bros. was more in tune with the working class, and might have lent Eisenstein a more sympathetic ear.

It was to Sternberg that Paramount turned to direct *An American Tragedy*, which Eisenstein, naturally, found 'very poor. So poor in fact that I could not sit through the picture to the end . . . The idea of "inner monologue" never occurred to Sternberg . . . he confined himself to a "straightforward" detective story.'[54] Leaving aside how much Eisenstein's disappointment might have tempered his criticism, his assessment was correct. Sternberg eliminated the sociological elements, reducing the novel to a flat and perfunctory drama, culminating in a hammy court scene, though it has two moving performances from Phillips Holmes and Sylvia Sidney.

Dreiser was so enraged when he saw what Sternberg had done to his story that he sued Paramount for damages, although he had received around $80,000 for the film rights. He lost the case but for many years he continued to hope that Eisenstein would one day make the film in the Soviet Union. Neither Eisenstein nor Dreiser lived to see George Stevens' romantic version, *A Place in the Sun*, made in 1951. In it, Clyde, for some reason renamed George Eastman (Montgomery Clift), is visited in his death cell by Sondra (Elizabeth Taylor), who declares her love, whereas in the book she refuses to visit him, thus demonstrating the inhumanity of the values of her class.

One has only to watch the conventional murder sequence in the boat in both Sternberg's and Stevens' films and read Eisenstein's version to realise what an opportunity was missed. The passage below is from the 'first treatment'.

'As the boat glides into the darkness of the lake, so Clyde glides into the darkness of his thoughts. Two voices struggle within him – one: "Kill!-kill!" the echo of his dark resolve, the frantic cry of all his hopes of Sondra and society; the other: "Don't-don't kill!" the expression of his weakness and his fears, of his sadness for Roberta and his shame before her. In the scenes that follow these voices ripple in the waves that lap from the oars against the boat; they whisper in the beating of his heart; they comment, underscoring, upon the memories and alarums that pass through his mind, each ever struggling for mastery, first one dominating then weakening before the onset of its rival . . .

' . . . the boat overturns. Once more rings out the long-drawn booming cry of the bird. The overset boat floats on the surface of the water. Roberta's head appears above the surface. Clyde comes up. His face showing terrible fright, he makes a movement to help Roberta. Roberta, terrified by his face, gives a piercing cry and, splashing frantically, disappears under the water. Clyde is about to dive down after her, but he stops and hesitates. And the third time the long-drawn booming cry of the faraway bird. On the mirror-like calmness of the water floats a straw hat . . .'[55]

Some of his earlier notes reveal how he might have shot certain scenes such as Clyde in the death cell. 'Clyde visited by a preacher (terrifying coming out of darkness only the face of a skeleton) *Necessary*: that Clyde's cell be flooded with light, like a stage but the corridor, from where the visitors come – must be in semi-darkness.'[56]

A month before his Paramount contract was terminated, Eisenstein addressed a symposium devoted to the problems of the wide screen, which was organised by the Technicians' Branch of the Academy of Motion Picture Arts and Sciences. In a witty and insightful speech, printed under the title The Dynamic Square, he made the cases for vertical and horizontal screens, before opting for the square.

'This vertical tendency can be traced in their biological, cultural, intellectual and industrial efforts and manifestations . . . [But] in the heart of the super-industrialised American, or the busily self-industrialising Russian, there still remains a nostalgia for infinite horizons, fields, plains and deserts . . . This nostalgia cries out for horizontal space . . . [The square is] the one and only form that is equally fit, by alternately suppressing right and left or up and down, to embrace all the multitude of expressive rectangles in the world.'[57]

*

The Paramount contract was cancelled early in October 1930. It cost the studio over $30,000 in compensation to Eisenstein, but that was a modest sum in the scheme of things. They had already invested three times that amount in securing the property and the company had grown accustomed to years of writing off 'abandoned' or 'worthless' scripts.

In order for the three Russians not to leave Hollywood without having made a film, they made a last desperate suggestion, put to both MGM and Universal, for a film of Edgar Lee Masters' *Spoon River Anthology*. What Eisenstein liked about the book was the way 'there occurs a change in the point of view towards the events being recounted. The author wanted to create an image of a small American town with many characters and extremely complex, interlacing events. He creates a collection of poems in the form of epitaphs in the town's cemetery. Each epitaph is written as a monologue spoken by the deceased person . . .'[58] This demonstrates how much Eisenstein was still gripped by the notion of 'inner monologue'. Needless to say, the proposal was rejected.

Perhaps the best films are those that are never made, those that remain in the mind. There was a cinema in Prague when Franz Kafka was a young man called The Cinema of the Blind. This strange name (though not as strange as the cinema for dogs suggested to Eisenstein in Berlin) was more banal than it sounded. It was called that because it was owned by a charitable association for the support of the blind. Kafka believed that all cinemas should be called The Cinema of the Blind because their flickering images blind people to reality. We can only see Eisenstein's unrealised dreams in our imaginations. It was really the studio bosses who were blind, unable to 'see' the screenplays Eisenstein offered them.

Eighteen months after his departure from Moscow and six months after his arrival in the USA, Eisenstein's hopes of making a film in Hollywood were dead. It was time to return home.

11

Trouble in Paradise

*What is so amazing about Mexico is the vivid sense that there
you can experience things which you only know about otherwise from books and philosophical conceptions opposed to
metaphysics. I imagine that when the world was in its infancy
it was full of exactly the same supremely indifferent laziness,
coupled with the creative potential of those lagoons and
plateaux, deserts and undergrowth; pyramids you might
expect to explode like volcanoes . . .*

As permission to travel to the West had in fact been granted to the
three Russians for a maximum period of twelve months, their plans
had been faithfully reported to, and approved by, the Soviet film
authorities – Sovkino in Moscow and Amkino in the USA. It was
assumed that after the Paramount contract had been cancelled they
would return home at once.

There was a plan to go back to Russia via Japan to make a film
there, a proposal that was not only supported by Ivor Montagu but
formally approved by Lev Monosson, the Amkino representative in
the USA. All was set for their departure after Paramount bought
three one-way tickets to the USSR. However, before he left
Hollywood, Eisenstein had a significant encounter with Robert
Flaherty, 'the father of the documentary film'.

In the last eight years, Flaherty had only made two features as
sole director, *Nanook of the North* (1922) and *Moana* (1926). He
had left both *White Shadows of the South Seas* and *Tabu* because
of disagreements with their co-directors (W.S. Van Dyke and F.W.
Murnau respectively), and was now looking for another project.

Despite his own struggles, Flaherty convinced Eisenstein of the virtues of independent film-making. He had a fund of ideas which cried out to be made into films. 'There, I'll make you a present of that one,' he said to Eisenstein, referring to a story set in Mexico. Flaherty, in turn, was inspired by Eisenstein to go to the Soviet Union. 'The old man [forty-six years old!] was fired . . . with determination to work in Russia on a series of films devoted to the national minorities.'[1]

Flaherty had an indirect influence on Eisenstein's approach to *Qué Viva México!* with its synthesis of the style and structure of a fictional film, while filming real people and situations. Eisenstein wanted passionately to work in Mexico, a country that had gripped his imagination since 1922 when he had designed the sets for the Proletkult's production of the Jack London story, *The Mexican*. He had read Ambrose Bierce, who went missing during the Mexican Civil War in 1914, the reportages by John Reed on Mexico and the stories of the American writer Albert Rhys Williams whom he had met in Moscow in 1928. Then there were the frescoes of Diego Rivera, who corresponded with Eisenstein and urged him to make a documentary film called *Life in Mexico*.

It was at the Hollywood Book Store that Eisenstein nurtured his attraction to Mexico. The shop was owned by a mysterious man called Odo Stade, either 'a Hungarian Swiss' or 'Tyrolean Czech', who was writing a book on Pancho Villa, with whom he had fought in the Mexican Revolution. Stade spoke to Eisenstein about Mexico, 'and the offshoots of my fascination with this country, which took root when I saw some photographs of the Day of the Dead . . . I had a burning desire to go there.'[2]

Eisenstein recalled seeing a picture some years before, in a German magazine, of 'a human skeleton astride the skeleton of a horse. He wore a broad-brimmed sombrero, with a bandolier over one shoulder . . . And there was a photograph of a hat-shop window – skulls sticking out of collars and ties. The skulls wore neat straw hats in the latest style . . . What could it be? A madman's delirium, or a modern version of Holbein's *Danse Macabre*? No! These were photographs of the Day of the Dead in Mexico City. The skeletons were . . . children's toys!!! . . . This impression lodged with me like a splinter. My desperate longing to see this in reality

217

was like a chronic sickness. And not only this. But the whole of a country that would take its amusements in such a way! Mexico!'[3]

He also read *The Mexican Maze* by Carlton Beals, whom Eisenstein subsequently met in a bookshop in Mexico City. Eisenstein quoted Beals' definition of *vacilada*, a form of Mexican wit, not unlike his own. 'The *vacilada* is a combination of the ridiculous and the sublime, of vulgarity and purity, of beauty and ugliness, of spirituality and animality, disconcertingly tripping over each other, showering the world with passing glory, like the spray of a rocket flame. The Mexican's approach to life, death and sex . . . is shot through with poetic irresponsibility, it defies direct logic, takes serious things lightly, and insignificant things with great gravity. This is a gracious and self-protective distortion, a creative destruction of values cherished by the European mind.'[4] Is not this description one of the most accurate summings up of the whole of Eisenstein's oeuvre?

Suddenly, Hollywood no longer interested him (the feeling was mutual), and the idea of making a film in Mexico was now dearest to his heart. He expressed his desire to Chaplin, who told him to approach Upton Sinclair, the left-wing novelist and would-be governor of California, to help finance the project. (Chaplin had based his 1917 film *The Adventurer* on a work by Sinclair.) When the idea was put to Sinclair, he recommended it to his wealthy wife, Mary Craig Sinclair, persuading her to back the project, together with a number of her rich friends in Pasadena. The thought of financing a film by a great radical Soviet director appealed to the politically active author.

Eisenstein also tried to obtain the financial support of William King Gillette, the inventor of the safety razor, but the shrewd Gillette decided not to invest in the film. 'He was obsessed with building villas in desert regions. A house, a palace would rise above the sand; he would plant orchards around it; but then the builder would dash off to a new part of the desert to construct a new palace, and so on and so on,' Eisenstein wrote. 'I have lived in much the same sort of way, in relation to the events in my personal life. Like a pack animal or horse that has a sheaf of corn hanging in front of him which he chases, headlong, hopelessly, for ever.'[5] At the time, Eisenstein could not have foreseen that *Qué Viva México!*

would be one of those abandoned palaces built on sand, the completion of which he would pursue in his mind forever after.

Delighted at the prospect of making a film in Mexico, Eisenstein paid little attention to the clauses of the contract, signed on November 24, 1930. It stipulated a period of three to four months of filming, which Eisenstein was determined to stick to. As he wrote to Esther Shub: 'My leave of absence expires in February and I expect not to delay overmuch. I may perhaps stop off in Japan on the way.'[6]

The contract also stipulated that Eisenstein should have a completely free hand in the shooting, that the film was to be apolitical and that world rights as well as positive and negative copies should belong to Mary Sinclair. At Eisenstein's request, the rights for the USSR were granted to the Soviet government. That neither Sinclair nor his wife knew anything about the economics of filming would play a detrimental role in the whole sorry affair that ensued.

'I quarrelled with Eisenstein over the Mexican project,' recalled Ivor Montagu in 1971. 'I could not believe that the enterprise could succeed, and my reason was that Upton Sinclair tried to keep it in his own hands – not for bad motives (for his motives were the best) but partly in order to save money, and partly because his brother-in-law (Hunter Kimbrough), whom he appointed as production manager, knew almost nothing about how films are made and costed. Moreover, Eisenstein, strange as it may seem, knew absolutely nothing at all. He knew of film direction. He knew everything that in those days could possibly be known technically and artistically. But in the Soviet Union the essential elements of production had been in the hands of others. He had no idea how much a film would cost in his own country, and even less about its cost anywhere else. But Upton Sinclair had quite fairly asked that very essential question. What could he do? In the event what he did was a singularly silly thing; he went to a bookseller in Hollywood who was well known to us all and who fought with Villa in Mexico, and asked him how much it would cost to make a reasonably priced documentary film in that particular country. Of course he got an absurd answer, but he passed it on to Sinclair in all sincerity. So, when the costs began to rise, Sinclair began to worry, and in his panic he spread the legend that Eisenstein was ludicrously over-shooting and was running up costs that were quite unjustified. All of which was unfair and untrue. According to Sinclair, Eisenstein had shot 35 miles of film; but I myself can recall – and I think most of us who know anything about the cinema can recall – that for a normal feature film in those days we often shot 45 miles. In any case these were rushes designed to be cut to length in the editing room. But there was poor ignorant Sinclair, sitting in Hollywood and seeing shot after shot and re-take after re-take . . . and saying to himself, "Is this man mad?" Whereas in truth the work was extremely economical, and its total cost would have compared very favourably with such a simple documentary as the British film *Man of Aran*. Eisenstein's *Qué Viva México!* was about the whole of a country and its social history, and was full of mass-scenes, whereas *Man of Aran* was concerned with a few people on a tiny island. But the eventual cost of *Man of Aran* was between £17,000 and £20,000; and Eisenstein's completed Mexican project would have cost Sinclair, by his own admission, about £15,000.'[7]

On the day of his departure for Mexico, Chaplin showed Eisenstein the first edited version, without sound, of his new film, *City Lights*. While Eisenstein watched the film from Chaplin's armchair, Chaplin himself sat at the piano, explaining his plan for the sound and humming the melodies. Then friends took Eisenstein, Alexandrov and Tisse to the station, where the former left, as one of them, the American journalist Seymour Stern recalled, looking 'like a little boy taking his first long trip . . . Eisenstein, the king and master of flaming images of turmoil and the world's war for freedom – seemed so completely, so pathetically and tragically, innocent. This was what stared from the Pullman window.'[8]

Eisenstein could have had no premonition of the tragedy that would haunt him for the rest of his life. Indeed, he set off for Mexico in a mood of innocent expectation. In a letter at the time of Eisenstein's departure, Sinclair wrote, 'This will be the first time in Eisenstein's life that he has been entirely free to make a picture according to his own ideas.'[9] And so it would have been.

Typical of the kind of improbable brief encounters in Eisenstein's life were two on the train trip from Los Angeles to Mexico City.

Eisenstein found his reserved berth in the wagon-lit already occupied. A vain attempt to sort out the situation ended up with Eisenstein, Alexandrov and Tisse forcibly ejecting the intruder, an incident which would have potentially serious consequences a little later. The second encounter on the train was the one in which Eisenstein shared a sleeper with Maurice Tessier, who, under the *nom de plume* of Maurice Dekobra wrote detective stories, including *The Madonna of the Sleeping Cars* (*La Madonne des sleepings*, 1925), which, in Eisenstein's words, 'broke all records – in terms of both print run and banality. Dekobra had written an equally banal book about Indian rajahs, *Les Tigres parfumés* . . . This 'Madonna' wrote her books with particular ease on trains, and on sheets of complimentary hotel writing-paper.'[10]

About two weeks after their arrival in Mexico City, the three Russians were summoned before the Chief of Police, to be confronted by their adversary from the wagon-lit – who turned out to be none other than the Chief of Police's brother, and on whose evidence they were arrested. It culminated in demands for Eisenstein's deportation. Again it was Major Frank Pease and his 'patriotic' cronies who were responsible for having written to the Mexican authorities to warn them of the Communist 'danger' that Eisenstein represented. Mexico, which had recognised the Soviet Union some years before, had broken off relations with them in 1930.

Eisenstein and his two companions spent the night at the hotel under police surveillance. However, immediately the news reached Sinclair he contacted Chaplin, Fairbanks and some US senators, two of whom, Senators Borah and LaFollette, intervened with the Mexican authorities, and the detainees were released. According to Eisenstein, twelve American senators intervened, as well as Chaplin and Albert Einstein. The Mexican authorities apologised and declared the visitors honoured guests, the President himself shaking them by the hand at an anniversary celebration in Mexico City.

Eisenstein immediately set out to explore Mexico. He saw the thousand-year pyramids at Yucatan and sat at the foot of the ruins of the Temple of a Thousand Columns. He was impressed by the Catholic churches on the sites of Aztec and Toltec temples. At the same time he met many of Mexico's leading artists: Fernando Gamboa, José Clemente Orozco, David Alfaro Siquieros and Diego Rivera, adding to his knowledge of the country.

'People who have been to Mexico greet each other like brothers. For people who have been to Mexico catch the Mexican fever. Anyone who has ever seen the Mexican plains has only to close his eyes to picture something like the Garden of Eden . . . And this despite the mangy curs licking the dirty cooking pots with food, the universal graft and exasperating irresponsibility of incorrigible sloth, the terrible social injustices and rampantly arbitrary actions of the police force, and age-long backwardness, which coexist alongside highly sophisticated forms of social exploitation.'[11]

He then set about writing a rough outline of *Qué Viva México!*, which was sent to Upton Sinclair and approved by him. He prepared the earliest of his scenarios in April 1931. It consisted of a prologue, six novellas and an epilogue, each of which was to be dedicated to an artist. Eisenstein explained: 'It was constructed like a necklace, like the bright, striped colouring of the *serape* or Mexican cloak, or like a sequence of short novellas. This chain of novellas was held together by a set of linking ideas, proceeding in a historically based sequence, but not so much by chronological epochs as by geographical zones.'[12]

The Prologue embodied the composition of David Alfaro Siquieros' unfinished, mutilated fresco, *The Worker's Burial*. 'The time of the prologue could be today or twenty years ago or a thousand years ago; because the people of Yucatan, a land of ruins and immense pyramids, have preserved the features and forms of their ancestors, the great ancient race of the Mayas. Stones. Gods. Men. Act in the Prologue.' After a 'strange' funeral ceremony, 'a young girl with bare breasts drifting along the river in a boat. She combs her long black hair and goes to see her lover, offering herself to him with simple joy.'

The first novella was entitled *Conquest*, in which Eisenstein filmed the Stations of the Cross. 'Preceded by three skulls, a group of penitent monks leads the procession. On the way to the cross, an old woman offers water to a thief.' *Sandunga* was the marriage of a young Mexican Indian girl. 'Old women examine the bridal dress while friends bring the girl gifts. After the ceremony, the men perform a marriage dance in honour of San Diego la Sandunga. Young girls watch the ceremony. The faces of the young couple are full of joy and tenderness.'

Fiesta (for which only part of a bullfight was filmed), was dedicated to Goya. It was a triangular drama – husband, wife and picador – which takes place during an afternoon of bullfighting. *Maguey*, set during the dictatorship of Porfirio Diaz at the beginning of the century, centred on the tragedy of the wedding of two young Mexican victims of Spanish colonialism. 'The action takes place on the day of Corpus Christi. During the ceremony, cock fights mingle with Christian rites. A penitent submits himself to ceremonial chastisement. As the ceremony reaches its climax, the young peon Sebastian goes to present his fiancée, Maria, to the owner of the hacienda. Custom demands that any peon wanting to marry must ask his master's permission. Maria is raped by one of the guests and kept prisoner. Guards beat up Sebastian and throw him out. At nightfall he returns with three other peons to free Maria. A volley of shots greets them, and they run away. One of them is killed, the others beaten and tied up. They stand waiting for their graves to be dug. Buried in the sand up to his chest, Sebastian is trampled to death by horses. Crazed with grief, Maria discovers the mutilated body of her lover.

Soldadera (none of which was shot), inspired by José Clemente Orozco's fresco *Las Soldaderas*, was to have been the story of the wives of the soldiers of Zapata's revolutionary army of 1910, and the overthrow of Diaz. 'An army of soldiers is preceded by an army of soldiers' wives . . . The *soldadera* scoured the deserted battlefield, searching among the corpses for the wounded body of her soldier-companion, side by side with whom she frequently fought, in order to carry him away on her shoulders, or bury him and make a cross of coloured stones on his grave, after which she would become the wife of another soldier.'

The epilogue was set during a carnival in contemporary Mexico on All Saints' Day. 'On this day, Mexicans show their contempt for death. Life reaffirms itself under the cardboard skulls; life surges forward, death retreats and vanishes.'[13]

Because Eisenstein's fatal attraction to the Day of the Dead had first prompted him to go to Mexico, 'it is natural enough that my last word on that country – the ending of the film – should be expressed in images from that same Day of the Dead. The more so as the theme of life and death expressed ultimately by a living face and skull, is the key, basic theme which informs the whole film.'[14]

Shooting actually started long before the script was sent to Sinclair. As his centre for filming, Eisenstein chose Tetlapayac, an old Spanish plantation situated eighty miles or so south-east of Mexico City and owned by Don Julio Salvidar, 'an extremely kind and courteous man'. Between shooting sessions, Eisenstein would retire to the monastic seclusion of his room and bury himself in his studies and reading. Simultaneously he was working on his book of film aesthetics.

'The stupefying aroma of fermented maguey juice filtered up from the pulque (the Mexican type of vodka) distillery, which was lit by candles and with a tawdry madonna, and permeated my temporary sleeping quarters on the first floor . . .' It was there that they filmed the scenes of peon uprisings on the estates. 'We filmed, many days running, episodes where the revolting peasants exchanged fire with the landowners' police, the *charros*, in the overgrown cactus palms, or among the sparse foliage of agave bushes . . . the acting was unusually realistic. Because the actors were real peons and real *charros*, retained by the young Señor Julio [Salvidar]. Give both sides free rein, substitute the blank cartridges with loaded ones . . . The estate manager, Señor Nicolas from Santander, Spain, allowed only the owner, Señor Julio, to shoot off pieces of cactus (in close-up near his face) . . . At evening the tall gates were shut. And no one from the administration block dared to go out in the fields by night.'[15]

In the course of shooting, Eisenstein expanded his ideas in the scenario, sometimes developing brief passages into long and detailed scenes and transforming other episodes. On April 15, 1931, Sinclair wrote to Hunter Kimbrough, his brother-in-law and personal representative with the film unit, 'We are not in the least worried about the design or story of the picture; we are quite cheerfully leaving that to him.' The same day, Eisenstein wrote to Sinclair: 'It is true that you are in the same position as was Sovkino when we were shooting *Potemkin* – we had such a lot to do that nobody in Moscow knew what we were doing! . . . The more because it is very complicated for me to expose on paper what and how the film will become and is becoming.'[16]

The fact that the film was taking much longer than scheduled could not be blamed on Eisenstein. Many of the delaying factors were the impossibly difficult filming conditions, the language barrier, the attitude of the Mexican extras who regularly turned up late or disappeared at crucial moments, and of the Mexican authorities whose permission to shoot certain scenes was required.

During the filming, Felix Olvera, who played the boy who witnesses the execution of his older comrades, was arrested for accidentally shooting his sister with the large-bore pistol, a 1910 model, which he used in the film. In order that Felix could complete his scenes, the police had to be bribed to bring him each day to the filming.

Then there was the torrid heat that had members of the unit literally falling over and frequently brought filming to a halt. This was followed by the rains and a new series of obstacles. Finally Eisenstein succumbed to an illness that immobilised him for a period. All the time, he was working in the dark with the help of only a few simple rushes, since the filmed material was sent straight to California for processing.

Still the filming was not finished and the time limit was extended again and again. The expenses too were mounting, and Sinclair once more sent his brother-in-law, who had returned to the USA, to supervise the activities of Eisenstein and his team. Kimbrough's arrival was followed by a sharp clash with Eisenstein that gave rise to a whole crop of misunderstandings and arguments. In Hollywood, meanwhile, where Sinclair arranged a showing of some 10,000 metres of the rushes sent by Eisenstein, the film aroused the enthusiasm of everyone who saw it, including Seymour Stern, Chaplin and also, apparently, Albert Einstein.

But Sinclair had his doubts, as he expressed in a letter to Lev Monosson, the head of Amkino. 'Things have come to a crisis with the Eisenstein picture . . . Having had the advantage of seeing the rushes so far, I can tell you pretty definitely that the hacienda story is the only one in the whole picture which is consecutive and interesting to the public. The so-called first story is nothing but pictures of Mayan ruins and an Indian funeral; the second story is simply a village wedding with a dance; the fourth story is the daily life of a bullfighter, with preparation for the ceremony and the scenes in the ring; the fifth story I cannot judge because this has not been taken. But the third story, which is the hacienda picture . . . is what Hollywood calls a "story". It has some suspense and excitement, and so it will be possible to get the trade to consider it. I do not want for a moment to give the impression that I am discouraged about Eisenstein's picture, as he plans it. I know that it will be a beautiful and magnificent work of art.'[17]

Although it is absurd to evaluate the quality of a film by its rushes, particularly one by Eisenstein, where the editing is so fundamental to the conception, Sinclair's views were understandable in the circumstances.

On October 26, 1931, Sinclair wrote enthusiastically to Stalin: 'You may have heard that I have taken the job of financing a moving picture which the Soviet director Sergei Eisenstein is making in Mexico. It is going to be an extraordinary work, and I think will be a revelation of the moving-picture art . . . Some day you will see the picture which Eisenstein is making, and realise that Soviet technique has advanced another step and been crowned with fresh laurels.'[18]

Four days after Sinclair's comments to Stalin, Eisenstein's loyal friend, the Mexican critic, Augustin Aragon Leiva, confided to Seymour Stern in a letter, that Eisenstein was 'facing troubles', that he was 'in danger of producing an unfinished symphony.' Sinclair began to panic, and gave Hunter Kimbrough more authority to watch every penny spent. Kimbrough, a former stock and bond salesman, was a repressed, humourless Southern gentleman, who knew nothing about films or filming.

Eisenstein begged Sinclair in letter after letter (no less impassioned for his spelling errors) to get Kimbrough, whom he accused of spending the film's money on women, drink and gambling, off his back. 'At the actual moment all my personal contact with Hunter has seased – I think it quite natural after his declaring me a dishonest person and my behaviour towards you as blackmailing. You understand very well that these statements cannot affect me when said by a person who was put in jail in Merida for public indecency in a bordell, after a wild adventure with throwing whores in the swimming pool. Well in his story the rabelasian inclination towards liquor plaid its positive part.'[19]

Meanwhile, Eisenstein had lost the confidence of the Soviet authorities. On November 21, 1931, Sinclair received a cable from Stalin.

EISENSTEIN LOOSE HIS COMRADES CONFIDENCE IN SOVIET UNION STOP HE IS THOUGHT TO BE DESERTER WHO BROKE OFF WITH HIS OWN COUNTRY STOP AM AFRAID THE PEOPLE HERE WOULD HAVE NO INTEREST IN HIM STOP AM VERY SORRY BUT ALL ASSERT IT IS THE FACT STOP MY REGARDS STOP STALIN.

In a reply to Stalin, the very next day, Sinclair made a sturdy defence of Eisenstein.

' . . . your statements concerning Eisenstein . . . have caused me both distress and bewilderment . . . I have never heard Eisenstein speak a word of disloyalty to the Soviet government . . . Eisenstein had a contract with Paramount by which they were to pay him $3,000 per week when he started work. This would have been a very comfortable start in the bourgeois world, and all he had to do was to sacrifice to a slight degree his artistic integrity. He was ferociously attacked in Hollywood by the Fascist element here . . . He made no attempt to protect himself from this, as he could very easily have done by making a few concessions . . .'[20]

Sinclair, who has always been cast as the villain of the piece, went on to explain to Stalin that the delays in filming were not Eisenstein's fault, that he had insisted the rights of the film should be given to the Soviet Union free, and that he had every intention of returning to the Soviet Union when the film was completed.

Despite this defence, Sinclair continued to rely on reports from his brother-in-law on the spot, causing Eisenstein to react once more. 'I cannot until now conceive how you could impose us Kimbrough with absolute and irrevocable autority [sic] after all the things that happened between us. Even the most hard-boyled [sic] business man would never do such a thing . . .'[21] Kimbrough remained, writing to Sinclair that Eisenstein and Co were 'a bunch of homos'.[22] What provoked this remark, a specific incident or a general perception by Kimbrough of their behaviour, has never been adequately explained.

Salka Viertel explained the seriousness of the situation in her book, *The Kindness of Strangers*. 'The year had passed quickly and the money was about gone . . . Eisenstein asked me to persuade his Pasadena sponsors to invest more money in the film. Through Upton I succeeded in the difficult task and the millionairesses agreed to increase the financing. But Mrs Sinclair insisted that the "irrational artist" be put under the strict control of her brother, Mr Kimbrough. There were telephone calls and letters, and finally Eisenstein agreed, appointing me to be his representative when the rushes were shown in Los Angeles . . . My job was to explain to the Pasadena ladies why Eisenstein had photographed this or that from different angles (for example, the bare breasts of a dark Mexican girl . . .)'[23]

But there was still a danger that the Sinclairs would withdraw all financial support from Eisenstein. He therefore wrote a desperate letter to Salka, whom he called Zalka, on January 27, 1932: 'You know that instead of the four months schedule and $25,000, which would have merely resulted in a pitiful travelogue, we have worked 13 months and spent $53,000, but we have a great film and have expanded the original idea. This expansion was achieved under incredible difficulties inflicted upon us by the behaviour and bad management of Upton Sinclair's brother-in-law, Hunter Kimbrough . . . Mr Kimbrough was recalled and then sent back with "increased powers" *as my supervisor*, which means that now he has the right to interfere with everything I do and make all the cuts! He presented me to Sinclair as a liar, a blackmailer, and God-knows-what-else . . . Now to our practical achievements: We have 500 soldiers, which the Mexican army has given us for 30 days, 10,000 guns and 50 cannons, *all for nothing* . . . We need only $7,000 or $8,000 to finish it, which we could do in a month, and then we would have a truly marvellous film . . . And all that has to be sacrificed because of $8,000 . . . Sinclair stopped the production and intends to throw before the people a truncated stump with the heart ripped out! I have exhausted my powers of persuasion. I shall do everything he wants . . . I accept Kimbrough, everything, anything . . . if only they let me finish this film. I've worked under most incredible harassment, no, not worked, fought . . . We, all three of us, are convinced that this is our best film and that it must not be destroyed. I beg you, Zalka, go to Sinclair . . . a film is not a sausage which tastes the same if you eat three-quarters of it or the whole Wurst . . . Our only hope is that meanwhile a miracle will happen and that the *Soldadera* episode will be filmed. Help us, Zalka! No, not us, help our work, save it from mutilation!'[24]

But the Sinclairs called a halt to the production in mid-January when Eisenstein was about to shoot *Soldadera*, the last of the six episodes. Among the reasons which influenced his decision was that he was clearly told that the USSR did not want the picture. In his autobiography, Sinclair explained that he broke with Eisenstein under pressure from his wife and family. There must have been further pressure on Sinclair to sequester all the material already shot, and to exclude Eisenstein from the editorial process.

'I gnash my teeth with hatred for those film people who, through stupidity and lack of culture, have not allowed us to complete our 14 months of intensive work which, by all objective criteria, represents an enormous stage in the creative activity of our collective.'[25]

Consequently, without money and with all the film shot to date in Sinclair's possession, Eisenstein was forced to leave Mexico for the USA. With his two friends he set off in their old De Soto but got no further than the small border town of Nuevo Laredo, where they were refused entry visas by the American immigration authorities.

'Anyone who has seen the film *Hold Back the Dawn* will remember Charles Boyer's confinement to the border,' wrote Eisenstein. 'Three weeks was not so long in Nuevo Laredo. Even four. Five. Six. People spent months here. Years, sometimes. The quota. And the whole flyblown town of Nuevo Laredo was made up of people like this, waiting. They have set up in business.'[26] (In fact, the trio had to wait for their transit visas for almost a month, from February 17 to March 14.)

The situation reminded Eisenstein of another film, the final scene from Chaplin's *The Pilgrim* (1923), which had the sheriff escorting the convict Charlie near the Mexican border. The sentimental sheriff wants Charlie to escape, and therefore asks his charge to pick a

229

flower for him across the border in Mexico. 'Charlie obligingly crosses the border. In relief the sheriff spurs on his horse. But . . . Charlie catches him up with the flower. The film ends with a kick up the backside and a shot of Chaplin running off with one foot in the USA and the other in Mexico. In the middle is the border. There is no solution . . .'[27]

Stranded in Mexico and unable to gain access to the footage he had sent to Hollywood for processing, Eisenstein tried, during this frustrating enforced stay, through official Soviet channels in America, to make arrangements for cutting the film in Moscow. Sinclair agreed to this in a telegram to Eisenstein in which he promised to ship both the film and his luggage to the USSR. However, he added a caveat. 'Your statements that picture incomplete are damaging. Insist you do not make such statements again. If New York papers question you you will be wise and explain it was your proposal to cut in Russia.'

While in Nuevo Laredo, Eisenstein was paid a visit by the owner of a cinema in San Antonio in Texas, who had had the courage to show *The Battleship Potemkin* to his redneck audience, losing money in the process. The elderly German-born man asked Eisenstein if he would be interested in making a film of the 1945 war between Texas and Mexico. He told Eisenstein: 'My friends who own the biggest ranches in these parts, will be only too glad to let you have as many horses as you need.' When Eisenstein explained that making a film required more than horses, he came back with another idea. He had heard of a singer called Señora Montoya, 'the idol of Latin America'. 'Do you understand the magic in this name, the effect it would have on the film's success in South America?'

Coincidentally, she happened to be performing the very next night in Monterey, not far to the south of Nuevo Laredo. Eisenstein declined to go, but Edouard Tisse who 'did not mind where he went, or why . . .' travelled to see Señora Montoya with the Texan.

'My theatre lovers returned from the performance late. Tisse was bent double with mirth. The gentleman from San Antonio spat angrily and suddenly lapsed into the language of his forebears. "*Alte*

Hure!!" [old whore!!], he furiously muttered through clenched teeth.'[28] The man drove back to San Antonio in his old Ford, and they never saw him again.

The next day, the head of immigration control on the American border ran across to the Mexican side and shouted, 'The visas are ready!' In a few hours, they were driving through Texas, the beginning of a nineteen-day drive across the country to New York. En route, Eisenstein accumulated a number of comic books, and cut out comic strips and articles from newspapers in an attempt to analyse American humour. In New Orleans, he was invited to lecture to black audiences at the Negro Straight College there, making contact with a number of black intellectuals at the time.

While he had been waiting for sunshine in Merida, where he was filming the bullfight sequence, Eisenstein had begun to sketch key scenes for a film about the Haitian Revolution, an idea inspired by John Vandercook's *Black Majesty*, something for which he had already thought of Paul Robeson before leaving Europe.

In New York, Eisenstein was determined to enjoy as much of the bourgeois delights of capitalism as he could before his return home. He saw the *Ziegfeld Follies*, the 'college' musical *Good News*, and the Barnum and Bailey circus; he visited nightclubs in Harlem, and was at the Max Schmeling-Primo Carnera heavyweight fight at Madison Square Gardens 'in the presence of the Prince of Wales', as he noted. He spent time with the dancer Sara Mildred Strauss, once improvising a ballet with her, Tisse and Alexandrov at her studio. He also introduced Sergei Yutkevich's *The Golden Mountains* that had opened in New York.

'The speech gave me a chance to say some harsh words about the emptiness and shallowness of American works, contrasting that with the problematic and deeply philosophical issues which, admittedly, are minor and embryonic, but at least touched upon in *The Golden Mountains*. In the same speech I mentioned the enhanced subject matter of ideology as the single and crucial means of escape from the dead ends of form and production, which was where American cinema was logically heading. You will appreciate the political significance that this speech had especially in the American context: the American press reacted quite violently to my statement.'[29]

But what preoccupied Eisenstein most was getting hold of the processed reels of film he had shot for *Qué Viva México!*, some of which he managed to see in New York in the form of rushes in the laboratory before it was edited and spliced together.

On April 19, 1932, Eisenstein left the USA permanently, on board the *Europa*. On the ship he shared a table with Noël Coward and Alexander Woollcott, two homosexuals whose waspish wit he enjoyed. Just before sailing he had received a cable from Sinclair, which cheered him up. BON VOYAGE. ALL FILM WILL FOLLOW ON NEXT SHIP. For the rest of his life, Eisenstein kept this broken promise in a black frame on display above his desk, along with a more positive reminder written on a card of the *Europa* – '"Réaliser!" – Cézanne.'[30] For Cézanne, it meant 'Create!'; for Eisenstein, it also meant 'Direct!', something he would find increasingly difficult to be allowed to do.

While on the *Europa*, Eisenstein was blissfully unaware of another storm raging around him. In Mexico, during the months of shooting, he had found time to make many of his finest drawings, most of them, in Ian Christie's words, 'delirious conflations of the spiritual and the erotic.'[31] The fact that their eroticism was principally homosexual, mingled with blasphemy, added spice to the scandal that their discovery provoked. The drawings, as well as photos of nude males, were found in the trunks and boxes Eisenstein sent to Hollywood from Mexico and were seized by US Customs agents. Sinclair was alerted to these drawings when he was given some samples by Hunter Kimbrough. In an indiscreet letter addressed to the Soviet authorities dated March 19, 1932, Sinclair wrote:

'It appears that Eisenstein spends all his leisure time in making very elaborate obscene drawings. I have a specimen of his work brought from Mexico. It is identified as Eisenstein's by his handwriting on it. Believe me, it is not an anatomy study nor a work of art or anything of that sort; it is plain smut. Hunter tells me that Eisenstein presented a series of such drawings to the young owner of the hacienda, and they were so bad that this educated young Mexican refused to put them up in his den.'[32]

One drawing which Sinclair saw was 'a parody of Christian paintings showing Jesus and the two thieves hanging on crosses; the penis of Jesus is elongated into a hose, and one of the thieves has the end in his mouth.'[33] (Actually, this was Eisenstein's private joke on the scene of the Mexican version of the Passion in the film.) The customs men apparently informed Sinclair on discovery of the drawings that 'they were the worst they had ever seen in their lives,' and 'they wanted to confiscate the whole shipment'.[34] As the trunks also contained property of Sinclair's, he claimed that Eisenstein had put these drawings in there in the hope of damaging him. One of Eisenstein's most endearing traits was his complete shamelessness with regard to his erotic/pornographic drawings, seeming not to care who saw them.

The fourteen-month sojourn in Mexico may not have produced a completed film, which, to make matters worse, was mutated in other people's hands, but the country had a profound influence on Eisenstein as a man and an artist. In his private diary, in which he jotted down idle thoughts in Mexico, he attempted to analyse the mystery that Mexico held for him, trying to make a connection between the ideas of dialectical materialism and the reality of Mexico. He elaborated on his ideas of progress and regression, impossible in the Soviet Union, which knew only progress; the past was wrong, only the future was beautiful and the present only a time of transition before the Communist Millennium. The primitivism of Mexico made him call into question this interpretation of history.

'I think that it was not that my consciousness and emotions absorbed the blood and sand of the gory *corrida*, the heady sensuality of the tropics, the asceticism of the flagellant monks, the purple and gold of Catholicism, or even the cosmic timelessness of the Aztec pyramids; on the contrary, the whole complex of emotions and traits that characterise me extended infinitely beyond me to become an entire, vast country with mountains, forests, cathedrals, people, fruit, wild animals, breakers, herds, armies, decorated prelates, majolica on blue cupolas, necklaces made of gold coins worn by the girls of Tehuantepec and the play of reflections in the canals of Xochimilco . . . Here my passions seemed to surge in the crimson groves of the cardinal's robes, which were gilded by the incense smoke at high mass as autumn gilds the leaf. They bore fruit in the form of amethyst crosses and tiaras, whose split tops looked like overripe pomegranates that had burst open in the sun.'[35]

Qué Viva México! was shot by Tisse in black and white but Eisenstein invariably saw the film in his mind's eye in colour. 'The reason for this is very simple (I would say tragically simple!): its shots have remained in my memory not as photographic pictures but as the very objects themselves as they were caught by the lens as they actually appeared in front of the camera.'[36] Mexico was a 'paradise regained' of graphic art; its elaborate primitivism and religiosity interlaced with sensuality clearly reconnected Eisenstein with some thread broken during the emotional traumas of his childhood.

'It was in Mexico that my drawing underwent an internal catharsis, striving for mathematical abstraction and purity of line,' Eisenstein declared.[37] This was derived directly from the Mexican landscape, and from the outlines – square and round – of the dress of the peons.

According to the painter Jean Charlot, who watched Eisenstein drawing in Mexico, the sketches were done 'very quickly so as not to disturb the subconscious elements.'[38] Among the drawings he did in Mexico was a series of hundreds of variations on the killing of Duncan by Macbeth, emphasising the savagery of the regicide, and the erotic excitement produced by the act. Eisenstein never forgot that Shakespeare was a contemporary of Ivan the Terrible, as he himself was a contemporary of Stalin. There was also 'Ten Aspects of the Death of Werther', and Samson and Delilah, again concentrating on the violent facets of these stories, as well as a cycle of Salome sketches, one of which has Salome drinking through a straw from the lips of John the Baptist's severed head.

These were slightly less directly influenced by his Mexican surroundings than those he called Adoration of the Matador, Crucified Bull, and Synthesis: Eve, Europe, Jesus, Torero. There were further series of drawings with equally sado-masochistic themes: the subject of the martyrdom of St Sebastian (the pre-eminent saint in homosexual mythology) merged with that of the bullfight, such as the crucified bull pierced with arrows, and St Sebastian as a dying matador. However, these drawings, though open to psychological interpretation (the Freudian Hanns Sachs thought they demonstrated that Eisenstein had a 'womb complex' or *Mutterleibsversenkung*), did not derive solely from the perverted psyche of a 'blazing decadent', as Kimbrough once described Eisenstein. As Eisenstein noted: 'Do not blame me for any of this. It was Mexico: in one element of the Resurrection festival they mix the blood of Christ from the morning mass in the cathedral, with the streams of bull's blood in the afternoon *corrida* in the city's arena.'[39]

The tableau of male coupling, which takes place around the central figure that is identifiable as a self-portrait, with a vulture biting his penis, is a wry reference to Freud's analysis of Leonardo's dream of a vulture stinging him with a tail, considered a fantasy of fellatio.

Not only did Mexico liberate Eisenstein's drawing, but also his libido. 'The latent wanderings of sensuality seemed incarnate in the interweavings of bronzed bodies . . . Washed by moonlight, the regularly breathing abundance of bodies of the *soldadaras* and their husbands – soldiers – held in close embraces seemed embodied in me . . . the bodies breathed regularly and in unison; the very earth seemed to be breathing; here and there a white blanket showed up, modestly thrown over a pair lying among the others, black in the moonlight, bodies covered by nothing; bodies not knowing shame; bodies for whom what is natural is natural and naturally needs no concealment . . .'[40]

Eisenstein admitted to finding himself drawn to this 'bronze race' of Mexican Indian, seeing them as hermaphrodites. 'The masculine frenzy of temper, the feminine softness of outline hiding a steel musculature and the outer muscles flowing around it; and the disposition to forgive coupled with a childish naughtiness . . . Adult men and women seem adolescent in comparison with other races; a race of young people, where the men have not yet lost their early femininity, nor the women abandoned their puerile pranks and both seem charmingly childish . . . Mexico is tender and lyrical, but brutal too,' Eisenstein remarked, a composite that found an echo in his own character. 'Physical brutality, whether in the "asceticism" of flagellant monks, or in their torturing of others; in the blood of bull or man, which after mass each week douses the sands of countless Sunday corridas in a sensual communion; or the pages of history telling of the unexampled brutality used to suppress countless uprisings of peons, whipped to a frenzy by unforced paid labour; and the brutal reprisals of the leader of the revolt: Villa who ordered the prisoners to be hanged naked so that he and his soldiers could be entertained by the sight of their last physiological reactions, peculiar to hanged men.'[41]

The subsequent history of *Qué Viva México!* was almost as brutal. Upton Sinclair never kept his promise to send the film material to Moscow for Eisenstein to edit. In order to recover his losses, Sinclair, no doubt under pressure from his wife and her Pasadena group, allowed several films to be mined from the material shot by Eisenstein in Mexico.

Even after learning of vicious attacks made on him by Sinclair with the aim of blackening his reputation with the Soviet authorities, Eisenstein, back in Moscow in May 1932, still hoped to obtain the film. In August, he heard of Sinclair's shocking decision to allow the American producer Sol Lesser to assemble some of the raw material into a film called *Thunder Over Mexico*. It used footage from the Prologue, Epilogue and the Maguey episode, which was cut together by editor Don Hayes for Lesser.

At the opening performance in Los Angeles on March 1, 1933, Sinclair declared that the picture followed Eisenstein's scenario and that the scenes had been selected in proper proportion to make practicable footage. An International Defence Committee for Eisenstein's Mexican Film was set up, and the editors of the magazine *Experimental Cinema* immediately published a manifesto. 'We decry this illegitimate version of *Qué Viva México!* and denounce it for what it is – a mere vulgarisation of Eisenstein's original conception put forth in his name in order to capitalise on his renown as a creative artist . . . We denounce the cutting of *Qué Viva México!* by professional Hollywood cutters as an unmitigated mockery of Eisenstein's intention. We denounce *Thunder Over Mexico* as a cheap debasement of *Qué Viva México!*'[42] There was even a petition organised against Sinclair's nomination for the Nobel Prize for Literature.

Eisenstein referred to it as 'the ill-starred, emasculated version of my film, *Qué Viva México!* . . .. transformed by someone's grubby hands into the pitiful gibberish of *Thunder Over Mexico* . . . [by] the enterprising Yankees.'[43]

The American producer Sol Lesser defended himself thus: 'We had a mass of film, several hundred thousand feet, along with duplicate shots. I was able to make a film out of it, but the Communists started to attack me for invading the cutting rights of Eisenstein. They said I was desecrating the master's touch. The night we previewed the picture in Los Angeles, they threw stink bombs in the theatre. I received all kinds of threatening letters. In any event we took the picture to New York. Everywhere I went there was publicity about it. And some organisations announced a boycott. At last, one of the theatres down around 14th Street agreed to run only the original uncut version as Eisenstein had delivered it, eighty or ninety reels of uncut film. I agreed, but under one condition: the exhibitor would really show it all. I numbered the reels, and the theatre advertised the original uncut version. People came and brought their lunches. After a couple of hours, they began to drift out and others came in. Before it was a third over, the house was empty. No one ever asked for the uncut version again. The boycott stopped. I went to Europe with a salesman, and we were able to sell the rights nearly everywhere. Upton Sinclair got out. I handled the picture for a while until there was no more demand for it. We deposited the film at the Museum of Modern Art; we gave it to them. They were making money on it, and they would occasionally send Mr Sinclair a little cheque. They were not obligated to do so, but they felt they should. The film is actually very good.'[44]

Lesser failed to add that he produced two short films, *Eisenstein in Mexico* and *Death Day* derived from different footage in 1934. Five years later, Eisenstein's well-meaning British friend, Marie Seton, went to Hollywood and discovered original footage in a 'stock shot' vault. From there she went to Mexico to check with various Mexican advisers on the footage Eisenstein had shot, with the object of having it sent back to him in Moscow. She claimed, however, that the outbreak of World War II prevented her from doing so. Thus, without Eisenstein's knowledge, she decided to edit the material as *Time in the Sun*, maintaining that she followed the basic scheme of Eisenstein's screenplay. Though it was more faithful to the original conception than *Thunder Over Mexico*, the cutting was crude, the music mere accompaniment, and the narration banal. In 1941, there was *Mexican Symphony* (1941), a series of educational shorts issued by the Bell and Howell Company, taken from much of the same material. (In the late 1970s, Alexandrov re-edited it, with no more success.)

When Eisenstein finally saw some of these educational films many years later, he wrote: 'Passer-by! Do not look for my thoughts here in cinematographic discordances cobbled together by the filthy hands of money-makers. Those films, which have been compiled from the material filmed by us on the wondrous soil of Mexico, do not belong to me.'[45]

Nevertheless, *Qué Viva México!*, even in these foetal forms, made a tremendous impact on Mexican cinema, which until then had exposed audiences to mostly popular melodramas and crude comedies, as well as Spanish-language versions of Hollywood movies. Eisenstein's visit inspired directors like Emilio Fernandez and cameraman Gabriel Figueroa, and the number of Mexican-made films increased and improved in quality. Again, there is a direct line from *Qué Viva México!* to Buñuel's Mexican films with their surreal images, anti-clericalism and ambivalent attitude to religion.

Since Eisenstein neither had the opportunity to complete the shooting nor to edit the film as he would have wanted, the various versions, no matter how mutilated, have enabled audiences to catch glimpses of some of the elements that would have made up the film. They disclose much of Eisenstein's bizarre humour – setting profiles of the present-day Indians against the statuary of their ancestors, a group of mourners at a funeral with their chins resting on a coffin, from which breast-like objects protrude, and the death masks, revealing further death masks beneath during a *danse macabre*.

Eisenstein's obsession with religious rituals is given full rein in the parade of penitents walking on their knees, while following three young men on their way to Calvary, later echoed by the three bound peons suffering their own Golgotha as they stand on a hill awaiting execution. Intermingled with religion are the rites of courtship and marriage, to which scenes Eisenstein and Tisse brought an exotic sensuality; as a young couple swing gently in a hammock, light and shadow play upon her bare breasts. (One remembers, in a very different context, the sweaty male bodies swinging in their hammocks below deck in *The Battleship Potemkin*.)

Fruitless as it is to speculate on how the completed *Qué Viva México!* would have turned out, the received wisdom is that it might have been Eisenstein's masterpiece. Unlike the extant sequence of stills from *Behzin Meadow*, for which greater claims could be made, there is enough evidence – to judge from the over-ambitious, overly-episodic screenplay, with its didactic and pedagogical overtones, its travelogue element and the elaborate posing of the 'noble savages' – that the completed film might have been seriously flawed. There is also confirmation that the deprivation of Eisenstein's montage, serious as it is, does not hamper our appreciation of the individual shots as much as its absence would have done in his previous films.

According to Eisenstein, 'When I had finished investigating montage, and foreseeing a unity of laws both in montage and shot, which I examined in stages, I dedicated all my work (from its formally academic point of view) to the question of the nature of shot composition: *Qué Viva México!* – my film about Mexico. As if punishing me for virtually leaving montage out of the scheme of things, this picture is frequently open to the most diverse of montage interpretations by different editors, although it does bear up to audience perception, probably simply because it was planned primarily on the basis of the shot.'[46]

A letter from Eisenstein in French in July 1934 to Victorio Ocampo, the Argentinian writer, and editor of the literary periodical *Sur*, gives some idea of the agony Eisenstein suffered on account of the aborted film.

'Very dear friend. My entire Mexican adventure ended in total disaster, as you probably already know. The photography (and it's very beautiful) is all that remains – but the entire composition, montage etc are completely destroyed by the imbeciles who contrived it. As well as the total epic conception. I so loved Mexico and I find it painful not to be able to express it in this film which is destroyed . . . I hope you will discern where Eisenstein ends and Hollywood idiocy begins! This whole affair has broken my heart to the point where I have become disgusted with cinema and have not made a film since . . .'[47]

But this situation was not a matter of choice, and there was more heartbreak to come.

PART III

BACK IN THE USSR

12

The Rules of the Game

Soviet cinema has been so intimidated by the Ku-Klux-Klan of 'Formalism' that it has almost eradicated creativity and creative searches in the field of form. If Formalism as a scientific literary tendency invites attack and censure, it has first and foremost a complete and formulated platform. But in cinema 'Formalism' was rather created 'by analogy' – and not so much by the film workers themselves as by the critics who were looking for a label to attach themselves to.

Eisenstein had already received a pointer as to how things were changing for the worse in the Soviet Union when a letter from his mother reached him in Mexico. She told him that she had been visited several times by the KGB, who had confiscated the family jewels. She pleaded with him to come back to Moscow as soon as possible to relieve the pressure on her. Pera also wrote, informing Eisenstein that his mother was in danger because of rumours that he was not going to return to the Soviet Union. As a result, Eisenstein departed from New York without delay, leaving Alexandrov and Tisse to stay a little longer.

After the *Europa* docked at Cherbourg in May 1932, Eisenstein went on to Hamburg where he hoped to take delivery of the rushes of *Qué Viva México!*, only to learn that they had not been sent from the USA as Sinclair had promised. Apparently, Mrs Sinclair had stopped the shipping of the reels, claiming that if the material got into Eisenstein's hands, they would never get any money back on the film from the Soviets. Disappointed, he travelled to Berlin, stopping at the Golf Hotel where Hitler was rumoured to be occupying a suite two floors above him. During his brief stay in Berlin, he discussed various projects, including a travel film on the USSR, and *A Modern Götterdämmerung*, with German producers.

'The film was to show the decline of capitalist society, and I proposed to base it on the sensational stories about the recent disappearance of the "match king" Ivar Kreiger, the financier Lowenstein, who threw himself out of an aeroplane, and a number of other sensational catastrophes that overtook the representatives of big capital.'[1]

On the train to Moscow, he met Bertolt Brecht, Margarete Steffin, Brecht's collaborator and lover, and Slatan Dudow, on their way to Moscow for the premiere of *Kühle Wampe*, the only film with which Brecht was ever involved that did not distort his intentions. Directed by Dudow and written by Brecht, it was a co-operative venture using actors drawn from the theatre, supported by real workers. The film had fallen foul of the German censors who felt it 'endangered the safety of the State', not realising that the true danger was approaching in the form of the Nazi party. Like Eisenstein, Brecht was also thought to be a formalist by the dominant and conservative Moscow critics, but neither man was aware how much the arts were in the grip of Stalin's iron fist. During the three years that Eisenstein was abroad, he had changed, the Soviet Union had changed, and so had his country's attitude towards him.

The entry on him in the 1932 edition of the *Soviet Encyclopaedia* reads: 'In his works *October* and *The General Line*, Eisenstein, despite his great ability, yet gave no deep analysis of the decisive stages of the Socialist Revolution and made a diversion to formal experiments. Eisenstein is a representative of the ideology of the revolutionary section of the petty bourgeois intelligentsia which is following in the path of the proletariat.'

While Eisenstein was gallivanting over Europe, the USA and Mexico, the Soviet Union was experiencing forceable collectivisation in agriculture and forceable proletarianisation in the arts. This was the period when all the nation's resources, human and material, were conscripted in the service of the one great objective: fulfilment of Stalin's Five-Year Plan. In 1930 signs of trouble began to appear. Factories were erected with no machines available, machines were delivered to plants unable to house them. Hastily recruited and untrained workers ruined shiny new machines in one place, while skilled workers sat idle for want of equipment in another. In the last quarter of 1930 there was an attempt to overcome all difficulties at once. October, November, December were proclaimed a special 'shock quarter' – Stalin's effort to wheedle and frighten workers and technicians into greater exertion.

There was a trial in 1930 of the so-called 'Industrial Party', whose members included Professor Ramzin and other engineers accused of working for France; and in 1931 a number of ex-Mensheviks, headed by Professor Groman of the State Planning Commission who was said to have acted for emigré Mensheviks, were put on trial. The accused were intimidated but not liquidated. Stalin was merely trying to frighten the trained specialists of pre-revolutionary days into doing what he demanded of them. As the Five-Year Plan approached its final year, the strain became intolerable. Industrial workers were on subsistence wages and forced collectivisation, jammed through under high pressure, produced the terrible famine of 1932–1933.

In two years, the arts were laid to waste like the fertile Ukrainian farmlands. The most notorious case was the dictatorship exercised over literature, with Stalin's blessing, by the RAPP (Russian Association of Proletarian Writers). Its chief was Leopold Averbakh, whose brother-in-law was Henry G. Yagoda, chief of the secret police. Calling for the creation of a 'literary front' in the struggle to fulfil the first Five-Year Plan, Averbakh inaugurated a literary dictatorship. Some of the most independent and original of Soviet intellectuals were now attacked for their 'anarchism' and for their 'Trotskyist-left deviations'.

Writers were called upon to become 'shock workers' in 'art brigades' in the service of the first Five-Year Plan. Boris Pilniak was chastised for publishing a novel abroad and for other failings. He attempted to set things right with a large work glorifying the Five-Year Plan called *The Volga Falls To The Caspian Sea*. The writers who wanted to go on publishing, hastened to write 'Five-Year Plan novels'. Fyodor Gladkov produced *Cement and Energy*, Valentin Katayev wrote *Time Forward!*

Vladimir Mayakovsky had been one of the earliest writers to satirise this utilitarian attitude to the arts in his 1929 futurist play *The Bedbug*. When the hero-villain requests books on roses and daydreams, he is told that 'nobody knows anything about what you asked for. Only text books on horticulture have anything on roses, and daydreams are dealt with only in medical works – in the section on hypnosis.' In 1930, Mayakovsky's play *The Bathhouse* (*Banya*) was a direct assault on the bureaucracy that was closing in on him. The cultural bureaucrats had tolerated his satire on the Communist Millennium in *The Bedbug*, but they were determined not to let him get away with attacking the present regime.

After a first reading in February 1930, Glavrepertkom, the theatre censorship committee, declared the play was unacceptable in its present form. Only Mayakovsky's formidable reputation saved it from being scrapped altogether. After some alterations, it was produced the following month but failed as badly as *The Bedbug* had. This time, his enemies were more outspoken in the press and at public meetings. The critic and official of RAPP, Vladimir Ermilov, insinuated in *Pravda* that Mayakovsky was playing the game of the Trotskyite opposition, an accusation once levelled at Eisenstein. Always hypersensitive to criticism and stricken by failure, Mayakovsky believed he was now the victim of persecution. With the purges of the intelligentsia at hand, he sensed he would be among the first to be condemned.

At the beginning of April 1930, Mayakovsky was taken to the Kremlin Hospital for a few days with a breakdown that was diagnosed as nervous exhaustion, and on April 14, he shot himself. Part of his suicide note read: 'Do not blame anyone for my death and don't gossip. The deceased terribly dislike this sort of thing. Mamma, sisters, comrades, forgive me – this is not a way out (I do not recommend it to others), but I have none other . . . Seriously – there was nothing else I could do. Greetings.'

At 8 p.m. on the day of his death the State Institute for the Study of the Brain extracted Mayakovsky's brain; it weighed 1,700 grams as against an average of 1,400, and was put in the Institute's 'Pantheon'. Five years later Stalin declared, 'Mayakovsky was and remains the best and the most talented poet of our Soviet epoch . . . Indifference to his memory and to his work is a crime.'

As the first Five-Year Plan neared its completion, the Party Central Committee again intervened in the literary scene in April 1932. RAPP was abolished and replaced by a single Union of Soviet Writers. The policy of Averbakh as leader of RAPP was condemned for alleged leanings towards idealism. Stalin blamed RAPP for the suicide of Mayakovsky, who had been driven to the grave by 'enemies of the people'. Stalin expressed his willingness to forget the past errors of the old intelligentsia, who should be utilised for 'socialist construction'.

By the end of 1932 the slogan 'Socialist Realism', a phrase attributed to Stalin himself, was *de rigeur* in the arts. Socialist Realism had a dialectical antithesis, 'formalism' – in other words experimental or modern art. Soviet art must be understandable and loved by the masses, but it must be worthy of its ancestry in classic Russian and world art, and by its strength and optimism it must help to build socialism. In architecture it meant classical colonnades, in painting the academic French school of the previous century; the major experimental formalist painters – Natan Altman, Pavel Filonov and Kazimir Malevich (absurdly accused of being a German spy) were under intensifying attack. In literature Soviet Realism was exemplified by the banal novels of Alexis Tolstoy, and in music the tuneful marching songs of Ivan Dzerzhinsky.

The Union of Soviet Composers was established to safeguard 'Social Realism' in Soviet music. Stalin admonished Dmitri Shostakovich for his discordant modern technique, ordering him to compose melodies which the toiling masses could whistle on their way to work. Art had to function as an opiate not a stimulant. Where now Eisenstein's Ciné Fist?

The Civil War operas *The Black Crag* (*Cherny yar*) by Andrei Pashchenko and *The Break-Through* (*Proriv*) by Sergei Pototsky were composed in an old-fashioned nationalist idiom. The senior Soviet composer of symphonies for thirty years, Nikolai Myaskovsky, a student of Rimsky-Korsakov, wrote in a late-Romantic style. His Eighth (1925) was based on appropriate folk-songs; his Tenth (1927) was regarded as a deviation in the direction of 'false modernism', and number Eleven (1932), he admitted, was 'subjective'. He made amends in the same year in his Twelfth, conceived as a 'Collective Farm' symphony and dedicated 'To the Fifteenth Anniversary of the October Revolution'. Shostakovich's Second Symphony (1927) was subtitled 'To October: symphonic dedication.'

Some of the episodes in Shostakovich's Third were meant to represent the Young Pioneers, and others the excitement of a vast May Day meeting. (He could just as well have labelled them Stalin's birthday or Lenin's funeral.) On February 15, 1932 Shostakovich announced that he had begun 'a great symphonic poem with orchestra, chorus and solo vocal numbers, its theme being "From Karl Marx to our own days."'

There were two operas written at the same time on the subject of an uprising by serfs in 1606 against Dmitri Shuysky. One, *Ivan Bolotnikovan* by Vassili Nechaev, had been accepted for production in 1932 by Stanislavsky, but it had leanings towards 'modernism' and never reached the stage. The other, Valeri Zhelobinsky's *Kamarinsky Muzhik*, modelled on Mussorgsky's *Boris Godunov* – there was even a Polish scene with mazurka – was produced in 1933. However, it was criticised for its failure to show the hero's connection with the people and for Zhelobinsky's 'grotesque and ironical' treatment of the boyars, almost the identical criticism that would be levelled at Eisenstein's *Ivan the Terrible Part II* thirteen years later.

Sergei Prokofiev, who had been abroad since 1917, returned to the Soviet Union in 1932, having decided to settle in Moscow permanently. His musical language during his twenty-five-year absence, nine of which were spent in Paris, was marked by jagged tonal shifts, aggressive harmonies, humour and mordant satire. He had grown increasingly disillusioned with what seemed to him the artificial nature and narrowly restricted appeal of contemporary music in Western Europe, and became more aware of the ties that bound him to his native country and the possibilities that it promised him as a composer. Later in his life he wrote: 'The cardinal virtue (or sin, if you like) of my life has been the search for an original musical language, a musical language of my own. I detest imitation; I detest hackneyed methods. I always want to be myself.'[2] As he was to discover, the Soviet Union was not the ideal climate in which any 'original' artist could thrive.

The sterility of the Soviet cinema was of more direct relevance to Eisenstein. In the spring of 1930, a *piatiletka*, or plan, had been announced for theatre, cinema, sculpture and painting. The *piatiletka* for cinema was implemented by a decree bringing all branches of the movie industry under the centralised control of a new organisation – Soyuzkino (All-Union Soviet Film Trust). At the head of Soyuzkino, Stalin placed Boris Shumyatsky, an energetic thirty-two-year-old bureaucrat, whose authority over directors was absolute. His chief concern was to make sure the industry could fulfil its fantastic production quotas.

In the summer of 1931, when the cinema had been brought almost to a standstill by the combined problems of censorship, bureaucracy and the technicalities of sound, Shumyatsky announced that Soyuzkino planned to make five hundred full-length films in 1932, eighty of them in sound and twenty in colour, which was more than all the studios in Hollywood produced in an average year. Two months later, he was talking even more wildly: 'By the end of 1932, we shall need 75,000 projection-machine operators . . . We have today only three theatres in the whole of the Soviet Union equipped to show sound pictures. By the end of the year we shall have 100. Next year, there shall be 5,000.' Lenin had a word for this: *komchvanstvo* meaning communist swagger. However, within a year, the movie industry had slumped both qualitatively and quantitatively.

From 1929, Soviet film directors struggled to solve two major problems. One was technical – the use of sound. The other was how to treat a new theme: the everyday life of the Soviet Union. The problem was that although film-makers at that period knew the rules they were never sure how to interpret them. The two most notable films on collectivisation, *The General Line* and Dovzhenko's *Earth* (1930) came in for semi-official criticism.

Izvestia had a three-column article denouncing *Earth* as 'counter revolutionary', 'defeatist', and 'too realistic' in its portrayal of the peasantry. The article was even more damaging as it was written by

Demyan Bedny (the pseudonym of E. Pridvorov), a writer who was close to Stalin and lived in the Kremlin. There were other 'spontaneous' protestations against *Earth*, which was not seen in its entirety until 1958.

Pudovkin's last silent film, *A Simple Case (Prostoi Sluchai)* aka *We Live Well* (in December 1930) aka *It is Necessary to Live Well* (in February 1931) aka *Life is Beautiful* (at its release in the summer of 1931) was condemned as 'elitist, overly-abstract and pseudo-significant.' Paradoxically, Pudovkin set out to make a film with wide appeal. It concerned a triangular love conflict during the Civil War: a married Red Army commander falls for another woman. He is condemned by his friends for betraying their 'comrade citizen' and returns to his wife.

In December 1931, an official decree criticised 'ultra-leftist tendencies' in cinema. As the better-known directors failed to adjust themselves to the demands of the bureaucracy, the members of the Stalin School began to push them aside. *The Road to Life*, directed by Nikolai Ekk, was the first Soviet film to be conceived and made as a talkie. Although it contained remnants of the montage techniques Ekk had learned from his teacher Eisenstein, the film moved towards a more personalised kind of Soviet cinema. It told of the thousands of homeless orphans who roamed the countryside as vagabonds in the chaotic aftermath of the Civil War. At a children's collective, they are rehabilitated and taught a trade.

In the same year, 1931, Sergei Yutkevich produced his first talkie, *The Golden Mountains*. Eisenstein had introduced the film to audiences in New York, an occasion which provided him with the opportunity to get in some digs at Hollywood. This rather tedious affair with long stretches of slow dialogue was hailed by Professor Yesuitov, the Kremlin's voice on cinema aesthetics, living up to the first syllable of his name, as 'a picture of great ideological significance.' *The Soviet Culture Bulletin* added, 'Its greatness lies in its profound and earnest social thematics.'

In 1932, Ermler and Yutkevich collaborated on *Counterplan* for which Shostakovich wrote the score. The theme was the foiling of a sabotage attempt in a steel plant, and the film was the showpiece of the celebration of the fifteenth anniversary of the Revolution. It took its text from one of Stalin's sayings, 'The realisation of our

Plan depends on us, on living men.' No expense was spared on the film, which was to show the world, and particularly other Soviet directors, just what Stalin wanted in the cinema. Ermler studied at the Communist Academy for two years to prepare himself for his great task. *The Soviet Culture Bulletin* (1932) described it thus: 'It freely combines elements of healthy romance with joyous comedy, dramatic intensity with lyric warmth . . . unimpeachable pictures of Leningrad's white nights . . . Special mention should be made of the work of the painter-architect Dubrovsky-Eshke, who built within the studio a giant department of a metal factory with all of its machines and lathes.'

Counterplan, wrote Professor Yesuitov, 'was the first victory of Socialist Realism in the Soviet cinema.'

Despite the best efforts of the Stalin School, the cinema refused to thrive. In 1933, Pudovkin's *The Deserter* opened. Having taken two years to finish, he had started before Socialist Realism took hold so he had to alter it in the cutting room to conform to the new dogma. As a result, the film was marred without making it politically acceptable. *The Deserter* was taken off the screens of Moscow's two biggest movie theatres after a week because of the film's 'Leftism' and 'Formalism', and because it dealt too much with politics!

This was the environment in which Eisenstein, already *persona non grata* with the authorities, found himself on his return to the Soviet Union. Although his international reputation could not be ignored, he was attacked by the Soviet press and in film circles for his involvement in the Mexican scandals, his altercation with Upton Sinclair, a radical writer respected in the Soviet Union, his long absence which had generated rumours of defection, whispers about his sexual preferences, and his deviation from the endorsed tenets of Socialist Realism.

13

'The Old Man'

In recent years I have become self-absorbed. I have retreated into my shell. The country fulfilled its Five-Year Plans. Industrialisation took giant steps forward. I remained in my shell. My alienation from life was, it is true, not complete. It was in those years that I was intensely involved with the younger generation, devoting all my energies to my work at the Institute of Cinema. But this was also a retreat within the walls of an academic institute; there was no broad creative exit towards the masses, towards reality.

The period after his return home was one of Eisenstein's most painful. Cramped in his uncomfortable bedsitter (with shared kitchen and lavatory) on Chysti Prudi, ruminating on the warm days in Beverly Hills and Mexico, he still believed that the negatives of *Qué Viva México!* would soon follow him to Moscow. Negotiations with Upton Sinclair through friends continued until Eisenstein learned that his film had been turned over to other hands. There were rumours that Sinclair had sold some footage of *Qué Viva México!* to MGM for *Viva Villa*, the biopic on Pancho Villa which was begun in Mexico by Howard Hawks at the hacienda in Tetlapayac, but finished by Jack Conway in Hollywood. But Eisenstein, after seeing (and liking) the film, could recognise none of his material. However, there were scenes that had been influenced by his aborted film, such as where honey is spread over a prisoner's face to attract ants.

Soon after his return to Moscow, he received a letter from his Mexican friend Augustin Aragon Leiva. 'Where is Eisenstein?' he wrote. 'Tetlapayac is waiting for him . . . that corner room is filled with his thoughts and his tremendous devilish dreams . . .'[1] Inconsolable over the abortion of the project in which he had invested so much time and energy, frustrated as an artist, and bitterly disillusioned, Eisenstein spent over a month at Kislovodsk Sanatorium with a serious nervous condition.

On October 13, 1932, Eisenstein wrote to Kenneth MacPherson, editor of *Close Up*: 'At the present time I am finishing the licking of my Mexican wounds – it looks as if the picture is lost for ever . . . as soon as the thing is definite you will get an article about this *chef d'oeuvre inconnu* – the film that nobody will see.'[2] Almost a year on, when his American student Jay Leyda asked why he had so far made no films since his return to Moscow, 'He gave me the most genuinely anguished look I ever saw on his face and shouted at me: "What do you expect me to do! How can there be a new film when I haven't given birth to the last one!" Eisenstein felt himself now "too old" and "done for."'[3]

Four years later, he was writing to Salka Viertel: 'I am slowly recovering from the blow of my Mexican experience. I have never worked on anything with such enthusiasm and what happened to it is the greatest crime, even if I have to share the guilt. But there are things that have to be above all personal feelings. Let's not talk about it anymore.'[4]

Besides having to live with his deep disappointment, Eisenstein was also subjected to derogatory comments by Boris Shumyatsky, who had little time for the 'intelligentsia illusions' of the avant-garde and even less for someone like Eisenstein who had gone abroad for a protracted period when he was needed at home, and had not made a feature film for three years. Eisenstein felt an odd man out, and was perceived as already part of an older generation of film-makers, someone who belonged to the silent cinema.

Yet, such was his residual reputation that less than six months after his return to the Soviet Union, he was made Head of the Director Department at the State Institute of Cinematography where he had already been a lecturer before his visit to the West. 'It was some compensation in all those years, when after the Mexican trauma, I was not able to make a single film,' he remarked.[5]

Many of his students testified to his talents as a teacher. The director Grigori Rostotsky: 'He was an extraordinary teacher, who never talked down to his students, and never taught them to imitate him. He knew perfectly well that none of us could possibly make films the way he made them, and he quite rightly preferred to develop what was best in each of us. Always he tried to raise each student to his own level, never himself sinking to the level of the person he was speaking to. Whenever you talked to him you became, quite involuntarily, more intelligent because you were receiving so much new information, new knowledge, new observations.'[6]

Rostotsky had met Eisenstein first when he was thirteen, then again at sixteen, when he asked him if he had the makings of a film director. '[Eisenstein] never gave a straight reply . . . his response was to begin teaching me, there and then, and in a most unexpected way. He made me read certain books, he told me to look at particular paintings by particular artists, and he made me listen to selected pieces of music. What he was doing, of course, was to give me a general education in the arts, and after reading the books and studying the paintings I would be invited to his Moscow flat and we would have long and detailed talks about my own reactions to all those discoveries. Those conversations were a reward as well as a lesson, and as lessons they were the greatest in my whole life.'[7]

Herbert Marshall, a lanky red-headed cockney with a Hitler moustache, was the only foreign student to go right through the course, starting in 1932 and graduating in 1935. On his master's teaching methods, Marshall later wrote: 'To Eisenstein editing was much more than usually conceived. It was the basic method of artistic composition applied to all works of art; the creation of a higher dimension from the conflict of opposing forces within a lower dimension. The creation of an abstract idea from the collision of concrete ideas. His favourite example was from Chinese hieroglyphs, where: Door plus ear = to eavesdrop. Mouth plus birds = to sing. Knife plus heart = sorrow. Which is montage in a nutshell, as he used to tell us . . . Eisenstein insisted that every director must be able to explain visual ideas visually to his art director and his cameraman . . . When we graduated, Eisenstein's final words to us were: "When you come to make your first film, forget all about montage and about me! Here you have learned, but there you must do. And the doing should reveal the learning.'"[8]

As most of the students were mainly workers and peasants, Eisenstein once turned to Marshall and remarked, in English, 'Thank goodness, you at least have heard of the Sistine Chapel and Sigmund Freud.'[9] Jay Leyda, who had heard him lecture at Columbia University in 1931, arrived at the school two years later. He noted in his diary of October 13: 'Lectures by tireless Eisenstein. His pupils adore him. He keeps them excited with new ideas expressed by his short, sturdy body, his rasping voice, and his amazing indicative face and head.'[10]

The director Mikhail Romm came to Eisenstein for advice in 1933 when he was starting his first film, *Boule de Suif*, based on the Guy de Maupassant novel, which Eisenstein knew almost verbatim. But Eisenstein refused to give Romm advice after disagreeing with him about his approach to the adaptation. Then, the day before shooting began, Romm dared to approach him once more.

'Sergei Mikhailovich, tomorrow I start shooting. Please give me some advice. Say something. Anything.'

'Very well, then, what's your first shot?'

'I'm beginning with the simplest of all. A close-up of a pair of boots standing by the door.'

'Excellent. Now this is my advice. You must film those boots in such a way that if you happened to fall under a tram tomorrow night I'd feel justified in taking your shot to the Institute and saying to my students, "Now you can see what a great director we've lost. He took only one shot of a pair of boots, but on the basis of that shot I intend to put those boots in our Museum."'

'Thank, you. I'll do as you say. I'll shoot those boots in exactly that way.'

'But try not to fall under a tram afterwards.'

'I'll do my best. And then? What do I do after that?'

'Then you must make every shot in that same way, and every film, and every script. And you must continue like that for the rest of your life. That is all the advice I can give you.'[11]

Eisenstein's lectures were stenographed by Vladimir Nizhny, a student and later a lecturer at the Institute. Nizhny's transcriptions endorse the eulogies of former pupils to Eisenstein's gifts as a teacher. Nizhny wrote: 'For Eisenstein the work at GIK had multiple uses: his production inactivity in those years left him with a quantity of theories to be aired and tested; there were also teaching methods in a new field to be tried; and he grew profoundly involved in the problems and potentialities of his students.

'"The Institute exhausts me," he often remarked. But he had a need and love of teaching. It was one of his basic tenets as an instructor that the teacher is no more than *primus inter pares* – first among equals. He demanded absolute precision from his students, sometimes snapping, "Don't say 'I think!' Until you know, I will not listen to you!" He invariably opened the course with a light-hearted discussion, listening to his students' tales and launching into reminiscences of his own travels. Each new section of the course opened with several concrete problems to be solved, supplemented by a vast variety of illustrative material produced from his enormous yellow briefcase. Hokusai sketches, Daumier engravings, reproductions of Serov, exotic ritual masks from all over the world, books, photographs. "Always try to define things plastically," was a method he urged his students to adopt.'[12]

Although teaching satisfied Eisenstein's desire to communicate his ideas to others, he had every intention of continuing his career as a film director. In order to do so, he had to prove not his artistic credentials, but his ideological ones. In one of the first of his essays cautiously toeing the party line, he wrote, 'As far as my personal creativity is concerned, my systematic scientific and pedagogical practice are inseparably intertwined . . . My *Weltanschauung* appears to have taken shape. I have accepted the Revolution. My activity is devoted entirely to furthering its interests . . . Abroad is the severest test that biography can set a Soviet man whose development is automatically and indissolubly linked with the development of October. It is the test of free choice. Abroad is the severest test for a "master of culture" to examine consciously "whom he is for and whom he is against". Abroad is the severest test for a creative worker as to whether he is on the whole capable of creation outside the Revolution and whether he can go on existing outside it. This test appeared for us when we were confronted by the golden hills of Hollywood and we passed it, not with a heroic pose of arrogant rejection of the earth's charms and blessings, but with our creative and instructive instincts modestly and organically rejecting the opportunity to create in a different social atmosphere and in the interests of a different class. This inability to create on the other side of the demarcation line between the classes reflects the strength and power of the revolutionary pressure of the proletarian revolution as a whirlwind sweeping away all those who oppose it, and as a still more powerful whirlwind engulfing those who have chosen to march in step with it. That is how everyone in the galaxy of active Soviet artists acts, feels and thinks. Many of us have come through the Revolution to art. All of us summon you through art to the Revolution!'[13]

Grigori Alexandrov arrived back in Moscow in June, and took on a Hollywood-style musical, *Jazz Comedy* aka *Jolly Fellows*, using a pre-recorded music track, and making use of his experience on *Romance Sentimentale* and his previous work with Eisenstein. Eisenstein's only contribution to the film was the sketches he made for the comic musical instruments. *Jazz Comedy*, which was a tremendous success, starred Alexandrov's wife, Lyubov Orlova, who became the first popular star of the Soviet cinema. Alexandrov, whom Eisenstein had come closer to loving than anyone else, became immediately acceptable to the Soviet establishment, and became far less close to his old friend and colleague.

Jazz Comedy had originally been proposed to Eisenstein who turned it down. It seemed as though he was being deliberately offered subjects he would be forced to reject, while he seemed deliberately to offer subjects that would be rejected. For example, during the winter of 1932/1933, Eisenstein worked on a satirical comedy called *MMM*. It was a Mayakovskian idea, originally planned in 1928 when it might still have been possible to make. Now, given the sort of escapist and Socialist Realist films the Soviet Union was making in the early 1930s, Eisenstein was swimming against the tide.

Maxim Strauch was to play Maxim Maximovich Maximov, the

257

MMM of the title, a newly appointed head of Intourist in an unnamed Russian city. Strauch's wife, Judith Glizer, was cast as the vaudeville actress married to Maxim. The film, in which 'the Russian boyars would be transplanted into the life of modern Moscow, giving rise to various possibilities of comic quid pro quo', was intended to satirise the realities of everyday life by alternating them in a grotesque way with the fantasies of the hero. The action of *MMM* ranges (in the hero's nightmare) through Russian history, with echoes of the *Don Juan* myth.

At one point in the script, Eisenstein the director was to play chess against Eisenstein the screenwriter. 'The camera pulled back. The black and white tiled floor was like a chessboard. On the alternate squares stood the tired characters, looking for a way out of the utter mess of the action. And above the board, tugging at their hair, sat the writer and the director, trying to make sense of these labyrinthine human relations. A solution was found. The action proceeded. The paths of the characters converged and diverged fluidly.'[14] (The Tsar Ivan demonstrates his tactics by using a chessboard in *Ivan the Terrible*, many years later.)

Eisenstein produced a scenario and shooting script of *MMM*, gave screen-tests to potential actors, and even rehearsed some of them. But, predictably, the project was 'postponed' by the new administrator of the Soviet cinema, Boris Shumyatsky.

MMM came out of the theoretical analyses and researches Eisenstein had been making into the sources of comedy, and by 'combining logic with intuition', he formed a theory of Soviet film comedy. 'I work in a very academic way,' Eisenstein explained. 'I throw up ramparts of erudition to accompany the work . . . I do the accounts, the computations and draw conclusions. I like to imagine the music as I work. Sometimes I get ahead of myself . . . The screenplay halts and pages of film research build up instead. I do not know which is the more useful. But the cross that I often have to bear is that problems of creative production extend into matters of scientific analysis. Often when I have decided upon the principle, I lose interest in the application! Which is what happened with the comedy [*MMM*] . . . Perhaps I was not destined to make a Soviet comedy.'[15]

*

On June 6, 1933, Edouard Tisse wrote to Ivor Montagu in London: 'We are hard at work. The comedy that we were planning with Sergei Mikhailovich has been postponed, and we are now preparing a grandiose production, a big historical film, *Moscow*. The work is big. Shooting is to start in February 1934 . . . We are now in the category of "elders". Therefore, we have resolved to turn away from light comedies and to make huge screen canvasses as befits our age.'[16]

After the fruitless work on *MMM*, Eisenstein made detailed notes and drawings for *Moscow*, whose theme was no less than four centuries of the city's history, intercut with the story of several generations of a working family. Structurally, it followed the panoramic picture of Mexico's history in *Qué Viva México!* – different contrasting epochs within a historical unity. (Eisenstein knew Noël Coward's episodic pageant of patriotism, *Cavalcade*, written three years earlier, which followed an English family through three decades of British history.) *Moscow* was envisaged as history seen through the four elements: water (the origins of the city), earth (Ivan the Terrible and Peter the Great), fire (the peasant rebellions, the fire of 1812, the class struggle and the Revolution) and air (the construction of the new Moscow).

Among the number of sketches Eisenstein made to accompany the treatment, he again revealed a sado-masochistic interest: after the Tartar victory, a naked young Russian prisoner is lying prone, his bound feet turned upwards waiting to be whipped by a malicious looking Tartar, busy rolling up his sleeves for the task.

On the occasion of the 17th Party Congress in January 1934, Eisenstein wrote: 'I am developing my activity in three spheres: 1) the creative 2) the academic and 3) research . . . Contrary to the gossip . . . that in terms of creativity I have become overgrown with grass like a burial mound, my creative work does of course come first (or, rather, my creative works – all three of them). The subject of my work is *Moscow* . . . My work on this theme has so far not been greeted by my immediate superiors with any great enthusiasm, encouragement, interest, or – most important of all – understanding.'[17]

The congress was called the Congress of Victors, at which Stalin announced complacently, 'There is nothing more to prove and, it seems, no one to fight.' There was 'no-one to fight' because most of the regime's opponents, including peasants and workers, had been starved, killed or frightened into submission.

The proposal for *Moscow* was also turned down by Shumyatsky's office as being counter to 'the current needs of the Soviet cinema'. As stubborn – or as naive – as ever, Eisenstein then considered a second idea to be called *Moscow the Second*, to be made in conjunction with his direction of Nathan Zarkhi's play of the same title. It was about the relationship between a worker-hero and a public statue erected in his honour, prefiguring the Stakhanovite ideal the following year. As Eisenstein explained, 'a whole gamut of contradictory feelings and actions, which reflect the conflict between the old and new emotional concepts. Thus the theme of the play becomes the struggle for the new man, the new personality and new attitude towards labour and fame.'[18] But this project ended tragically in June 1935 when Nathan Zarkhi, known best for his scenarios for Pudovkin, was killed in a car accident in which Pudovkin was injured.

In March 1934, Eisenstein wrote an open letter to Dr Goebbels in reply to a speech which the head of Nazi propaganda in Germany had made, complimenting him and wishing for a 'National Socialist *Battleship Potemkin*.' Eisenstein advised Goebbels that what he needed was 'the whole Soviet system. Because in our days great art, the truthful depiction of life, the truth of life even life itself, are possible only in a land of Soviets . . . But truth and National Socialism are incompatible. He who stands for truth can have no truck with National Socialism. He who stands for truth stands against you . . . Because, despite the mellifluous tones of your speeches, you are keeping your art and culture in the same iron shackles as the thousands of inmates in your hundreds of concentration camps. Works of art are not produced in this way, as you imagine them to be. A genuine work of art is the formally organised striving of a class to consolidate its struggle, its achievements, its social profile in the lasting images of art. The higher the work of art, the more fully the artist has succeeded in comprehending, feeling and communicating this creative burst of the masses themselves . . . It is only the genuine socialist system of the

Soviet Union that is capable of giving birth to the grandiose realistic art of the future and the present.'[19]

Two months later, in the 'genuine socialist system of the Soviet Union', the secret police came for the poet Osip Mandelstam. He was arrested because an epigram he had written for a small circle of friends had somehow fallen into the hands of the secret police. In it, he had called Stalin a 'murderer and peasant-slayer.' Mandelstam was granted temporary clemency, with the order to 'isolate, but retain'. (He died in a detention camp in 1938.) Under this system, a novelist and playwright like Mikhail Bulgakov was allowed to write but not to be published. 'I was the one and only literary wolf. I was advised to dye my fur. An absurd piece of advice. Even with its hair dyed or clipped a wolf simply cannot be mistaken for a poodle,' wrote Bulgakov later.[20]

In August 1934 at the first Congress of the new Union of Soviet Writers, Andrei Zhdanov, a close advisor to Stalin, declared: 'Soviet literature must know how to portray our heroes, it must be able to look into our tomorrow.' Karl Radek of the Central Committee made clear his attitude to non-political foreign literature by calling the work of James Joyce 'a heap of dung' and denouncing the 'morbid interest' of certain Soviet writers in Joyce, John Dos Passos . and Marcel Proust. There was a chosen list of Western classics, such as plays by Shakespeare and Molière, and later works of some 'social significance' by Dickens, Balzac and Mark Twain. It was at this conference that the guidelines of Socialist Realism in literature were laid down and, by implication, those of the other arts as well.

In 1934, the condition of the Soviet cinema was beginning to cause alarm even in official circles. The film critic of the *Moscow News* wrote that the past year and a half 'has been, not to mince words, perhaps the most arid period in the history of the Soviet film.' *Izvestia* surveyed the recent films and found them dull, lacking in artistry, and overburdened with propaganda.

There was a revival of literary adaptations, exemplified by Grigori Roshal and Vera Stroyeva's *A Petersburg Night* (from Dostoevsky), Vladimir Petrov's *Thunderstorm* (Ostrovsky) and Mikhail Romm's *Boule de Suif* (Maupassant). The film that set the pattern of political conformity and hero-worship films was

Chapayev by Sergei and Georgi Vasiliev (unrelated despite their shared surname). The film was about Red Army Commander Chapayev fighting against Czech and Kolchak forces during the Civil War. He has to resist the attempts of a commissar to tame his impulsive and heroic nature.

Shown as the highlight of the fifteenth anniversary of Soviet cinema, it was the first great Soviet success of the sound era, at home and abroad. The Vasilievs spent two and a half years on the film, more than twice as long as Eisenstein had spent on *Potemkin* and *October* combined. Ivor Montagu saw it as a sign of 'an expanding delight in individualism and personalisation in all art fields of the Soviet Union, corresponding to the flowering of the individuality consequent on the raising of the level of living accompanying the Second Five-Year Plan . . . No picture so simple, so innocent of a desire to prove points, or even of a feeling that they needed proving . . . could possibly have been produced anywhere but in a society that had long lost its doubts about itself.'[21]

Although Eisenstein praised *Chapayev* in public as a 'remarkable achievement', privately he was expressing doubts about the current 'hero-worship' films. When he was reproached by a Party member for never having made a film about individual heroes of the Revolution, but only its masses (presumably not counting the peasant heroine in *The General Line*), Eisenstein retorted by quoting the *Internationale* back at him. 'Nobody will give us freedom, neither God, nor the Tsar, nor a hero . . .'[22]

Despite *Chapayev*, Eisenstein felt that the best Soviet film of 1934 was Alexander Medvedkin's *Happiness*, which was far closer to his own preoccupations. Using burlesque, music-hall jokes, surrealism, masked figures and folk-tale images, the film succeeded in producing what the title promised. Although finally orthodox in its praise for collectivisation (how could it not be?), it recalled the radical Soviet cinema of a decade earlier – surprising during the period of strict Socialist Realism.

Eisenstein wrote: 'Today I saw Medvedkin's comedy *Happiness*, and I cannot keep quiet about it, so to speak. Today I saw a Bolshevik laughing . . . This picture has not yet been released . . . It has not yet been through all the proper procedures. Not yet been approved. Not yet been tried out on an audience . . . A Chaplin gag is individually illogical. A Medvedkin gag is socially illogical . . . I feel that joy that is also possible only in a country where money-grabbing can serve as an object of laughter. I am glad that Medvedkin has resolved the problem of our humour in the same way that I would have done, had I been filming and making it!'[23]

During the summer of 1934, Eisenstein met H.G. Wells at the dacha of Maxim Litvinov, People's Commissar for Foreign Affairs, whose English-born wife, Ivy Low, was a writer. He then left for several weeks rest in the Caucasus as his health was frail, and then went to the Crimea as production consultant on Mikhail Chiaureli's *The Last Masquerade*. It was not unusual for directors from the centre, especially those actively involved in teaching, to travel to provincial studios in this consultative capacity. A few years before, the Georgian Chiaureli had made *Kharbada*, a sharp satire on personality cults; now he was perpetuating them through his films.

While staying at Yalta, Eisenstein visited the Young Pioneers' camp at Artek, and revisited the Alupka Palace where he had filmed the stone lions for *The Battleship Potemkin*, his one and only real success. There he met a group of American engineers, whom he fooled by pretending to be an American tourist who began running down Eisenstein.

On October 27, 1934, Eisenstein married Pera Attasheva with little publicity. Their relationship was a purely platonic one – in fact, Eisenstein later told a friend that during their many years of friendship, they had 'never even kissed' – but their affection for each other ran deep. Pera was one of the few people Eisenstein trusted totally, and she stuck to him faithfully through the good and the bad times. The following year, when he went down with smallpox while filming *Bezhin Meadow*, she stayed with him in the hospital, defying quarantine rules at the risk of her own health. She always called him 'The Old Man' and he called her 'Pera Soldadera', after the women soldiers of Mexico's revolutionary army, because of what he saw as her toughness. In the milieu of the cinema, she was greatly respected and loved, and friends often reproached Eisenstein for his frequently cool treatment of her. Although

Eisenstein incomprehensibly fails to mention her once in his published memoirs (she is referred to intermittently in the diaries), Pera was his guardian angel, and probably the most important person in his life and beyond.

Actually, at the time of the marriage, they were less close than they had been two years previously, but it happened to coincide with the strengthening of the laws against homosexuality. It was convenient for Eisenstein to marry and Pera wanted to protect him from the rumours, but she also hoped that marriage might cement their relationship. However, their union failed to silence the rumours about his sexuality, although they became less overt. While, in the 1920s, Eisenstein had never made a secret of his attraction to Grisha Alexandrov, and they were seen everywhere together, a similar liaison would have been dangerous in the climate of the 1930s.

Anal and genital contact between consenting males became a criminal offence in the Soviet Union on December 17, 1933. On April 1, 1934, a punishment of up to five years imprisonment was instituted. On May 23 of the same year, Maxim Gorky published an article declaiming that homosexuality was the result of pernicious influences from the Western bourgeoisie and German Fascism. 'Destroy homosexuality, and Fascism will disappear,' he wrote. There was a rumour that Gorky's adopted son had been seduced by a man, and that Gorky's personal petition to Stalin led to the subsequent prohibition. Another of Stalin's favourite authors, Alexei Tolstoy, was anti-homosexual, and anti-Semitic.

From January 1934, homosexuals were arrested *en masse* in the main cities. They were called *opushchennye*, literally downcast, but in slang meaning those who have been beaten up and pissed upon. Homosexual rape was rife in the prison camps, and there were numerous suicides. (It was not until January 1994 that Russian law permitted homosexual acts in private between adults over the age of sixteen.)

When André Malraux came to the Soviet Union for the Writer's Congress in September 1934, there were discussions about the filming of *La Condition Humaine*, and Malraux joined Eisenstein in the Crimea where they developed a screen treatment. In fact, they signed a contract with Mezhrabpomfilm studio. One scene developed from the novel showed a number of Chinese children laughing in close-up. What are they laughing at? 'A man has fallen on to a bed. Seemingly drunk. And a small Chinese woman is slapping him on the face with unremitting energy. The children are seized by uncontrollable laughter. Although the man is their father. And the small Chinese woman is their mother. And the big man is not drunk at all. And the small woman is not hitting him in the face for drunkenness. The man is dead. And she is hitting the corpse in the face just because he has died, and abandoned her, and these small children laughing so melodiously, to starve to death.' For Eisenstein it was a scene that illustrated the way Chaplin saw life: 'To see the most terrifying, the most pitiful, the most tragic phenomena through the eyes of a laughing child.'[24]

Malraux had awakened an old dream of Eisenstein's to make a film about China. It was a project never far from his thoughts, continually nourished as it was by his reading and the Chinese music in his record collection. His passion was fired most significantly when he met the famous Chinese actor Mei Lan-fan, who was in Moscow with his troupe later that year. Lan-fan derived his worldwide reputation from the playing of *dan*, the female characters in Peking Opera, elevating the female role to the position previously held by the *laosheng* or elderly male role. (Eisenstein had first heard of Mei Lan-fan from Charlie Chaplin.)

At the same time Bertolt Brecht, who had been invited to Moscow by Erwin Piscator to attend the Fifth International Decade of Revolutionary Art, also met Lan-fan. It was this meeting that eventually led to the writing of his play *The Good Woman of Setzuan*, and the concept of the 'alienation effect', which he first delineated in an essay entitled 'Estrangement-effect in Chinese Acting'. In a letter to his wife Helene Weigel, Brecht wrote, 'I've seen the Chinese actor Mei Lan-fan with his troupe. He plays girls' parts and is really splendid.'[25]

Eisenstein, too, was as influenced by the Chinese actor, which can be seen most directly in the wild dance at the Tsar's banquet in *Ivan the Terrible Part II*. In an essay titled 'To the Magician of the Pear Orchard', Eisenstein described the symbolic traditions of Chinese theatre as contrasted with Socialist Realism, a style to which Eisenstein was forced to pay lip service.

'*Our* [author's italics] position is quite different. *Our* artistic aim is realism and realism of the very highest form and development. Socialist Realism. The question arises, can we learn from an art that is symbolic, and seemingly incompatible with our premise of an intellectual system?' Answering in the affirmative, he concluded, 'The experience of Chinese culture and art on this remarkable level must give us plenty of material for study and for the enrichment of our artistic methodology which has been decided and resolved in completely different ways and means.'[26]

Eisenstein arranged a film session at the Newsreel Studio (now the Kiev station) to shoot Mei Lan-Fan and his troupe performing one of their plays, *Duel at Rainbow Pass*. They filmed all night, but the next day Shumyatsky informed Eisenstein that he was not to proceed with the film. Eisenstein was too ashamed to tell Mei Lan-Fan the truth, so he explained that he did not have the time to complete it, and made the only copy from the positive of what had been shot (the negative was never cut) and gave it to the Chinese actor. Sadly, though photographs exist of Eisenstein talking to Mei Lan-Fan and watching a rehearsal, the film, like *The Storming of Sarraz*, seems to have been lost forever. There were rumours that Mei Lan-Fan's son had it, but it might have been destroyed during the Cultural Revolution. However, a few shots from it did turn up in a newsreel about Mei Lan-Fan's visit to Moscow.

The range of Eisenstein's cultural interests continues to astonish. Parallel with his absorption in Chinese culture, he was planning a film on the slave revolt against French rule in Haiti in 1791, and its leaders Toussaint L'Ouverture, Henri Christophe and Jean-Jacques Dessalines (the last two of whom became emperors of the island).

In 1932, Eisenstein had signed a contract with Soyuzkino for a film based on the novel *The Black Consul* by Anatoli K. Vinogradov. While he was still at Paramount, he had bought a cheap reprint of John W. Vandercook's *Black Majesty* for one dollar at the Hollywood book store he frequented. It was about Henri Christophe, whom he saw as a Shakespearean hero because of the breach between the emperor and the Haitian revolutionary masses; 'the transformation of a leader into a despot'. (Something

Eisenstein was to have direct experience of on his return to the Soviet Union, and which was the subject of *Ivan the Terrible*.) The idea was never put to Paramount, and only came up as a wild possibility for independent finance when he and his colleagues were clutching at straws after they had been sacked by the studio. 'Quite obviously it did not appeal to those in America who could have financed the film,' remarked Ivor Montagu.[27]

In Mexico the theme had returned to his imagination, as a series of sketches made at the time attest. For days and nights on end he elaborated the scenes, reading, sketching and making notes. The theme stayed with him when he returned to Moscow, and he talked over the project with Boris Shumyatsky, who allowed him to feel encouraged.

Eisenstein envisaged the film as a vehicle for the great black actor-singer Paul Robeson, with whom he corresponded. (Sources differ as to which of the three leaders Eisenstein suggested Robeson should play.) Meanwhile, he devoted several working lectures to *The Black Consul* at the Institute. For a number of days, Eisenstein encouraged his students to imagine how they would film a conspiracy by the French command to kill Dessalines. As quoted by his student Vladimir Nizhny, Eisenstein told his class, 'When I was in America I wanted to make a film of this rising in Haiti, but it was impossible: nowadays Haiti is virtually a colony of the USA . . .'

Eisenstein showed the class photographs of Robeson, saying how sorry he was that 'they can only inadequately convey the rich temperament of this splendid actor' and recommended the students to 'imagine Dessalines looking just like this, with just such a physique and marvellous face.'[28]

Robeson's only film yet released was *The Emperor Jones* (1933), based on the Eugene O'Neill play in which he had made such an impact on stage in 1921. One of the rare Hollywood movies of that particular period to star a black performer, the title role bore certain similarities to that which Eisenstein was proposing – Brutus Jones escapes from a chain gang to a Caribbean island where he sets himself up as its megalomaniac ruler.

Eisenstein daydreamed of having colour sequences in *The Black Consul*. 'I hope that it may be a theme in which white and black take on the full-blooded forms of human beings, a theme that has long excited me, the theme of the racial problem, in which the "whites" clash with the "blacks", and where the "black" will be played by that incomparable master of the screen, Paul Robeson.'[29]

Ever optimistic, despite the failure of Shumyatsky to sanction his two previous projects, Eisenstein sent Paul Robeson a letter inviting him to the USSR as a guest of the Administration for Films to discuss making a picture on the Haitian revolution.

'I never had an opportunity to meet you and I was allways [sic] sorry of it, because you are one of the personalities I allways [sic] liked without knowing them personally . . .. I am enthusiastic to see you here. As soon as you'll be in this country we will have an opportunity to talk (at last!!) and we will see if finally we will get to do something together.'[30]

In December 1934, Robeson, his wife Eslanda ('Essie'), and Marie Seton, the English writer, arrived in Moscow from London. Seton had met Eisenstein in 1932, when she carried some books to him in Moscow from Maurice Dobb, the Marxist economist, and had acted as a go-between for Eisenstein with Robeson. They were met at the Moscow station by Eisenstein, Tisse, Alexander Afinigonov, the head of VOKS and his mulatto American wife Genia, and several black Americans living in the USSR.

Eisenstein and Robeson took to each other immediately. During his two weeks in Russia, Robeson saw Eisenstein almost every day. There were even rumours going around that Robeson was bisexual and was having an affair with his Russian host. There was no truth to the gossip, but Eisenstein was enchanted by this 'black Mayakovsky' as he nicknamed Robeson. To Robeson *The General Line* was 'easily the finest film I've ever seen.'

Eisenstein arranged introductions, accompanied the Robesons on visits, took them on a tour of the Film Institute where he introduced Robeson to selected students. Essie reported that Eisenstein was 'marvellous company. He is young and great fun, with brains and a sense of humour.'[31]

Far into the night, Eisenstein and Robeson discussed subjects such as the so-called primitive people of Central Asia – the Yakuts, Tadzhiks and Kirghiz. Eisenstein said he disliked the unfair implications of inferiority which the term primitive conveyed –

which was why he explained the Soviets preferred the phrase 'national minorities'. Robeson, who expressed his admiration for Communism, said that he felt like 'a human being for the first time since I grew up. Here I am not a negro but a human being.'[32] Still waiting for Shumyatsky's decision on the project, Robeson left in January 1935, expressing his wish to return for the filming.

Eisenstein had hardly said his farewells to the Robesons when he was called to account at the All-Union Creative Conference of Cinematographic Workers, under the slogan 'For A Great Cinema Art', which was held in Moscow from January 8–13, 1935. Eisenstein, who had not completed a film since 1929, was under considerable pressure to prove his credentials. The conference, attended by the leading Soviet directors, cameramen, scenarists, actors and film executives, was held against a background of five years of sterility and failure. Morale was low, nerves were frayed, tempers short. Since it was out of the question to discuss frankly the political roots of the problem, scapegoats had to be found. Just as Soviet engineers were punished when the bureaucracy's high-pressure methods and impossible production quotas caused breakdowns in industry, so Eisenstein, Dovzhenko and Pudovkin were publicly humiliated. The current success of *Chapayev* gave all the sharper an edge to the attack. At the conference, the three directors made sure to pay it homage.

Eisenstein: The intellectual cinema . . . is too vulgar to consider. *The General Line* was an intellectual film . . . *Chapayev* is the answer to the very deep solving of Party problems in art.

Dovzhenko: *Chapayev* is tied up with the future of the cinema.

Pudovkin: In *Chapayev* we see how a real class character is made.'

Pudovkin's last film, *The Deserter*, had been sharply criticised two years previously, and he had been working for several years on *The Happiest*, a film about the rivalry of two Soviet aviators in setting a round-the-world speed record. It was never made. After his serious injury in the car accident that killed Nathan Zharki, and a long convalescence, he made no films for three years, after which he turned to a conventional narrative form. Dovzhenko had not

made a film since *Ivan* three years before, but was about to go off
to Siberia to make *Aerograd* for Mosfilm.

'I don't think that the Soviet cinema is only made up of heroes
like Eisenstein and Dovzhenko,' said Sergei Yutkevich, declaring he
spoke 'for the great army of cinema workers.' He liked American
films 'because they appeal to a great public, for in the best meaning of the word, cinema is a popular art.' In conclusion, he made a
'friendly criticism' of Eisenstein, 'spoken as a practical man', for
theorising too much and producing too little. Turning to Eisenstein,
he quoted a letter from George Sand to Flaubert. 'You read, study,
work more than I, more than a great many others. You have gained
an education such as I will never have. You are a hundred times
richer than all of us. You are rich but you complain like a beggar.
"Give to a beggar, whose mattress is stuffed with gold, but who
wants to feed on beautifully turned phrases and choice vocabulary." But you are a fool who roots around in his straw and eats his
gold. Eat the ideas and emotions found in your head, in your heart;
the words and phrases, the form which you are so full of, will
themselves appear as a result of digestion . . .' Eisenstein merely
smiled in response.

Trauberg also called on his old master to stop theorising and get
down to work. He criticised *October* for the 'stupid poetry' of its
palaces and statues. 'Chapayev is a hero, but he is not above the
heads of the audience. He is their brother. But in *October* the
people were very high up.'

Sergei Vasiliev expressed the fear that Eisenstein's theoretical
work might lead to 'isolation from practical work.' Dovzhenko
attacked Eisenstein for his erudition. 'If I knew as much as he does
I would literally die. (Laughter and applause.) I'm sorry you're
laughing. I'm afraid . . . I'm convinced that in more ways than one
his erudition is killing him. No, I should have said disorganising
him . . . Sergei Mikhailovich, if you fail to make a film within
twelve months at the latest, I beg you never to make one at all. We
will have no need of it and neither will you . . .'

Only Lev Kuleshov spoke in Eisenstein's defence. 'You have
talked about him here with very warm, tearful smiles as if he were
a corpse which you are burying ahead of time. I must say to him,
to one who is very much alive, and to one whom I love and value

greatly: Dear Sergei Mikhailovich, no one ever bursts from too much knowledge but from too much envy. That is all I have to say.'[33]

Kuleshov had, by that time, become a victim of Stalinism, his emphasis on internationalism having made him unpopular. Kuleshov's last film was made in 1934 and he was not to direct another for six years, but by then the spark had gone from his work.

Attempting to keep the peace was the Kremlin's liaison officer for cinema, Sergei S. Dinamov, then editor of *International Literature*, and a literary critic who specialised in American literature. A humourless, zealous young functionary, he doled out a certain amount of diplomatic praise for the older generation, among them Eisenstein, then two weeks short of his thirty-seventh birthday. He then proceeded to give 'ideological directives' to the assembled cinema workers. Some of his main points were:

1) Beauty is to be reinstated.
2) The cinema must be 'optimistic'.
3) One of the chief elements in Soviet film style is its true reflection of life.
4) There must be more emotion. 'Without love and hate there can be no art. One cannot separate thought from passion . . . What is wrong with Eisenstein's theory is that he separated thought from feeling.'
5) There must be more heroes. 'I once gave an address at the Academy of Aviation. One of the commandants asked me a question, "When will our artists show us the best people of the country?" I answered, "When the artists themselves are the best people in the country."'
6) The individual must replace the mass as hero. 'Learn from Shakespeare, in whose works the epoch becomes the man, the events of an epoch the acts of a man.'
7) There must be more passion. 'One must not be afraid of being passionate, for, after all, true Party art is truly passionate art.'
8) The film must be built around the professional actor. 'The film without a hero was only an experiment. We need

actors with great passions. Without actors, we can do nothing. We cannot base our cinema on *typage*.'

9 The important thing now is to think about the style of the Soviet cinema.

(Dinamov was to be imprisoned and shot in 1939.)

The first of Eisenstein's two speeches in his own defence was extra-ordinarily wide-ranging and erudite, seeming more so in that much of the discussion going on around him was too insular and arcane to be of wider interest today.

'You know my speech-making is a poor affair and I talk badly. I had hoped to get away with just a few words in this speech but, as our preparatory conference and indeed Sergei Sergeyevich [Dinamov] showed, I shall have to speak of a whole range of matters which I should have thought had long since sunk into oblivion, but which will continue to trouble people from time to time and even to insinuate themselves into discussions long after they have, properly speaking, ceased to exist.'

He promised 'to re-examine some of the positions I once held,' explaining, rather sententiously, that his films with their *typage*, mass heroes and formalistic tendencies, were necessary developments towards the cinema of the day. As for 'intellectual cinema', it was misunderstood. 'When we spoke of intellectual cinema, we meant first and foremost a construction that might convey an idea to the audience and at the same time perform the particular function of *emotionalising the thought process*.' Eisenstein then went on to cover Shakespeare, Gogol, James Fenimore Cooper, Balzac, Victor Hugo, Hegel, the philosophy of the Indians of Brazil and the language of the Bushmen to define the nature of art and classicism, and how cinema should be a synthesis of the other arts. He concluded: 'I think we are now entering a most remarkable period: our cinema's era of classicism – the best period, in the highest sense of the word . . . When spring comes, I shall plunge into production work as vigorously as I conduct my academic work, so that I shall have my place in this embryonic classicism and make my contribution to it as well.' (Applause.)[34]

On January 11, 1935, two days before the end of the conference, the climax of the fifteenth anniversary celebrations, a presentation of honours was held at the Bolshoi Theatre, and those who expected Eisenstein's name to be announced had to wait a long time. The Order of Lenin, the highest of the honours, was presented to Shumyatsky, Pudovkin, Dovzhenko, Kozintsev, Trauberg, Ermler and the Vasilievs. Two of Shumyatsky's assistants were among those who received the second award, the Order of the Red Banner of Labour, and Alexandrov and Vertov were given the Order of the Red Star, one degree lower. The Award of People's Artist was then announced, and still there was no mention of Eisenstein. His turn came even later and lower, when with Tisse and Kuleshov, he received the minor Award of Honoured Art Worker. It was a formal statement of his position in the Soviet film industry in 1935. It was clear which way the tide had turned.

On the night of the awards, when Eisenstein made his entrance, Shumyatsky rose to greet him, and said, 'Sergei Mikhailovich, let us kiss.' They embraced and kissed three times. Then Shumyatsky said, 'Sergei Mikhailovich, I hope that this was not the kiss of Judas.' Eisenstein replied, 'Not at all. It was the kiss of two Judases.'[35]

The next day Eisenstein, again apologising for being no public speaker, gave his closing address.

'Comrades, the first, highest class of society is now the proletarian class. (Applause) . . . Comrade Yutkevich has co-opted George Sand as his assistant; I wonder which girl I should take as an accomplice. (Laughter) . . . I think that I must make a picture, and I will make pictures, but I feel that this must be worked on in parallel with equally intensive theoretical work and theoretical research. (Voice from the floor: "Well said!") I want to say something about this to Sergei Vasiliev . . . When you talk to me about my Chinese robe with its hieroglyphs, which I'm supposed to wear as I sit in my study, you make one mistake: there are no hieroglyphs. Nor do I gaze at a statuette in abstract meditation when I am sitting in my study. I work at the problems that will confront the up-and-coming generation of film-makers. I am a director and teacher. There may be cases where I have acted without realising that I might break someone's heart. Comrades, my heart has not been broken, and it has not been broken because no heart that beats for the Bolshevik cause can be broken.' (Prolonged applause, standing ovations.) . . .[36]

On January 12, Eisenstein wrote in *Pravda*: 'A series of remarkable films is coming onto the screens and they are greeted with lively excitement by the many millions of Soviet cinemagoers. Informed by a great sense of purpose, our cinema has won over the proletariat of the entire world and hearts and minds even beyond our border. And today, when those who work in cinema are so favoured by the attentions of Stalin, our Party, our government and the whole country, we can sense that it is only thanks to the vital link with all of them that our cinema can say that on its fifteenth birthday cinema has really become the most important of the arts as Lenin ordained.'[37]

Following the conference, from February 21 to March 1, 1935, a film festival was held in Moscow, the first international film festival in Eastern Europe. Its chief purpose was to stimulate sales of Soviet films abroad, which had fallen off since the advent of Socialist Realism. Hollywood sent King Vidor's *Our Daily Bread* and Cecil B. DeMille's *Cleopatra*, and France, René Clair's *The Last Millionaire*.

The major prize given by the jury, comprising Eisenstein, Dovzhenko and Pudovkin, was awarded to Leningrad's Lenfilm Studios. The jury greatly appreciated *Chapayev*, Kozintsev and Trauberg's *The Youth of Maxim*, and Ermler's *Peasants*. An honorary prize was given to *The Song of the Fisherman* by Chu-sheng, which took up the cause of the Yangtse fisherman.

After the Festival, Shumyatsky led a delegation of film officials to Hollywood, where they spent six weeks learning how to make movies 'in the American style'. Shumyatsky returned home with grandiose plans for a mass-entertainment industry on the American scale, compartmentalising output into standard genres.

The month before the 1935 cinema conference, on December 1, 1934, a young Communist named Nikolaiev had assassinated Sergei Kirov, one of Stalin's chief lieutenants. A rising young star in the Party apparatus, Andrei Zhdanov, was promptly sent to replace Kirov, and in the early months of 1935 whole trainloads of 'Kirov murderers' were deported to Siberia, though it was likely that Stalin himself instigated Kirov's murder. There were those in the Central Committee who wanted Kirov to replace Stalin as General Secretary. Against the background of further arrests for alleged Trotskyism, from the middle of 1935 to the middle of 1936, Stalin made many public appearances, smiling at little children and bestowing awards. He declared, 'Life is gayer, comrades, now that Socialism has been achieved in Russia!' As the hero of Milan Kundera's novel *The Joke* seditiously suggests, 'Optimism is the opium of the people.'

14

Crimes and Misdemeanours

How could it have happened that more than ten years after the victory of The Battleship Potemkin, *on the twentieth anniversary of* October, *I came to grief with* Bezhin Meadow. *What caused the catastrophe that overtook a picture I had spent two years working on?*

At the cinema conference in January 1935, Eisenstein announced that he was beginning work on a new film, *Bezhin Meadow*, which was to be the answer to the 'friendly critics' who urged him to implement theory with action. At last a project of his would go beyond the planning, scripting and casting stages. It meant interrupting his lectures, but four of his students joined him as apprentice directors, among them Jay Leyda, who kept a production diary until his return to the USA in 1936.

The author of the original script of *Bezhin Meadow*, commissioned by the Young Communist League, was Alexander Rzheshevsky, who had worked with Pudovkin on *A Simple Case*. Its genesis was one of the short stories by Ivan Turgenev in the collection *A Sportsman's Notebook*, which told of how the author, one summer evening, loses his way while returning from one of his hunting trips, and stays the night at a bonfire kept by the peasant boy horse-herders, who tell each other ghost stories to keep awake. Although the film has the same title as the story, the plots bear virtually no relation to each other. What *is* retained from Turgenev, however, is the writer's pantheistic evocation of the Russian countryside, and the almost supernatural sense of foreboding that hovers over the innocent youths.

After spending two years in the village of Bezhin Meadow (Bezhin Lug), Rzheshevsky had written a script based partly on the Turgenev tale and partly on the true story of Pavlik Morozov, the young village hero who was killed by his relatives in the northern Urals in 1932 because he had denounced his father to the village soviet for speculating. In the script, the action of which takes place over twenty-four hours, from the morning of one day until the following day of harvesting, the young village boy, now called Stepok, has organised the local Young Pioneers to guard the harvest of the farm collective each night, thereby frustrating the plans of his own father to sabotage it. In the film's climax, the father kills the son. Rzheshevsky stated that his intention was to draw a comparison between the peasant children in the 19th-century story and those of his own time. Eisenstein was delighted by the screenplay's simplicity, which he described as 'about children and adults for adults and children'. It was an 'emotional scenario' aimed to give the director 'emotional stimulus'.

The part of the father was given to Boris Zakhava, an actor trained by Meyerhold and the Director of the Vakhantangov Theatre. The grandmother was played by someone Eisenstein found in an old people's home. Elisabeta Teleshova, an actress of the Stanislavsky school from the Moscow Arts Theatre, took the part of the president of the Co-operative and advised Eisenstein about other parts. Teleshova had become very close to Eisenstein, so much so that she was often thought to be his wife. This misunderstanding came about because she accompanied him to various formal occasions, since she was more at ease in society and rather more decorative than the homely Pera. However, both women had the type of female figure that appealed to Eisenstein – fat and round, like his mother. Eisenstein's relationship with Teleshova was one that pained Pera, who was working on *Bezhin Meadow* as an assistant. (Teleshova died during the war in 1943, having appointed Eisenstein her heir.)

The most difficult task was to find a Stepok. Eisenstein's assistants had whittled two thousand boys down to six hundred 'possibles'. Eisenstein himself, in the course of twice-weekly sessions of four hours each, got the number down to two hundred. Still Stepok had not been found. Suddenly, at one of the final sessions he caught sight of Vitka Kartachov, who was from Moscow. 'He is Stepok!' Eisenstein exclaimed. The boy, according to Jay Leyda, 'seemed to have everything against him. His hair grew in the wrong way, insufficient pigmentation of the skin gave him great white blotches on his face and neck, and at the test his voice grew stiff and dull – until he was told to ask us riddles, when he produced a clear, fine, almost compelling voice. Only Eisenstein was able at once to see the positives, later clear to all.'[1]

Parallel to the casting, a search went on for suitable locations as the village of Bezhin Meadow itself was unsatisfactory. Eisenstein drew up a map of a 'synthetic village' and sent out parties to scour for sites. Eventually, the shooting of Eisenstein's first sound film began, with the prologue, in the apple orchards of Kolomenskoye on May 5, 1935. With Tisse as cameraman, Eisenstein attempted to show how Turgenev, attracted by the French Impressionists, saw things around him. The opening lines of Turgenev's story read: 'It was a beautiful July day, one of those days that come only after long spells of settled weather. From the earliest morning the sky is clear; the dawn does not blaze and flame, but spreads out in a gentle blush. Instead of the flaming incandescence that goes with sultriness and drought, or the dark crimson that precedes the storm, the sun has a bright and friendly radiance, as it swims peacefully up from a long narrow cloud, shines out briskly, and then veils itself in the lilac-coloured mist.'

On June 15, at six in the morning, Eisenstein flew from Moscow with six of his team and all their equipment en route for Armavir and the Stalin State Farm near the Sea of Azov, fifteen hundred kilometres from Moscow.

One of the first scenes to be filmed was an episode in which four fugitive incendiaries, who have been forced out of the refuge in the village church, are being taken away under guard by two militiamen. They try to cut across the highway, along which peasants holding pitchforks are moving to the harvesting camp. When the harvesters learn who these men are, they threaten to lynch the saboteurs. 'They wanted to bring back the Tsar!', shouts a peasant woman, but the boy Stepok, stepping between the two groups, relaxes tension with a little dance. Everybody laughs, and the militiamen are able to proceed with their prisoners.

Jay Leyda wrote: 'Taking advantage of the generosity of the State Farm and the fine weather, and because we were way ahead of schedule, we used the marvellously filmic acres of ripe grain to film some shots for the finale of the film, when the body of the murdered Stepok is brought back to the village. Young Pioneers salute from their watchtowers as the body is carried past, in a series of unusually beautiful and bare compositions . . .'[2]

Generally speaking the film progressed well. They shot from six in the morning to seven at night, when the unit retired to their hotel to discuss the next day's work. In the course of the filming, Eisenstein had at last been allocated new accommodation in a four-roomed fourth-floor flat at Potylikha, not far from Mosfilm Studios on the edge of Moscow. He would joke that if he cut a cucumber in his kitchen, only half of it would be in Moscow. His mother moved into the small rooms in Chysti Prudi. He finished furnishing his new flat by September. 'Once only one room was designated for books. But insidiously, room by room, my flat was filled with books which loop themselves around things like hoops on a barrel. So, after the "library", the study was taken over; after the study, the walls of my bedroom . . .'[3] He also had a room for the woman who, as his devoted housekeeper, would look after him for the rest of his life. Totisha 'Aunt' Pasha was a dark-haired woman, in early middle age, who had come to Moscow in the 1920s from Sigorsk. At the same time a dacha was built for him in Kratov, a small village about forty kilometres from Moscow. Things seemed to be looking up for Eisenstein. He even dared to feel that the black days were over.

Then the first of a series of misfortunes arrived to cast a shadow over the film. Eisenstein went down with ptomaine poisoning. Then towards the end of October, he caught smallpox. He was said to have succumbed, according to Leyda, because 'in his personal selection of every object that was to decorate the next interior set, the church, one germ, waiting on an icon or holy banner, chose the atheist Eisenstein for the only case of smallpox known in Moscow for about two years.'[4] After a quarantine of three weeks, he convalesced for a month in the Caucasus. However, he still intended completing the film by May 1936.

On January 28, 1936, *Pravda* launched its celebrated attack on Shostakovich. It accused his music of being 'un-Soviet, unwholesome, cheap, eccentric, tuneless and "leftist"', and advised him to emulate Glinka and write tunes that could be whistled. The onslaught was aimed specifically at *Lady Macbeth of Mtsensk* and his recent collective-farm ballet *Clear Stream*. 'From the first minute the listener to *Lady Macbeth* is dumbfounded by a deliberately discordant, confused stream of sounds.' The music was 'modernist formalism' of the worst kind. The attack was entirely unexpected – Shostakovich for several years had been considered, inside as well as outside the Soviet Union, the country's greatest living composer.

A few days later, the notorious 'modernist-formalist' Alexander Mosolov, made a public protest in a Moscow restaurant. The Union of Soviet Composers unanimously voted to expel him for drunken brawling and he withdrew to Mongolia, reappearing as a composer of simple, conservative music in 1939.

Pravda also denounced modern architecture as 'monstrous trick architecture', while Joyce's *Ulysses*, one of Eisenstein's favourite books, was 'written in English that can hardly be understood by Englishmen . . . Its style reminds one of the delirious babblings of a mad philosopher who has mixed all the known languages into one monstrous mess.'

In literature, the works of Mikhail Sholokov were published in quantity, and his four-volume *And Quiet Flows the Don*, a realistic novel about the Civil War, became perhaps the most popular single work in Soviet literature. It was made into an opera by Ivan Dzerzhinsky, first produced in 1935 as a result, ironically, of the help and encouragement of Shostakovich, to whom it is dedicated. The opera was publicly approved by Stalin and Molotov as a model Soviet opera.

The onslaught against formalism and leftism continued unabated. Demyan Bedny, the erstwhile Stalin favourite, was denounced for his libretto to the opera *The Bogatyrs* on the grounds that it failed to evaluate positively the contribution

Christianity had made to Russia in the tenth century. (A criticism Stalin later levelled at *Ivan the Terrible*, regarding the fifteenth century.)

Meanwhile, Meyerhold, Eisenstein's 'spiritual father', incurred the displeasure of the authorities for his production of *Camille* in which his wife, Zinaida Raikh, played the title role. He was charged with having a 'pernicious foreign influence' on other theatre directors. Things would subsequently become more dangerous for Meyerhold.

Boris Shumyatsky called together a number of directors and scenarists, warning them against formalism – 'an abnormal outgrowth of form in a work of art to the detriment of its content' – and scrapped a great number of completed films while inspecting those in progress for traces of the deadly disease. *Bezhin Meadow* was one of these.

After his second long absence due to illness, Eisenstein was informed that he would have to revise the scenario. Shumyatsky expressed dissatisfaction with the film so far shot. He felt that the characters were 'not images of collective farmers, but biblical and mythological types.' He felt that the 'smashing of the church' episode was 'a veritable bacchanalia of destruction.'

For the revisions – the destruction of the church was replaced by the destruction by fire in the granary – Eisenstein called upon his old friend Isaac Babel, whom he greatly admired. Filming resumed in the Crimea towards the end of the year, with changes in the cast such as Nikolai Khmelyov of the Moscow Arts Theatre, replacing Boris Zakhava as the father. In January 1937, Eisenstein again succumbed to illness – influenza this time – and was forced to spend three weeks in bed.

In February, in a letter to Leyda in New York, Eisenstein, though working, expressed his feeling of isolation since his return to the Soviet Union. 'Strange as it may seem, I am missing you here! You know I was never too sentimental – I'd say on the contrary – but you formed a certain link with things I even have no opportunity to talk to anybody now! . . . Most of the time with you I was pretty . . . disagreeable – but that was a sort of self-protection against oneself: against things that drive me mad – things I cannot put down in book form . . . You were allways [*sic*] provoking and touching my most secret wounds . . . So that's why our intercourse had a certain mixture of pain and pleasure as well as any masochistic pass time! [*sic*] Now nobody and nothing is tickling me in this way . . . I hope that in three or four weeks I'll be through with the shooting. Quite a few people have seen the rushes and are very highly impressed – all of them feel in it a return and revival of film poetry . . .

'Another feeling of sorrow overcame me in another direction. Your letter made me feel out of touch with the outer world. I felt myself in no connection with what is going along on the other side of the ocean – what people think about, what they write about, what is going along in the arts and sciences . . . Couldn't you hold me a little bit *au courant* of what is happening in the fields I am interested in. May be it would not be too difficult to send me from time to time even the *Times Book Review* so as to know what is published and printed over there . . . You are in the centre of all that there . . .'[5]

A month later, with shooting completed but cutting yet to commence, came the crippling body blow. On March 17, 1937, Shumyatsky decided to veto *Bezhin Meadow*. Everything was to be shut down, and Eisenstein and the crew were ordered to return to Moscow. Two years' work and two million roubles had been thrown away. Almost immediately Shumyatsky explained his reasons in an article in *Pravda*.

'From the beginning Eisenstein associated his work on *Bezhin Meadow* with the need for a complete reassessment of his own artistic methods, and indeed he had promised to recognise the new principles that had been developed during the years of his silence . . . He could hardly ignore the fact that the most recent works of Soviet art, in all the media, have become more and more politically responsible. Because of this he readily declared his intention of working in the new way, in the true spirit of Socialist Realism, and of correcting his serious mistakes of the past. Yet, despite this, Eisenstein was enthusiastic about Rzheshevsky's script, even though it contained serious flaws . . . the plot was badly constructed and didactic, the characters were poorly drawn, and the

entire script lacked the essential drive that gives a film its true ideological and artistic purpose . . . Unfortunately Eisenstein paid no
attention to the suggestions we all gave him . . . From the very first
shot it was clear he was treating his subject matter both subjectively
and arbitrarily . . . He should have presented our enemies as the
opponents of both the people and of socialism, but he preferred to
turn them into creatures living in a world of religious mythology
that is a million years away from the ideas of our own time . . . He
transformed the personality of the chief of the political section into
a man with a totally expressionless face, a big beard, and features
that are indisputably biblical . . . Moreover, the young hero, the
pioneer Stepok, was presented in pale and luminous tones, with the
face of some kind of holy youth whose fate was already decided by
a supernatural destiny. Indeed in many of the shots the lighting is
so contrived that this pale boy in his white shirt seems to be
wrapped up in a halo . . . The film's conception is not in any true
sense based on the class struggle, but on a conflict of more ele-
mental forces, or a fight between "good" and "evil" . . . Eisenstein
was so sure of his own unanswerable authority that he completely
declined to respect public opinion. He refused to study a world of
which he was ignorant, preferring to rely on his own academic erudition. And in the end, he discovered that the task was quite
beyond him.'[6]

A few days later Eisenstein wrote a long self-criticism and 'confession'. It was published in *Sovietskoye Iskusstvo* under the
heading 'The Mistakes of *Bezhin Meadow*'.

'Where lay the original error in my world view that flawed the
work, so that, despite the sincerity of my feelings and dedication, it
turned out to be patently groundless politically; and anti-artistic in
consequence? Asking myself that question again, and with much
soul-searching, I have begun to see my error and understand it. My
error is rooted in a deeply intellectual, individualist illusion . . . an
illusion that can make something that is genuinely revolutionary
purely "off your own back" rather than in the thick of a collective,
marching resolutely in step with it.'

Of the father's killing of the son, it 'was more reminiscent of
Abraham's sacrifice of Isaac than it is of the themes that are bound
to stir the viewer: the final battle to ensure the lasting triumph of

collective farming . . . I needed the withering and harsh criticism with which the catastrophe of *Bezhin Meadow* was discussed in the press and among the activists of GUK [the State Directorate for the Cinema and Photographic Industry] and Mosfilm . . . the criticism of my comrades helped me towards a clear perception of how wrong my slant on the matter had been . . . Work should have been stopped. No amount of takes and retakes could have saved it . . . Speeches from our Mosfilm collective of workers saved me from the worst . . . the collective helped open my own eyes above all to my own mistakes, to the mistakes in my method and the mistakes in my socio-political conduct . . . I feel very acutely the necessity finally to overcome the errors of my world view, the necessity for a radical reconstruction [*perestroika*] and mastery of Bolshevism . . .[7]

According to Alexandrov, this 'confession' was written under the threat of arrest. Anyone reading it with the slightest knowledge of Eisenstein's philosophical and aesthetic views would be struck by the vast disparity between them and the above. It is rather like a naughty boy found misbehaving, and saying 'I'll be good in future,' knowing he will not.

Naum Kleiman believes that Eisenstein was being satiric under cover of the confessional. 'It's so pathetic that its parodic,' he claims.[8] There were many other occasions where one discovers Eisenstein playing dangerously ironic games, sending signals to those who knew him well that what he was saying could be interpreted on two levels. James Agee was convinced that both *Alexander Nevsky* and *Ivan the Terrible* were satires on Stalinism in the spirit of Swift's *Modest Proposal*, which suggests the opposite conclusion to the one postulated. Certainly, *Ivan the Terrible Part II*, banned by Stalin, can be read as the last of Eisenstein's passing shots at his 'father oppressor'.

In 1937, Eisenstein got a call from *Pravda* asking him to write an article for them giving his opinion on the Trotskyist show trials. Pera later explained that this was tantamount to an order from on high and, had he refused, his silence would have condemned him. What he wrote was: 'Shame on the traitors and killers!' without specifying to whom he was referring. Pera and his few intimate friends knew exactly whom he was accusing.

Waclaw Solski remembered a conversation he had with Eisenstein in his apartment. 'I examined photographs stuck on the walls . . . two photographs of the same woman, one depicting her laughter, the other with her face contorted in tears. I asked Eisenstein what these pictures meant . . . "The woman laughs and then she cries. But the basic expression on her face in both cases is almost the same. Why? Well, I don't know why. Maybe because it is caused by the convulsion of the same muscles. Or, maybe because, after all, there is not such a difference between laughter and tears, revolution and counter-revolution" . . . It wasn't healthy to carry on such a conversation in Moscow. Someone quickly changed the subject.'[9]

Like a number of 'dissident' artists and 'counter-revolutionaries', *Bezhin Meadow* disappeared in mysterious circumstances. What happened to *Bezhin Meadow*? The thought that a completed version still exists somewhere has tantalised film historians since it was banned in 1937. It seems that Eisenstein's montage assistant, Esther Tobak, handed it over one night to a chauffeur from the Ministry of Cinema, whence all trace of it was lost. Tobak maintained that Eisenstein once told her that he had another copy, so thoroughly hidden, that no one would be able to find it, and she supposed he had buried it in the grounds of his dacha. There were also rumours that Eisenstein's personal copy was among the cans of film removed from his Potylikha apartment the morning after his death.

It seems most likely that the positive copy was burned on the orders of the ministry in 1937, while the confiscated negative and work-print were kept in the vaults of Mosfilm Studios until the studios were damaged in a German air-raid during World War II. It was thought that a bomb fell near the vault and its contents were subsequently destroyed by the firemen's hoses.

In the early 1950s, when Sergei Yutkevich, who was made head of a committee to administer Eisenstein's legacy, was collecting the writings with Naum Kleiman, they found small clips from nearly every shot of *Bezhin Meadow* in Pera's archives.

'What happened was that during the shooting of the film he had for some unexplained reason given orders for several frames to be cut from each roll of film,' explained Yutkevich. 'About a thousand of them altogether. Kleiman had the clips enlarged into lengths of one or two metres each, and he and I began to use these bits of film in an attempt to restore something of what Eisenstein had managed to achieve . . . I tried to edit those bits of film as Eisenstein himself might have done. I began to sort out their sequence, capture their rhythm, discover the subtle visual connection between each one and the next. We needed music, and we were lucky to have the services of Boris Volsky, who had recorded the sound track for both parts of *Ivan the Terrible* and was an experienced sound director as well as musician in his own right. Together he and I devised a musical background from the Third and Fifth symphonies of Prokofiev.'[10]

Thus, using the 'frames' from the material that had been preserved, Yutkevich and Kleiman secretly constructed a montage of 'stills' from the film, ready for showing at the Moscow Film Festival of 1967. The remnants of *Bezhin Meadow* were pompously introduced on film by the Soviet critic Rostislav Yurenev, who had published a book on Eisenstein. He explained that the film remained incomplete because Eisenstein had taken ill, and that the existing reels were then destroyed during the war. Not a word about the real reason for its tragic fate.

Attending the first screening was Vitka Kartachov, who had played the boy Stepok and was now an engineer of around forty-four years old. He had been a soldier in the war, had been wounded, and had lost his memory for some years. Some of his recollections of the making of the film came back to him as he watched himself as a child on screen for the first time. He remembered it as a very happy time, and how wonderful it was to work with Eisenstein, who seemed to understand exactly what the boy was feeling. However, he found it painful to talk about, because of the sadness he felt at the film's destruction.

Although watching *Bezhin Meadow* in this ghostly form increases the sense of loss more than if it had never been seen at all, Yutkevich and Kleiman created a masterpiece of reconstruction. So powerfully persuasive is the conjunction of the surviving frames that it almost makes redundant any discussion of *Bezhin Meadow* in the conditional. Therefore, the little blond boy *is* one of the great child performers in the cinema – the way he cheers up the workers, the way his eyes light up with joy at the liberation of the pigeons from the fire, his nobility in facing his cruel father – and his death, like a valedictory aria in an opera, when he is allowed time to expire.

The desecration of the church *is* one of the great set-pieces in cinema, in which the earlier visual metaphors – at their most extreme in *October* (Kerensky = mechanical peacock) – have given way to more ambiguous compositions. On one level, the audience is encouraged to sympathise with the peasants robbing the church of its relics, squabbling over an icon, sacrilegiously trying on vestments, heretically laughing at the statuary – while Eisenstein's profound admiration and knowledge of religious art creates a parallel revulsion at the vandalism. A young girl is framed in a mirror as if in a picture of the Virgin Mary, a young child is a cherub, a statue of the crucified Christ is held as in a Pietá. (Buñuel attempted a similar effect with his evocation of Leonardo's *Last Supper* enacted by a group of beggars in *Viridiana* in 1961.)

The film is so skilfully cut, retaining an Eisensteinian rhythm, combined with the most felicitous use of Prokofiev's music – part of *The Fiery Angel* matches the images of the burning of the tractor fuel by the *kulaks* – it is often easy to forget that there is no movement within the shots themselves. The heart-breakingly beautiful images in the close-ups of faces are equalled only by Carl Dreyer, while the luminous diurnal and nocturnal landscapes evoke the classicism of Claude Lorraine despite the monochromatic photography. Eisenstein's use of black and white in the film is also an expression of the feelings the film evoked in him, and a reflection of his own dichotomous nature, though not everything is black and white.

Eisenstein described the way he visualised the film thus: 'The *kulaks* took on black colouring; white was reserved for the murdered boy. On a bright sunny day the blazing barn burned with black smoke – the *kulaks'* handiwork – while tones of white characterised everyone connected with the positive forces in the village, who extinguished the fire: the ash-blond Stepok; the Komsomol member dressed in white, the white shirt of the political instructor and the white headscarves of the women; the white horses of the fire brigade; and finally, the white pigeons rescued by Stepok against a background of a wall of black smoke. Black was the night of *Bezhin Meadow* and like a white, other-worldly spectre, the injured Stepok wandered through it to his death. There were people who liked to see in this the materialisation of the line from Turgenev's *Bezhin Meadow*, "The darkness did battle with the light."[11]

Léon Moussinac saw Eisenstein in Moscow shortly after *Bezhin Meadow* had been cancelled. 'It was one of the most bitterly painful experiences of my creative life,' Eisenstein told him, though he tried to avoid any mention of contemporary politics and said that 'he wanted to rest and complained about his heart.'[12] He was also in financial difficulties, because, following the accusations against *Bezhin Meadow*, he was driven out of the Institute and deprived of his professiorial salary.

One day in May 1937, Eisenstein locked himself in his bedroom, refusing to leave it even for meals. 'Aunt' Pasha, Eisenstein's housekeeper, was so worried that she called Pera, who was living with her mother, saying that she was worried about 'the Old Man'. Pasha, who was anti-Semitic, didn't like Pera, but she nevertheless knew that she was the person whom Eisenstein trusted more than any other. Pera arrived and tried to persuade Eisenstein to come out and eat, but she got no response. After repeated requests from her that he should at least say something, he suddenly called out from behind the door that, if he did come out, it would only be so that he himself could go and tell 'Them' exactly what he thought of 'Them', and 'bugger the consequences.'

After further pleas from Pera, Eisenstein told her that he was busy writing a sharp letter of complaint to Stalin. Pera was terrified and decided to telephone Isaac Babel, to whose advice Eisenstein usually listened. Eisenstein let Babel into his bedroom immediately. Babel set about toning down Eisenstein's letter. Then the two men came out together and Eisenstein handed Pera an envelope on which he had written the address: 'J.V. Stalin, The Kremlin, Moscow', asking her to do him a favour and deliver it. Pera took the typed envelope to Red Square and put it in the special postbox there.

The letter to which Babel had contributed pleaded with Stalin for the chance to continue making films. 'I feel I have within me the strength to make many more *Potemkins* . . . I am asking not for privilege but for trust.' Babel then advised Eisenstein to leave Moscow as soon as possible. Sometimes when the NKVD (The People's Commissariat of Internal Affairs) came in the night, people were saved by the simple fact that they were not at home. It was always possible that the executioners would move on to their next victims the following night.

Eisenstein left immediately for a sanatorium in Kislovodsk, a city in the Northern Caucasus. It was here, far away from criticism, that he began a book on film theory which occupied him for almost a month. He then moved on to another spa town, Pyatigorsk, that summer and autumn.[13]

Isaac Babel was arrested shortly afterwards. He refused to defend himself, believing that an artist had the right to remain silent, but Stalin's reply was 'Silence is treachery'. On the morning of his arrest, the police took all his manuscripts, including the new short stories he was working on. Babel embraced his wife, and told her to say goodbye to their two-year-old daughter. 'We'll see each other one day again,' he said. It is thought that he was sent to a Gulag, where he died or was executed in 1941. Alexander Rzheshevsky, the scenarist of the first version of *Bezhin Meadow*, was damned for writing like 'an American decadent, especially Hemingway (!)' He was sent to a prison camp, from which he emerged ill, and died prematurely. Vladimir Nilson, Tisse's camera assistant on *October* and *The General Line* was sent to a labour camp, taking a photo of Katharine Hepburn with him.

Over the next decade, the writer Boris Pilniak and his wife (a pupil of Eisenstein's) disappeared, as did D.S. Mirsky, the foremost historian of Russian literature and a former prince (Prince Peter D. Sviatopolk Mirsky), who had been converted to Communism while in Britain and had thereupon returned to his homeland. Konstantin Eggert, the film director, and Mikhail Koltsov, editor of the German-language magazine *Das Wort*, were arrested. Marshal Tukhachevsky and other military men were executed.

Sergei Tretyakov, one of the earliest Soviet playwrights and friend and translator of Brecht, was 'liquidated' in the purges of 1939 as a 'Japanese spy'. On Tretyakov's death, Brecht wrote the following poem, which could stand equally for others, such as Babel:

> *My teacher*
> *The great-hearted, the kind-hearted*
> *Has been shot, condemned by a people's court,*
> *As a spy. His name is damned.*
> *Talk about him is suspect and silenced.*
> *Supposing now – if he is innocent.*

Eisenstein survived. His survival was explicable for a variety of reasons, not the least of them being Stalin's respect for Lenin's view about the importance of the cinema as an art form in a socialist society, his personal liking for the director as a man, and the letter he had received from Eisenstein. Eisenstein's statement at the Fifteenth Anniversary Conference and his public apology for the 'errors' of *Bezhin Meadow* also went some way towards appeasing the rulers of the film industry.

A few months after his 'confession', Eisenstein wrote a rave review of Mikhail Romm's hagiographic film *Lenin in October*, the sort of 'plot-based' film that he would have attacked earlier. 'The film's exceptional achievement lies in the apparently most profound unity between this creative collective and our people. This organic merger with the people, with their feelings, with all the shades of their emotions about the memory, deeds and the continuation of the cause of Ilyich [Lenin], was uniquely capable of teaching the scriptwriter and director, the leading actor and the whole collective that fundamental and unrepeatable phenomenon that makes the film so enthralling.'[14]

Eisenstein was among hundreds of artists who were forced to pander to the status quo – those such as the novelist and playwright Alexei Tolstoy, who wrote works pleasing to the regime. Tolstoy told Eugene Lyons in his own study, 'When I enter this room I shake off the Soviet nightmare. I shut out its stink and horror . . .

Some day, believe me, all Russia will send them to hell . . .!' While he lived, however, Tolstoy, like many of his colleagues, prostituted any ideals he might have had in return for a luxurious life and the opportunity to write. He had written two plays about Ivan the Terrible, in which the elements of an apologia for Stalin show clearly through the guise of a 16th-century setting.

Shostakovich withdrew his Fourth Symphony, deciding that it did not exemplify Socialist Realism. The Fifth Symphony of 1938 was described by the composer as 'A Soviet artist's practical creative reply to just criticism.'

In July 1946, almost a decade after the tragedy of *Bezhin Meadow*, Eisenstein was still circumspect *vis á vis* that *film maudit*, almost always referring to it as 'a failure'. 'The theme of "father and son" informs my entire opus . . . that completely crushed the objective theme, namely the struggle to establish the collective farm system. Figures and situations were here ossified in biblical stylisation. Abraham, Isaac, Rustum and Sohrab all came together in one character on screen . . . And the social value of the film was lost in the alleyways of "private" subject matter.'[15]

Throughout the rest of his life, still with a threat hanging over him, Eisenstein referred to the 'catastrophe of *Bezhin Meadow*', repeating what his 'mistakes' had been. Jay Leyda noted that 'Eisenstein himself, who was archive conscious and normally saved all significant documents, kept none of the hundreds (possibly thousands!) of work drawings that I had seen and watched him work on through the first version of the film.'[16]

The American essayist and film critic Dwight Macdonald, in the *Partisan Review* in 1942, wrote:

'There is a modern sentimentality about the artist and intellectual which pictures him as a Prometheus defying the gods of totalitarianism in the name of Art and Culture. Such defiances are not unknown, but they are generally delivered from a safe distance. When, as in Russia, the artist-intellectual has remained within the totalitarian borders, he has reacted pretty much as Eisenstein did, submitting in aesthetic as well as political matters.'

An article by emigré Georgy Adamovich, published in the Paris

Russian-language newspaper *Latest News* in February 1937, expresses the situation clearly.

'There are precious few grounds for supposing that the qualitative, moral composition of the intelligentsia is any different there from what it is here. It is entirely possible, then, that were we ourselves presently in Moscow, we would be signing the same proclamations. The burden of guilt, then, lies in all of us, and we cannot parade the purity of our cotton socks until such time as we can demonstrate that they would have been equally snowy white at any time in any place and under any circumstances. We must be fully cognisant of this, if only to have a right to discuss those who are signing their names, living in an atmosphere far different from ours, suffering a different misfortune than our substantial rootless emigré freedom.'

15

Heroes and Villains

We had only one opportunity for his genius to dazzle – that was in the strategy of the Battle on the Ice, the famous pincer movement in which he crushed 'the iron swine' – the Teutonic Knights – the pincers entirely surrounding the enemy. This is a manoeuvre all generals in history have dreamed of, it brought unfading glory to the first person to employ it . . . It brought hundred-fold more glory to the generals of the Red Army . . .

'The courtroom. My case is being tried. I am on the stand. The hall is crowded with people who know me . . . I try to shrink by gazing at my feet. I see nothing but all around me I hear the whisper of censure and the murmur of voices. Like blow upon blow fall the words of the prosecuting attorney's summing up . . . My return from prison. The clang of the gates closing behind me as I'm released. The astonished stare of the servant girl who stops cleaning the windows next door when she sees me enter my old block . . . There is a new name on the mail box . . . my door is closed in my face by the former acquaintances who now occupy my apartment . . . I turn back. The hurriedly raised collar of a passerby who recognises me . . .' This revealing passage, not published until 1943, is not, as one might imagine, by Franz Kafka, but by Eisenstein, expressing palpable fears of what might be his own trial, disguised in the form of an objective, academic essay on Word and Image in his first book, *The Film Sense*.[1]

Apart from his three women friends, Pera Attasheva, Elizabeta Teleshova, Esther Shub, and his faithful housekeeper, 'Aunt' Pasha, who stood by Eisenstein during this 'grey atmosphere', the only prominent cultural figure to give him support was the writer Alexander Fadeyev. Fadeyev sent him an admiring and encouraging letter begging him not to pay overmuch attention to the slanders and attacks, ending up, 'I clasp you warmly, warmly by the hand.'[2] It marked the beginning of a close friendship. Eisenstein was frequently to seek Fadeyev's advice in moments of crisis and was among the few people he addressed in the familiar form.

The dramatist Vsevolod Vishnevsky, who was brave enough to defend Eisenstein publicly regarding *Bezhin Meadow*, sketched two scenarios for Eisenstein to direct: *We, the Russian People* and an untitled film about the war in Spain, treated as a battle against fascism. Eisenstein mentioned this in his letter to Jay Leyda in February 1937, 'Primo: There are plans for Spain. Secundo: Paul Robeson who was with a concert tour here has put himself at my entire disposition for the time from July to October. Now both these things can fit marvellously together – taking the race and national problem within the film about revolutionary Spain . . .'[3]

A few months later, Pera was writing to Ivor Montagu: 'What do you think about Robeson playing the part of a Moroccan soldier in Spain – that is the new idea, instead of *Black Majesty* (sweet dreams! while Shumyatsky sleeps!).'[4] Eisenstein made a few sketches, indicating roles for Robeson, Pera, Maxim Strauch, Judith Glizer and others, showing a church, a Madonna, and an army tank in a town square with snipers on the roofs.

About *We, the Russian People* Eisenstein was enthusiastic, and after a favourable reception by a group of actors, scenarists and the artistic council of Mosfilm to whom Vishnevsky read it, he looked forward to starting work on the film. He often visited Vishnevsky for a meal, after which they would retire to the writer's study and spend long periods looking at each other in silence.

Among those who saw a rough cut of *Bezhin Meadow* was the German novelist Lion Feuchtwanger, who was in Moscow to discuss a film version of *The Oppenheim Family* with the Jewish director, Grigori Roshal. He and Eisenstein discussed the possibilities of a film of Feuchtwanger's historical novel, *The Ugly Duchess*, and the staging of his play, *The False Nero*, for which Eisenstein made sketches and designs. Because of the problems he had had in completing films, or even getting them made, Eisenstein began to consider going back to directing for the theatre. Most of the plays suggested were fairly weighty, but while in America he had obtained the Russian theatrical rights to George Kaufman and Moss Hart's *Once in a Lifetime*, which he wanted to direct with Maxim Strauch and Judith Glizer. This 1930 lampoon of the havoc caused by the coming of sound to Hollywood, would have finally satisfied Eisenstein's desire to direct a comedy. Unfortunately, it was not to be, though his grotesque humour was apparent, in varying degrees, in all the various manifestations of his talent.

On May 18, 1937, Yelena Sokolovskaya, the head of Mosfilm, wrote and informed Eisenstein that she was trying to secure a script by Pyotr Pavlenko about the hero of 13th-century Russia, Saint Alexander Nevsky. A little later, Boris Shumyatsky offered Eisenstein the choice of two historical subjects about patriotic heroes, either Ivan Susanin (the hero of Glinka's opera *A Life for the Tsar*) or Alexander Nevsky. Perhaps Eisenstein's letter to Stalin had had some effect because, behind this proposal, lay an instruction from the Leader himself, who would 'entrust' Eisenstein with one more production. Despite the heartache, literal and figurative, that he had suffered over the assassination of *Bezhin Meadow*, Eisenstein was elated to be given another opportunity, no matter what the subject. He had not completed a single film since *The General Line* in 1929, and a director's fee would help pay off a number of creditors.

If Eisenstein had had the choice, the historical subject that he really wanted to make was that of the 12th-century Prince Igor of Severski, which Borodin had treated in his grand opera, *Prince Igor*. Unlike Borodin, who played down the clashes between the different Russian princes, Eisenstein wanted to stress the internecine conflicts. However, *Prince Igor* was suggested to, and rejected by, Mosfilm.

One afternoon in the summer of 1937, Eisenstein was at his dacha in Kratov, living next door to Mikhail Romm, when he called to Romm over the garden fence. He told Romm about the choice of two subjects he had been given. Romm expressed surprise that Eisenstein was thinking of going back so far in history. 'Oh, I knew you'd regard both these ideas as irrelevant and out of date,' Eisenstein retorted. 'But why should you? What is it that makes you regard history as dead and useless? I happen to know that despite what you say I'll enjoy doing it.' He asked Romm which of the two subjects he would choose. Romm said Ivan Susanin. Eisenstein asked his reason. 'Because for one thing you have a good plot, the dramatic story of a peasant. Then the period of history is well researched and well documented. But Alexander Nevsky is largely a mystery.' 'Precisely!' Eisenstein replied. 'And that is exactly why it appeals to me. Nobody knows much about him, and so nobody can possibly find fault with me. Whatever I do the historians and the so-called "consultants" won't be able to argue with me. They all know as well as you and I do the evidence is slim. So I'm in the strongest possible position because everything I do must be right . . . I'll find an actor and cast him as Alexander Nevsky, and the whole world will soon believe that the real Nevsky was just like my actor. If I choose a fat actor, then Nevsky was fat. If I have a thin actor, then he was thin. Then and now, always and forever.'[5] Eisenstein was always proud to have created (or imagined) history with the Odessa Steps sequence from *The Battleship Potemkin*.

Actually, 'then and now, always and forever', Alexander Nevsky is assumed to have looked like Nikolai Cherkassov, who reluctantly agreed to play the title role. Cherkassov had just come from great successes – in Alexander Zarkhi and Josef Heifitz's *Baltic Deputy* and in the role of Alexei, the son of Peter the Great in *Peter the First*. It was difficult to believe that this commanding thirty-four-year-old actor of great height and deep voice, had actually started his career as a comic actor in music hall.

In 1990, *The European* newspaper obtained a distorted version of Judith Glizer's memoirs published in an obscure quarterly *Kinovedcheskie Zapiski* (*Diaries of the Cinema*). The correspondent, Jeanne Vronskaya, claimed that Glizer had written that Eisenstein and Cherkassov were lovers, and that Cherkassov's wife knew of the affair. What Vronskaya's motive was in misquoting Glizer remains obscure. Factual errors in the article headed 'How the Casting Couch Survived Under Stalin: Eisenstein made his male lover a star – and Uncle Joe approved', add to the suspicion that the whole piece might have been concocted in order to defame the memory of both Eisenstein and Cherkassov. According to Vronskaya (falsely attributed to Glizer), Pera Attasheva was 'his childhood sweetheart from Riga' and Cherkassov was an 'obscure film extra' in 1933 when Eisenstein's 'eye fell upon him'. In fact, Cherkassov had already had substantial roles in a number of films, including Zarkhi and Heifitz's *Hectic Days* (1935). It is also implied that Eisenstein had to get Stalin's approval for the casting of the 'unknown' Cherkassov as Alexander Nevsky. Actually, Cherkassov was a member of the Supreme Soviet and a State Artist, more in favour than the director. The actor, whom Eisenstein called, enigmatically, a 'Holy Nag', forbade his face to be photographed from certain camera angles – behaving like certain Hollywood sex symbols.

Eisenstein began work on *Alexander Nevsky* with his co-author, Pyotr Pavlenko, in the late summer of 1937. Pavlenko was a Stalinist and probably a KGB agent; the Kremlin was taking no chances with Eisenstein this time. To protect him from the temptations of formalism, and any 'deviation' from the accepted tenets of Socialist Realism, Eisenstein was surrounded by collaborators faithful to Party policy; he was 'assisted' by Dmitri Vassiliev (who had also recently watched over the making of Mikhail Romm's *Lenin in October*) and had been given, in addition to Cherkassov, 'politically correct' stars like Nikolai Okhlopkov, formerly Chief Director of Moscow's Realist Theatre, who would play Vassili Bouslai. Another factor which would contribute to making political 'errors' impossible, was that the Kremlin's views on the subject were well known.

The increasing threat from Nazi Germany had led to further official encouragement of patriotic art, and the victory of the Novgorod nobles, led by Prince Alexander Nevsky, over their Teutonic rivals, was considered the first victory of democracy over fascism. The official announcement of the film described it as 'dealing with the struggles of the Russian people against the German knights,' being filmed 'to make workers conscious of what they had to defend.' These were the pressures and restrictive conditions under which Eisenstein embarked on *Alexander Nevsky*.

In November 1937 the first version of the scenario, entitled *Rus*, was completed and published in *Znamya*, after the inclusion of a series of suggestions volunteered by Vishnevsky. As *Prince Igor* still lingered in Eisenstein's mind, he had included a battle between Russians in Novgorod before Alexander Nevsky arrives to stop the feuding. The script ended with Nevsky being killed by the Mongol chief before the climactic triumph of the Russian army. Following publication, a whole avalanche of suggestions from historians, teachers, students and even schoolchildren flooded in. When Stalin received the second version of *Rus*, he cut the battles between the princes and refused to condone the death of the hero.

It was while he was doing preparatory research on locations that Eisenstein heard the news of the downfall of his nemesis, Boris Shumyatsky.

In the first six months of 1937, very few Soviet pictures had been produced. Alexandrov was enjoying a vogue with his comedy-musicals, and there was a football comedy called *The Goalkeeper of the Republic*, reviewed by the *New York Times* as 'a rollicking if by no means first rate production, strongly reminiscent of American college comedies.' Other releases of 1937 acceptable to Stalin were Grigori Roshal's *People of the Eleventh Legion*, about the Paris Commune; Vladimir Petrov's *Peter the First*, based on Alexei Tolstoy's novel, the hero of which Stalin identified with; Romm's *Lenin in October* ('This remarkable and momentous film', according to Eisenstein's review), and *Baltic Deputy*, starring Cherkassov as the distinguished Russian scientist Klement Timiriazev, who became a hero of the Revolution.

But the Soviet film industry was on the brink of bankruptcy. A notebook kept at Lenfilm studio in 1936 stated, 'Filming of the picture *Peter the Great* was stopped because of the cold in the studio . . . actor Cherkassov refused to be filmed wearing only a shirt . . . sound recording for *The Youth of the Poet* was delayed four hours because the roof leaked . . . It is discovered that an actor is holding a different script today. A search begins for yesterday's script . . .'

A version of *Treasure Island* that had been produced by the Children's Film Trust was denounced as 'bourgeois' by *Soviet Art*, the organ of the Central Art Committee. In this case, criticism may have been justified, because in order to get love interest, Jim Hawkins had been changed into Jenny Hawkins, with whom Dr Livesey falls in love, and, to give it a class angle, the Irish revolutionary movement had been dragged in. A reference in the review to Shumyatsky as 'the former chief' of the cinema industry was the first public intimation of his fall.

However, in a country with so Machiavellian an infrastructure, it would have been too rational merely to fire Shumyatsky for incompetence. If he had simply been dismissed, it would have reflected on the regime which had kept him in office for eight years. Therefore he was charged with having permitted 'savage veteran spies, Trotskyite and Bukharinist agents, and hirelings of Japanese and German fascism to perform their wrecking deeds in the Soviet cinema.'

In January 1938, Boris Shumyatsky was arrested, and was shot in July of the same year. Although Eisenstein did not openly express any glee at Shumyatsky's demise, he must have felt some satisfaction that he had outlived the man who had led the campaign against *Qué Viva México!*, had taken pride in the aborting of *MMM*, *Moscow* and *The Black Consul* and, most wounding of all, who banned *Bezhin Meadow* after two versions of the film had been virtually completed. Yet, Eisenstein's satisfaction would have been qualified by the knowledge that nobody was safe in the climate of the times, and that his turn might come.

Nevertheless, with optimism again triumphing over experience, Eisenstein could only hope that he would now be able to make more films in the future, relatively unimpeded, and that he would be thoroughly rehabilitated as a Soviet artist. However, celebrations were premature because the Kremlin replaced Shumyatsky with Semyon Dukelsky, who came straight from the NKVD or Secret Police. He was appointed 'to introduce firm Bolshevik order' into the cinema.

Developing a technique used in *Qué Viva México!*, Eisenstein made sketches for *Alexander Nevsky* before shooting because, as he wrote, 'without some concrete notion of act and gesture it is impossible to be specific about individual behaviour. The drawing is very often the search for something. Sometimes the scene you shoot has apparently no longer anything in common with the drawing: sometimes it will be even two years later, the drawing itself comes to life.'

Although stylistically much less experimental than his previous work, *Alexander Nevsky* has what Eisenstein called a 'symphonic structure', derived from his close collaboration with Sergei Prokofiev. Prokofiev and Eisenstein had met many times in the past, but few could have predicted the extraordinary success of their collaboration. (Even closer than that of Alfred Hitchcock and Bernard Herrman, Federico Fellini and Nino Rota.) Prokofiev welcomed the opportunity of working on the score of a film. He had spent some time in Hollywood film studios, making a careful study of film music techniques with the thought of applying them to his work in Soviet cinema.

'The cinema is a young and very modern art that offers new and fascinating possibilities to the composer,' Prokofiev commented. 'These possibilities must be utilised. Composers ought to study and develop them, instead of merely writing the music and then leaving it to the mercy of the film people.'[6]

As the action of the film takes place in the thirteenth century, there was a temptation to make use of the actual music of the period, but the Catholic choral singing was considered far too remote from contemporary audiences to have much effect.

Prokofiev would watch the rushes, note the timing of a sequence, and then leave around midnight, promising to deliver new music at noon the following day. True to his word, he would arrive punctually on the morrow, in his little blue car, with music that harmonised perfectly with the images he had seen. For the 'Battle on the Ice' sequence the composer produced a brilliant 'tone poem' in a matter of days, merely on the basis of Eisenstein's sketches and spoken ideas.

When it came to recording the sound track, Prokofiev was actively involved at all the stages, experimenting with dramatic microphone distortions and using the Mosfilm bath-tub as a percussion instrument. Eisenstein explained: 'There are sequences in which the shots were cut to a previously recorded music track. There are sequences for which the entire piece of music was written to a final cutting of the picture . . . in the battle scene where pipes and drums are played for the victorious Russian soldiers, I could not find a way to explain to Prokofiev what precise effect should be "seen" in his music for this joyful moment. Seeing that we were getting nowhere, I ordered some "prop" instruments constructed, shot these being played (without sound) visually and projected the results for Prokofiev – who almost immediately handed me an exact "musical equivalent" to that visual image of pipers and drummers which I had shown him.'[7]

Because of the difficulty of its execution, The Battle on the Ice was filmed first, paradoxically, during a summer heatwave at a lake near Moscow. Tisse converted the summer sky into a wintry one by means of filters, artificial snow was spread over one bank and the trees were painted white and covered with cotton wool. The 'ice' on the lake was supported by air-filled balloons from which the air was released when the ice blocks had to give way under the weight of the drowning German knights. Unlike the non-factual Odessa Steps sequence in *The Battleship Potemkin*, The Battle on the Ice had really taken place, on Lake Peipus, on April 5, 1242.

Alexander Nevsky was made with extraordinary speed. Shooting began in the spring of 1938, and the completed film was ready by November of the same year, five months ahead of schedule. To achieve this, Eisenstein worked as many hours in the editing room as the day would allow.

One night a telephone call came from the Kremlin – Stalin wanted to see the film. Without waking Eisenstein, his assistants gathered up the reels and hurried them off to the command screening. When the film was returned to the editing studio, it was discovered that one reel was missing. One theory put forward to explain its disappearance, was that the reel had been left behind in the studio by mistake, and Stalin did not notice its absence. Afterwards, when this was brought to the attention of the official in charge of the Kremlin screening, it was decided that the film would be better if released in the version that had been seen and approved by Stalin. Therefore, the spare reel was destroyed. A more likely explanation is that suggested by Esther Tobak, Eisenstein's assistant, who controlled the lights at the showing for

Stalin. She believed that the complete film was shown, but that Stalin objected to scenes involving a brawl on the bridge at Novgorod. The reel on which it appeared was extracted and eventually destroyed.

However, whatever the cause of its disappearance, the missing reel has never been found. The reason the gap was (and is) hardly noticeable is due to the way many films were still being made with a single projector in mind. The technique, dating from the silent era, was to have the end of a reel coincide with the end of a sequence so as not to interrupt the action.

Alexander Nevsky is Eisenstein's most straightforward and linear film, whatever the complexities behind its conception and making. Although Nikolai Cherkassov has the charisma and stature to hold the film – and the Russian army – together, Nevsky is presented as a one-dimensional figure, a conqueror striking heroic poses at the centre of a grandiloquent historical fresco. A Russian icon, in fact. Eisenstein's watchdogs (Dmitri Vassiliev was given a co-director's credit) made sure that he kept to the straight and narrow of the tenets of Socialist Realism, and that Nevsky was the kind of hero the times required, princely and patriotic, not revolutionary. If one were to imagine Eisenstein's works as animated films in the manner of the best of Walt Disney, *Alexander Nevsky* would need the least modification. There is even a Russian folk tale, about a vixen and a hare, told by a soldier in *Nevsky*, that would benefit as a cartoon sequence because, on English ears at least, it falls flat as it stands.

In other hands, this patriotic pageant would have been unwatchable. What one sees is how much Eisenstein (as in *The General Line*) tried to get away with while confined within the strict formula of the propaganda film. The costume designs alone conjure up a fantastic folk tale: the Germans wear bucket helmets with slits in the form of a cross for their eyes, while their leaders have even more fanciful helmets, with stag's horns or eagle's wings and claws on either side. As black smoke billows behind an evil-looking Catholic priest speaking of God (in the dictatorial manner of the father in *Bezhin Meadow*), a sinister Savonarola-profiled monk in a black cowl plays an organ outside the German camp, in what can be seen today as 'camp' in another sense. (In an echo of the priest in *The Battleship Potemkin*, the monk also pretends to be dead as he cowers behind his cowl.) Nevsky's helmet has elements of the goggles of a pilot's cap (as was worn by the tractor driver in *The General Line*.)

If one analyses the film in terms of grand opera, the surface simplicity is deepened further. Nevsky's orations can been seen as arias, the scenes between Vassili and Gavrilo as duets. There are trios (Olga, Gavrilo, Vassili), choruses (the fishermen, the masses), the dying men on the battlefield each crying (or singing) out in a fugue for their loved ones, and a ballet (the Battle on the Ice), underlined by the dramatic use of Prokofiev's score, including songs (all of which the composer developed into his symphonic cantata, *Alexander Nevsky*). The music often takes a broadly satirical approach, switching briskly from the uplifting (the Russians) to direful, menacing chords (the Germans), and there is a comic 'glug, glug' coda to the drowning of the enemy under the ice.

However, the music is used in the manner of a silent film score, accompanying the images rather than integrating with them, and cutting off after each sequence. Indeed, *Alexander Nevsky* has many of the elements of a silent film, with the camera hardly moving throughout, apart from a few effective tracking shots. Although Eisenstein still relies on montage to advance the action, there are a number of uncharacteristic long takes, such as one which picks out the German army as tiny figures on a hill, advancing slowly towards the camera. The violent and bloody clash between the two armies could have come from Uccello's *Battle of San Romano*. Despite some occasional speeding up, the battles, which take up the greater part of the film's running time, are excitingly choreographed, and influenced many subsequent screen battles, notably Laurence Olivier's *Henry V* and Orson Welles' *Chimes at Midnight*.

Ominous tuba chords sound the overture to The Battle on the Ice, as the thin ice on the lake gives way beneath the weight of the Germans' heavy armour, and the white knights are swallowed up by the waters, desperately – and a little comically – trying to cling to the blocks of ice under the broad, white expanses of the sky. (Eisenstein is here making an allusion to the climax of D.W. Griffith's *Way Down East*, when Lillian Gish is rescued from the swirling ice-floe.) The battlefield strewn with the dead refers back to the film's prologue, where skulls and skeletons on the 'field of death' echo the Day of the Dead in *Qué Viva México!*.

Just as it was inevitable that the scenes after the Odessa Steps sequence in *The Battleship Potemkin*, despite their fervour, would be anticlimactic, the prolonged post-battle scenes of celebration in *Alexander Nevsky* cannot avoid bathos. The great leader with small children clinging to him (reminiscent of another 'great leader'), the resolution of which of the two friendly rivals will be chosen by Olga, rapidly solved by Vassili's pairing off with the warrior goddess Vassilissa, and the final patriotic speech, are the nearest Eisenstein ever came to the conventional.

Alexander Nevsky opened in Moscow on November 23, 1938. At the premiere, held in Stalin's presence, Eisenstein sat between Prokofiev and Cherkassov. He was amused by Prokofiev's whispered query as to who the man was on his other side – the composer had failed to recognise Cherkassov without his make-up, small beard and flowing locks in the film. After the performance, Stalin personally congratulated Eisenstein and shook him by the hand. With Stalin's endorsement, *Alexander Nevsky* and its director were given the official stamp of approval, increasing Eisenstein's confidence in his future as a film director. (During the war, Stalin instituted an Order of Alexander Nevsky for Bravery.)

On February 20, 1938, Hitler had made his most anti-Soviet speech to that date. 'There is only one State with which we have not sought to establish relations, nor do we wish to establish relations with it: Soviet Russia. More than ever do we see in Bolshevism the incarnation of the human destructive instinct . . .'

By 1938, the Soviet Union appeared thoroughly isolated and ignored. On the day after Hitler's speech, Chamberlain declared that peace would depend on 'the four major powers of Europe: Germany, Italy, France and ourselves.' In September came the Munich agreement, and the belief that appeasement had succeeded.

Because *Alexander Nevsky* was conceived as a piece of history with contemporary overtones, and was first shown only two months after the Munich Pact, the defeat of the invading Teutonic Knights by Nevsky's army became, by implication, a comment on

Nazi aggression and, more ominously, proved to be a prophecy of what was to happen to Soviet Russia three years later.

While still working on the film, Eisenstein, in his mandatory bombastic (parodic?) vein, wrote an article entitled 'Alexander Nevsky and the Rout of the Germans' for *Izvestia*. In the piece, published on July 12, 1938, he made a correlation between Nevsky and Stalin, and presented Nevsky's victory over the Germans as a warning to their present-day counterparts.

'The only miracle in the battle on Lake Peipus was the genius of the Russian people, who for the first time began to sense their national, native power, their unity: a people able to draw from this awakening self-awareness an indomitable strength; able to advance, from their midst, a strategist and commander of genius, Alexander; and with him at their head, to defend the motherland, having smashed the devious enemy on foreign territory and not allowed him to despoil by his invasion their native soil. "The swine are finally repulsed beyond the Russian frontiers," wrote Marx. Such will be the fate of all those who dare encroach upon our great land even now. For if the might of our national soul was able to punish the enemy in this way, when the country lay exhausted in the grip of the Tartar yoke, then nothing will be strong enough to destroy this country which has broken the last chains of its oppression; a country which has become a Socialist Motherland; a country which is being led to unprecedented victories by the greatest strategist in world history – Stalin.'[8]

This was followed a few months later by an equally rhetorical article called 'My Subject is Patriotism', effectively playing dummy to Stalin's ventriloquist. This Eisenstein was unrecognisable to friends, and not to be found in his letters, diaries or memoirs.

'The great ideas of our Soviet Fatherland endow our art with unusual fecundity. We have tried to serve these great ideas of our Socialist Fatherland in all the films we have made in the course of nearly fifteen years. These were themes about the underground struggle, collectivism, the October Revolution, collectivisation. And now, in this picture [*Alexander Nevsky*], we have approached the national and patriotic theme, which dominates the attitude of Socialist creativity not only in our country, but in the West as well, for the guardians of national esteem, pride and independence, and true patriotism throughout the world are none other than the Communist Party and Communism . . . Now as I write this article, the picture *Alexander Nevsky* is finished. Our entire collective, imbued with the lofty ideas of the picture, worked on it enthusiastically; we are sure that the close of this film, Alexander Nevsky's splendid speech, will resound in our day as a terrible warning to all enemies of the Soviet Union. "Should anyone raise his sword against us, he shall perish by the sword. On this the Russian land stands and shall stand!"; These words express the feelings and will of the masses of the Soviet people.'[9]

The film and these public pronouncements did the trick. On February 1, 1939, a decree of the Presidium of the Supreme Soviet of the USSR awarded Eisenstein the Order of Lenin. The following March he was accorded the title of Doctor of the Science of Art Studies.

On this occasion, as if to consolidate his position as one of Stalin's darlings, Eisenstein wrote a piece in *Izvestia* called 'We Serve the People' in which he maintained, 'Living in conditions that are exceptionally conducive to creativity, unlike artists and craftsmen in the West, our artist does not always realise the extent to which these conditions oblige him to rise to the occasion.'

In contrast, early in 1939, Eisenstein wrote to Jay Leyda, 'I'm still so tired after *Nevsky* – who was a hell of a job to be made on so short a schedule . . . Please write me *as much as you can* and *about everything of importance* and *interest* in *books*, in the *arts* and so on . . . What about the 'snobbishness' around *Nevsky*? [The film had recently opened in the USA] I'd like to know as much as possible about everything – unfavourable even more than favourable. What is written in *Nation* and *New Republic*, what in magazines? What do people say about him? The next film will be not *so very* soon . . .'[10]

Though not yet fully recovered from the exhaustion induced by *Alexander Nevsky*, Eisenstein was nonetheless immersed in his next film project. *Perekop* (aka *Frunze*), which he was writing with his novelist friend Alexander Fadeyev. It was to retell the story of

Mikhail V. Frunze's 1920 victory against the White forces at the Battle of Perekop in the Crimea. Since his Proletkult days he had been familiar with Isaac Babel's *Red Cavalry* stories, Frunze himself, and other veterans of the campaign.

However, in May 1939, Pyotr Pavlenko, his co-scenarist on *Alexander Nevsky*, returned from a trip to Uzbekistan and enthused to Eisenstein about the construction of the Ferghana Canal. Eisenstein discussed the project with Tisse early in June, when the decision seems to have been taken to make a 'half-documentary, half-acted' film about it. On June 18 he obtained official blessing, and at the suggestion of the Committee for Cinematographic matters, he, Tisse and Pavlenko set off by plane for Tashkent to look into the filming possibilities.

The next few weeks were spent touring the area by car, covering some thousands of miles and visiting the historic cities of Bukhara and Samarkand. After all his travels and researches, Eisenstein and his colleagues returned to Moscow on July 12. Soon after, Eisenstein wrote to Prokofiev asking him to write the music for *The Great Ferghana Canal*. 'We shall be making a long and complex film . . . I cannot imagine such a film without you and therefore without delay I took the liberty of sending you an expanded libretto . . . In my opinion the stuff is damned fascinating and might prove very substantial.'[11]

The scenario was completed before the end of July and the first form of the shooting-script was edited in record time at Eisenstein's dacha during the first three days of August. 'The plan of the scenario was for an epic film dealing with the fertilisation of the deserts from Tamburlaine's time to the building of the Ferghana Canal in the modern Soviet of Uzbekistan,' Eisenstein announced. 'This will be the story of humanity's epic struggle against the deserts and sands of Asia and of the spectacular fight for water . . . another hymn to collectivist unification through socialist labour.'[12]

A reading of the imaginative shooting script reveals that *The Great Ferghana Canal* would have been far more than 'another hymn to collectivist unification through socialist labour.' The main action – the fight for water and the fertilisation of the desert with the help of the Ferghana Canal – is preceded by an historical prologue showing the invasion of Tamburlaine, who, in the fourteenth century, diverted the water, thus condemning the country to drought and death. Each episode was to be linked by songs from Tokhtasin, an aged and popular Uzbek singer, who evokes the drama and greatness of his country.

'The singer Tokhtasin sings, gazing into the desert . . . singing a song of a flowering land, such as was known in the days of the ancient land of Kharesm . . . Before Tokhtasin spreads the endless desert . . . Over the words of the song *dissolve to* . . . a spray of delicately flowering bush . . . And lo! before us a whole shady oasis is disclosed . . . its trees reflected in a broad artificial lake . . . intricate patterns of silvery channels irrigate fertile fields . . . we see in the lake the inverted reflection of a sky-blue cupola [Eisenstein was hoping to use colour] . . . The lake reflects the domes of the mosque . . . the intricate pattern of silvery channels dissolves into the complex arabesques of the ornamental tiles of the facade of a magnificent mosque, and before us is the square of the rich ancient city . . .'

There follows a brutal episode of Tamburlaine oppressing the people. As the people cry out for water, the cruel Emir of Kharesm orders that their blood be used to mix the mortar for his buildings. 'Scimitars flash through the frame . . . The stretched neck of a prisoner . . . Blood drips into a tub . . . From the desert comes the black cloud of the attacking army of Tamburlaine . . . The city square is strewn with dead. In the middle of the square a single crawling figure strains upwards crying, "Water!" . . . The warriors of Tamburlaine burst through the breach in the city wall, laying waste everything in their path . . .'[13]

The scenario was delivered on August 23 and the film unit left for Uzbekistan, where shots of the construction of the canal were taken. By October, Eisenstein had designed part of the decor and costumes and even began casting. But on the eve of shooting, a halt was suddenly called, leaving everything in mid-air. Eisenstein returned home with only the preliminary footage (later edited into a short documentary) to show for months of minutely detailed and laborious work. Another project had, like the city in *The Great Ferghana Canal*, become engulfed by sand.

One of the reasons given for the abandonment of the film, besides the apprehension that the monumental project would be too expensive to accomplish, was the signing of the infamous Nazi-Soviet Pact by foreign commissar Wenceslas Molotov and German foreign minister Joachim von Ribbentrop on August 23, 1939. The public text was simply an agreement of non-aggression and neutrality. The real agreement was in a secret protocol which, in effect, not only partitioned Poland, but much of Eastern Europe, Finland, Estonia, Latvia and Bessarabia were allotted to the Soviets; to the Nazis went everything to the west of those regions, including Lithuania. The Pact, coupled with a trade treaty and arrangements for a large-scale exchange of raw materials and armaments, amounted to an alliance. The Soviet Union obtained immunity from attack by Hitler, the opportunity of considerable expansion, and non-involvement in the war which began with Hitler's *blitzkrieg* against Poland on September 1.

The foreign reaction to the Nazi-Soviet Pact was one of shock and rage, while the Communist parties abroad who had had no official warning of the Soviet switch, reacted in confusion. Until the middle of 1941, the Soviet Union was to some degree in military, trade and cultural alliance with Nazi Germany, the rest of the West 'in an enemy camp'.

Naturally, *Alexander Nevsky*, a patriotic pageant depicting the defeat of Teutonic invaders, was withdrawn quietly from distribution and was only reshown, appropriately, when the Nazis invaded the Soviet Union. Ironically, the opening pastoral scenes of *Alexander Nevsky* are imbued with a Nordic savour – tall and fair-haired men and women, in contrast to the dark and shifty-eyed Tartars who descend on the peaceful village, are interchangeable with the iconography of some of the Nazi films being made in Germany during the same period. Vassilissa, the heroine in chain mail, who fights as bravely as any man, seems to have stepped out of *Die Walküre*.

Anti-Nazi films such as Adolf Minkin and Herbert Rappaport's *Professor Mamlock* and Grigori Roshal's *The Oppenheim Family* were also discreetly withdrawn from circulation. The former, about a brilliant surgeon publicly degraded because he is a Jew, was also banned in Britain in 1938 because of its anti-Nazi stance.

*

Not long before the signing of the Pact, Stalin had told H.G. Wells, 'Fascism is a reactionary force which is trying to preserve the old world by means of violence. What will you do with the Fascists? Argue with them? Try to convince them?'

How hollow Eisenstein's article 'My Subject is Patriotism' (written before the Pact) rings in retrospect. He wrote: 'It is hard to believe your eyes when you read of the unbridled ferocity of the Jewish pogroms in Germany, where the whole world watches as hundreds of thousands of people, denied their rights and deprived of human support, are being wiped from the face of the earth. The Communists have led, and are leading the front line against this bloody nightmare . . . . The mighty voice of the Soviet Union is the only one to have rung out unwaveringly, insistently, and uncompromisingly for a decisive struggle against this obscurantism . . . We want our film [*Alexander Nevsky*] to mobilise even more those who are in the very thick of the worldwide struggle against Fascism . . . there is no force of ignorance and darkness that can resist the united forces of all that is best, healthy, progressive and forward-looking in humanity.'[14]

Meanwhile, the Soviet government continued to wage war on its own citizens. In 1938, Meyerhold's theatre was closed down after its director was accused in *Pravda* of consistently producing anti-Soviet plays, as well as allowing formalism, nepotism and favouritism to flourish in his theatre. Nevertheless, Stanislavsky invited the humiliated but still proud Meyerhold to direct at the Opera Theatre, where he revived Mayakovsky's *The Bed Bug* in an abridged form. But the death of Stanislavsky, whose Moscow Arts Theatre had been above criticism, deprived Meyerhold of his protector and exposed him to the full force of the purges.

Not long after Eisenstein received the Order of Lenin, the sixty-five-year-old Meyerhold was given an ovation at the First All-Union Conference of Directors on June 13, 1939. A few days later he was arrested, and a month later his wife, the actress Zinaida Raikh, was found brutally murdered with her throat cut. In February the following year, Meyerhold was executed in a Moscow prison.

Eisenstein only made one oblique reference in print to Meyerhold's arrest. In his account of one of his first meetings with his mentor, Eisenstein wrote: 'Let everyone know how they treated Meyerhold . . . So far, nothing in particular had happened to Meyerhold . . .'[15] In spite of the real danger to himself, Eisenstein remained faithful to Meyerhold, visiting his home frequently during 1938 and 1939, and he saved Meyerhold's papers and notes by hiding them in the walls of his dacha.

After Eisenstein's death, Pera immediately called the State Archives and informed them that she had some material of Meyerhold's that she would like to donate to them secretly. She never told them that Eisenstein had hidden anything, only that he had been a student of Meyerhold's and had kept a few papers of his. Two weeks later some KGB agents turned up at Pera's apartment to ask if she had any papers belonging to anyone else. Somehow, she managed to convince them that she had nothing of interest to them, and Eisenstein's papers and the rescued frames from *Bezhin Meadow* remained safeguarded.

On 3 September 1939, Britain declared war on Germany. The world would be torn apart by World War II for five long years, during which the USSR would become a once unlikely ally of the West, and Stalin would be fondly known as 'Uncle Joe' to the British. This, however, did not happen until mid-1941, and February 19, 1940, saw the following report in the *New York Times*.

'Sergei Eisenstein, one of the most prominent Soviet film directors, today launched a Soviet-German cultural co-operation program over the Comintern Radio Station. Broadcasting especially to Germany, Mr Eisenstein said that friendly Russian-German relations established last year formed a solid base for "increased cultural co-operation between the two peoples."' But Eisenstein's private diary at the time was filled with anxiety and dread about the rapprochement with Nazi Germany.

In 1940, political imperatives dictated that there should be pro-German films like Dovzhenko's *Liberation*. As part of a government policy to put Russia's best film directors in positions of creative authority, Dovzhenko was assigned the studios in Kiev, and Eisenstein became the Head of Productions at the Mosfilm Studios, somewhat alleviating his disappointment over the cancellation of *The Great Ferghana Canal*.

Now Eisenstein, the man who once wrote, 'Soviet cinema must cut through to the skull! It is not Ciné-Eye that we need, it is a Ciné-Fist', was celebrating, in print, 'the final victory of Socialist Realism in cinema'. After tracing the road to this victory, the price of which was paid with 'kilometres of wasted film; lists of failures, gradually fading from memory' (including *Bezhin Meadow*, we assume), he proclaimed: 'For cinema, unlike the other arts, can capture and reflect with the greatest clarity and resourcefulness both the leading tendencies and the subtlest nuances and shades of the progressive movement of history . . . And this is probably because one and the same genius is tirelessly nourishing both the most progressive movement of the whole country and at the same time the arts that reflect this movement – above all, cinema. That genius lies in the genius of our great people and in the genius of the wise leadership of the Bolshevik Party.'[16]

There is in Eisenstein's public actions an echo of Bertolt Brecht's *The Life of Galileo*, completed in November 1938, which was written under the impact of the Soviet show trials that had resulted in the execution of, among others, Nikolai Bukharin, whose confessions of his 'crimes' was to no avail. Galileo yielded to the Inquisition because he felt both his life and the survival of his work were threatened. Brecht saw Galileo going down on his knees before the Inquisition out of 'an historical necessity'.

Brecht has Galileo say: 'Shortly after my trial a number of people who had known me before, treated me with a certain degree of indulgence, in that they attributed to me all sorts of high-minded intentions. I rejected all of them . . . After a careful consideration of all the circumstances, the extenuating ones as well as the others, one cannot but conclude that a man would find no other ground for such submission but in the fear of death . . . No less than a threat of death is generally needed to deflect a man from that to which his intellect has led him – this most dangerous of all the gifts of the Almighty.'

Eisenstein himself, in a self-revealing passage in his memoirs, tells a Persian legend: 'It concerned a certain strong man who would become a hero and who had felt, since childhood, a calling to accomplish some very great task. Preparation for this future accomplishment meant conserving his strength until he had attained his full might. He went to a bazaar, where some tanners, as I recall, pressed around him. "Get down on your knees before us and lie in the filth of this bazaar, so that we can walk over you," they jeered. And the hero-to-be, saving his strength for the future, humbly lay at their feet in the filth. This is said to have happened as many as three times. Later the hero reached manhood, attained the full mastery of his unprecedented strength and performed all the feats of unheard-of difficulty that lay before him. I found this episode with the tanners utterly captivating: his unheard-of self-control and sacrifice of everything, including his self-esteem, as he readied himself for the achievements to come, where he would accomplish what had already been primordially ordained and decreed. In my personal, too personal, history, I have had on several occasions to stoop to these levels of self-abasement.'[17]

16

The Earthly Tsar

Step by step, page by page – the historical records open up before us not only a profound rationale, but also a simple and historical necessity for Ivan to act in the way he did, in his dealings with those who sought to ruin, sell off cheap, or betray their fatherland for their own selfish ends. The father-land, which the great statesmanlike mind of Ivan the Terrible had gathered up, strengthened and victoriously led into battle. It was not my intention to whitewash him in the collective memory, or to turn Ivan the Terrible into Ivan the Sweet.

As early as 1933, Sergei Prokofiev had wanted to write a 'heroic and constructive' opera on a Soviet theme. Eventually he found this in a story by Valentin Katayev, *I, Son of the Working Class*, a peasant drama of the Civil War played out in 1918 when the Communists in the Ukraine still had to contend with German troops as well as counter-revolutionaries.

In Prokofiev's opera *Semyon Kotko*, the Germans are charac-terised, as they had already been in *Alexander Nevsky*, by viciously dissonant harmony. Although less successful when consciously attempting the broad gestures required to express bluff, optimistic Communist emotions, the work also finds room for some lyrical love music and some vividly colourful ensembles.

But, as Dmitri Shostakovich wrote in his memoirs: 'As . . . *Semyon Kotko* deals with the occupation of the Ukraine by the Germans in 1918, it had no chance in the improbable but inescapable context of a Moscow-Berlin axis. It was put into pro-duction at the Stanislavsky Opera Theatre by Meyerhold. It was his last work in the theatre. In fact, he never finished it; he was arrested in the middle of it, and he was no longer Meyerhold but Semyonich. That was his alleged underground saboteur's nickname. That's quite ridiculous. It was probably the interrogator who invented the name, having read something about *Semyon Kotko* in the papers. The director was arrested but the work went on as though nothing had happened. This was one of the terrible signs of the age; a man disappeared but everyone pretended that nothing had happened. A man was in charge of the work, it had meaning only with him, under his direction. But he was no longer there, he had evaporated, and no one said a word. The name Meyerhold immediately disappeared from conversations. That was all . . . Prokofiev turned to Eisenstein, his friend. The word "friend" is used as a convention here, particularly when it's used for two men like Eisenstein and Prokofiev. I doubt that either of them needed friends. They were both remote and aloof, but at least Prokofiev and Eisenstein respected each other. Eisenstein had also been a student of Meyerhold's, so Prokofiev asked the film director to bring the production of *Semyon Kotko* to completion. Eisenstein refused. The political climate had changed by then, and in that wonderful era attacks on Germans, if only in an opera, were forbidden. The opera's future looked doubtful. Why get mixed up in a politically dubious venture? So Eisenstein said, "I don't have the time." He found time, as we know, for *Die Walküre* . . .'[1]

The Bolshoi Theatre had, in fact, invited Eisenstein to stage Richard Wagner's *Die Walküre* 'in the mutual interests of German and Russian cultures.' He eagerly accepted the new challenge as it presented him with an opportunity to apply Wagner's idea of combining theatre, music, literature and myth into one medium, which concurred with his own vision of film as synthesis; film had become the new *Gesamtkunstwerk*.

Eisenstein wrote a long enlightening article, with only the occasional sloganising, on his ideas behind the staging of *Die Walküre*. 'After a period of intensive "retheatricalisation" of cinema, which is just as great a bastardisation as the mechanical "cinematographisation" of theatre, there comes a new, beneficial cross-fertilisation of film and theatre . . . I devoted the whole conception of the last piece,

The Magic Fire, to searching for ways of combining the elements of Wagner's score with a changing play of coloured light on stage. Despite the extremely limited technical resources and the far from perfect lighting and the lighting equipment of the Bolshoi's stage, which drastically reduced the range of colours available for the fire, we nevertheless achieved an extremely convincing rendering in colour of Wotan's Farewell . . . One way or another, I take the first practical steps in chromophonic – a synthesis of sound and colour – counterpoint on the stage of the Bolshoi for myself.'[2]

Like George Bernard Shaw's socialist interpretation of the tetralogy in *The Perfect Wagnerite*, Eisenstein saw 'hatred of private property' as one of the themes of *The Ring*. He quotes from Wagner's *The Art-Work of the Future*: 'The task of the contemporary state is to preserve the inviolability of property throughout the ages, and that is precisely what has impeded the creation of a free future.' Put simply, the price of economic power is the renunciation of love, and that the possession of the ring and its wealth will ruin those who aspire to possess it can be seen as the over-riding theme of *The Ring*. But Eisenstein concluded that 'Wagner's characters are not abstractions or mouthpieces for proclaiming the author's programmatic statements. They are intriguing, multifaceted living beings who, in addition to their philosophical significance, also embody a complex of human emotions which are revealed in the element of Wagner's incomparable music. And so they can be interpreted in different ways.'[3]

Die Walküre is the least 'political' of the four operas, and Act One is the only act in the whole cycle consisting of mortals rather than gods – a triangle of husband, wife and lover. Eisenstein attempted to give his production a humanist, and by implication, an anti-Nazi interpretation. The first act was dominated by a 'Tree of Life' that took up the entire expanse of the stage. (Eisenstein worked very closely with the designer Peter Williams aka Pyotr Vilyams.) The tree motif continued throughout the following two acts. 'Wotan's appearance was preceded by toppling pine trees. Then, near the curtain, they rose up from the ground once more, joining the Valkyries' final upward flight and their divine father's furious departure. I had identified the Valkyries with pine trees. Probably because I first heard their frenzied flight on someone's piano among the giant pines in the forests of Finland . . . And I came to know the structure of leitmotif and counterpoint among the bases of even greater trees – the famous Redwoods around San Francisco.'[4]

Eisenstein would have liked The Ride of the Valkyries, which opens Act Two, to 'envelop the entire audience via a system of loudspeakers, reverberating "as if in flight" from the rear of the stage to the back of the auditorium and back; and roll around the auditorium, up the steps and along the aisles and corridors. But I was not able here to overcome the traditions of the opera theatre!' (Eisenstein was here anticipating The Ride of the Valkyries as used in the stereophonic Dolby system by Francis Ford Coppola, an Eisenstein devotee, in *Apocalypse Now*, almost four decades later.)

Die Walküre opened at the Bolshoi Theatre on November 21, 1940, and was greeted coolly by both the public and the critics. The coolest reception of all was given by the Germans. Alexander Werth, the English historian, on leaving the premiere, overheard two officers from the German embassy remark: 'Deliberate Jewish tricks,' and that it was 'a terrible example of *Kulturbolschewismus* (cultural Bolshevism).'[5]

Eisenstein was not only disappointed by the reception but by some of the effects. 'There was no dazzling sunlight to hasten the joyous song of love into the audience; instead a yellow spotlight shone from behind a curtain, saturating the auditorium with light. And the wind machine beneath the stage always failed to blow – they never once fanned the tongues of fire, which hung limply in the blue and scarlet light, looking more like streamers above a butcher's shop than the play of fire that was supposed to protect Brünnhilde's sleep, until Siegfried came to wake her . . . what I derived of infinite emotional value from this work, with its burning aspirations, inspired strivings and tragic achievement, was condemned by insuperable technical difficulties to crawl where it should have burst into the heavens . . .'[6]

He had hoped to have been able to complete *The Ring*, and had already made sketches for *Das Rheingold* – the drawing for the opening scene shows a submerged and inverted Paramount-like mountain, the water being 'Disney-like blue' – but he abandoned the idea of proposing it to the Bolshoi administration. However, his experience with working on an opera was another factor that influenced his conception of *Ivan the Terrible*.

Eisenstein returned to his work as Head of Productions at Mosfilm. (Yelena Sokolovskaya, the director of Mosfilm, had been arrested, a victim of guilt by association, because her husband, a member of the Central Committee, was suspected of being anti-Soviet.)

According to Mikhail Romm, Eisenstein enjoyed walking around the studio 'generally playing the part of the Artistic Boss of the studio.' Romm, who won five Stalin prizes in his career, was at Mosfilm filming *Dream* at the time. 'In the course of the production, he [Eisenstein] visited every set and watched part of the shooting of almost every sequence,' Romm recalled. 'If he was pleased with what he saw, he made a joke. If there was something he disliked, he still made a joke, but it was much more caustic. Often he left the poor director guessing if he was pleased or otherwise. This of course was typical of Eisenstein's general personality. His own thought processes were extremely complicated, and it was usually a tough exercise in intelligence and imagination to understand his real meaning. For anyone who made the effort it was a great pleasure to talk to him and to hear what he had to say. But, unfortunately, his erudition and his sharp wit were poor helpmates to clarity.'[7]

Meanwhile, Eisenstein was at work on a scenario by Lev Sheinin called *The Beilis Case* about Mendel Beilis, a Jew from Kiev who had suffered a long trial on the charge of ritual murder of a Russian boy. There was also the possibility of a film on Lawrence of Arabia, whose psychology greatly interested Eisenstein. 'True, the only colour here is in the green of the Prophet's flag and the green turbans of the generals. And also the remarkable description of the old Arab woman, who had never seen blue eyes before and asked the intelligence officer whether his eyes were blue because the sun shone through them . . . And in order to treat the material more freely, the film was not to be too factually biographical . . .'[8] A colour film about Giordano Bruno was also proposed. 'Italy . . . Renaissance costumes . . . Burning at the stake . . .'[9] Eisenstein mused with relish, but it too got no further than the proposal stage. Nevertheless, the committee was determined he make a big colour film. Following the Bruno idea, there was a suggestion about Tommaso Campanella – 'The colourful past was inevitably sought on the border between the Middle Ages and the Renaissance'[10] – and one about the Black Death. Eisenstein was fascinated by one episode – a banquet held in the midst of a raging plague. 'It would be a film about the colour black, the blackness of the plague inexorably spreading everywhere, swallowing everything in its wake, the engulfing blackness of the funeral cortège smothering the motley colours of the carnival.'[11]

One idea which came closer to fruition was a proposed biopic of Pushkin to be called *A Poet's Love*. Pushkin had fascinated Eisenstein ever since he had seen an amateur performance of *Eugene Onegin* during his childhood in Riga. Later he had read and re-read Pushkin's poems and, while he was busy with *Die Walküre*, he sketched out the life story of the writer for a film which was described in the language of colour. 'I devoted the summer [of 1940] to Alexander Sergeyevich. I reached the point where I felt I knew my hero well enough to call him by his first names . . .'[12]

Esther Shub recounted Eisenstein's words to her about wanting to make a film about 'a great lasting and wonderful love', and simultaneously to rehabilitate Pushkin by killing off once and for all his Don Juan image and replacing it with that of the genuine, intensely passionate lover. Shub had advised him to read Yuri Tynanov's *A Nameless Love*, which suggested that the nameless love of Pushkin's life was Yekaterina Karamzina, the wife of the famous Russian historian Nikolai Karamzin. 'Did she really, in the spring of 1940, see herself playing Karamzina to my . . . Pushkin?' Eisenstein commented, echoing his earlier remark that she saw herself as George Sand to his Chopin. 'A picture of such love. A love hidden and illicit. But illicit rather than hidden. But of such strength. And inspired.'[13] Sadly the film proved impossible to make because of the inadequacy of the technical equipment available for colour filming. 'We were not prepared from the technical point of view,' he commented. 'My first colour film to be worked out in detail [was] "archived" as soon as it became clear that the technology was still in its infancy.'[14] Around the same time, in France, Jean Renoir was hoping to make *La Régle du Jeu* in colour, but the cost of the process was exorbitant. Technicolor was still rare enough even in Hollywood. Yet Eisenstein still dreamt of making a colour film.

In the outline of *A Poet's Love*, he had pictured the monologue in Pushkin's play, *Boris Godunov* with 'Tsar Boris, clad in thick gold, with flecks of silver in his black beard . . . The red carpets of the cathedral. The red candlelight. And, illuminated by it, seemingly splashed with blood, the icon frames. The Tsar rushes about his apartments. Dark blue. Cherry red. Orange. Green . . . the multi-coloured brightness of the apartments and towers of the Kremlin palace burst upon the Tsar, a nightmare of colour, as the camera lunges this way and that.'[15] This was another colour dream that disappeared on waking to the monochrome reality of Soviet life.

On March 15, 1941, Eisenstein was awarded the Stalin Prize. But, as a previous biographer, Yon Barna put it, 'his personal satisfaction was tempered with sadness as he noted that eight out of ten of the recipients of top awards were former students of Meyerhold – of that great personality who had so senselessly and tragically been wiped out of existence.'[16] Perhaps to delay having to join Meyerhold, a month later Eisenstein published a short sycophantic piece in *Pravda* entitled 'The Heirs and Builders of World Culture' which eulogised the system that liquidated Meyerhold.

'The land around is aglow. Thanks to the wisdom and foresight of the Soviet government and Comrade Stalin, our Union is the only place in the world where the artist can create in peace, where the builder can build in peace, and the inventor can solve his problems in peace. The rest of the world is in the furnace of war . . . A great task lies before us, the artists of the land of the Soviets; to continue and advance the cause of world culture. For, we apart, there is no one in the world working at this; everything beyond our Soviet soil is aimed at the annihilation and destruction of culture. Let our ranks stand all the more firmly together! We shall carry out our task with a new strength and energy! I shall wholly devote my personal creativity in the coming year to the creation of a film about the great builder of the Russian state in the sixteenth century: *Ivan the Terrible*.' The article was signed, 'S. Eisenstein, Film Director and Stalin Prize Winner.[17]

*

During the summer of 1941, Eisenstein was at his dacha at Kratov when news came through of the German attack on Russia. The Nazis, with the aid of Finnish and Romanian troops, invaded the Soviet Union. On the day before the invasion, Stalin was still acting as if he considered Hitler his partner. Prokofiev, who was also at Kratov working on his ballet *Cinderella*, described the day.

'On the warm, sunny morning of June 22, I was sitting at my desk when suddenly the watchman's wife appeared, looking greatly upset. "The Germans have invaded us," she gasped. "They say they're bombing our cities." The news staggered me . . . I hurried over at once to see Sergei Eisenstein who lived not far from us. Yes, it was true.'[18]

From June 22 to July 3, 1941, Stalin did not utter a word in public. He then commandeered the people to conduct guerrilla warfare in Nazi-occupied areas, and said he would wage a 'national patriotic war.' He warned that 'there must be no room for whimperers and cowards, for panic-mongers and deserters . . .' Thousands of prominent political prisoners were hastily executed, and other potential dissidents were selected for front-line service.

To prevent the population at large from hearing German propaganda, radio receivers were gathered in wholesale. Soviet citizens of German descent were rounded up. The entire population – almost half a million – of Volga Germans was uprooted and 'deported' by methods which few survived. Conceding that it might be wondered how the Soviet government could have 'consented' to sign a pact with 'such perfidious people, such fiends as Hitler and Ribbentrop,' Stalin gave the answer, 'We secured to our country peace for a year and a half and the opportunity of preparing our forces.'

With unwitting prescience, there was an unrealised part of the *Alexander Nevsky* screenplay that stands as a metaphor for Stalin's wooing of Hitler, and even Eisenstein's grovelling behaviour. It was summarised thus: 'After the Germans had been routed on Lake Peipus, the Tartar horde advanced on Russia once more, to exact vengeance. The victor, Nevsky, hastened to meet them. He walked submissively between the purifying fires in front of the Khan's pavilion and humbled himself on one knee before the Khan. His meekness gained the time needed to build up strength so that later this enslaver of our land could be overthrown, too . . .'[19]

In a speech delivered on November 7 in Red Square to troops marching directly to the front, Stalin invoked the shades of medieval saints and tsarist generals in an unequivocal appeal to Russian nationalism. 'Let the manly images of our great ancestors – Alexander Nevsky, Dmitri Donskoi, Kuzma Minin, Dmitri Pozharsky, Alexander Suvorov and Michael Kutusov – inspire you in the war!' In effect, he begged his soldiers to fight for Mother Russia not for Communism. *Pravda* replaced the phrase 'Workers of the World unite!' on its masthead with 'Death to the German invader!'

Suddenly the bad guys who had become the good guys were the bad guys again. *Alexander Nevsky* was back on the cinema screens, and anti-Nazi films became the order of the day. The emphasis turned to documentary films, a field that had lain relatively dormant for a number of years. Cameramen were despatched to the fronts and the material they sent back was edited into morale-boosting compilation films. In 1942, the first full-length war documentaries appeared: Leonid Varlamov and Ilya Kopalin's *The Defeat of the German Armies Near Moscow*, Roman Karmen's *Leningrad in Combat*, and Mikhail Slutsky's *Days of War*. Dziga Vertov, once the leading documentary film-maker in the Soviet Union, now out of favour, found himself editing conventional *News of the Day* newsreels under Esther Shub. Eisenstein was appointed consultant for a documentary on the war effort.

During the Nazi-Soviet Pact, dismissals of Jews and restrictions on them had been increased. Now Moscow's public policy of anti-Nazism was a time of consolidation for many Soviet Jews. In July 1941, together with four other prominent Jewish intellectuals and artists – the writer Ilya Ehrenburg, the playwright Perets Markish, the actor Solomon Michoels and the physicist Pyotr Kapitsa – Eisenstein took part in an anti-Fascist meeting broadcast over the American radio network. In a newsreel he called for United States intervention in the war. Speaking in his high voice in English, his hair standing up like a peacock's fan, he declared, 'As a representative of the Russian intelligentsia, and working as I do in the field of Russian cinematography and Russian art, the very principle of racial hatred is foreign and loathsome to me . . . The triumph of humanism over brutality, barbarism, infamy and violence, is a matter of a bright future for all humanity irrespective of nationality . . . but the time of indignation and condemnation has passed, the time has come to fight.'

The coming of the 'Great War for the Fatherland' inaugurated a period of relative freedom in the arts. In literature, the regime, with scant regard to ideological criteria, encouraged the use of nationalism, religion, love – anything which might sway the emotions of the reading public into identifying themselves with the struggle against Hitler. There was also a great upsurge in patriotic feeling which found an outlet in musical expression. Opera composers drew inspiration from national heroes of the past. Prokofiev began work on his *War and Peace*. Shostakovich produced his seventh symphony, the so-called *Leningrad*, in 1941, the first movement of which suggested the inexorable advance of the invading armies.

It was against this background that Eisenstein embarked on a monumental film entitled *Ivan the Terrible* ('terrible' in the sense of 'Awe-inspiring' or 'Redoubtable'), a three-part epic – *Ivan Grozny*, *The Boyars' Plot* and *The Battles of Ivan* – about Ivan IV, the 16th-century Tsar who first unified all the lands of Russia. By April 1941, the main lines of the scenario were sketched out, though Eisenstein devoted two further years to historical research, the analysis of Ivan's character and related drawings, of which he made over two thousand.

'The basic idea of the film is to show Ivan in the full context of his tremendous efforts on behalf of the Russian state in and around the city of Moscow, and I must say quite bluntly that a great deal of what he did, and the ways in which he did it, were as bloody as they were grandiose,' explained Eisenstein. 'Nor shall we ignore a single drop of all the blood that was shed during the life of Ivan IV. Our aim is not to whitewash but to explain. In this way, without hiding anything or modifying anything in the story of Ivan the Terrible, and also without denying his extraordinary and romantic popular image, we hope to present him, complete and as he truly was, to cinema audiences throughout the world.'[20]

In the autumn of 1941, Moscow came under heavy bombardment, and one midnight in mid-October Eisenstein and other film makers received instructions to evacuate the city. The very next morning the exodus began by the train which was to take them twelve days and nights into the heart of Central Asia, to Alma Ata, the capital of Kazakhstan. This was not far from the Chinese border where other evacuated members of Mosfilm and Lenfilm Studios were hard at work on morale-boosting projects.

Using the former Palace of Culture as a studio were Pudovkin, Ermler, and the Vasilievs. The size of the rooms allowed for only the most cramped of stage sets – sets totally unsuited to the massive filming of *Ivan the Terrible* that Eisenstein had in mind. The three parts would have to be filmed simultaneously, because the studio could accommodate only one large set at a time and the same set was required throughout.

Eisenstein was not given separate living accommodation, but had to make do with 'eleven square metres' as he wrote to Elisabeta Teleshova in a letter dated March 3, 1942. He suggested that if she were to come they could have a room to themselves of twice the size. Another problem, he added, was his 'completely catastrophic' financial situation.

In the same month, Eisenstein wrote to Prokofiev, who was in Tblisi, the capital of Georgia, asking him to compose the music for *Ivan the Terrible*. In a letter of March 29, 1942, Prokofiev replied: 'Am finishing up the last bars of *War and Peace*, thus very shortly I'll be ready to submit to your bondage.'[21]

Although the bulk of the music was composed after the film had been shot, Prokofiev travelled to Alma Ata in May, bringing with him the score of his opera *War and Peace* to continue its orchestration. As the latter work progressed, Prokofiev acquainted Eisenstein with the opera, scene by scene – until Eisenstein was making suggestions for the production. Semyon Samosud, conductor and artistic director of the Bolshoi, recalled, 'Eisenstein was the man to stage the opera . . . Knowing how the completion of *Ivan* was the most urgent task, our theatre offered him the position of consulting director.'[22]

Prokofiev telegraphed Samosud: 'Eisenstein consents to work as director, not consultant. Requests urgent arrival of [Peter]

Williams to work out plans for the sets. Prokofiev.'[23] Eventually, however, the Bolshoi decided that a new production of such a large-scale work was unwise in wartime, and *War and Peace* was first heard in a concert version in Moscow in the summer of 1945. Eisenstein and Samosud met at that performance and agreed that only a full staging would do justice to the opera. Eisenstein was too ill to take it on when it was finally staged in Leningrad in June 1946, though many of the designs were based on the sketches he made in Alma Ata. Eisenstein's experience on *Die Walküre* and his work on *War and Peace*, helps explain much of the 'operatic' aspect of *Ivan*.

Luckily, Nikolai Cherkassov had been evacuated with the Pushkin Theatre to Novo Sibirsk, not too far from Alma Ata, so was available to play the title role. (Curiously, Eisenstein confided to a friend that he would have preferred the less heroic-looking Mikhail [Michael] Chekhov to play Ivan had he not emigrated to the USA some years earlier.) Pudovkin was cast as the beggar simpleton Nicholas, and Serafima Birman, from Stanislavsky's Moscow Arts Theatre, took the role of Euphrosinia, the Tsar's aunt. Eisenstein wanted prima ballerina Galina Ulanova to play the Tsarina Anastasia. Though she herself was enthusiastic and made successful screen and make-up tests, travelling difficulties forced her to decline. Ludmilla Tselikovskaya, a theatre actress from Moscow, took the part.

Eisenstein had been reinstated at The Institute of Cinematography, which had also been evacuated to Alma Ata, and he continued to teach there while working on the film. In August 1942 his first book, *The Film Sense*, was published in the USA, translated and edited by Jay Leyda. (A year later it was published in England.) A copy reached Eisenstein in Alma Ata, on January 22, 1943, his forty-fifth birthday.

'This must be the first time in my life that I'm absolutely satisfied – with my first book and how it came out,' he wrote to Leyda. 'I can't imagine how it could be better . . . Even the dust jacket . . . is the one I would have chosen; absolutely boulevard in appearance – yellow with black, like the cover of a detective novel. On it my face with an absolutely obscene glance and a Gioconda smile. This was cut from a photo by Jiménez in Mexico in 1930. In my right hand near my shoulder I held a sugar skull from the objects associated with "death day". With the skull removed what is left is a semi-ironic expression on my face and a lustful eye looking out from under a slightly raised left eyebrow . . .'[24]

Eisenstein's writings in general, from his return to the USSR in 1934 onwards, though as erudite, wide-ranging, and full of unexpected insights, were more cautious and conservative than his earlier innovative and enthusiastic essays. One noticeable aesthetic change was his attitude to montage. In a complete reversal of many of his theories (and practices), he now claimed that the 'basic aim and function' of montage is 'connected and sequential exposition of the theme, the material, the plot, the action . . . the simple matter of telling a connected story'; he who had once characterised montage as 'collision' and 'conflict'. 'From the collision of two given factors arises a concept. Linkage is, in my interpretation, only a possible special case . . . Thus montage is conflict. The basis of every art is always conflict.'

But, as Dwight Macdonald suggested in 1942, 'Eisenstein's change of mind about montage has nothing to do with aesthetic theory; it is simply an adaptation to the political pressures which have crushed all Soviet art in the last decade . . . The cinema is a dramatic art form, and dramatic structure depends largely on the tension created by conflict; but there cannot be conflict in a totalitarian state, since there is only one principle, one set of values authorised to be publicly expressed.'[25] There was a revolutionary quality to the conflict-montage in Eisenstein's *October*, whereas Socialist Realist films i.e. Stalinist films, were, in a sense, counter-revolutionary.

While working on the script of *Ivan* in Alma Ata, Eisenstein also found time to write a number of essays, a perceptive comparison between Charles Dickens and D.W. Griffith, and another on Charlie Chaplin. Neither did the work on *Ivan* stop him from contemplating future film possibilities. He exchanged letters with Leopold Stokowski, whom he had met in Mexico, and who he invited to Russia after the war to discuss 'an idea for a musical film.' Eisenstein had seen and admired Disney's *Fantasia* three years previously in which the conductor played straight-man to Mickey Mouse.

Eisenstein and Pudovkin were, in turn, jointly approached by the newly-knighted Alexander Korda about co-directing a film of *War and Peace* for which Orson Welles was suggested as Pierre Bezukhov. (Welles boasted that he had corresponded with Eisenstein, but no letters to or from him have ever turned up.) Both directors were enthusiastic and sent a detailed summary of their ideas for the film. As the USA and Great Britain were now allies of the Soviet Union, contacts with the West were allowed. (A few years previously, Korda had made *Knight Without Armour*, a sort of *Thirty-Nine Steppes*, in which Robert Donat rescues Countess Marlene Dietrich from execution by the Bolsheviks.)

In 1937, Eisenstein had written: 'The aspiring film director could derive enormous benefit from studying the change of levels, the interplay of details in close-up, the glimpses of the behaviour of heroes and episodic characters, the type-casting and crowd scenes in long shot that unfold on the grandiose canvas of the Battle of Borodino in Tolstoy's *War and Peace*.'[26] (There had been two silent film versions in 1915, one of which was directed by Vladimir Gardin and starred Olga Preobrazhenskaya as Natasha. But modern audiences had to wait until King Vidor's 1956 version, and then Sergei Bondarchuk's mammoth eight-hour film of 1966.) During 1943, Eisenstein reread *The Brothers Karamazov*, noting in his diary ideas for a possible screen version. It was the first time he had read it since the time, aged seventeen, when he had prepared himself for his meeting with Dostoevky's widow.

The filming of the three parts of *Ivan the Terrible* began in April 1943, in the evenings only when electricity could be spared from the more urgent needs of wartime industry. Tisse photographed the exteriors for *Part I*, but the cameraman for the interiors – the bulk of the film – was Andrei Moskvin. Moskvin had been a member of the FEKS group, and photographed most of the films directed by Kozintsev and Trauberg.

The twenty-eight-year-old Pavel Kadochnikov, who played Vladimir Staritsky, was asked by Eisenstein to play two different roles in *Part III* because Staritsky had been murdered in the previous part. 'And that was not all,' recalled Kadochnikov. 'One day during the preparation for the 'Fiery Furnace Play' (staged in the cathedral to intimidate Ivan) he [Eisenstein] suddenly asked me, "Can you do a cartwheel?" "I certainly can," and thus I was cast . . . as one of the evil clowns in the play . . .'[27]

Serafima Birman, who played the formidable Euphrosinia, recalled: 'The filming of *Ivan the Terrible* was for me a time of shadow as well as light, and I still think the shadow was more powerful than the light. Yet, in retrospect, I doubt whether those shadows were real ones, for Eisenstein worked with such passion, such spontaneous inspiration, and ultimately with such true comradeship that to distress him unnecessarily, as some of us did, was to slap his superb talents in his face. For the truth is that, despite all, we loved this man, but with a love that we never expressed in words, either to him or to ourselves, but by working long and hard, by day, by night, and often on our so-called holidays as well.

'So we agreed to do the most extraordinary things for him; for instance Cherkassov, in the Kazan sequence, had to wear a very heavy metal costume, and he willingly stood in it on the edge of a precipice, for take after take, in a temperature of sixty degrees centigrade. Poor Ludmilla Tselikovskaya once spent a whole night in a coffin because Eisenstein refused to let her get out of it. Why did we do these things without protest? I have already suggested one reason in our deep professional respect for Eisenstein as an artist. But another cause, and of equal importance, was a reflection of the war. Elsewhere in a country, people were fighting and being maimed for something they believed in, and perhaps the only way we could compensate for the privilege of our own safety was to fight a battle for what we regarded as serious and lasting art. For these reasons, and despite our quarrels with him, we eventually did whatever Eisenstein asked us to . . .

'One aspect of his extremely complex personality never failed to surprise me, if only because I've known so many lesser men without it, and that was his completely natural way of treating, say, a young lighting assistant as though he were as important to the production as Prokofiev. Consequently, such people were transformed in his presence, and if he ever shouted at them in a fit of temper they immediately forgave him and were never angry or offended. I was often very angry myself, but they never were.'[28]

When Michael Chekhov saw *Ivan The Terrible Part II* in America, he couldn't believe that his former colleague at Stanislavsky's Moscow Arts Theatre, Serafima Birman, could have accepted such a 'betrayal' of all their lessons without protest.

With the Germans on the retreat and facing defeat, and Moscow no longer threatened, Mosfilm returned to the capital in the autumn of 1944. Eisenstein took with him a huge metal-lined wooden crate filled with his sketches and carefully bound folders. At the end of the year, he completed editing *Part I*, and it had its first showing in January 1945 to general acclaim. Chaplin sent a telegram extolling it a year later as 'the greatest historic film that has ever been made.'

Bosley Crowther in the *New York Times* wrote that it was 'a film of awesome and monumental impressiveness in which the senses are saturated in medieval majesty.'

Following the success of *Part I*, Eisenstein resumed work on *Part II* and the projected *Part III* throughout 1945. There was one sequence – the banquet – in *Part II* to be filmed. 'Why couldn't this explosion be . . . in colour? Colour would participate in the explosion of the dance. And then at the end of the feast, imperceptibly flow back into black and white photography . . .'[29]

Having managed to lay his hands on a small quantity of colour negative film captured from the Germans, Eisenstein would at last be able to put his theories on the use of colour into practice. (*The Stone Flower* was the first Soviet film to be made with the captured AGFA colour system taken when Russian troops occupied the plant at Wolfen, and which was adapted as Sovcolor.)

It was inevitable that Eisenstein, who had dreamt of working in colour long before it was in general use, should have grabbed the opportunity to apply it to *Ivan*. 'Colour. Pure. Bright. Vibrant. Ringing . . . the penetrating choir of pink flamingos, standing out against the pale blue background of the Gulf of Mexico, picked up the refrain where Van Gogh's canvases in the Hague Museum left off with their whirlwind of colour produced in Arles . . . the green square of the tablecloth in the lemon room flooded with light, the dark blue teacup among red cups, the golden buddha against the azure walls or the books in their orange and black binding on the green and gold brocade of the round table. I always surround myself with such spots of colour . . . I find it dull when there is no yellow pencil next to the blue one to set it off; no red and green striped pillow lying on the blue couch . . .'[30]

Eisenstein, in his copious writings on the subject, was conscious of the symbolic connotations of colours. Of the banquet scene from *Ivan the Terrible: Part II*, he wrote: 'At first all the colour themes are tied up in a knot. Then the red theme is gradually teased out, then the black, then the blue. What counts is that they are torn away from their original association with an object. Suppose that the red theme begins with a red sleeve; it is repeated with the red background of candles; when Vladimir Andreyevich goes to his death, the theme is picked up by the red carpet . . . I wanted there to be red drops of blood in the black-and-white part, after the murder of Vladimir Andreyevich; but Fira [Esther] Tobak would not have it; saying that would be Formalism . . .'[31]

In January 1946, Eisenstein, while also working on another book on film theory (*Film Form*), wrote to Jay Leyda: 'I was (and still am for about three weeks) busy like hell; just finishing to shoot and cut the second part of *Ivan*. This part includes two reels made in colour. Colour used in quite different a way than it is usually done – so that it gives a big additional chapter to what is nearly ready in book form. If everything is all right here with the picture I expect to take a vacation and finish the book – three quarters of which is ready for print. Most of the stuff is unpublished (part of it even unwritten yet!) and is mostly concerned with the development of the principles started by *Potemkin* during these twenty years in different media (is that the way to say it?) – treatments of sound, music, colour . . .'[32]

Apart from his work on *Part II*, Eisenstein had completed the script, many sketches, and shot four reels of *Part III*. Among the production stills is one in which Mikhail Romm, in full regalia, makes an extremely convincing Elizabeth I of England. *Part III* would have opened up the trilogy with more exteriors, more crowd movements and more battle scenes than the claustrophobic *Part II.*

One sequence which survived shows an ageing Ivan interrogating a haughty one-eyed German knight about his false papers, while Dickensian clerks ponder the papers in a dark cellar-like hall. Another that was filmed, but lost, was the confrontation between Ivan, the Earthly Tsar, and the Heavenly Tsar, in a fresco of the Last Judgement, while the names of Ivan's victims are intoned. 'He accounts as his a fearful responsibility. Sweat pours in streams from his forehead. Scorching tears stream from his closed eyes. The Tsar has grown thin, emaciated. And seems yet older by a dozen years . . .'[33]

In order to get the Tsar's appearance as he imagined it, Eisenstein presented the chief make-up artist Vassili Goryunov with a pile of sketches. On looking through the sketches Goryunov remarked, 'These sketches can never be realised . . . they are pure formalism.' 'I'll supply you with an idea for an image, and it will be up to you to realise it,' replied Eisenstein. 'But you must always work with the face of the player . . . You must lengthen Cherkassov's head. You'll have to make a stiff wig, and think about his chin while you do it . . . Have you noticed that Cherkassov's torso and arms do not harmonise with the shape of his head? It actually should have a shape like this.'[34] Eisenstein then drew Ivan's head in what Goryunov described as the shape of a cucumber, not recognising the wig as the continuing influence of the Chinese opera on the work as a whole.

Ivan the Terrible is the peak of Eisenstein's achievement, fulfilling his ambitions of a synthesis of all the arts – a *gesamtkunstwerk* in the Wagnerian sense – a film opera combining music, poetry, painting, sculpture, architecture, literature and dance. All the individual components complement each other, arresting the eye, the ear, the mind and the emotions; 'the montage of attractions' has matured from the often too schematic, frenetic and didactic 'intellectual montage' of the earlier films. If the sets, costumes, lighting or colour are stylised then so are the performances, a blend of classical Russian acting and that of the Chinese opera, while the text is written in blank verse. Yet, in no way can *Ivan* be 'accused' of 'formalism' because everything is used in the service of the historical narrative, with its contemporary undertones, the psychology of the characters, and the atmosphere which informs their actions.

Ivan the Terrible, which should be seen as a single work, with its unifying and continually developing plot, characters, themes, and pictorial style, assembles all of Eisenstein's preoccupations, obsessions, and motifs of his films, drawings and writings, so that his final film is his most personal. The simultaneous attraction and aversion to religious rites and the aura of the church; the themes of regicide and Oedipal patricide, the exercising power, whether for good or evil; martyrdom and sado-masochism; fraternalism bordering on the homo-erotic, and the existential isolation of the individual – all are in evidence.

Each of these strands is woven into a tapestry of haunting images: the tenebrous church and chambers through which people move in conspiratorial groups; the vast shadow of the Tsar projected on the wall, a symbol of his overweening power; the Tartar prisoners tied to the walls of Kazan, pierced by the arrows of their own people and dying like so many Saint Sebastians; boyars' necks in close-up waiting for the sword, and the Tsar clinging to his handsome, young devotee Fyodor. The final scene of *Part I*, one of the most memorable in all cinema, has Ivan appearing at the portal of his retreat, having calculated on the masses coming to seek his return to power. In profile, his pointed beard lowers into the frame, while in the background thousands of people, literally behind and below him, weave their way towards him across the snowy countryside, stopping to kneel and pray.

The colour sequence, with its dominating reds and golds punctuated with black, explodes onto the screen, as Fyodor in a female Oriental mask dances and sings surrounded by a chorus of young men (many of them chosen by Eisenstein from the Red Army) as a pagan prelude to midnight mass. As the dancing gains in tempo, Ivan discovers from Vladimir, the drunken simpleton, that his mother has arranged for him to become Tsar. There is then a mock coronation, as Ivan dresses Vladimir in his regalia with orb and sceptre, resulting in the assassin mistaking his prey. The dazzling choreographic sequence, leading to the denouement, demonstrates the Tsar's dependence on the *oprichniki* (the chosen few around him), the precariousness of his power, his political shrewdness and his personal vulnerability.

The magnificent Nikolai Cherkassov, who has the lean angularity of an El Greco portrait come to life, dominates every scene, his body taking on positions one thought only possible in an animated film. The other characters, too, move in a similar manner, every gesture a meaningful one. Ivan's faithful follower Malyuta sits at his master's feet, becoming his 'ginger dog' waiting to be stroked; Vladimir, a brother to Harry Langdon and Stan Laurel, is an overgrown baby, being sung a lullaby as he is cradled in his mother's arms. But more than a film of posture and gesture, *Ivan* is a film of glances; eyes move up and down, from left to right, penetrating, suspicious, adoring, watchful. There are eyes, too, staring from the icons on the walls, and one gigantic eye watching everyone like Big Brother.

As Eisenstein celebrated the success of *Ivan the Terrible: Part I*, and the coming of 1946, he had no inkling of the bitter struggle which loomed against two enemies – Stalin and Death.

17

Danse Macabre

It is doubtless unwise for anyone who is not a Mexican to laugh at death. Whoever dares to mock her is punished by the terrible goddess of death. Her reward to me was the death of that scene and the death of the entire film. But even if I never managed to realise fully my conception of death, in the film as a whole I paid the homage due to her!

On February 2, 1946, Eisenstein completed the editing of *Ivan the Terrible Part II*. He put the final touches to it that night, leaving the studio to attend a dinner-dance to celebrate the award of the Stalin Prize for *Part I*. In jubilant mood, he joined in the dancing until, at two in the morning, while dancing with the actress Vera Maretskaya, he collapsed with a heart attack and was taken by ambulance to the Kremlin Hospital. Despite the doctor's warning that if he moved he would be 'a dead man', he walked unaided to the car that took him to the hospital.

When Eisenstein described the fateful evening to friends who visited him in hospital after the first critical weeks of total immobility, he jokingly added, 'I'm dead right now. The doctors say that according to all rules I cannot possibly be alive. So this is a post-script for me, and it's wonderful. Now I can do anything I like.'[1]

In March he was allowed to sit up in his armchair and several days later to take his first steps. Towards the end of May he was moved to a sanatorium at Barvikha outside the city, and a month later was allowed to convalesce in his dacha at Kratov, where he occupied himself by reading, sketching, writing and watching films, many of them American. These were supplied to him by Elizabeth

Eagan of the US Embassy, who brought or sent 16mm copies to him, along with a steady flow of books. Part of a letter to her reads:

' . . .Bring me the picture *Meet Me In St Louis*. I'm terribly fond of Judy Garland! And don't you have by any chance a copy of *Forever Amber*? I'd like to read that very much. Is there no way to find Agatha Christie's *Murder of Roger Ackroyd* in Moscow (the old detective story).' Another letter reads: 'Dear Miss Eagan! I want to thank you so much for the enormous pleasure you provided in sending me the *National Velvet* and Lewis Jacobs' book [*The Rise of the American Film*]. Always eager to see more films and books . . .'

Eisenstein's appetite for Hollywood films was insatiable. While in hospital, he had asked to see *Harvey*, obviously intrigued by the story of a gentle alcoholic (James Stewart) who believes he is being accompanied everywhere by a giant rabbit. His diary of March 27 to June 11, 1945, indicates the films he had seen, many marked with either an X for approval or a G for *govno* (crap). Eisenstein's wide-ranging tastes were well known. Apart from the British-made *Henry V*, his eclectic list of American films reveals a hunger for top-rate escapist entertainment.

Of those, he gave three cheers (or crosses) to Clarence Brown's *The Human Comedy*, starring Mickey Rooney, an over-sentimental William Saroyan-scripted family drama. Of Victor Fleming's *A Guy Named Joe*, a wartime fantasy in which a dead pilot (Spencer Tracy) is sent back to earth to watch over fledgling pilots, Eisenstein noted, 'American inventiveness and skill at extracting from situations a range of possibilities – from lyricism to farce, from low comedy to tragedy . . . the idea that the hands of each trainee would be guided by the thousands that perished before him attains the height of pathos.'

One can only suppose that his enjoyment of Paramount's *Star Spangled Rhythm* was one of nostalgia, born of recognition of a multitude of stars, and the musical numbers, including a literally flag-waving routine, 'Old Glory', sung by Bing Crosby and company against a studio backdrop of Mount Rushmore.

The films to which he gave the thumbs down were those that strayed into his own territory, and/or had artistic pretensions.

William Dieterle's *The Hunchback of Notre Dame*, starring Charles Laughton, was not Eisenstein's idea of the Victor Hugo novel; he failed to be flattered by a direct homage to the Battle on the Ice from *Alexander Nevsky* in Laurence Olivier's *Henry V*, and disliked *The Kid from Spain*, despite the Busby Berkeley numbers, of which the opening one was supposed to be in a college girls' dormitory, where the students (!) rise from their sumptuous satin beds in transparent nightdresses. Perhaps he found it painful to watch the absurd bullfighting scenes in Mexico, where saucer-eyed Eddie Cantor is mistaken for a celebrated matador.

Among the other films he saw, and sometimes marked, while recuperating were Esther Williams in *Bathing Beauty*, Otto Preminger's *Laura*, the all-black musical, *Stormy Weather* (X), the Chopin biopic *A Song to Remember* (G), Walt Disney's *Bambi* (X), which had the rabbit Thumper battling on the ice; Charles Boyer and Ingrid Bergman in George Cukor's *Gaslight*; Boyer waiting on the Mexican border in *Hold Back the Dawn* (X), reminding him of his own similar predicament; Claude Rains in *Phantom of the Opera*, Ronald Colman and Greer Garson in *Random Harvest*, Deanna Durbin in *It Started with Eve*, Billy Wilder's *Five Graves to Cairo*, Alfred Hitchcock's *Shadow of a Doubt*, an army comedy *See Here Private Hargrove* (G), the boy-and-horse movie *My Friend Flicka*, and Betty Grable in *Moon Over Miami*.[2]

In 1945, Eisenstein wrote a chapter on *Young Mr Lincoln* (1939) for a collection of essays on John Ford in the series *Materials on the History of World Cinema*. He claimed that if there was one American picture he would like to have made, it was *Young Mr Lincoln*. 'Some pictures are more effective, richer. Some pictures are more entertaining and enthralling. Some are more stunning. Even those by Ford himself . . . But – why do I love this film so much? First of all because it has that marvellous quality that a work of art can have: a striking harmony among all its component parts . . . I think that our epoch yearns for harmony . . . Henry Fonda, amazing actor that he is, has caught this sorrowful gaze, the bend of this spine, the childlike simplicity, wisdom, and childlike cunning in a miraculous character. But the maker of the film, John Ford, looked at the recreated images of the epoch with such a gaze before realising them on screen . . .'[3] There is indeed a striking Eisensteinian moment at the rhetorical end of *Young Mr Lincoln* when Henry Fonda, still years from becoming president, marches up a hill during a storm, which cuts to rain falling on the Lincoln statue in Washington. In appreciation of the article, John Ford sent Eisenstein a letter and a still from *Young Mr Lincoln.*

Watching many of the better films made under the Hollywood system, Eisenstein, though it was fruitless to replay his own American tragedy, must have regretted not having been able to make at least one example of the kind of 'bourgeois' entertainment that he so enjoyed towards the end of his life. Regarding freedom of expression, however, as Eisenstein knew from personal experience, there were certain similarities between Hollywood autocracy and Soviet autocracy – although the 'Siberia' to which one could be sent in America was purely metaphorical.

In July 1946, Eisenstein wrote to Ivor Montagu: 'I'm recovering very very slowly from my heart attack in February – and expect to return to my film activities sometime around October or November. Things were so drastic that even up to now I'm nearly out as to what might be labelled my writing activity – although I expected to give away most of the time of my reconvalescence to writing. (Four and a half months I had just to lay on my back – just waiting for my heart muscle to piece itself together, after it had split as a result of overworking. Now laying for months on one's back and not being exactly a harlot – is not much fun?)'[4]

On September 30, 1946, Eisenstein was offered the making of a film, entirely in colour, to celebrate the eight-hundredth anniversary of the founding of the city of Moscow. He eagerly accepted, and started sketching two aspects of *Moscow 800* that particularly interested him: the function of colour in films and the 'montage of epochs' that he had been trying to realise since *Qué Viva México!* 'The spiral development of historical events, repeating and revealing new qualities and aspects in certain crucial moments of history.'[5]

Moscow would be seen saving Europe from 'three hordes – the Tartars, Napoleon and the Germans.' Eisenstein also noted down: '1) the Moscow of icons 2) Wooden Moscow 3) Moscow of white stone 4) Iron Moscow 5) Moscow of steel (planes, tanks – war)

6) Moscow of the rainbow (celebration of war's end. A peaceful rebirth) 7) Moscow of growth and strength.' However, *Moscow 800* was to remain another tantalising film of the mind.

'The war on fascism ends, the war on capitalism begins', was one of the slogans of the Party after the armistice. During the war, the Soviet Government and the Central Committee of the Communist Party had not paid close attention to literary and artistic orthodoxy and, with control thus relaxed, artists had insensibly begun to take liberties; the old evils of 'formalism' and 'subjectivism' had started creeping back.

Early in 1946, Stalin decided to bring Andrei Zhdanov from Leningrad to conduct a full-scale ideological attack on those who had expressed admiration for the West and, by implication, dissatisfaction with the regime. He thundered: 'Does it suit us, the representatives of the advanced Soviet culture, to bow before bourgeois culture, which is in a state of miasma and corruption!'

At the start, Zhdanov's fire was directed at literature, especially the poet Anna Akhmatova, whom he called 'a harlot and a nun who mixes harlotry and prayer.' Michael Zoshchenko, perhaps the most popular Soviet humorist, he labelled 'a literary swindler.' In August, the Party Central Committee passed a resolution declaring that 'Soviet literature neither has nor can have any other interests except those of the people and of the State. Hence all preaching of that which has no idea-content, of the apolitical, of "art for art's sake", is foreign to Soviet literature, harmful to the interests of the Soviet people and State.' Charges of neglect of ideology and subservience to Western influence were levelled at men prominent in the other arts. The Union of Composers did not fail to notice the danger signals.

While awaiting the release of *Ivan the Terrible Part II*, Eisenstein was recuperating at his country home, watching 'harmful' bourgeois films. It was then that he heard from Cherkassov that Stalin had seen the film and disliked it. There were those who believed, and still believe, that the reason for his dislike was, that as the story developed, the Tsar's acts of cruelty in the name of a unified Russia came uncomfortably close to home.

Many of Eisenstein's friends had warned him to change *Part II*, with its pointed allusions to Stalin in Ivan, to Lavrenti Beria, chief of the secret police, in Malyuta, and in the *oprichniki*, to Stalin's hatchet men. Pera commented, 'We tried to persuade Eisenstein not to try and produce *Part II* as per script he had prepared. He was firm, though he had a sick heart. He was told it would be the end of him. But he would not retreat.'[6] Herbert Marshall believed that Eisenstein deliberately and consciously risked his freedom and his life to expose the degeneration of Stalin and his regime.[7] But *Ivan the Terrible Part II* was not the only film severely criticised, and in some cases banned, in 1946; others were Kozintsev and Trauberg's *Simple People*, Pudovkin's *Admiral Nakhimov*, and Leonid Lukov's *A Great Life Part II*. The most successful film of the year was Chiaureli's *The Vow*, a flattering review of Stalin's work.

On September 4, the Central Committee issued a statement attacking a number of Soviet film-makers, including Ivan Bolshakov, the first Minister for Cinema. The Committee maintained that he had 'poorly managed the work of the film studios, and the work of their directors and scriptwriters . . . doing little to raise the quality of the films being released, uselessly squandering large resources.' The Committee's main reprimand was reserved for Leonid Lukov's *The Great Life Part II*, the first part of which had been released in 1940 and, like *Ivan the Terrible Part I*, had won the Stalin Prize. 'The film . . . champions backwardness, coarseness and ignorance. The film-makers have shown workers who are technically barely literate and hold outdated views and attitudes being promoted *en masse* to management positions . . . [it] shows Soviet people in a false, distorting light . . . the film is evidence that some workers in art, living among Soviet people [as if they were not part of them], fail to notice their high ideological and moral qualities and are unable to turn them into convincing characters in their works of art . . . the director Pudovkin has undertaken to put on a film about Nakhimov, but he has not studied the details of the matter, and he has distorted the historical truth. The result is not a film about Nakhimov, but one about balls, dances and scenes from Nakhimov's life . . . The director Sergei Eisenstein, in Part Two of *Ivan the Terrible*, has revealed his ignorance in his portrayal of historical facts, by representing the progressive army of Ivan the Terrible's *oprichniki* as a gang of degenerates akin to the American Ku Klux Klan: and Ivan the

Terrible, a strong-willed man of character, as a man of weak will
and character, not unlike Hamlet . . . Workers in the arts must
understand that those among them who continue to take an irre-
sponsible and flippant attitude to their work may easily find
themselves overboard as progressive Soviet art forges its way
ahead, or find themselves withdrawn from circulation . . . the Party
and the State will continue to inculcate good taste in the people,
and high expectations of works of art.'[8]

It was clear, given Stalin's later conversation with Eisenstein,
that these were the dictator's own opinions of the film. (It was
said that Stalin's favourite films at the time were the wartime
weepie *Waterloo Bridge* and *The Great Waltz*, nicknamed by some
wag 'The Great Schmaltz'.)

On the evening of February 25, 1947, Eisenstein and
actor/Supreme Soviet member Cherkassov were summoned to the
Kremlin for a meeting at 11 p.m. At 10.50 they entered the reception room. At precisely eleven o'clock, Poskrebyshev, Stalin's
principal secretary until his arrest in 1952, came out to take them
into the study. Stalin, Molotov and Zhdanov were at the back of
the study. They went in, shook hands and sat at the table. As
recorded by Eisenstein in his diary immediately afterwards, the
following grimly comic encounter took place:

Stalin: (to Eisenstein): How is your heart?

Eisenstein: Much better, Comrade Stalin.

Stalin: You look very well. You wrote a letter. The answer has
  been somewhat delayed. I thought of replying in writing, but
  then decided it would be better to talk it over, as I am very busy
  and have no time. I decided after considerable delay to meet
  you here. I received your letter in November.

Cherkassov: (reaching out for the box of cigarettes) Is it alright if
  I smoke?

Stalin: There is no ban on smoking, as such. (Chuckling) Perhaps
  we should take a vote on it. Go ahead. (To Eisenstein) Have you
  studied history?

Eisenstein: More or less.

Stalin: More or less? I too have a little knowledge of history.
  Your portrayal of the *oprichnina* is wrong. The *oprichnina* was

a royal army. As distinct from the feudal army, which could at any moment roll up its banners and leave the field, this was a standing army, a progressive army. You make the *oprichnina* look like the Ku Klux Klan.

Eisenstein: They wear white headgear; ours wore black.

Molotov: That does not constitute a difference in principle.

Stalin: Your Tsar has turned out indecisive, like Hamlet. Everyone tells him what he ought to do, he does not take decisions himself. Tsar Ivan was a great and wise ruler and, if you compare him with Louis XI (you have read about Louis XI, who prepared the way for the absolutism of Louis XIV?) he dwarfs Louis XI. Ivan the Terrible's wisdom lay in his national perspective and his refusal to allow foreigners into his country, thus preserving the country from foreign influence. In showing Ivan the Terrible the way you did, aberrations and errors have crept in. Peter I was also a great ruler, but he was too liberal in his dealings with foreigners, he opened the gates too wide and let foreign influences into the country, and this allowed Russia to be Germanised. Catherine even more so. And later – could you really call the court of Alexander I a Russian court? Was the court of Nicholas I really Russian? No, they were German courts. Ivan the Terrible's great achievement was to be the first to introduce a monopoly on foreign trade. Ivan the Terrible was the first, Lenin was the second.

Zhdanov: Ivan the Terrible comes across as a neurasthenic.

Molotov: There is a general reliance on psychologism; on extra-ordinary emphasis on inner psychological contradictions and personal experiences.

Stalin: Historical figures should be portrayed in the correct style. In Part I, for instance, it is unlikely that the Tsar would kiss his wife for so long. That was not acceptable in those days.

Zhdanov: The picture was made with a Byzantine tendency. That was also not practised.

Molotov: Part II is too confined to vaults and cellars. There is none of the hubbub of Moscow, we do not see the people. You can show the conspiracies and repressions, but not just that.

Stalin: Ivan the Terrible was very cruel. You can depict him as a cruel man, but you have to show why he *had* to be cruel. One of

Ivan the Terrible's mistakes was to stop short of cutting up the five key feudal clans. Had he destroyed these five clans, there would have been no Time of Troubles. And when Ivan the Terrible had someone executed, he would spend a long time in repentance and prayer. God was a hindrance to him in this respect. He should have been more decisive.

Molotov: The historical events should have been shown in the correct interpretation. Take Demyan Bedny's play *The Knights* for example. In that play, Demyan Bedny made fun of the conversion of Rus to Christianity, whereas the acceptance of Christianity was a progressive event at that particular historical period.

Stalin: We are not, of course, particularly good Christians. But it is wrong to deny the progressive role of Christianity at that stage. It had great significance, as it marked the point where the Russian state turned away from the East and towards the West. Recently liberated from the Tartar yoke, Ivan the Terrible was very keen to unite Russia as a bulwark against any Tartar invasions. Astrakhan had been subdued, but could at any point attack Moscow. As could the Crimean Tartars. We cannot scrap our history. Now, criticism is useful. Pudovkin followed our criticism and made *Admiral Nakhimov* into a good film.

Cherkassov: I am sure that we shall do just as well, because I am working on the character of Ivan, not only in cinema but also in theatre. I like the character very much and I am sure that our reworking of the script may turn out to be correct and truthful.

Zhdanov: I have held power for six years myself, no problems.

Stalin: Well, let's give it a try.

Cherkassov: I'm sure that the reworking will be a success.

Stalin (Laughing): God willing, every day would be like Christmas.

Eisenstein: It would be better not to rush the production of this film.

Stalin: On no account rush it. As a rule, we cancel films made in a hurry and they never go out on release. Repin spent eleven years painting *The Zaporozhian Cossacks*. If *Ivan the Terrible* takes eighteen months, two or even three years to produce, then go ahead, make sure of it, let it be like a work of sculpture. The overall task now is to improve the quality. Higher quality even if it means fewer pictures. Tselikovskaya was good in other roles. She acted well, but she was a ballerina.

Eisenstein: No other actress could make the journey from Moscow to Alma Ata.

Stalin: A director must be unyielding and demand whatever he needs. Our directors compromise too readily.

Eisenstein: It took two years to find our Anastasia.

Stalin: The actor Zharov did not bring sufficient gravity to his role, and the result was wrong. He was not serious enough for a military commander.

Zhdanov: He was not Malyuta Skuratov, more of a flibbertigibbet.

Stalin: Ivan the Terrible was more of a national Tsar, more circumspect. He did not admit foreign influences into Russia. It was Peter who opened the gates on to Europe and let too many foreigners in.

Zhdanov: The film overdid the use of religious ceremonies.

Molotov: Yes, it gave it a mystical edge which should not have been so prominent.

Zhdanov: The scene in the cathedral, with the 'bloody deed' was filmed too broadly, which was a distraction.

Stalin: The *oprichniki* looked like cannibals when they were dancing, reminiscent of Phoenicians or Babylonians.

Eisenstein: Do you have any specific instructions about the film?

Stalin: I am not giving instructions so much as voicing the thoughts of the audience.

Zhdanov: I think that Comrade Eisenstein's fascination with shadows distracted the viewer from the action, as did his fascination with Ivan's beard: Ivan lifted his head too often so that his beard could be seen.

Eisenstein: I promise that Ivan's beard will be shorter in the future.

Stalin: I thought in Part I, Kurbsky [Mikhail Nazvanov] was splendid. Staritsky [Pavel Kadochnikov] was very good. The way he caught flies was very good. He was a future Tsar but caught flies with his hands. You need details like that. They reveal a man's true character.

Cherkassov: What about Ivan's physical appearance?

Stalin: His appearance is fine and does not need changing. Ivan the Terrible's physical appearance is good.

Cherkassov: Can we leave the scene of Staritsky's murder in the film?

Stalin: Yes, murders did happen.

Cherkassov: There is one scene in the script where Malyuta Skuratov strangles Metropolitan Philip. Should we leave that in?

Stalin: It must be left in. It was historically accurate.

Molotov: Repressions could and should be shown, but it should be made clear what caused them and why. This requires a portrayal of how the State worked rather than scenes confined to cellars and enclosed spaces. The wisdom of statesmanship needs to be depicted.

Stalin: How will your film end?

Cherkassov: It will end with the rout of Livonia, the heroic death of Malyuta Skuratov and the expedition to the sea, where Ivan the Terrible will be surrounded by his soldiers and say, 'We stand on the seas and always will.'

Stalin: Which is what happened. And more besides.

Cherkassov: Does the outline of the future script need to be shown to the Politburo for reading and approval?

Stalin: There is no need to submit it for approval. Sort it out for yourselves. It is always difficult evaluating a script; it is easier to talk about a finished work. (Turning to Molotov) You, of course, very much want to read the script?

Molotov: No, I specialise in a somewhat different area. Let Bolshakov read it.

Stalin: Well then, that is sorted out. Comrades Cherkassov and Eisenstein will be given the chance to complete their project and the film. Pass that on to Bolshakov. I wish you luck, and may God help you.

(They all shook hands, and the meeting ended at 1.10 a.m.)[9]

As a result of the meeting, permission was given to modify the film to comply with official demands. On March 14, 1947, Eisenstein sent a telegram to Jay Leyda: 'Everything okay. Continue working *Ivan*.'[10] But, although attempting to make the suggested alterations to *Part II*, he lacked the strength to make the new sequences that were needed. There were no further discussions or plans about completing *Part III* – all materials including four edited reels had, by then, been destroyed. Only one reel survived. It would be ten years after Eisenstein's death before *Ivan the Terrible Part II* would be shown to the public.

It was finally released in 1958. The same year, as part of Khrushchev's 'thaw', it was shown in the West under the title *The Boyars' Plot*. But according to Ian Christie, 'the world in which this Rip Van Winkle appeared was very different from the one in which Eisenstein had carved his tortured, dangerous and intensely personal epic. It could scarcely appear other than an anachronism – the long-awaited completion of the Eisenstein canon, itself something perceived as firmly rooted in the silent era of heroic montage and only reluctantly accommodating synchronised sound . . . And of course it was equally inevitable that the shadow of Stalin would lie across the film. How could it not be seen as either a brave critique of Ivan's latter-day heir, or as an apologia for that tyrant?'[11]

Bosley Crowther of the *New York Times*, who had called *Part I* 'a film of awesome and monumental impressiveness,' found the second a 'murkily monolithic and monotonous series of scenes with little or no dramatic continuity . . . The musical score of Serge Prokofiev fails to be much more than sound behind scenes . . . The place for this last of Eisenstein's pictures is in a hospitable museum.'

Dwight Macdonald wrote: '*Ivan the Terrible, Part II* is the last work of the greatest talent the cinema has yet known . . . [It] is the late, final decadence of this talent . . . but the dying lion is still a lion . . . Its current release is part of the post-Stalin "thaw". I applaud the decision of Khrushchev's bureaucrats but I think Stalin's were smarter . . . The film shows the disintegration of Eisenstein's personality under the frustrations and pressures he had endured for fifteen years . . .'

What particularly disturbed Macdonald was that 'his homosexuality now has free play . . . There are an extraordinary number of young, febrile and – there's no other word – pretty males, whose medieval bobbed hair makes them look startlingly like girls. Ivan has a favourite, a flirtatious, bold-eyed police agent [Fyodor], and many excuses are found for having Ivan put his hands on the hand-some young face . . . There are two open homosexuals in the film, both villains. The minor one is the King of Poland, who is shown in his effete court camping around in a fantastically huge ruff . . . The major one is the very odd character of Euphrosinia's son, Vladimir . . . It is too much to speculate that Eisenstein identified himself with the homosexual Vladimir, the helpless victim of palace intrigues who just wanted to live in peace (read: to make his films in peace) . . .'[12]

It is extremely doubtful that Eisenstein, in that he identified with any character in the film, would have chosen the simple-minded, cowardly and effeminate Vladimir. Parker Tyler describes Vladimir as 'pretty as a Hollywood starlet . . . constantly pursing his lips or batting his eyelashes.'[13] For Thomas Waugh, 'Gay artists have often been able to express an explicit interest in homosexuality only within the safe limits of the dominant stereotype of gayness.'[14]

Ivan's relationship with the young Fyodor is not necessarily closer than that with his faithful follower Malyuta, and no more than can be seen between close friends in productions of Shakespeare's plays, and other Elizabethan classics. Fyodor's coquettish dance, wearing a woman's mask and breast plates, is related to the style of female impersonation in Chinese Opera, as well as being a slightly risqué comical musical number for the all-male guests at the banquet. The effete Sigismond, King of Poland, is merely a classical convention and, in no way, is he an 'open' homosexual. However, Andrew Britton described the scene between the traitor Kurbsky and Sigismond as 'decadent homo-sexual flirtation, Kurbsky presenting his sword and Sigismond stroking it languidly with jewelled gloves.'[15] Was Eisenstein really planting a clandestine gay time-bomb under a perilously homo-phobic society?

Ivan the Terrible can be read as an anti-Stalinist, gay fantasy, or a classical historical drama, with many of the genre's traditions, about a heroically strong leader who had to be cruel to defend his power and the unity of his country – after all, he is more plotted against than plotting – or a Macbethian despot 'in blood stepped in so far that, should I wade no more, returning were as tedious as go o'er.' Yet, one question keeps hovering above one's head. Although the rules of the game in the Soviet Union kept being changed by the referee mid-match without the players being told, how did Eisenstein ever imagine he could have got away with such a bold, often outrageous, all-encompassing work of art such as *Ivan the Terrible* or, for that matter, *The General Line* or *Bezhin Meadow*, in the stultifyingly conventional atmosphere of the times.

Eisenstein, who was never able to complete a film that he himself instigated, always made the film as close to his own conception as possible, wherein lay the danger. In contrast, most of his contemporaries ended up making exactly what they were asked to do.

Echoing his 'confession' after the condemnation and termination of *Bezhin Meadow*, Eisenstein published a magazine article in 1947 which generally accepted the criticism of *Ivan the Terrible Part II*. 'I must admit that we artists . . . forgot for a time those great ideals which our art is summoned to serve . . . the honourable, militant and educational task . . . to build a Communist society. In the light of the resolutions of the Central Committee, all workers in art must . . . fully subordinate our creative work to the interests of the education of the Soviet people. From this aim we must not take one step aside nor deviate a single iota. We must master the Lenin-Stalin method of perceiving reality and history so completely and profoundly that we shall be able to overcome all remnants and survivals of former ideas which, though long banished from consciousness, strive stubbornly and cunningly to steal into our works whenever our creative vigilance relaxes for a single moment. This is a guarantee that our cinematography will be able to surmount all the ideological and artistic failures . . . and will again begin to create pictures of high quality, worthy of the Stalinist epoch.'[16]

In 1952, while Stalin was still alive, Cherkassov also expressed his doubts about *Ivan the Terrible Part II* in his ghosted autobiography. 'My confidence in the film waned and my worries grew with each passing day. After watching scenes of the second part run through, I criticised some episodes but Eisenstein brushed my criticisms aside, and in the end stopped showing me edited bits altogether.'[17] In addition, he complained of the painful positions that he had been forced to maintain. In fact, Nina, Cherkassov's widow (he died in 1966) said he hated the book and was ashamed of it, and had later stoutly defended the film.

'A small, ridiculous woman died today. Thursday evening. She was seventy-two. And for forty-eight of those seventy-two years she was my mother.' Thus did Eisenstein note the death of Yulia Ivanovna in his diary dated August 8, 1946. In the same entry, he dispassionately recounts that they were never close, and argued a lot. But, she did mean a great deal to him, and the sadness at her parting is disguised by a certain forced flippancy he adopted to hide his emotions.

'I had, to my horror, known all month that Yulia Ivanovna was dying . . .' When Eisenstein visited her for the last time on her death bed, he was shocked to see 'a small, white, old lady' lying before him, more reminiscent of his grandmother, as he remembered her.

Four months later, Eisenstein observed his embarkation on a 'comic autobiography . . . in that super-exact manner ['stream of consciousness'] of Joyce's description of Bloom.' 'Today I start to write my *Portrait of the Author as a Very Old Man*,'[18] Eisenstein wrote on December 24, 1946. In fact, encouraged by Prokofiev, he had begun his memoirs on May 1 in the Kremlin Hospital, three months after his heart attack, but had been scribbling down notes for this undertaking since 1927. For Eisenstein, who sensed that he had not long to live, his 'Post Scriptum' period was the best time to put his thoughts down on paper, quoting Mark Twain's *Autobiography* as he did so. 'I am writing from the grave. On these terms only can a man be approximately frank. He cannot be straitly and unqualifiedly frank either in the grave or out of it.'

In March 1947, Eisenstein finally saw *Thunder over Mexico* and *Time in the Sun* – the films made by others from his footage for *Qué Viva México!* It was a last blow to his continuing hopes that something still might be recovered from the Mexican tragedy. He wrote an angry introduction to the Mexican script for the (unpublished) French edition of his writings. On May 10, in a letter to Georges Sadoul, the French film critic, he remarked: 'The way they cut my film is more than heart-breaking.'[19]

For most of 1947, Eisenstein's health prevented him from further film-making. He wrote some new essays and edited old ones, kept in touch with his students and wrote reminiscences. His last project for the stage was a ballet that Prokofiev had composed in 1936, based on Pushkin's story *The Queen of Spades*. He supplied a libretto and sketched a choreography for the entire ballet, but this last collaboration between Prokofiev and Eisenstein was to remain unrealised.

There had been a time when he spoke of following *Ivan the Terrible* with *The Brothers Karamazov*, but he now knew he would make no more films. In one of his last essays, written in November 1947, he again felt the need to sing the praises of the regime, though neither he nor almost anybody else believed in it any longer.

'I think that the basis of what our cinema has achieved, in its thematic, stylistic, ideological and artistic aspects, can be said to lie in the profound sense that every moment of our daily active existence is of the greatest historical significance – the emergence of Communism in our country and of the Communist future of a liberated mankind, with the Soviet Union in the vanguard . . . Fortunate the art born in such a country and such a people . . . It is to this country alone, to this people alone and to those people and countries alone who travel with us, along our path, that the Future of Emancipated Mankind belongs.'[20]

As his fiftieth birthday approached he became increasingly depressed, although outwardly he continued to make jokes, even about his own imminent death. When his friend, the director Grigori Rostotsky, planned to make a speech at a birthday celebration, Eisenstein told him, 'You know, of course, that your speech will in fact be for my funeral, not for my birthday.'[21]

Despite being cared for by 'Aunt' Pasha, who slept in a room near his study, Eisenstein kept a monkey-wrench by the radiator, so in an emergency he could strike it to summon Tisse who had the flat below. Some weeks after his birthday he was immersed in his writings on the theory of colour. He broke off for a moment to doodle a maze on the paper, then he continued writing. But the writing suddenly petered out, to be followed by a single word in red crayon – 'Attack!' Maxim Strauch, who visited the flat on February 10, was shown the page by Eisenstein who told him, 'That is the graph of my disease.'[22] After Strauch had left, Eisenstein continued to work into the early hours of February 11, 1948. In the morning, 'Aunt' Pasha found him dead at his desk. On the desk was a letter. 'All my life I've wanted to be accepted with affection, yet I've felt compelled to withdraw . . . and thus remain forever a spectator.'

Legend has it that the young doctor who was assigned to do the postmortem, and who did not know whom he was examining, was struck by the dead man's brain. He asked, 'Who was that man?' 'He was a film director.' 'How many films did he direct?' 'Eight.' 'What a pity! A man like that could have discovered a new theory of relativity.'

In his will, Eisenstein left his brain to science and his oeuvre to posterity.

Epilogue

Taking Tea in Eisenstein's Brain

Birds fly to some saints: Francis of Assissi. Beasts run to some legendary figures: Orpheus. Pigeons cluster around the old men of St Mark's Square in Venice. A lion followed Androcles wherever he went. Books cluster around me. They fly to me, run to me, cling to me.

It has taken me longer than Eisenstein did to get here. I'm standing at Eisenstein's grave in the Novodevichy cemetery, the Père Lachaise of Moscow, on a biting cold April day. There are a few wilted flowers lying across it, unlike the fresh wreaths I saw yesterday on Stalin's grave beside the Kremlin wall. Pera Attasheva, who died in July 1965, is buried here beside her husband.

Some of the smaller gravestones are covered entirely by a snow shroud. I find it strange to be in a predominantly atheist cemetery where crosses and other symbols of religion are rare. Nevertheless, I am fascinated by the tradition of having either a bust of the deceased on the tomb or a likeness sketched on the stone, from which one can gain some impression of what the person was like when alive. It is rather like walking through a gallery or a museum and looking at sculptures and portraits of famous, not-so-famous and unknown people. Many here were obviously government officials, but the attempt to make them look important has given them the appearance of stony pomposity. Yet there is a surgeon peeling off his gloves, an orchestra conductor conducting, a painter painting . . .

Carved onto a large, black granite stone, vaguely shaped like the prow of a ship (*Potemkin?*), is a picture of a youngish serious-looking Eisenstein in profile. It is disappointing in that it has failed to capture any of his personality as seen in photographs, films and self-portraits, or as described by others. René Clair once called Eisenstein 'a smiling lion, loaded with hair, and always laughing.' That is how he should have appeared on his tomb. Across the bottom in bold block cyrillic letters, is one word: EISENSTEIN. There is no epitaph, though Eisenstein had suggested 'I lived, I contemplated, I admired.'

I don't think I would have found Eisenstein's grave very easily, if at all, in this vast cemetery, had Naum Kleiman not guided me here. I probably would not have recognised the face, though I could read the name in Russian.

The icy wind cuts into my cheeks. An hour ago I was drinking boiling hot tea in apartment 160, Smolenskaya Ulitsa, known for want of a better expression, as the Eisenstein Museum. The dictionary gives the definition of a museum as 'a repository for the preservation and exhibition of objects illustrating human or natural history, especially the arts and sciences.' I suppose, then, that this small two-roomed flat conforms to the definition – though there is no old woman sitting at the entrance suspiciously watching the visitors, nor is there room for a party of bored schoolchildren or noisy tourists. There is hardly capacity for any kind of party. In addition to the living room, the apartment consists of a pokey entrance hall (lined with bookshelves and pictures), a basic kitchen, a lavatory, a bathroom whose tub is filled with knick-knacks, and a study strewn with piles of books, manuscripts and magazines relating to Eisenstein's work.

However, it is to the living room that pilgrims come to pay homage, or academics and biographers scavenge for information on their subject. The four walls (I don't recall a window) are covered with bookshelves jammed with Eisenstein's books. Pera had all his books, pictures and *objets d'arts* transported to her flat in Smolenskaya. There, with Kleiman's assistance, she kept as closely as possible to Eisenstein's own arrangement in his larger apartment in Potylikha, where he died.

Looking at the books, I have the sensation of sharing the effect they had on their owner, who wrote, 'I slowly go past the books; it is a road through the whole of my life . . . Currents flow from the small cells of grey matter of the brain, through the cranium and the sides of bookcases, through the walls of bookcases and into the hearts of the books . . . in response to the flow of thoughts they hurl themselves at my head . . . I feel like a latter-day St Sebastian, pierced by arrows flying from the shelves. And the small sphere of bone, containing splinters of reflections like Leibnitz's reflecting monad, seems no longer a cranium but the outer walls of the room, and the layer of books covering the surfaces of its walls are like stratifications extending inside my own head.'

So there I sat in Eisenstein's brain, a warm and cosy space, taking tea at a round table, encircled by his choice of books. Mostly in their original languages, they are arranged with both interior and exterior logic, indicating different strata of significance. Some, like the photos, drawings and paintings, are connected with friends, others with his work, and still others with his 'unborn children', the films that never got made: copies of Theodore Dreiser's *An American Tragedy*, Blaise Cendras' *L'Or* (*Sutter's Gold*), Edgar Lee Masters' *Spoon River Anthology*, among the forlorn reminders of might-have-beens. There are a couple of shelves on American humour containing books by O. Henry (the Complete Stories), Mark Twain, and James Thurber (*Men, Women and Dogs*), another on the theatre (Henry Irving, Gordon Craig). There is a shelf of works about men whom Eisenstein called 'The Great Abnormals' – Genghis Khan, Nero, Tamburlaine, Guy Fawkes, and the Emperor Claudius (Robert Graves' *I Claudius* and *Claudius the God*).

There are also more cryptic sequences of books. It was Eisenstein's wry comment on different attitudes to art, life and religion to place Stanislavsky's *An Actor Prepares*, considered the Bible of the theatre, beside the real Bible. Next to it are Poulain's *Back to Ecstasy* and *Loyola* by Degraisse d'Horizon, the former on the excesses of religion, and the latter the more practical theologian whose 'Spiritual Exercises', a system of rules, prayers and self-examination, echo Stanislavsky's similar approach to acting, while Diderot's *The Paradox on Actors* establishes a more rational context. Finally, a book on the migration of birds seems to put the aforementioned in perspective, making a claim for nature above the artificial. And did he not, perhaps, envy those birds that could fly away from the Soviet Union?

Scattered around, wherever space allows, are further reminders of Eisenstein's life. There are pictures of Chaplin, Paul Robeson, Meyerhold, the French mime Deburau, and his contemporary the Romantic actor Frédéric Lemaître; a photo of a handsome unknown young Mexican soldier; the director Joris Ivens; the 'typage' photo of the three Daughters of the American Revolution (part of his research for *An American Tragedy*), Chinese and African masks, and a mask that resembles that worn by the coquettish Fyodor during the wild dance in *Ivan the Terrible Part II*; a Buddha (like the one in *October*), a Mexican rug, and the wickerwork Mexican horseman and horse given to him by Ernst Toller.

I was also able to see the dedication (*Car moi aussi j'aime les gros bateaux et les matelots*) that the dancer Kiki of Montparnasse made to Eisenstein in her memoirs in *Le Boeuf sur le Toit* – she had drawn a roof on the top of the T of Toit. And I handled the copy of *Les Enfants terribles* signed 'To the person who astounded me by showing me what I had touched with the fingers of a blind man. To Eisenstein, his friend Jean Cocteau.' And there was the photo inscribed 'To Eisenstein from Einstein.'

As I paged through the first edition of *L'Or*, a piece of paper fell out. On it was a limerick which someone had written out for Eisenstein in America, which obviously appealed to his schoolboy's smutty sense of humour:

> *There was a young girl called Miss Boyd*
> *whom no prick could ever avoid.*
> *But her cunt was unpleasant*
> *as the nest of a pheasant*
> *so crept out every damn spermatoid.*

I also came across a pornographic drawing he did in Alma Ata in 1942 of a young man, sporting a huge penis wrapped around Queen Elizabeth I. In the same place at the same period, he drew Tsar Ivan on one side of a page and, on the reverse, a caricature of

G.K. Chesterton's Father Brown, the antithesis of the fanatical priests in Eisenstein's films. Another sketch found in a book was of a grotesquely fat woman with five legs whose face resembles Pera's. Make of it what you will. In contrast, there is a photo of the pleasant, rather chubby, smiling face of Pera on the wall. Suffering from diabetes and partially blind, Pera was in and out of hospital and bedridden for much of her last years, but continued to laugh and to take an interest in anything that concerned 'The Old Man'.

One of the most magnificent volumes in the room is a tome of reproductions of the paintings and drawings of Leonardo da Vinci. Curiously, when Andrei Tarkovsky was making *Mirror* in 1974, and wanted to photograph Leonardo's *A Young Lady with a Juniper* for the film, he insisted that it should come from Eisenstein's book and no other. Curious, because Tarkovsky always claimed to find Eisenstein's work anathema. In *Sculpting in Time*, he wrote, 'I am radically opposed to the way Eisenstein used the frame to codify intellectual formulae . . . Eisenstein's montage dictum contradicted the very basis of the unique process whereby a film affects an audience. It deprives the person watching of that prerogative of film, which has to do with what distinguishes its impact on his consciousness from that of literature and philosophy, namely the opportunity to live through what is happening on the screen as if it were his own life.'[1]

Naum Kleiman, who is understandably protective of Eisenstein's reputation, believes Tarkovsky, whose *Andrei Roublev* owed a great deal to *Ivan the Terrible*, was afraid of Eisenstein's influence, and reacted against him as a son against a father. Kleiman says he watched Tarkovsky during the screening of the reconstruction of *Bezhin Meadow*, and could see he was obviously extremely moved by it despite himself.

When André Bazin, the co-founder of the influential magazine *Cahiers du Cinéma*, formulated a theory of cinema in opposition to Eisenstein's theory of montage in the early 1950s, critics came down on one side or another. Bazin considered that the realistic nature of the film image was best evolved through *plan-séquences*, extended shots edited in the camera rather than in the cutting room. One method which assisted this technique was deep focus, which enabled a scene to be shot with both foreground and background in full view. For Bazin, this represented 'true continuity' and 'objective reality', leaving the interpretation of a particular scene to the spectator rather than to the director's viewpoint through editing.

But this is a largely bygone battle. Nowadays, it is difficult to think of Eisenstein in the narrow terms delineated by Bazin and his followers. They also failed to take into account that Eisenstein virtually abandoned the so-called 'intellectual montage' after *The General Line* in 1929. Neither of his two further completed films, *Alexander Nevsky* and *Ivan the Terrible*, can be analysed in the earlier manner, mainly because the use of synchronised dialogue limited the possibilities of dynamic montage. Although he rejected the replacement of montage by long takes, by the mid-1930s Eisenstein was already moving towards montage as an active method of narrative, rather than the juxtaposition of images that comment on the narrative rather than advance it. There is nothing stylistically in either *Alexander Nevsky* or *Ivan the Terrible* that would have been unacceptable in a Hollywood movie, whereas *The Battleship Potemkin* and *October* were far too avant-garde for the commercial cinema to have tolerated.

Behind much of the criticism of Eisenstein's films, there was also, in the words of French critic Noël Burch, 'the myth, for so long universally accepted in the West, of the cinema's "naturalistic" vocation. But the young Eisenstein who wanted the cinema to reveal its artifices, and who consequently pushed them to their ethical and aesthetic extremes, helped to lay the foundations for all the constructions which are now [1986] permitting the cinema to rediscover *its* reality.'[2]

Eisenstein would have been delighted by the range of international film people who have grazed in this apartment. Robert Wise was so animated that he broke the chair he was sitting on. Derek Jarman filmed the room for his short, *Imagining October*, and Francis Coppola sat silently taking in the atmosphere while his children ate watermelon. Coppola claimed that it was seeing *October* at New York's Museum of Modern Art in 1956 which made him decide to become a film-maker.

Among the disparate names in the visitors' book of film luminaries from all over the world are Sacha Vierny, Alain Resnais' and

Peter Greenaway's cinematographer, who wrote that Eisenstein was *'mes racines'* ('my roots'); Robert Redford, who noted that his being there was to 'return to the reason we started'; Bo Widerberg, Hiroshi Teshigahara, Masaki Kobayashi, Nanni Loy, Mrinal Sen, Krzysztof Zanussi, John Boorman, King Vidor, Wim Wenders, Elem Klimov, Tomás Gutiérrez Alea, Terry Gilliam, Lindsay Anderson, Phil Kaufman, Claude Lelouch, Claude Chabrol . . . all made this journey into Eisenstein's brain.

Sometimes Kleiman plays a game with his guests. He asks them to name any particular interest of theirs and bets they will find some allusion to it in the room. On one occasion, Jean Rouch, the French ethnologist and documentary film-maker, accepting the challenge, said, with pity for Kleiman, that he was actually researching the Revolt of the Slaves of Haiti at the end of the 18th century. Rouch almost fainted when Kleiman proudly pointed to a row of books on the very subject, explaining that Eisenstein had wanted to make a film about it starring Paul Robeson.

Feeling at home, I could have curled up like a cat on one of the chairs and remained there for the rest of my stay in Moscow, but I knew my journey had to end soon – and I knew *where* it had to end. After putting on our coats, fur hats, gloves and scarves, Kleiman and I went out into the street and began our long walk towards the Novodevichy cemetery.

En route, Kleiman helped me to read the different layers of this often enigmatic city, mostly through examples of architecture from many of Moscow's epochs, which recalled one of Eisenstein's plans to film four centuries of Moscow's history. We saw stylish *art nouveau* houses, not so different from those of Eisenstein *père* in Riga; grandiose Stalinist Gothic; a small church undergoing restoration after being abandoned for years; the rustic-type house where Gogol had written *Dead Souls* (greatly admired by Eisenstein), and the Novodevichy (New Maiden's) Monastery, a superbly preserved ensemble of 16th and 17th-century Russian architecture, much of it contemporary with Ivan the Terrible's reign.

The Novodevichy cemetery was only opened to the general public in 1987. Kleiman did not lead me directly to the grave, he took me on a tour of the supporting actors in my biography. All around Eisenstein were the tombs of those he had known in life: Gorky, Mayakovsky, Stanislavsky, Dovzhenko, Vertov, Prokofiev, Alexandrov (the object of Eisenstein's unrequited passion), Yutkevitch and Romm, the latter sketched on the stone with a cigarette in his hand. I felt I could hear the chattering of all these old colleagues around me, though it might have been the wailing wind.

Karl Marx wrote, 'The bourgeoisie created the world in its own image. Comrades, we must destroy that image.' Eisenstein, in his writings and films, led the storming of the palaces of bourgeois culture, only to find himself continually trampled underfoot in the manner of his beloved Charlie the Tramp. But the eccentric polymath with the *Eraserhead* hair, mischievous simian features, big head and stocky body, always retained his irreverent sense of humour, and his dream of creating 'an unheard-of form of cinema which inculcates the Revolution into the general history of culture, creating a synthesis of science, art and militant class consciousness.'

Now, appropriately, standing before Eisenstein's grave, I have arrived at where he ended his journey.

I remain silent.

Filmography

COMPLETED FILMS

Glumov's Diary

Proletkult Theatre 1923. Film interlude in production of the play *Enough Folly in a Wise Man* by Alexander Ostrovsky. *Photography*: Boris Frantzisson. *Cast*: Grigori Alexandrov (Glumov), Maxim Strauch (Mamayev), Vera Yanukova (Mamayeva).

The Strike

Goskino 1924. *Scenario*: Eisenstein, Valeri Pletnyov, Grigori Alexandrov, the Proletkult Collective. *Photography*: Edouard Tisse. *Cast*: Alexander Antonov (Organiser), Mikhail Gomarov (Worker), Maxim Strauch (Spy), Grigori Alexandrov (Foreman), Judith Glizer, Boris Yurtzev and Proletkult Actors.

The Battleship Potemkin

Goskino 1925. *Scenario*: Eisenstein, Nina Agadjanova-Shutko. *Photography*: Edouard Tisse. *Cast*: Alexander Antonov (Vakulinchuk), Vladimir Barsky (Captain Golikov), Mikhail Gomorov (Matushenko), Alexander Levshin (Petty Officer).

October

Sovkino 1928. *Scenario*: Eisenstein, Grigori Alexandrov. *Photography*: Edouard Tisse. *Cast*: Nikandrov (Lenin), N. Popov

(Kerensky), Boris Livanov (A Cabinet Minister), the Soldiers of the Red Army, Sailors of the Red Fleet.

The General Line (aka The Old and the New)

Sovkino 1929. *Scenario*: Eisenstein, Grigori Alexandrov. *Photography*: Edouard Tisse. *Cast*: Marfa Lapkina (Marfa), Vasya Buzenkov (Co-operative leader), Kostya Vasiliev (Tractor Driver).

Alexander Nevsky

Mosfilm 1938. *Scenario*: Eisenstein, Pyotr Pavlenko. *Photography*: Edouard Tisse. *Music*: Sergei Prokofiev. *Cast*: Nikolai Cherkassov (Alexander Nevsky), Nikolai Okhlopkov (Vassily Buslai), Alexander Abrikosov (Gavrilo Olexich), Vera Ivasheva (Olga), Anna Danilova (Vassilissa), Dmitri Orlov (Ignat).

Ivan the Terrible Part I

Central Cinema Studio 1944. *Scenario*: Eisenstein. *Photography*: Edouard Tisse (exteriors), Andrei Moskvin (interiors). *Music*: Sergei Prokofiev. *Cast*: Nikolai Cherkassov (Ivan), Ludmilla Tselikovskaya (Anastasia), Serafima Birman (Euphrosinia), Pavel Kadochnikov (Vladimir), Mikhail Nazvanov (Prince Andrei Kurbsky), Alexander Abrikosov (Fyodor Kolychov), Mikhail Zharov (Malyuta), Alexander Mgebrov (Archbishop Pimen).

Ivan the Terrible Part II

Mosfilm 1945 (released 1958).
Credits as above. *Additional Cast*: Erik Pyriev (the Young Ivan), Pavel Massalsky (Sigismond, King of Poland).

INCOMPLETE FILMS

Qué Viva México!

Mexican Pictures Trust (Upton and Mary Sinclair) 1931. *Scenario*: Eisenstein. *Photography*: Edouard Tisse.

Bezhin Meadow

Mosfilm 1936–1937. *Scenario*: Eisenstein, Alexander Rzheshevsky (first version), Eisenstein, Isaac Babel (second version). *Photography*: Edouard Tisse. *Cast*: Vitka Kartachov (Stepok), Boris Zakhava (Father – first version), Nikolai Khmelyov (Father – second version), Elisabeta Teleshova (President of the collective).

THEATRE (AS DIRECTOR)

The Mexican (1920–1921)

First Workers' Theatre of the Proletkult. Based on Jack London.

Enough Simplicity In Every Wise Man (1922–1923)

Proletkult Theatre. Based on Ostrovsky's play.

Can You Hear Me, Moscow! (1923)

Proletkult Theatre. Written by Sergei Tretyakov.

Gas Masks (1923–1924)

Proletkult Theatre. Written by Sergei Tretyakov.

Die Walküre (1940)

Bolshoi Opera. Setting and costumes by Peter Williams after sketches by Eisenstein. N.D. Schpiller (Sieglinde), Marguerite Butenina (Brünnhilde), Innokenti Redikultzev (Wotan), Alexander Khanayev (Siegmund), Vassili Lubentzov (Hunding), Elena Slivinskaya (Fricka).

Bibliography

BY EISENSTEIN

The Film Sense (Faber and Faber, 1943)
Film Form (Dennis Dobson, 1951)
Film Essays (Dennis Dobson, 1968)
Notebooks of a Film Director (Lawrence and Wishart, 1959)
Eisenstein: Writings 1922–1934 (BFI, 1988)
Eisenstein: Towards a Theory of Montage (BFI, 1991)
Eisenstein: Writings 1934–1947 (BFI, 1996)
Beyond The Stars: The Memoirs of Sergei Eisenstein (BFI, 1995)

ABOUT EISENSTEIN

Eisenstein by Yon Barna (Secker and Warburg, 1973)
Sergei M. Eisenstein: A Biography by Marie Seton (The Bodley Head, 1952)
Sergei Eisenstein and Upton Sinclair: The Making and Unmaking of Qué Viva México! by Harry M. Geduld and Ronald Gottesman (Thames and Hudson, 1970)
With Eisenstein in Hollywood by Ivor Montagu (Seven Seas, 1968)
Sergei Eisenstein by Léon Moussinac (Cinéma d'Aujourd'hui, Seghers, Paris, 1964)
Eisenstein: A Documentary Portrait by Norman Swallow (George Allen and Unwin, 1976)

Lessons With Eisenstein by Vladimir Nizhny (George Allen and Unwin, 1962)

The Complete Films of Eisenstein (Weidenfeld and Nicolson, 1974)

Eisenstein At Work by Jay Leyda and Zina Voynow (Methuen, 1982)

Eisenstein At Ninety edited by Ian Christie and David Elliott (Oxford, 1988)

Eisenstein Rediscovered edited by Ian Christie and Richard Taylor (Routledge, 1993)

GENERAL

Inside the Film Factory: New Approaches to Russian and Soviet Cinema 1896–1939, edited by Richard Taylor and Ian Christie (Cambridge, Mass, 1988)

Masters of the Soviet Cinema: Crippled Creative Biographies by Herbert Marshall (London, 1983)

The Politics of the Soviet Cinema 1917–1929 by Richard Taylor (Cambridge, 1979)

Kino, a History of the Russian and Soviet Film by Jay Leyda (Allen and Unwin, 1960)

Notes

ABBREVIATIONS

Barna: *Eisenstein* by Yon Barna (Secker and Warburg, 1973)
BTS: *Beyond the Stars: The Memoirs of Sergei Eisenstein* (BFI Publishing, 1995)
EA: Eisenstein Archives at TsGALI (State Archives of Literature and Arts), Moscow
EC: Eisenstein Collection, Museum of Modern Art, New York
E1: *Eisenstein's Writings* Volume 1 (BFI Publishing, 1988)
E2: *Eisenstein's Writings* Volume 2 (BFI Publishing, 1991)
E3: *Eisenstein's Writings* Volume 3 (BFI Publishing, 1996)
Geduld-Gottesman: *Sergei Eisenstein and Upton Sinclair: The Making and Unmaking of* Qué Viva México! by Harry M. Geduld and Ronald Gottesman (Thames and Hudson, 1970)
IM: Ivan Montagu Collection, BFI, London
Leyda: *Eisenstein At Work* by Jay Leyda and Zina Voynow (Methuen, 1982)
Montagu: *With Eisenstein in Hollywood* by Ivor Montagu (Seven Seas, 1968)
Moussinac: *Sergei Eisenstein* by Léon Moussinac (Crown, 1964)
Nizhny: *Lessons With Eisenstein* by Vladimir Nizhny (Allen and Unwin, 1962)
Seton: *Sergei M. Eisenstein: A Biography* by Marie Seton (The Bodley Head, 1952)

Swallow: *Eisenstein: A Documentary Portrait* by Norman Swallow (Allen and Unwin, 1976)

NOTES

*The quotes at the beginning of each chapter are all from Sergei Eisenstein. Their sources are indicated below after an asterisk.

Prologue: Yo!

1 BTS (p. 797) 2 BTS (Foreword) 3 BTS (Acknowledgements) 4 BTS (p. 439) 5 *S. M. Eisenstein*, Jean Mitry (Paris, 1961) 6 *Eisenstein and the English*, Richard Taylor (Journal of European Studies, 1990) 7 *Masters of the Soviet Cinema*, Herbert Marshall (London, 1984) 8 Naum Kleiman to author 9 Nizhny (Foreword) 10 BTS (p. 306) 11 BTS (p. 350)

1 The Childhood of Sergei Mikhailovich Eisenstein

*BTS (p. 21) 1 BTS (p. 43) 2 BTS (p. 18) 3 Swallow 4 EA 5 BTS (p. 725) 6 BTS (p. 527) 7 EA 8 BTS (p. 290) 9 EA 10 Swallow 11 Nizhny (Foreword) 12 BTS (p. 526) 13 BTS (p. 530) 14 BTS (p. 531) 15 BTS (p. 535) 16 BTS (p. 492) 17 BTS (p. 535) 18 BTS (p. 536) 19 BTS (p. 24) 20 BTS (p. 563) 21 BTS (p. 60) 22 BTS (p. 62) 23 BTS (p. 61) 24 EA 25 *Ibid.* 26 BTS (p. 36) 27 BTS (p. 446) 28 BTS (p. 125) 29 BTS (p. 126) 30 BTS (p. 432) 31 BTS (p. 433) 32 EA 33 E3 34 Swallow 35 *Masters of the Soviet Cinema*, Herbert Marshall (London, 1984) 36 BTS (p. 544) 37 BTS (p. 424) 38 BTS (p. 9) 39 BTS (p. 409) 40 EA 41 BTS (p. 493) 42 BTS (p. 99) 43 BTS (p. 100) 44 BTS (p. 390) 45 EA 46 BTS (p. 544) 47 Swallow 48 BTS (p. 73) 49 BTS (p. 76) 50 EA 51 Swallow 52 *Ibid.* 53 EA 54 *Ibid.* 55 Swallow 56 BTS (p. 576) 57 EA 58 BTS (p. 577) 59 E3 60 EA 61 E2 62 *Ibid.* 63 Swallow 64 *Ibid.* 65 *Ibid.* 66 *Ibid.*

2 Revolution!

*EA 1 E1 2 BTS (p. 85) 3 BTS (p. 290) 4 BTS (p. 344) 5 Nizhny 6 BTS (p. 85) 7 BTS (p. 89) 8 BTS (p. 16) 9 EA 10 BTS (p. 100) 11 Swallow 12 EA 13 *Ibid.* 14 *Ibid.* 15 BTS (p. 521) 16 EA 17 BTS (p. 654) 18 EA 19 Barna 20 BTS (p. 62) 21 BTS (p. 67) 22

BTS (p. 67) 23 BTS (p. 67) 24 BTS (p. 66) 25 BTS (p. 72) 26 BTS (p. 27) 27 E1 28 BTS (p. 462) 29 BTS (p. 28) 30 EA 31 E1 32 BTS (p. 141)

3 Agitka!

*EA 1 BTS (p. 83) 2 Swallow 3 Introduction by Patricia Blake to *The Bedbug and Selected Poetry* by Vladimir Mayakovsky (Meridian Books, 1960) 4 Swallow 5 E1 6 Montagu 7 *Kino* by Jay Leyda (Allen and Unwin, 1960) 8 E1 9 BTS (p. 243) 10 BTS (p. 269) 11 EA 12 BTS (p. 447) 13 BTS (p. 447) 14 BTS (p. 101) 15 E1 16 BTS (p. 433) 17 E1 18 *Ibid.*

4 Ciné-Fist!

*E1 1 *Ibid.* 2 *Ibid.* 3 *Ibid.* 4 *Ibid.* 5 *Ibid.* 6 *Kino* by Jay Leyda (Allen and Unwin, 1960) 7 *Ibid.* 8 Swallow 9 *Ibid.* 10 Barna 11 BTS (p. 687) 12 E1 13 *Ibid.* 14 E2 15 E1 16 Nizhny 17 E1 18 BTS (p. 147) 19 E3 20 BTS (p. 147)

5 Fire!

*BTS (p. 146) 1 BTS (p. 147) 2 E1 3 BTS (p. 152) 4 BTS (p. 148) 5 BTS (p. 149) 6 EA 7 *Ibid.* 8 Swallow 9 *Ibid.* 10 EA 11 BTS (p. 173) 12 *Black Sea* by Neal Ascherson (Vintage, 1995) 13 EA 14 Leyda 15 BTS (p. 157) 16 BTS (p. 167) 17 Swallow 18 BTS (p. 171) 19 Swallow 20 BTS (p. 168) 21 Barna 22 Swallow 23 Nizhny 24 EA 25 BTS (p. 165) 26 BTS (p. 166) 27 *The End of Sergei Eisenstein* by Waclaw Solski (*Commentary*, March 1949) 28 E1 29 BTS (p. 16) 30 *Memo from David O. Selznick* (Viking Press, 1972) 31 *Screening The Sexes* by Parker Tyler (Henry Holt, 1973) 32 *Film Comment* (1986) 33 E1 34 Solski as above 35 BTS (p. 327) 36 E1 37 *Ibid.* 38 *Ibid.* 39 *Ibid.* 40 *Ibid.*

6 Forward, Comrades!

*E1 1 EA 2 E1 3 EA 4 *Ibid.* 5 EA 6 Swallow 7 BTS (p. 473) 8 BTS (p. 396) 9 E1 10 *Ibid.* 11 Barna 12 BTS (p. 546) 13 Moussinac 14 Alfred Barr Archive, New York 15 E1 16 *In Close-Up* by Esther Shub (Moscow, 1959) 17 Barna 18 *Kino* by Jay Leyda (Allen and Unwin, 1960) 19 E1 20 Moussinac 21 BBC *Omnibus* (1988) 22 E1

Notes

7 Poet and Peasant

*E1 1 *Ibid.* 2 *Ibid.* 3 *Ibid.* 4 *Ibid.* 5 Moussinac 6 EA 7
Moussinac 8 BTS (p. 103) 9 BTS (p. 104) 10 BTS (p. 104) 11
BTS (p. 357) 12 Nizhny 13 Nizhny (Foreword) 14 *Ibid.* 15 Jay
Leyda Archive, New York 16 E1 17 E1 18 *Kino* by Jay Leyda
(Allen and Unwin, 1960) 19 E1 20 Naum Kleiman to author 21
BBC *Omnibus* (1988) 22 El

8 Western Approaches

*E3 1 EA 2 Moussinac 3 Barna 4 Montagu 5 *Ibid.* 6 EA 7 BTS
(p. 327) 8 BTS (p. 324) 9 BTS (p. 600) 10 EA 11 BBC *Omnibus*
(1988) 12 Seton 13 BTS (p. 113) 14 BTS (p. 46) 15 BTS (p. 47)
16 BTS (p. 515) 17 BTS (p. 184) 18 *George Bernard Shaw Letters*
(Max Reinhardt, 1965) 19 BTS (p. 187) 20 Index on Censorship
(1992) 21 BTS (p. 546) 22 BTS (p. 546) 23 BTS (p. 20) 24 EA
25 Swallow 26 *Ibid.* 27 Montagu 28 Swallow 29 BTS (p. 310)
30 BTS (p. 309) 31 BTS (p. 310) 32 BTS (p. 77) 33 Barna 34
BTS (p. 554) 35 EA 36 BTS (p. 185) 37 BTS (p. 637) 38 E2

9 A Russian in Paris

*BTS (p. 347) 1 BTS (p. 195) 2 EA 3 Moussinac 4 BTS (p. 364)
5 BTS (p. 250) 6 *Film Comment* (1986) 7 BTS (p. 250) 8
Montagu 9 BTS (p. 241) 10 BTS (p. 244) 11 BTS (p. 246) 12
BTS (p. 191) 13 E1 14 *Ibid.* 15 *Ibid.* 16 E3 17 BTS (p. 194) 18
BTS (p. 195) 19 BTS (p. 198) 20 BTS (p. 241) 21 BTS (p. 242)
22 BTS (p. 204) 23 BTS (p. 205) 24 BTS (p. 238) 25 BTS (p. 233)
26 BTS (p. 498) 27 BTS (p. 207) 28 The Marie Seton Archives,
BFI London 29 BTS (p. 367) 30 BTS (p. 663) 31 BTS (p. 369) 32
BTS (p. 214) 33 BTS (p. 244) 34 BTS (p. 216) 35 EA 36 Swallow
37 Barna 38 BTS (p. 237) 39 BTS (p. 285) 40 Moussinac 41
Montagu

10 Hollywood and Bust

*E1 1 BTS (p. 284) 2 BTS (p. 286) 3 *The Film Sense* (Faber and
Faber, 1943) 4 E1 5 BTS (p. 285) 6 BTS (p. 286) 7 BTS (p. 47)
8 BTS (p. 49) 9 Seton 10 Nizhny 11 EA 12 *Ibid.* 13 BTS
(p. 327) 14 BTS (p. 328) 15 BTS (p. 322) 16 *Fun in a Chinese*

Laundry by Josef Von Sternberg (Secker and Warburg, 1966) 17
BTS (p. 326) 18 BTS (p. 290) 19 Moussinac 20 EA 21 E3 22
Cinema: A Critical Dictionary (Secker and Warburg, 1980) 23 E3
24 BTS (p. 577) 25 Swallow 26 Ibid. 27 BTS (p. 331) 28 BTS
(p. 332) 29 E3 30 *Ibid.* 31 *My Autobiography* by Charles
Chaplin (Simon and Schuster, 1964) 32 BTS (p. 689) 33 BTS
(p. 709) 34 Naum Kleiman to author 35 EA 36 *Ibid.* 37
Montagu 38 EA 39 *Ibid.* 40 BTS (p. 292) 41 E1 42 EA 43
Montagu 44 BTS (p. 292) 45 BTS (p. 103) 46 Montagu 47 E1
48 Montagu 49 EC 50 *Memo from David O. Selznick* (Viking
Press, 1972) 51 Swallow 52 E1 53 Montagu 54 E1 55 EC 56
Ibid. 57 E1 58

11 Trouble in Paradise

*BTS (p. 412) 1 *In Close-Up* by Esther Shub (Moscow, 1959) 2
BTS (p. 372) 3 BTS (p. 411) 4 BTS (p. 421) 5 BTS (p. 8) 6 Shub,
op. cit. 7 IM 8 EC 9 Upton Sinclair Archive, Bloomington,
Indiana 10 BTS (p. 217) 11 BTS (p. 413) 12 E2 13 EC 14 BTS
(p. 629) 15 BTS (p. 376) 16 Geduld-Gottesman 17 *Ibid.* 18 *Ibid.*
19 *Ibid.* 20 *Ibid.* 21 *Ibid.* 22 *Ibid.* 23 *The Kindness of Strangers*
by Salka Viertel (Holt, Rinehart, Winston, 1961) 24 *Ibid.* 25
Geduld-Gottesman 26 BTS (p. 231) 27 E3 28 BTS (p. 224) 29 E1
30 EA 31 *Sight & Sound* (Summer 1988) 32 Geduld-Gottesman
33 *Ibid.* 34 *Ibid.* 35 BTS (p. 414) 36 EA 37 BTA (p. 579) 38
Seton 39 BTS (p. 581) 40 BTS (p. 418) 41 BTS (p. 420) 42 EC
43 BTS (p. 581) 44 *The Real Tinsel*, Bernard Rosenberg, Harry
Silverstein (Macmillan, 1970) 45 EA 46 E3 47 EA

12 The Rules of the Game

*E3 1 EA 2 *Prokofiev* by David Gutman (The Alderman Press
1988)

13 'The Old Man'

*E3 1 Seton 2 *Ibid.* 3 *Kino* by Jay Leyda 4 *The Kindness of
Strangers* by Salka Viertel 5 EA 6 Swallow 7 *Ibid.* 8 *Ibid.* 9
Masters of the Soviet Cinema by Herbert Marshall (London, 1984)
10 Jay Leyda Archive, New York 11 Swallow 12 Nizhny 13 E3
14 BTS (p. 34) 15 E3 16 IM 17 E3 18 Seton 19 E3 20 *Is*

Comrade Bulgakov Dead? by Mikhail Bulgakov (Methuen, 1993) 21 IM 22 Waclaw Solski (*Commentary*, March 1945) 23 E3 24 *Ibid.* 25 *Bertolt Brecht Letters* (Methuen, 1981) 26 E3 27 Montagu 28 Nizhny 29 EA 30 *Paul Robeson* by Martin Bauml Duberman (The Bodley Head, 1989) 31 *Ibid.* 32 *Ibid.* 33 E3 34 *Ibid.* 35 EA 36 E3 37 *Ibid.*

14 Crimes and Misdemeanours

*E3 1 Leyda 2 *Ibid.* 3 BTS (p. 350) 4 Leyda 5 *Ibid.* 6 Seton 7 E3 8 Naum Kleiman to author 9 Waclaw Solski (*Commentary*, March 1949) 10 Swallow 11 E2 12 Moussinac 13 As told to Naum Kleiman by Pera Attasheva 14 E3 15 BTS (p. 557) 16 Leyda Archive, New York

15 Heroes and Villains

*E3 1 *The Film Sense* (Faber and Faber, 1943) 2 *In Close-Up*, Esther Shub (Moscow, 1959) 3 Leyda Archive, New York 4 IM 5 Swallow 6 *Prokofiev* by David Gutman (The Alderman Press, 1988) 7 E2 8 E3 9 *Ibid.* 10 Leyda Archive, New York 11 Leyda 12 EA 13 *Ibid.* 14 E3 15 BTS (p. 270) 16 E3 17 EA

16 The Earthly Tsar

*E3 1 *Testimony*, The Memoirs of Dmitri Shostakovich (Hamish Hamilton, 1979) 2 E3 3 *Ibid.* 4 BTS (p. 663) 5 EA 6 BTS (p. 661) 7 Swallow 8 BTS (p. 671) 9 EA 10 *Ibid.* 11 *Ibid.* 12 BTS (p. 662) 13 BTS (p. 687) 14 EA 15 BTS (p. 712) 16 Barna 17 E3 18 *Prokofiev* by David Gutman (The Alderman Press, 1988) 19 E3 20 EA 21 Gutman as above 22 EA 23 *Ibid.* 24 EC 25 *Partisan Review* (November–December 1942) 26 EA 27 Leyda 28 Swallow 29 E3 30 BTS (p. 637) 31 E3 32 Jay Leyda Archive, New York 33 EA 34 Leyda

17 Danse Macabre

*EA 1 *Ibid.* 2 *Ibid.* 3 E3 4 IM 5 Leyda 6 Seton 7 *Masters of the Soviet Cinema* by Herbert Marshall (London, 1984) 8 E3 9 *Ibid.* (The author remarks: 'I have taken the liberty of putting all of Eisenstein's notes on the meeting into dialogue form, most of which was, in any event, written that way, as well as rearranging the sequence slightly where it was disjointed.') 10 Leyda Archive, New York 11 *Sight & Sound* (Summer, 1988) 12 *Esquire* (February, 1960) 13 *Screening the Sexes* by Parker Tyler (Henry Holt, 1973) 14 *Body Politic* (July–August 1977) 15 *Gay Times* (September, 1988) 16 E3 17 *Notes of A Soviet Actor* by N. Cherkassov (Foreign Language Publishing House, 1952) 18 EA 19 *Ibid.* 20 E3 21 Swallow 22 *Ibid.*

Epilogue: Taking Tea in Eisenstein's Brain

*BTS (p. 350) 1 *Sculpting In Time* by Andrei Tarkovsky (Faber and Faber, 1989) 2 *Cinema: A Critical Dictionary* (Secker and Warburg, 1980)

Index